TWO CLASSIC TAL[ES] OF AUSTRALIAN EXPLORATION

WATKIN TENCH was born in Chester, England on 6 October 1758. He joined the marine corps in 1776 and served in the American War of Independence before sailing to Botany Bay with the First Fleet. Tench returned to England in 1792. He stayed with the marine corps until retiring as a lieutenant-general in 1821. Watkin Tench died in 1833.

JOHN NICOL was born in Scotland in 1755, and first went to sea in 1776. He served in the American War of Independence, and later sailed to Greenland, the West Indies, the South Pacific, China, and the colony of New South Wales. He lived with the convict Sarah Whitlam in Port Jackson in 1790 after their son was born on the voyage to Australia. Later he served in the French Revolutionary Wars in Egypt and the Mediterranean until he settled in Scotland in 1801. He died in 1825.

TIM FLANNERY was born in Melbourne in 1956. He lives in Adelaide where he is director of the South Australian Museum. His books, which include *Throwim Way Leg*, *The Future Eaters* and *The Eternal Frontier*, have won numerous awards. He has made contributions of international significance to the fields of palaeontology, mammalogy and conservation.

Other TEXT PUBLISHING titles edited and introduced by Tim Flannery:

The Explorers, the bestselling anthology documenting the epic stories of courage and suffering across almost four centuries of exploration on the Australian continent;

The Birth of Sydney, another brilliant anthology, revealing the strange and secret life of one of the world's great cities from its unruly beginnings as a dump for convicts to its arrival as the 'queen of the south' a century later;

Terra Australis, Matthew Flinders' famous account of the first circumnavigation of Australia. Flinders writes about his meetings with Aborigines, his encounters with French explorers and Macassan fishing fleets and his adventures with the great Aboriginal leader Bongaree.

TWO CLASSIC TALES OF AUSTRALIAN EXPLORATION

1788 *by* Watkin Tench

Life and Adventures *by* John Nicol

EDITED AND INTRODUCED BY

TIM FLANNERY

The Text Publishing Company
171 La Trobe Street
Melbourne Victoria 3000

1788 first published 1789 and 1793
Text Publishing edition first published 1996

Life and Adventures 1776-1801 first published 1822
Text Publishing edition first published 1997

This edition published 2000, reprinted 2002

Printed and bound by Griffin Press
Designed by Chong Weng-Ho

National Library of Australia
Cataloguing-in-Publication data:

Two classic tales of Australian exploration: 1788 by Watkin Tench; Life and adventures by John Nicol

Bibliography.
Includes index.

ISBN 1 876485 61 2

1. Nicol, John, 1755-1825. 2. Seafaring life. 3. Sailors - Biography. 4. First Fleet, 1787-1788. 5. New South Wales - History - 1788-1851. 6. Australia - History - 1788-1851. 7. Botany Bay (N.S.W.) - History. 8. Port Jackson (N.S.W.) - History. I. Flannery, Timothy Fridtjof. II. Nicol, John, 1755-1825. Life and adventures, 1776-1801. III. Tench, Watkin, 1758 or 9-1833. 1788: comprising A narrative of the expedition to Botany Bay and A complete account of the settlement at Port Jackson. IV. Title: Complete account of the settlement at Port Jackson. V. Title: Narrative of the expedition to Botany Bay. VI. Title: Life and adventures, 1776-1801.

994.02

1788

comprising A Narrative of the Expedition to Botany Bay *and* An Account of the Settlement at Port Jackson

---

Watkin Tench

WATKIN TENCH

Contents

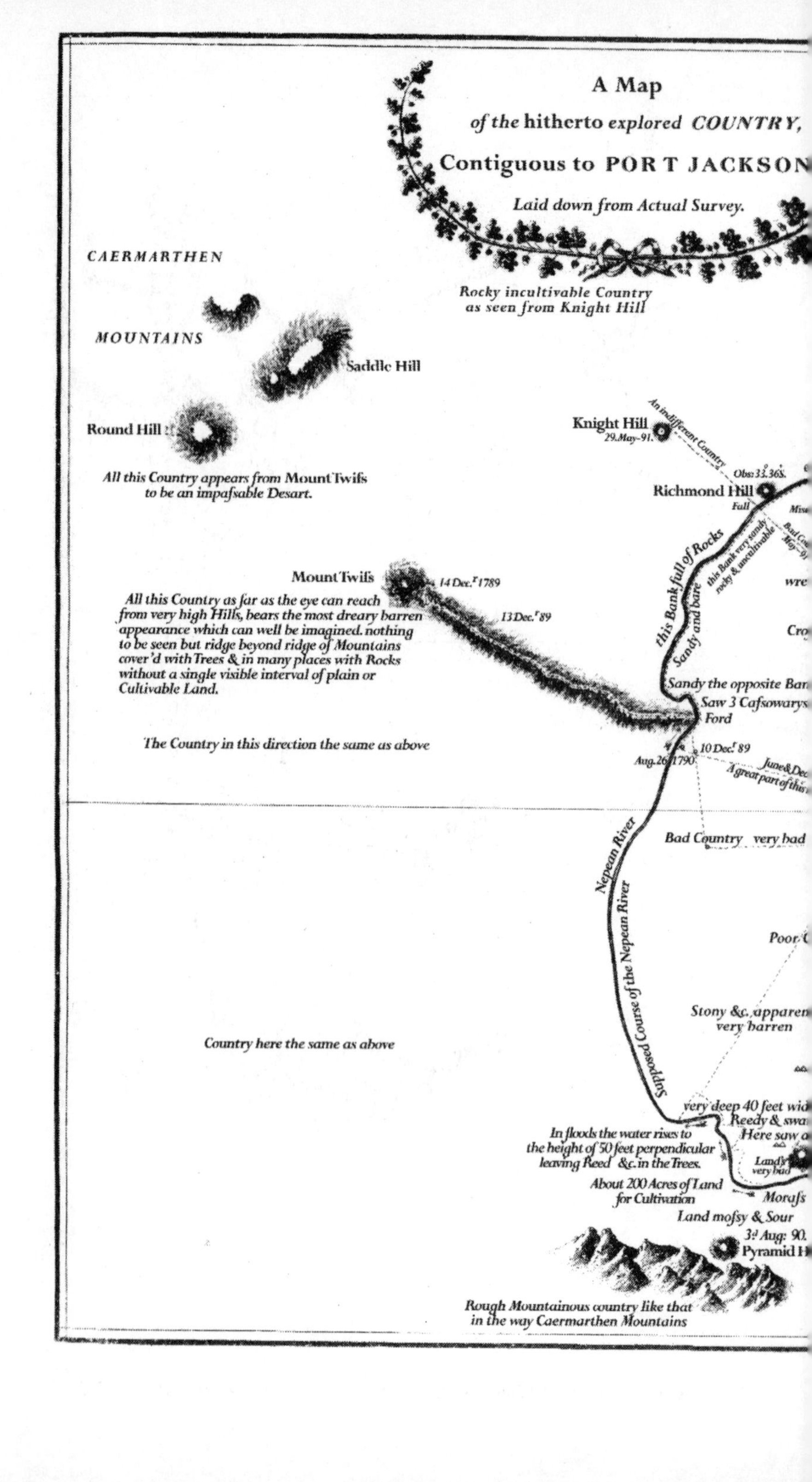
A Map
of the hitherto explored COUNTRY,
Contiguous to PORT JACKSON
Laid down from Actual Survey.
CAERMARTHEN
MOUNTAINS
Rocky incultivable Country
as seen from Knight Hill
Saddle Hill
Round Hill
Knight Hill
29.May-91.
An indifferent Country
Obs: 33.36S.
Richmond Hill
Fall
All this Country appears from Mount Twifs
to be an impafsable Desart.
this Bank full of Rocks
Sandy and bare
this Bank very sandy rocky & uncultivable
Mount Twifs
14 Dec.r 1789
13 Dec.r 89
All this Country as far as the eye can reach
from very high Hills, bears the most dreary barren
appearance which can well be imagined. nothing
to be seen but ridge beyond ridge of Mountains
cover'd with Trees & in many places with Rocks
without a single visible interval of plain or
Cultivable Land.
Saw 3 Cafsowarys
Ford
10 Dec.r 89
Aug. 26 1790
The Country in this direction the same as above
Nepean River
Bad Country
very bad
Supposed Course of the Nepean River
Country here the same as above
very barren
very deep 40 feet wi
Reedy & swa
In floods the water rises to
the height of 50 feet perpendicular
leaving Reed &c. in the Trees.
About 200 Acres of Land
for Cultivation
Morafs
Land mofsy & Sour
3d Aug: 90.
Rough Mountainous country like that
in the way Caermarthen Mountains

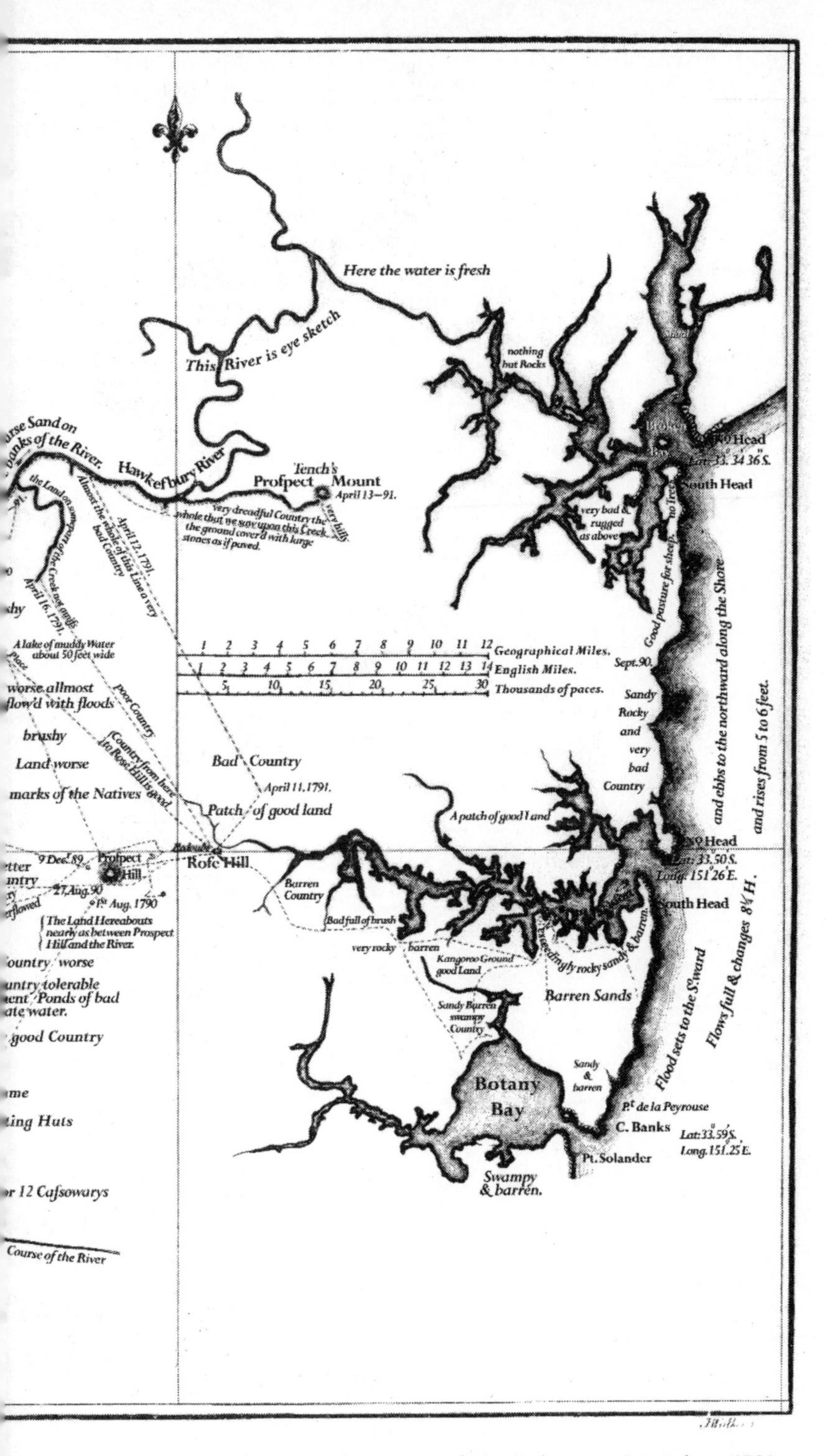

From Watkin Tench, *A Complete Account of The Settlement at Port Jackson*, 1793

Conversion table for weights and measures used by Watkin Tench

Length
1 inch = 25.4 mm
1 foot = 30.5 cm
1 yard = 0.914 m
1 mile = 1.61 km

Mass
1 ounce = 28.3 g
1 pound = 454 g

Area
1 acre = 0.405 ha

Volume
1 gallon = 4.55 litres

Temperature
$°C = \frac{5}{9} \times (°F - 32)$

The Extraordinary Watkin Tench

by Tim Flannery

Damn and bugger Captain Tench! So the overseer Henry Abrams was alleged to have said in 1790, during a dispute about convict labour. For his insolence, Abrams received warnings of 'the severest punishment'.[1] Yet posterity seems to have obliged him, for Watkin Tench's extraordinary account of the beginnings of modern Australia, a bestseller in its day, is virtually unknown to modern readers.

The story of Tench's works begins in early 1787. In that year a flurry of activity stirred in the publishing houses of London, for news was afoot that a fleet was soon to sail which would establish a British settlement in Australia. The venture must have seemed every bit as extraordinary as sending a man to the moon did almost two centuries later. In all, over one thousand Britons (759 of them convicts) were to sail in eleven ships to the antipodes, on a voyage which was to take eight months. The relatives and friends of the voyagers who remained in Britain waited anxiously for news of the settlement.

1. Moore, J., *The First Fleet Marines*, University of Queensland Press, St Lucia, 1987, 106.

Australia was the last of the habitable continents to be colonised by Europeans. Lying half a world away from Britain, its flora, fauna, geography and indigenous people were almost entirely unknown. Publishers were clearly not ignorant of the sales awaiting first-hand accounts of the settlement. They flocked to sign up the principals of the venture. Governor Arthur Phillip and Lieutenant-Governor John Hunter agreed to produce their own lavishly illustrated versions of events with the publisher John Stockdale of Piccadilly. Captain David Collins signed with Cadell & Davies in The Strand and Surgeon General John White was contracted to John Debrett of Piccadilly. But Debrett must have felt that White's account alone was insufficient for the occasion and, accordingly, contracted Watkin Tench, a humble captain-lieutenant of the marines, to write an 'interim report' on the state of the new colony.

Tench obliged in 1789 with *A Narrative of the Expedition to Botany Bay*. Published on 24 April, it beat all the others out. A pocket-sized pamphlet, the *Expedition* was by far the most modest of the five 'foundation books' of Australia's colonial history. But it was easily the most engaging. In 1793 his *A Complete Account of the Settlement at Port Jackson*, published by J. Nichol at Pall Mall, appeared. It too gave a vividly absorbing account of the infant colony. Tench's writings are unique for the understanding, humanity and eye for detail with which they record the earliest moments of Australia's European settlement. They are the most enduring and insightful eye-witness accounts that we have.

*

Apart from his period in Australia, very little is known of the life of Watkin Tench. It is surmised that he was born between May 1758 and May 1759. His father, the appositely named Fisher Tench, was a dancing master who, along with his wife Margaritta, ran a dancing academy and boarding school in

Chester.[1] Young Watkin was well-educated (as his fondness for quoting from Milton and Shakespeare attests) and he would be widely considered the most cultured mind in the colony at Port Jackson.

Tench entered the marine corps at the age of sixteen, and almost immediately saw active service during the American War of Independence. In 1778 he was captured by American forces and spent three months as a prisoner of war. The year 1783 saw the war end, and in 1786 Tench was placed on half pay. No doubt this predicament influenced him to apply, a few months later, for the three-year tour of service with the First Fleet.[2]

Tench returned to England from Australia in 1792. He served in the war against France during 1793–94, where he was again made prisoner (until exchanged in 1795) after a most heroic action. His ship, the *Alexander*, had resisted the advance of two French vessels when it was attacked by a third. By the time of her surrender, the *Alexander* had lost her main and three gallant top yards, all her other masts were damaged, the rigging cut to pieces, the hull badly damaged and set afire, and her hold filled with water. Forty of her men had been killed or wounded—but the French had lost 450.[3]

It was, perhaps, Tench's personal sense of valour which inclined him to admire the intrepid nature of the Aboriginal men of Port Jackson. Certainly, he viewed with admiration their utter disregard for death in the moment of crisis.

Tench subsequently saw sea service in various positions until 1802. As his writings show, he felt a profound loyalty to the marine corps. At this time the corps was considered very much a junior service, and was looked down upon by the army. While it suffered in both status and pay in comparison with the other services, it seems to have been a more disciplined and useful

1. Fitzhardinge, L. F. (ed.), Watkin Tench, *Sydney's First Four Years*, Library of Australian History, Sydney, 1979.

2. ibid., xvi.

3. ibid., xviii.

force.[1] Tench was well aware that marines had to be twice as good as regular troops if they were to earn any respect at all.

Some time after returning from Australia, Tench married Anna Maria Sargent. Apparently unable to have children, the Tenches adopted four of Anna's sister's children who had been orphaned, and brought them up as their own. Described as a 'gentleman' by the time of his death, Tench passed away at Devonport on 7 May 1833.

*

If details of Tench's life are sketchy, this is compensated in part by the rich picture of his personality revealed in his writings. For a young, unattached man like Tench, the voyage to Botany Bay was a great adventure. His detailed and lively descriptions of the Cape Verde Islands, Rio de Janeiro and Cape Town are just what one would expect from an intelligent, observant young man setting out on a tour of the world.

But it was upon reaching Australia that Tench's wide-ranging interests truly revealed themselves. There, he demonstrated considerable ability as an amateur naturalist, ethnographer, lawyer, soldier, agronomist and social commentator.

His writings in natural history, though not voluminous, were detailed and precise. His account of the internal anatomy of the emu, along with his description of its unusual double-shafted feathers, were the first notes of their kind. In his description of the kangaroo, he compares the actual animal with an illustration executed in 1770 during Cook's voyage, noting the merits and inaccuracies of the earlier work. His comment that 'the testicles of the male are placed contrary to the usual order of nature' doubtless refers to the fact that the testicles of marsupials are placed in front of the penis, a condition which must have seemed remarkable indeed at the time.

As the First Fleet was leaving England, Tench records the

1. *The First Fleet Marines*, 3-10.

reaction of the convicts on leaving their homeland, in all probability, forever:

> I strolled down among the convicts to observe their sentiments at this juncture. A very few excepted, their countenances indicated a high degree of satisfaction, though in some the pang of being severed, perhaps forever, from their native land could not be wholly suppressed. In general, marks of distress were more perceptible among the men than the women, for I recollect to have seen but one of those affected on the occasion. 'Some natural tears she dropp'd, but wip'd them soon.'

Tench's deep humanity, which is particularly apparent in his dealings with the convicts, was a rare attribute in the late eight–eenth century, especially in a military man. When he was told that he was at liberty to release the convicts from their fetters, he records that he 'had great pleasure in being able to extend this humane order to the whole of those under my charge, without a single exception'. The evident dismay with which he watched their punishment, particularly those who showed some penitence,is poignant. His transcription of the pathetic last letter of a condemned youth to his mother speaks eloquently of the inhumanity of the system within which he served.

Tench kept a daily journal (which is apparently now lost), from which he often quotes in writing. This sometimes gives his words an immediacy which suggests that he has just arrived breathless at his writing-table to narrate some extraordinary event. But Tench did not record everything. He makes no mention of his arrest in March 1788 by his superior, Captain Ross, for failing to reconsider the ruling of a military court case over which he had presided. This must have been a traumatic event for Tench. He remained technically under arrest in Australia for three years, and we know from other sources that the injustice of it long angered him.[1] A lesser man might have made much of the patent unfairness of his superior's actions.

1. *The First Fleet Marines*, 281.

While this incident goes unrecorded, it may account for Tench's minute detailing of the nature of the courts in the colony.

Watkin Tench had the ability to see an issue from perspectives as different as those of governor and Aborigine. Perhaps the most extraordinary events which Tench records (at least to the late twentieth-century reader) concern the Aborigines, or 'Indians' as he knew them. More than anyone else, except possibly his close friend Lieutenant Dawes, Tench was a friend and confidante of the Aborigines who attached themselves to the settlement. He learned their language, and they, apparently, reposed full confidence in him. Through Tench, some of the language of the Sydney Aborigines lives on in our own Australian idiom: *dingo* for native dog, and *gin* (or *dyin* as he rendered it) for woman.

As a military officer expected to defend the fledgling settlement, Tench was not in the best of positions to open friendly relations with the potentially hostile Aborigines. Indeed, he bears the unfortunate distinction of being the first European ordered to carry out an officially sanctioned massacre of Aborigines. In recording these events, his work takes on the touch of tragedy, for rarely has the conflict between private belief and the obligation of duty been conveyed with such deep feeling, yet outward restraint. Tench's horror at receiving the order remains implicit in his text, for as a soldier he could not be seen to betray his duty. We see Tench summoned to Governor Phillip's residence to be told of the hatchets and bags with which he is to cut off and carry away the heads of ten Aboriginal men. We hear Phillip give the gruesome order in his own words.

One wonders if it was something he saw in the expression on Tench's face which prompted Phillip to ask if Tench could propose any alteration to the order. Tench's suggestion that six Aborigines be captured (some to be executed, others to be released), rather than ten decapitated, was perhaps the best he felt he could negotiate. If so, he appears to have judged well, for his suggestion was accepted by Phillip. Tench's inability to carry out even this diminished order is not related with shame. Rather, he writes of the termination of the terrible episode with evident relief, and an almost comic sense of his hapless endeavours to capture a handful of Aborigines.

Tench's evolving view of the Aborigines is of enduring interest. It is typical of the way humans react to new and different cultures. At first fearful, perhaps even contemptuous of these 'fickle, jealous, wavering' people, Tench gradually came to know them individually, and to respect them. When he left Sydney in 1791, he also left firm friends behind.

The ignorance of Tench's initial assessment of the Aborigines is perhaps understandable when it is remembered that contacts with them were few during the first six months of the settlement (the period with which the *Expedition to Botany Bay* is concerned). Of the encounters which did take place over this period, a number were marked by violence. Indeed, in all, the Aborigines were able to kill or severely wound seventeen Europeans (including Governor Arthur Phillip himself), with no loss to themselves, before a reprisal was ordered.

Contact between European and Aborigine changed dramatically following the kidnapping of Arabanoo. Phillip had decided to take an Aborigine into custody because every other means of opening communication with them had failed. Tench was well aware that this was a desperate measure which would either make or break forever the chance for friendly contact between the two groups. In Arabanoo, Tench came to know an Aborigine personally for the first time, and his attitudes underwent a profound change. From this point on in Tench's writing one slowly loses sight of Arabanoo, Colbee and Bennelong as naked, black 'savages', and begins to see them as complex individuals. By the end of his time at Port Jackson, Tench could write: 'Man is the same in Pall Mall as in the wilderness of New South Wales.'

Arabanoo is a serious, somewhat ponderous person, with a gentle demeanour and a kindness to children which endears him to everyone. In contrast, Bennelong (who appears in Tench's narrative as Baneelon) is a mercurial character. Passionate, fearless and never slow to grasp an opportunity, he is the natural intermediary between his people and the new colonists. He plays the Europeans for all they are worth. Tench is patently fascinated by him:

> Baneelon we judged to be about twenty-six years old, of good stature and stoutly made, with a bold intrepid countenance which bespoke defiance and revenge...He quickly threw off all reserve, and pretended, nay, at particular moments, perhaps felt satisfaction in his new state. Unlike poor Arabanoo, he became at once fond of our viands and would drink the strongest liquors, not simply without reluctance but with eager marks of delight and enjoyment...Nor was the effect of wine or brandy upon him more perceptible than an equal quantity would have produced upon one of us, although fermented liquor was new to him...His powers of mind were certainly far above mediocrity. He acquired knowledge, both of our manners and language, faster than his predecessor had done. He willingly communicated information, sang, danced and capered, told us all the customs of his country and all the details of his family economy. Love and war seemed his favourite pursuits, in both of which he had suffered severely.

Tench did not demur at reporting events which show the Europeans in a poor light. During an expedition to the Hawkesbury, he reports how Boladeree refused to swim for a duck which the Europeans had shot. For days, the party had been shooting birds to feed themselves. All the while, the Europeans had reserved the ducks for themselves, giving the less palatable crows and hawks to the Aborigines.

This incident places in sharp focus just how distasteful the Aborigines found the English class system, a structure in which even fully initiated Aboriginal men were inevitably relegated to the bottom of the social ladder. They would simply not tolerate being treated so. Instead, they laughed at and mocked the Europeans for their clumsiness and stupidity in the bush.

When the exhausted Europeans (who in any case were carrying the supplies of the Aborigines) showed ill-humour at this, the Aborigines promptly called them *gonin-patta*—shit-eaters.

Tench's account of Arabanoo's first meals with Governor Phillip stands in contrast with the events of the Hawkesbury expedition. Although his acquaintance with his European abductors was but a few hours old, Arabanoo acquitted himself well at his first dinner, watching the others carefully in order to learn how to handle his food and napkin. His single mistake, not repeated, was to wipe his hands on his chair. Only at the end of his second meal did his performance become unstuck, for then he moved to throw his plate (one of the few in the colony) out the window, as one would a leaf or piece of bark. Rarely has the gulf between two cultures been so strikingly revealed.

One wonders, given the innate difficulties of their situation, how individuals such as Phillip and Arabanoo, or Tench and Bennelong, could have become such firm friends. Today, in comparison, the divide between black and white in Australia seems to have grown. Part of the equation, no doubt, was that the Europeans and Aborigines had yet to compete more than marginally for resources. The Europeans were fed largely out of their own stores, while the Aborigines still had their land. Because of this, neither group was dependent upon the other, and both retained their dignity. It was only when graziers and agriculturalists began to take the resources of the land wholesale from the Aborigines that the degradation of dispossession and dependency began.

For someone as vitally interested in the world's affairs as Tench, the isolation of Port Jackson was sometimes a cruel torture. This is amply revealed in Tench's reaction to the arrival of the transport *Mary Anne* at Port Jackson on 9 July 1791, while the French Revolution was in full swing:

> I was of a party who had rowed in a boat six miles out to sea, beyond the harbour's mouth, to meet them: and what was our disappointment...to find that they had not brought

> a letter...Nor had they a single newspaper or magazine in their possession...When I asked whether a new parliament had been called they stared at me in stupid wonder, not seeming to comprehend that such a body either suffered renovation or needed it.
>
> 'Have the French settled their government?'
>
> 'As to that matter I can't say; I never heard; but, damn them, they were ready enough to join the Spaniards against us.'
>
> We therefore quitted the ship, wondering and lamenting that so large a portion of plain undisguised honesty should be so totally unconnected with a common share of intelligence, and acquaintance with the feelings and habits of other men.

Tench not only missed the French Revolution by being in Australia. The opening night of Mozart's *Don Giovanni* and the madness of George III also occurred in his absence.

Many aspects of Watkin Tench's personality seem to sit more comfortably in our century rather than the eighteenth. Yet it would be a grave mistake to see him as a twentieth-century man, or to judge him by our own sensibilities. That he was well ahead of his time—in his regard for the Aborigines and his push to reform the cruel social practices of the eighteenth century, for example—is to be applauded. But it would be far too easy, and decidedly wrong, to condemn him for failing to espouse many other causes which have gained currency today.

So often we rewrite history to suit our own ends. For nations whose beginnings are shrouded in the mists of time, this is perhaps understandable. But in Australia we have the writings of Phillip, White, Tench and many others to inform us about how things were. We have no reason not to read them. It is merely our neglect of our own past that has led to the absurd idea that 'Australia has no history'. My normally languid blood boils at this notion, for no history is so extraordinary, nor so well documented, as that of Australia.

At times it has been convenient to forget that Australia's

European origins were as a penal settlement, or that the first European colonists suffered so many fatalities at the hands of the Aborigines without being able to strike back. At other times it has been unfashionable to remember that Aborigines and Europeans forged firm friendships in the first days of settlement. Today, many Australians will not wish to hear that Sydney's Aborigines expressed a desire to immigrate, *en masse*, to Norfolk Island, upon hearing that there was plenty of food there. Yet this, and much more, makes up the history of the people of this continent.

Tench's narrative records the disorientation that happens when old worlds and new come into collision. It is clear from his account that many convicts had no idea at all where they were as they laboured and starved at Sydney Cove. The attempt, in November 1791, by twenty convict men and a pregnant woman, to walk from Sydney to China, is perhaps the clearest proof of this. When questioned, they answered that they believed 'China might be easily reached, being not more than a hundred miles distant, and separated only by a river'.

This sense of disorientation was no less evident among the Aborigines who accompanied Europeans on journeys outside their tribal boundaries. Tench records that when Colbee and Boladeree joined him during the exploration of the Hawkesbury River they became

> very urgent in their inquiries about the time of our return...Their method of testifying dislike to any place is singular: they point to the spot they are upon, and all around it, crying *weèree, weèree* (bad), and immediately after mention the name of any other place to which they are attached (Rose Hill or Sydney for instance), adding to it, *budyeree, budyeree* (good). Nor was their preference in the present case the result of caprice, for they assigned very substantial reasons for such predilection. 'At Rose Hill,' said they, 'are potatoes, cabbages, pumpkins, turnips, fish and wine; here are nothing but rocks and water.' These comparisons constantly ended with the question of 'Where's Rose Hill? Where?'

Tench's own disorientation began on 21 January 1788, the day he first set foot on Australian soil. He walked along the beach at Botany Bay with a seven-year-old boy who held his hand. We do not know who this boy was or whether he was the child of a convict or a marine. As the pair strolled on the beach they met an elderly Aboriginal man who 'with great gentleness laid his hand on the child's hat, and afterwards felt his clothes, muttering all the while'. It is a moving image of the disorientation both the Aborigines and the Europeans would feel as they each experienced a world far broader than they had hitherto known. In this meeting of young and old was the beginning of that extraordinary process of adaptation which continues to define contemporary Australia.

*

My intention in editing this book has been to produce an accessible and inexpensive edition of Tench which I hope will be widely read, particularly by younger people. This book is not just for historians or specialists, who are much better served by L. F. Fitzhardinge's extensively annotated edition, first published in 1961.

I have used the text of the third edition of the *Expedition*, published in 1789, and the 1793 edition of the *Settlement*. I have modernised Tench's punctuation and spelling, corrected the occasional error (for example De Perrouse for La Perouse), and sometimes added a word or two of clarification or explanation in a footnote, marked by a dagger (†). Tench's own notes are indicated by an asterisk (*). Otherwise, Tench's text is given as it was first published.

Book One:
A Narrative of the Expedition to Botany Bay

IN offering this little tract to the public it is equally the writer's wish to conduce to their amusement and information.

The expedition on which he is engaged has excited much curiosity and given birth to many speculations respecting the consequences to arise from it. While men continue to think freely, they will judge variously. Some have been sanguine enough to foresee the most beneficial effects to the parent state from the colony we are endeavouring to establish, and some have not been wanting to pronounce the scheme big with folly, impolicy and ruin. Which of these predictions will be completed I leave to the decision of the public. I cannot, however, dismiss the subject without expressing a hope that the candid and liberal of each opinion, induced by the humane and benevolent intention in which it originated, will unite in waiting the result of a fair trial to an experiment no less new in its design than difficult in its execution.

As this publication enters the world with the name of the author, candour will, he trusts, induce its readers to believe that no consideration could weigh with him in an endeavour to mislead them. Facts are related simply as they happened and when opinions are hazarded they are such as, he hopes, patient inquiry and deliberate decision will be found to have authorised. For the most part he has spoken from actual observation, and in those places where the relations of others have been unavoidably adopted, he has been careful to search for the truth and repress that spirit of exaggeration which is almost ever the effect of novelty on ignorance.

The nautical part of the work is comprised in as few pages as possible. By the professional part of my readers this will be deemed judicious; and the rest will not, I believe, be dissatisfied at its brevity. I beg leave, however, to say of the astronomical calculations that they may be depended on with the greatest degree of security, as they were communicated by an officer who was furnished with instruments and commissioned by the Board of Longitude to make observations during the voyage and in the southern hemisphere.

An unpractised writer is generally anxious to bespeak public attention and to solicit public indulgence. Except on professional subjects, military men are, perhaps, too fearful of critical censure. For the present narrative no other apology is attempted than the intentions of its author, who has endeavoured not only to satisfy present curiosity but to point out to future adventurers the favourable as well as adverse circumstances which will attend their settling here. The candid, it is hoped, will overlook the inaccuracies of this imperfect sketch, drawn amidst the complicated duties of the service in which the author is engaged, and make due allowance for the want of opportunity of gaining more extensive information.

Watkin Tench, Captain of the Marines
Sydney Cove, Port Jackson, New South Wales, 10 July 1788

1

From the embarkation of the convicts to the departure of the ships from England

THE marines and convicts having been previously embarked in the river at Portsmouth and Plymouth, the whole fleet destined for the expedition rendezvoused at the Mother Bank on the 16th of March 1787 and remained there until the 13th of May following. In this period, excepting a slight appearance of contagion in one of the transports, the ships were universally healthy and the prisoners in high spirits. Few complaints or lamentations were to be heard among them and an ardent wish for the hour of departure seemed generally to prevail.

As the reputation equally with the safety of the officers and soldiers appointed to guard the convicts consisted in maintaining due subordination, an opportunity was taken, immediately on their being embarked, to convince them in the most pointed terms that any attempt on their side either to contest the command or to force their escape should be punished with instant death. Orders to this effect were given to the sentinels in their presence. Happily, however, for all parties, there occurred not any instance in which there was occasion to have recourse to so desperate a measure, the behaviour of the convicts being in general humble, submissive and regular. Indeed, I should feel myself wanting in justice to those unfortunate men were I not to bear this public testimony of the sobriety and decency of their conduct.

Unpleasant as a state of inactivity and delay for many weeks appeared to us, it was not without its advantages, for by means of it we were enabled to establish necessary regulations among the convicts, and to adopt such a system of defence as left us little to apprehend for our own security in case a spirit of madness and desperation had hurried them on to attempt our destruction.

Among many other troublesome parts of duty which the service we were engaged on required, the inspection of all letters brought to or sent from the ships was not one of the least tiresome and disagreeable. The number and contents of those in the vessel I was embarked in frequently surprised me very much. They varied according to the dispositions of the writers, but their constant language was an apprehension of the impracticability of returning home, the dread of a sickly passage and the fearful prospect of a distant and barbarous country. But this apparent despondency proceeded in few instances from sentiment. With too many it was, doubtless, an artifice to awaken compassion and call forth relief, the correspondence invariably ending in a petition for money and tobacco. Perhaps a want of the latter, which is considered a great luxury by its admirers among the lower classes of life, might be the more severely felt from their being debarred in all cases whatever, sickness excepted, the use of spirituous liquors.

It may be thought proper for me to mention that during our stay at the Mother Bank the soldiers and convicts were indiscriminately served with fresh beef. The former, in addition, had the usual quantity of beer allowed in the navy and were at what is called full allowance of all species of provisions, the latter at two-thirds only.

2

From the departure to the arrival of the fleet at Tenerife

GOVERNOR Phillip having at length reached Portsmouth, and all things deemed necessary for the expedition being put on board, at daylight on the morning of the 13th the signal to weigh anchor was made in the commanding officer's ship the *Sirius*. Before six o'clock the whole fleet were under sail, and the weather being fine and wind easterly, proceeded through the Needles with a fresh leading breeze. In addition to our little armament, the *Hyena* frigate was ordered to accompany us a certain distance to the westward, by which means our number was increased to twelve sail: His Majesty's ships *Sirius*, *Hyena* and *Supply*, three victuallers with two years' stores and provisions for the settlement, and six transports with troops and convicts.

In the transports were embarked four captains, twelve subalterns, twenty-four sergeants and corporals, eight drummers and 160 private marines, making the whole of the military force, including the major commandant and staff on board the *Sirius*, to consist of 212 persons, of whom 210 were volunteers. The number of convicts was 565 men, 192 women, and eighteen children. The major part of the prisoners were mechanics and husbandmen, selected on purpose by order of government.

By ten o'clock we had got clear of the Isle of Wight, at which time, having very little pleasure in conversing with my own thoughts, I strolled down among the convicts to observe their sentiments at this juncture. A very few excepted, their countenances indicated a high degree of satisfaction, though in some the pang of being severed, perhaps forever, from their native land could not be wholly suppressed. In general, marks of distress were more perceptible among the men than the women, for I recollect to have seen but one of those affected on the occasion. 'Some natural tears she dropp'd, but wip'd them soon.'† After this the accent of sorrow was no longer

† John Milton, *Paradise Lost*, XII, 645: 'Some natural tears they dropp'd...'

heard; more genial skies and change of scene banished repining and discontent, and introduced in their stead cheerfulness and acquiescence in a lot not now to be altered.

To add to the good disposition which was beginning to manifest itself, on the morning of the 20th, in consequence of some favourable representations made by the officers commanding detachments, they were hailed and told from the *Sirius* that in those cases where they judged it proper they were at liberty to release the convicts from the fetters in which they had been hitherto confined. In complying with these directions I had great pleasure in being able to extend this humane order to the whole of those under my charge without a single exception. It is hardly necessary for me to say that the precaution of ironing the convicts at any time reached to the men only.

In the evening of the same day, the *Hyena* left us for England, which afforded an early opportunity of writing to our friends and easing their apprehensions by a communication of the favourable accounts it was in our power to send them.

From this time to the day of our making the land, little occurred worthy of remark. I cannot, however, help noticing the propriety of employing the marines on a service which requires activity and exertion at sea in preference to other troops. Had a regiment recruited since the war been sent out, seasickness would have incapacitated half the men from performing the duties immediately and indispensably necessary, whereas the marines, from being accustomed to serve on board ship, accommodated themselves with ease to every exigency and surmounted every difficulty.

At daybreak on the morning of the 30th of May we saw the rocks named the Deserters which lie off the south-east end of Madeira, and found the south-east extremity of the most southerly of them to be in the latitude of 32° 28′ north, longitude 16° 17½′ west of Greenwich. The following day we saw the Salvages, a cluster of rocks which are placed between the Madeiras and Canary Islands, and determined the latitude of the middle of the Great Salvage to be 30° 12′ north, and the longitude of its eastern side to be 15° 39′ west. It is no less extraordinary than unpardonable, that in some very modern charts of the Atlantic, published in London, the Salvages are totally omitted.

We made the island of Tenerife on the 3rd of June, and in the evening anchored in the road of Santa Cruz, after an excellent passage of three weeks from the day we left England.

3

From the Fleet's arrival at Tenerife to its departure for Rio de Janeiro in the Brazils

THERE is little to please a traveller at Tenerife. He has heard wonders of its celebrated peak, but he may remain for weeks together at the town of Santa Cruz without having a glimpse of it, and when its cloud-topped head emerges the chance is that he feels disappointed, for from the point of view in which he sees it, the neighbouring mountains lessen its effect very considerably. Excepting the peak, the eye receives little pleasure from the general face of the country which is sterile and uninviting to the last degree. The town, however, from its cheerful white appearance, contrasted with the dreary brownness of the background, makes not an unpleasing *coup d'oeil.* It is neither irregular in its plan, nor despicable in its style of building, and the churches and religious houses are numerous, sumptuous and highly ornamented.

The morning of our arrival, as many officers as could be spared from the different ships were introduced to the Marquis de Brancifort, governor of the Canary Islands, whose reception was highly flattering and polite. His Excellency is a Sicilian by birth and is most deservedly popular in his government. He prefers residing at Tenerife, for the conveniency of frequent communication with Europe, to the Grand Canary, which is properly the seat of power, and though not long fixed there has already found means to establish a manufactory in cotton, silk and thread, under excellent regulations, which employs more than sixty persons and is of infinite service to the common people. During our short stay we had every day some fresh proof of His Excellency's esteem and attention, and had the honour of dining with him in a style of equal elegance and splendour. At this entertainment the profusion of ices which appeared in the dessert was surprising, considering that we were enjoying them under a sun nearly vertical. But it seems the caverns of the peak, very far below its summit, afford at all seasons ice in abundance.

The restless importunity of the beggars and the immodesty of the lowest class of women are highly disgusting. From the number of his countrymen to be found, an Englishman is at no loss for society. In the mercantile houses established here, it is from gentlemen of this description that any information is derived, for the taciturnity of the Spaniards is not to be overcome in a short acquaintance, especially by Englishmen, whose reserve falls little short of their own. The inland country is described as fertile and highly romantic, and the environs of the small town of Laguza mentioned as particularly pleasant. Some of our officers who made an excursion to it confirmed the account amply.

It should seem that the power of the church, which has been so long on the decline in Europe, is at length beginning to be shaken in the colonies of the Catholic powers. Some recent instances which have taken place at Tenerife evince it very fully. Were not a stranger, however, to be apprised of this, he would hardly draw the conclusion from his own observations. The bishop of these islands, which conjunctively form a see, resides on the Grand Canary. He is represented as a man in years and of a character as amiable as exalted, extremely beloved both by foreigners and those of his own church. The bishopric is valued at ten thousand pounds per annum, the government at somewhat less than two.

In spite of every precaution, while we lay at anchor in the road a convict had the address, one night, to secrete himself on the deck when the rest were turned below and, after remaining quiet some hours, let himself down over the bow of the ship and floated to a boat that laid astern, into which he got, and cutting her adrift, suffered himself to be carried away by the current until at a sufficient distance to be out of hearing, when he rowed off. This elopement was not discovered till some hours after, when a search being made and boats sent to the different parts of the island, he was discovered in a small cove to which he had fled for refuge. On being questioned, it appeared he had endeavoured to get himself received on board a Dutch East Indiaman in the road, but being rejected there, he resolved on crossing over to the Grand Canary, which is at the distance of ten leagues, and when detected was recruiting his strength in order to make the attempt. At the same time that the boats of the fleet were sent on this pursuit, information was given to the Spanish governor of what had happened, who immediately detached parties every way in order to apprehend the delinquent.

Having remained a week at Tenerife, and in that time completed our stock of water and taken on board wine etc., early on the morning on the 10th of June we weighed anchor and stood out to sea with a light easterly breeze. The shortness of our stay and the consequent hurry prevented our increasing much any previous knowledge we might have had of the place. For the information of those who may follow us on this service, it may not, however, be amiss to state the little that will be found of use to them.

The markets afford fresh meat, though it is neither plentiful nor good. Fish is scarce, but poultry may be procured in almost any quantity at as cheap a rate as in the English seaports. Vegetables do not abound, except pumpkins and onions, of which I advise all ships to lay in a large stock. Milch goats are bought for a trifle, and easily procured. Grapes cannot be scarce in their season, but when we were here, except figs and excellent mulberries, no fruit was to be procured. Dry wines, as the merchants term them, are sold from ten to fifteen pounds a pipe.† For the latter price the very best, called the London Particular, may be bought. Sweet wines are considerably dearer. Brandy is also a cheap article. I would not advise the voyager to depend on this place for either his hogs or sheep. And he will do well to supply himself with dollars before he quits England to expend in the different ports he may happen to touch at. Should he, however, have neglected this precaution, let him remember when he discounts bills or exchanges English money here not to receive his returns in quarter dollars, which will be tendered to him, but altogether in whole ones, as he will find the latter turn to better account than the former both at Rio de Janeiro and the Cape of Good Hope.

The latitude of the town of Santa Cruz is 28° 27½′ north, the longitude 16° 17½′ west of Greenwich.

4

The passage from Tenerife to Rio de Janeiro in the Brazils

IN sailing from Tenerife to the south-east, the various and picturesque appearances of the peak are beautiful to the highest degree. The stupendous height, which before was lost on the traveller, now strikes him with awe and admiration, the whole island appearing one vast mountain with a pyramidal top. As we proceeded with light winds, at an easy rate, we saw it distinctly for three days after our departure, and should have continued to see it longer had not the haziness of the atmosphere interrupted our view. The good people of Santa Cruz tell some stories of the wonderful extent of space to be seen from the summit of it that would not disgrace the memoirs of the ever-memorable Baron Munchausen.††

On the 18th of June we saw the most northerly of the Cape

† A large cask which held around 500 litres.

†† A fictional figure of the eighteenth century, famous for his wildly exaggerated stories.

Verde Islands, at which time the commodore gave the fleet to understand, by signal, that his intention was to touch at some of them. The following day we made Sao Tiago, and stood in to gain an anchorage in Port Praia Bay. But the baffling winds and lee current rendering it a matter of doubt whether or not the ships would be able to fetch, the signal for anchoring was hauled down and the fleet bore up before the wind. In passing along them we were enabled to ascertain the south end of the isle of Sal to be in 16° 40′ north latitude, and 23° 5′ west longitude. The south end of Boa Vista to be in 15° 57′ north, 23° 8′ west. The south end of the isle of Maio in 15° 11′ north, 23° 26′ west; and the longitude of the fort, in the town of Port Praia, to be 23° 36½′ west of Greenwich.

By this time the weather, from the sun being so far advanced in the northern tropic, was become intolerably hot which, joined to the heavy rains that soon after came on, made us very apprehensive for the health of the fleet. Contrary, however, to expectation, the number of sick in the ship I was embarked on was surprisingly small and the rest of the fleet were nearly as healthy. Frequent explosions of gunpowder, lighting fires between decks, and a liberal use of that admirable antiseptic, oil of tar, were the preventives we made use of against impure air; and above all things we were careful to keep the men's bedding and wearing apparel dry. As we advanced towards the Line the weather grew gradually better and more pleasant. On the 14th of July we passed the equator, at which time the atmosphere was as serene and the temperature of the air not hotter than in a bright summer day in England. From this period until our arrival on the American coast, the heats, the calms and the rains by which we had been so much incommoded were succeeded by a series of weather as delightful as it was unlooked for. At three o'clock in the afternoon of the 2nd of August, the *Supply*, which had been previously sent ahead on purpose, made the signal for seeing the land, which was visible to the whole fleet before sunset, and proved to be Cape Frio, in latitude 23° 5′ south, longitude 41° 40¼′ west.

Owing to light airs we did not get abreast of the city of St Sebastian, in the harbour of Rio de Janeiro, until the 7th of the month, when we anchored about three-quarters of a mile from the shore.

5

From the arrival of the fleet at Rio de Janeiro till its departure for the Cape of Good Hope, with some remarks on the Brazils

BRAZIL is a country very imperfectly known in Europe. The Portuguese, from political motives, have been sparing in their accounts of it. Whence our descriptions of it in the geographical publications in England are drawn I know not. That they are miserably erroneous and defective is certain.

The city of St Sebastian stands on the west side of the harbour, in a low unhealthy situation, surrounded on all sides by hills which stop the free circulation of air, and subject its inhabitants to intermittent and putrid diseases. It is of considerable extent. Mr Cook† makes it as large as Liverpool; but Liverpool, in 1767, when Mr Cook wrote, was not two-thirds of its present size. Perhaps it equals Chester, or Exeter, in the share of ground it occupies, and is infinitely more populous than either of them. The streets intersect each other at right angles, are tolerably well built and excellently paved, abounding with shops of every kind in which the wants of a stranger, if money is not one of them, can hardly remain unsatisfied. About the centre of the city, and at a little distance from the beach, the palace of the viceroy stands, a long, low building, no wise remarkable in its exterior appearance; though within are some spacious and handsome apartments. The churches and convents are numerous and richly decorated. Hardly a night passes without some of the latter being illuminated in honour of their patron saints, which has a very brilliant effect when viewed

† Captain James Cook, 1728–79.

from the water and was at first mistaken by us for public rejoicings. At the corner of almost every street stands a little image of the virgin, stuck round with lights in an evening, before which passengers frequently stop to pray and sing very loudly. Indeed, the height to which religious zeal is carried in this place cannot fail of creating astonishment in a stranger. The greatest part of the inhabitants seem to have no other occupation than that of paying visits and going to church, at which time you see them sally forth richly dressed, *en chapeau bras*,† with the appendages of a bag for the hair, and a small sword. Even boys of six years old are seen parading about, furnished with these indispensable requisites. Except when at their devotions, it is not easy to get a sight of the women and, when obtained, the comparisons drawn by a traveller lately arrived from England are little flattering to Portuguese beauty. In justice, however, to the ladies of St Sebastian, I must observe that the custom of throwing nosegays at strangers for the purpose of bringing on an assignation, which Doctor Solander and another gentleman of Mr Cook's ship met with when here, was never seen by any of us in a single instance. We were so deplorably unfortunate as to walk every evening before their windows and balconies without being honoured with a single bouquet, though nymphs and flowers were in equal and great abundance.

Among other public buildings, I had almost forgot to mention an observatory which stands near the middle of the town and is tolerably well furnished with astronomical instruments. During our stay here some Spanish and Portuguese mathematicians were endeavouring to determine the boundaries of the territories belonging to their respective crowns. Unhappily, however, for the cause of science, these gentlemen have not hitherto been able to coincide in their accounts so that very little information on this head, to be depended upon, could be gained. How far political motives may have caused this

† 'With tricorn hat under arm.'

disagreement I do not presume to decide; though it deserves notice that the Portuguese accuse the Abbe de la Caille, who observed here by order of the King of France, of having laid down the longitude of this place forty-five miles too much to the eastward.

Until the year 1770 all the flour in the settlement was brought from Europe, but since that time the inhabitants have made so rapid a progress in raising grain as to be able to supply themselves with it abundantly. The principal corn country lies around Rio Grande in the latitude of 32° south, where wheat flourishes so luxuriantly as to yield from seventy to eighty bushels for one. Coffee also, which they formerly received from Portugal, now grows in such plenty as to enable them to export considerable quantities of it. But the staple commodity of the country is sugar. That they have not, however, learnt the art of making palatable rum the English troops in New South Wales can bear testimony; a large quantity, very ill flavoured, having been bought and shipped here for the use of the garrison of Port Jackson.

It was in 1771 that St Salvador, which had for more than a century been the capital of Brazil, ceased to be so; and that the seat of government was removed to St Sebastian. The change took place on account of the colonial war at that time carried on by the courts of Lisbon and Madrid. And, indeed, were the object of security alone to determine the seat of government, I know but few places better situated in that respect than the one I am describing; the natural strength of the country, joined to the difficulties which would attend an attack on the fortifications, being such as to render it very formidable.

It may be presumed that the Portuguese government is well apprised of this circumstance, and of the little risk they run in being deprived of so important a possession, else it will not be easy to penetrate the reasons which induce them to treat the troops who compose the garrison with such cruel negligence. Their regiments were ordered out with a promise of being relieved and sent back to Europe at the end of three years, in conformity to which they settled all their domestic arrangements. But the faith of government has been broken, and at the expiration of twenty years all that is left to the remnant of these unfortunate men is to suffer in submissive silence. I was one evening walking with a Portuguese officer when this subject was started and, on my telling him that such a breach of public honour to English troops would become a subject of parliamentary inquiry, he seized my hand with great eagerness. 'Ah, Sir!' exclaimed he. 'Yours is a free country. We—' His emotions spoke what his tongue refused.

As I am mentioning the army, I cannot help observing that I saw nothing here to confirm the remark of Mr Cook that the inhabitants of the place, whenever they meet an officer of the garrison, bow to him with the greatest obsequiousness, and by omitting such a ceremony would subject themselves to be knocked down, though the other seldom deigns to return the compliment. The interchange of civilities is general between them and seems by no means extorted. The people who could submit to such insolent superiority would, indeed, deserve to be treated as slaves.

The police of the city is very good. Soldiers patrol the streets frequently, and riots are seldom heard of. The dreadful custom of stabbing, from motives of private resentment, is nearly at an end since the church has ceased to afford an asylum to murderers. In other respects, the progress of improvement appears slow and fettered by obstacles almost unsurmountable, whose baneful influence will continue until a more enlightened system of policy shall be adopted. From morning to night the ears of a stranger are greeted by the tinkling of the convent bells, and his eyes saluted by processions of devotees, whose adoration and levity seem to keep equal pace, and succeed each other in turns. 'Do you want to make your son sick of soldiering? Shew him the trainbands† of London on a field day.' Let him who would wish to give his son

† Companies of civilian soldiers.

a distaste to popery point out to him the sloth, the ignorance and the bigotry of this place.

Being nearly ready to depart by the 1st of September, as many officers as possible went on that day to the palace to take leave of His Excellency, the viceroy of the Brazils, to whom we had been previously introduced, who on this and every other occasion was pleased to honour us with the most distinguished marks of regard and attention. Some part, indeed, of the numerous indulgences we experienced during our stay here must doubtless be attributed to the high respect in which the Portuguese held Governor Phillip, who was for many years a captain in their navy and commanded a ship of war on this station, in consequence of which many privileges were extended to us, very unusual to be granted to strangers. We were allowed the liberty of making short excursions into the country, and on these occasions, as well as when walking in the city, the mortifying custom of having an officer of the garrison attending us was dispensed with on our leaving our names and ranks, at the time of landing, with the adjutant of orders at the palace. It happened, however, sometimes, that the presence of a military man was necessary to prevent imposition in the shopkeepers, who frequently made a practice of asking more for their goods than the worth of them. In which case an officer, when applied to, always told us the usual price of the commodity with the greatest readiness, and adjusted the terms of the purchase.

On the morning of the 4th of September we left Rio de Janeiro, amply furnished with the good things which its happy soil and clime so abundantly produce. The future voyager may with security depend on this place for laying in many parts of his stock. Among these may be enumerated sugar, coffee, rum, port wine, rice, tapioca and tobacco, besides very beautiful wood for the purposes of household furniture. Poultry is not remarkably cheap, but may be procured in any quantity; as may hogs at a low rate. The markets are well supplied with butcher's meat, and vegetables of every sort are to be procured at a price next to nothing. The yams are particularly excellent. Oranges abound so much as to be sold for sixpence a hundred, and limes are to be had on terms equally moderate. Bananas, coconuts and guavas are common, but the few pineapples brought to market are not remarkable either for flavour or cheapness. Besides the inducements to lay out money already mentioned, the naturalist may add to his collection by an almost endless variety of beautiful birds and curious insects, which are to be bought at a reasonable price, well preserved and neatly assorted.

I shall close my account of this place by informing strangers who may come here that the Portuguese reckon their money in *rees*, an imaginary coin, twenty of which make a small copper piece called a *vintin*, and sixteen of these last a *petack*. Every piece is marked with the number of *rees* it is worth, so that a mistake can hardly happen. English silver coin has lost its reputation here, and dollars will be found preferable to any other money.

6

The passage from the Brazils to the Cape of Good Hope with an account of the transactions of the fleet there

OUR passage from Rio de Janeiro to the Cape of Good Hope was equally prosperous with that which had preceded it. We steered away to the south-east, and lost sight of the American coast the day after our departure. From this time until the 13th of October, when we made the Cape, nothing remarkable occurred except the loss of a convict in the ship I was on board, who unfortunately fell into the sea and perished in spite of our efforts to save him by cutting adrift a life buoy and hoisting out a boat. During the passage a slight dysentery prevailed in some of the ships, but was in no instance mortal. We were at first inclined to impute it to the water we took on board at the Brazils, but as the effect was very partial some other cause was more probably the occasion of it.

At seven o'clock in the evening of the 13th of October we

cast anchor in Table Bay, and found many ships of different nations in the harbour.

Little can be added to the many accounts already published of the Cape of Good Hope, though if an opinion on the subject might be risked, the descriptions they contain are too flattering. When contrasted with Rio de Janeiro it certainly suffers in the comparison. Indeed, we arrived at a time equally unfavourable for judging of the produce of the soil and the temper of its cultivators, who had suffered considerably from a dearth that had happened the preceding season and created a general scarcity. Nor was the chagrin of these deprivations lessened by the news daily arriving of the convulsions that shook the republic, which could not fail to make an impression even on Batavian phlegm.†

As a considerable quantity of flour, and the principal part of the livestock, which was to store our intended settlement were meant to be procured here, Governor Phillip lost no time in waiting on Mynheer Van Graaffe, the Dutch governor, to request permission (according to the custom of the place) to purchase all that we stood in need of. How far the demand extended I know not, nor Mynheer Van Graaffe's reasons for complying with it in part only. To this gentleman's political sentiments I confess myself a stranger, though I should do his politeness and liberality at his own table an injustice were I not to take this public opportunity of acknowledging them. Nor can I resist the opportunity which presents itself to inform my readers, in honour of M. Van Graaffe's humanity, that he has made repeated efforts to recover the unfortunate remains of the crew of the Grosvenor Indiaman which was wrecked about five years ago on the coast of Caffraria.†† This information was given me by Colonel Gordon, commandant of the Dutch troops at the Cape, whose knowledge of the interior parts of this country surpasses that of any other man. And I am sorry to

† Batavian: Dutch.

†† Territory of the Bantu-speaking people of Southern Africa.

say that the colonel added, these unhappy people were irrecoverably lost to the world and their friends by being detained among the Caffres, the most savage set of brutes on earth.

His Excellency resides at the government house in the East India Company's garden. This last is of considerable extent and is planted chiefly with vegetables for the Dutch Indiamen which may happen to touch at the port. Some of the walks are extremely pleasant from the shade they afford, and the whole garden is very neatly kept. The regular lines intersecting each other at right angles in which it is laid out, will, nevertheless, afford but little gratification to an Englishman, who has been used to contemplate the natural style which distinguishes the pleasure grounds of his own country. At the head of the centre-walks stands a menagerie on which, as well as the garden, many pompous eulogiums have been passed, though in my own judgment, considering the local advantages possessed by the company, it is poorly furnished both with animals and birds. A tiger, a zebra, some fine ostriches, a cassowary, and the lovely crown-fowl are among the most remarkable.†

The tableland, which stands at the back of the town, is a black, dreary-looking mountain, apparently flat at top and of more than eleven hundred yards in height.†† The gusts of wind which blow from it are violent to an excess and have a very unpleasant effect by raising the dust in such clouds as to render stirring out of doors next to impossible. Nor can any precaution prevent the inhabitants from being annoyed by it as much within doors as without.

At length the wished-for day, on which the next effort for reaching the place of our destination was to be made, appeared. The morning was calm, but the land wind getting up about noon, on the 12th of November we weighed anchor and soon left far behind every scene of civilisation and humanised

† The tiger was possibly a leopard. The cassowary must have come from New Guinea.

†† Table Mountain.

manners to explore a remote and barbarous land and plant in it those happy arts which alone constitute the pre-eminence and dignity of other countries.

The live animals we took on board on the public account from the Cape for stocking our projected colony were two bulls, three cows, three horses, forty-four sheep and thirty-two hogs, besides goats and a very large quantity of poultry of every kind. A considerable addition to this was made by the private stocks of the officers, who were however under a necessity of circumscribing their original intentions on this head very much, from the excessive dearness of many of the articles. It will readily be believed that few of the military found it convenient to purchase sheep, when hay to feed them costs sixteen shillings a hundredweight.

The boarding houses on shore, to which strangers have recourse, are more reasonable than might be expected. For a dollar and a half per day we were well lodged and partook of a table tolerably supplied in the French style. Should a traveller's stock of tea run short, it is a thousand chances to one that he will be able to replenish it here at a cheaper rate than in England. He may procure plenty of arrack and white wine, also raisins and dried fruits of other sorts. If he dislikes to live at a boarding house, he will find the markets well stored and the price of butcher's meat and vegetables far from excessive.

Just before the signal for weighing was made, a ship under American colours entered the road, bound from Boston, from whence she had sailed one hundred and forty days on a trading voyage to the East Indies. In her route she had been lucky enough to pick up several of the inferior officers and crew of the Harcourt East-Indiaman, which ship had been wrecked on one of the Cape Verde islands. The master, who appeared to be a man of some information, on being told the destination of our fleet, gave it as his opinion that if a reception could be secured emigrations would take place to New South Wales, not only from the old continent, but the new one, where the spirit of adventure and thirst for novelty were excessive.

7

The passage from the Cape of Good Hope to Botany Bay

WE had hardly cleared the land when a south-east wind set in and, except at short intervals, continued to blow until the 29th of the month, when we were in the latitude of 37° 40′ south and by the timekeeper in longitude 11° 30′ east, so that our distance from Botany Bay had increased nearly an hundred leagues since leaving the Cape. As no appearance of a change in our favour seemed likely to take place, Governor Phillip at this time signified his intention of shifting his pennant from the *Sirius* to the *Supply*, and proceeding on his voyage without waiting for the rest of the fleet, which was formed in two divisions. The first consisting of three transports, known to be the best sailors, was put under the command of a lieutenant of the navy, and the remaining three, with the victuallers, left in charge of Captain Hunter of His Majesty's ship *Sirius*. In the last division was the vessel in which the author of this narrative served. Various causes prevented the separation from taking place until the 25th, when several sawyers, carpenters, blacksmiths and other mechanics were shifted from different ships into the *Supply*, in order to facilitate His Excellency's intention of forwarding the necessary buildings to be erected at Botany Bay by the time the rest of the fleet might be expected to arrive. Lieutenant-Governor Ross and the staff of the marine battalion also removed from the *Sirius* into the *Scarborough* transport, one of the ships of the first division, in order to afford every assistance which the public service might receive by their being early on the spot on which our future operations were to be conducted.

From this time a succession of fair winds and pleasant weather corresponded to our eager desires and on the 7th of January 1788 the long wished-for shore of Van Diemen gratified our sight.† We made the land at two o'clock in the

† Tasmania.

afternoon, the very hour we expected to see it from the lunar observations of Captain Hunter, whose accuracy as an astronomer and conduct as an officer had inspired us with equal gratitude and admiration.

After so long a confinement on a service so peculiarly disgusting and troublesome, it cannot be matter of surprise that we were overjoyed at the near prospect of a change of scene. By sunset we had passed between the rocks which Captain Furneaux named the Mewstone and Swilly. The former bears a very close resemblance to the little island near Plymouth whence it took its name. Its latitude is 43° 48′ south, longitude 146° 25′ east of Greenwich.

In running along shore we cast many an anxious eye towards the land on which so much of our future destiny depended. Our distance, joined to the haziness of the atmosphere, prevented us, however, from being able to discover much. With our best glasses we could see nothing but hills of a moderate height, clothed with trees, to which some little patches of white sandstone gave the appearance of being covered with snow. Many fires were observed on the hills in the evening.

As no person in the ship I was on board had been on this coast before, we consulted a little chart published by Steele of the Minories, London, and found it in general very correct. It would be more so were not the Mewstone laid down at too great a distance from the land and one object made of the Eddystone and Swilly, when in fact they are distinct. Between the two last is an entire bed of impassable rocks, many of them above water. The latitude of the Eddystone is 43° 53½′, longitude 147° 9′; that of Swilly 43° 54′ south, longitude 147° 3′ east of Greenwich.

In the night the westerly wind which had so long befriended us died away, and was succeeded by one from the north-east. When day appeared we had lost sight of the land and did not regain it until the 19th at only the distance of seventeen leagues from our desired port. The wind was now fair, the sky serene though a little hazy, and the temperature of the air delightfully pleasant. Joy sparkled in every countenance and congratulations issued from every mouth. Ithaca itself was scarcely more longed for by Ulysses than Botany Bay by the adventurers who had traversed so many thousand miles to take possession of it.

'Heavily in clouds came on the day' which ushered in our arrival. To us it was 'a great, an important day', though I hope the foundation, not the fall, of an empire will be dated from it.†

On the morning of the 20th, by ten o'clock, the whole of the fleet had cast anchor in Botany Bay, where to our mutual satisfaction we found the governor and the first division of transports. On inquiry we heard that the *Supply* had arrived on the 18th and the transports only the preceding day.

Thus, after a passage of exactly thirty-six weeks from Portsmouth, we happily effected our arduous undertaking with such a train of unexampled blessings as hardly ever attended a fleet in a like predicament. Of 212 marines we lost only one; and of 775 convicts put on board in England, but twenty-four perished in our route. To what cause are we to attribute this unhoped for success? I wish I could answer to the liberal manner in which government supplied the expedition. But when the reader is told that some of the necessary articles allowed to ships on a common passage to the West Indies were withheld from us; that portable soup, wheat, and pickled vegetables were not allowed, and that an inadequate quantity of essence of malt was the only antiscorbutic supplied, his surprise will redouble at the result of the voyage. For it must be remembered that the people thus sent out were not a ship's company starting with every advantage of health and good living which a state of freedom produces, but the major part a miserable set of convicts, emaciated from confinement and in want of clothes and almost

† Tench is remembering the opening lines of Joseph Addison's tragedy *Cato*: 'Heavily in clouds brings on the day, / The great, the important day, big with the fate / of Cato and of Rome...'

every conveniency to render so long a passage tolerable. I beg leave, however, to say that the provisions served on board were good and of a much superior quality to those usually supplied by contract. They were furnished by Messrs Richards and Thorn of Tower Street, London.

8

From the fleet's arrival at Botany Bay to the evacuation of it, and taking possession of Port Jackson. Interviews with the natives, an account of the country about Botany Bay

WE had scarcely bid each other welcome on our arrival when an expedition up the bay was undertaken by the governor and lieutenant-governor, in order to explore the nature of the country and fix on a spot to begin our operations upon. None, however, which could be deemed very eligible being discovered, His Excellency proceeded in a boat to examine the opening to which Mr Cook had given the name of Port Jackson, on an idea that a shelter for shipping within it might be found. The boat returned on the evening of the 23rd with such an account of the harbour and advantages attending the place that it was determined the evacuation of Botany Bay should commence the next morning.

In consequence of this decision, the few seamen and marines who had been landed from the squadron were instantly re-embarked, and every preparation made to bid adieu to a port which had so long been the subject of our conversation; which but three days before we had entered with so many sentiments of satisfaction and in which, as we had believed, so many of our future hours were to be passed. The thoughts of removal banished sleep, so that I rose at the first dawn of the morning. But judge of my surprise on hearing from a sergeant, who ran down almost breathless to the cabin where I was dressing, that a ship was seen off the harbour's mouth. At first I only laughed, but knowing the man who spoke to me to be of great veracity, and hearing him repeat his information, I flew upon deck, on which I had barely set my foot when the cry of 'another sail' struck on my astonished ear.

Confounded by a thousand ideas which arose in my mind in an instant, I sprang upon the barricado and plainly descried two ships of considerable size standing in for the mouth of the bay. By this time the alarm had become general and everyone appeared lost in conjecture. Now they were Dutchmen sent to dispossess us, and the moment after storeships from England with supplies for the settlement. The improbabilities which attended both these conclusions were sunk in the agitation of the moment. It was by Governor Phillip that this mystery was at length unravelled, and the cause of the alarm pronounced to be two French ships it was now recollected were on a voyage of discovery in the southern hemisphere. Thus were our doubts cleared up and our apprehensions banished. It was, however, judged expedient to postpone our removal to Port Jackson until a complete confirmation of our conjectures could be procured.

Had the sea breeze set in, the strange ships would have been at anchor in the bay by eight o'clock in the morning but, the wind blowing out, they were driven by a strong lee current to the southward of the port. On the following day they reappeared in their former situation and a boat was sent to them with a lieutenant of the navy in her to offer assistance and point out the necessary marks for entering the harbour. In the course of the day the officer returned and brought intelligence that the ships were the *Boussole* and *Astrolabe*, sent out by order of the King of France and under the command of Monsieur La Perouse. The astonishment of the French at seeing us had not equalled that we had experienced, for it appeared that in the course of their voyage they had touched at Kamchatka and by that means learnt that our expedition was in contemplation. They dropped anchor the next morning, just as we had got under weigh to work out of the bay, so that for the present nothing more than salutations could pass between us.

Before I quit Botany Bay I shall relate the observations we were enabled to make during our short stay there, as well as those which our subsequent visits to it from Port Jackson enabled us to complete.

The bay is very open and greatly exposed to the fury of the south-east winds, which when they blow cause a heavy and dangerous swell. It is of prodigious extent, the principal arm, which takes a south-westerly direction, being not less, including its windings, than twenty-four miles from the capes which form the entrance, according to the report of the French officers, who took uncommon pains to survey it. At the distance of a league from the harbour's mouth is a bar, on which at low water not more than fifteen feet are to be found. Within this bar, for many miles up the south-west arm, is a haven, equal in every respect to any hitherto known and in which any number of ships might anchor, secured from all winds. The country around far exceeds in richness of soil that about Cape Banks and Point Solander, though unfortunately they resemble each other in one respect, a scarcity of fresh water.

We found the natives tolerably numerous as we advanced up the river, and even at the harbour's mouth we had reason to conclude the country more populous than Mr Cook thought it. For on the *Supply*'s arrival in the bay on the 18th of the month they were assembled on the beach of the south shore to the number of not less than forty persons, shouting and making many uncouth signs and gestures. This appearance whetted curiosity to its utmost, but as prudence forbade a few people to venture wantonly among so great a number, and a party of only six men was observed on the north shore, the governor immediately proceeded to land on that side in order to take possession of his new territory and bring about an intercourse between its old and new masters. The boat in which His Excellency was, rowed up the harbour close to the land for some distance, the Indians keeping pace with her on the beach. At last an officer in the boat made signs of a want of water, which it was judged would indicate his wish of landing. The natives directly comprehended what he wanted and pointed to a spot where water could be procured, on which the boat was immediately pushed in and a landing took place. As on the event of this meeting might depend so much of our future tranquillity, every delicacy on our side was requisite. The Indians, though timorous, showed no signs of resentment at the governor's going on shore. An interview commenced, in which the conduct of both parties pleased each other so much that the strangers returned to their ships with a much better opinion of the natives than they had landed with; and the latter seemed highly entertained with their new acquaintance, from whom they condescended to accept of a looking-glass, some beads, and other toys.

Owing to the lateness of our arrival, it was not my good fortune to go on shore until three days after this had happened, when I went with a party to the south side of the harbour and had scarcely landed five minutes when we were met by a dozen Indians, naked as at the moment of their birth, walking along the beach. Eager to come to a conference, and yet afraid of giving offence, we advanced with caution towards them. Nor would they, at first, approach nearer to us than the distance of some paces. Both parties were armed, yet an attack seemed as unlikely on their part as we knew it to be on our own.

I had at this time a little boy, of not more than seven years of age, in my hand. The child seemed to attract their attention very much, for they frequently pointed to him and spoke to each other; and as he was not frightened I advanced with him towards them, at the same time baring his bosom and showing the whiteness of the skin. On the clothes being removed they gave a loud exclamation and one of the party, an old man with a long beard, hideously ugly, came close to us. I bade my little charge not to be afraid and introduced him to the acquaintance of this uncouth personage. The Indian, with great gentleness, laid his hand on the child's hat and afterwards felt his clothes, muttering to himself all the while. I found it necessary, however, by this time to send away the child, as such a close connection rather alarmed him, and in this, as the conclusion verified, I gave no offence to the old gentleman. Indeed it was but putting ourselves on a par with them, as I had observed from the first that some youths of their own, though considerably older than the one with us, were kept back by the grown people.

Several more now came up, to whom we made various presents, but our toys seemed not to be regarded as very valuable; nor would they for a long time make any returns to them, though before we parted a large club with a head almost sufficient to fell an ox was obtained in exchange for a looking-glass. These people seemed at a loss to know (probably from our want of beards) of what sex we were, which having understood, they burst into the most immoderate fits of laughter, talking to each other at the same time with such rapidity and vociferation as I had never before heard. After nearly an hour's conversation, by signs and gestures they repeated several times the word *whurra*, which signifies 'begone', and walked away from us to the head of the bay.

The natives being departed, we set out to observe the country, which on inspection rather disappointed our hopes, being invariably sandy and unpromising for the purposes of cultivation, though the trees and grass flourish in great luxuriancy. Close to us was the spring at which Mr Cook watered, but we did not think the water very excellent, nor did it run freely. In the evening we returned on board, not greatly pleased with the latter part of our discoveries, as it indicated an increase of those difficulties which before seemed sufficiently numerous.

Between this and our departure we had several more interviews with the natives, which ended in so friendly a manner that we began to entertain some hopes of bringing about a connection with them. Our first object was to win their affections and our next to convince them of the superiority we possessed: for without the latter, the former we knew would be of little importance.

An officer one day prevailed on one of them to place a

target, made of bark, against a tree, which he fired at with a pistol at the distance of some paces. The Indians, though terrified at the report, did not run away, but their astonishment exceeded their alarm on looking at the shield which the ball had perforated. As this produced a little shyness, the officer, to dissipate their fears and remove their jealousy, whistled the air of 'Malbrooke', which they appeared highly charmed with, and imitated him with equal pleasure and readiness.† I cannot help remarking here, what I was afterwards told by Monsieur La Perouse, that the natives of California, and throughout all the islands of the Pacific Ocean, and in short wherever he had been, seemed equally touched and delighted with this little plaintive air.

9

The taking possession of Port Jackson, with the disembarkation of the marines and convicts

OUR passage to Port Jackson took up but few hours and those were spent far from unpleasantly. The evening was bright and the prospect before us such as might justify sanguine expectation. Having passed between the capes which form its entrance, we found ourselves in a port superior in extent and excellency to all we had seen before. We continued to run up the harbour about four miles in a westerly direction, enjoying the luxuriant prospect of its shores covered with trees to the water's edge, among which many of the Indians were frequently seen, till we arrived at a small snug cove on the southern side, on whose banks the plan of our operations was destined to commence.

The landing of a part of the marines and convicts took place the next day, and on the following the remainder was disembarked. Business now sat on every brow and the scene, to an indifferent spectator at leisure to contemplate it, would have

† '"Malbrooke s'en va-t-en guerre", an old French song, to the same air as "We won't go home till morning".' *Sydney's First Four Years*, 97.

been highly picturesque and amusing. In one place a party cutting down the woods; a second setting up a blacksmith's forge, a third dragging along a load of stones or provisions; here an officer pitching his marquee, with a detachment of troops parading on one side of him, and a cook's fire blazing up on the other. Through the unwearied diligence of those at the head of the different departments, regularity was, however, soon introduced and, as far as the unsettled state of matters would allow, confusion gave place to system.

Into the head of the cove on which our establishment is fixed runs a small stream of fresh water, which serves to divide the adjacent country to a little distance in the direction of north and south. On the eastern side of this rivulet the governor fixed his place of residence with a large body of convicts encamped near him, and on the western side was disposed the remaining part of these people, near the marine encampment. From this last, two guards, consisting of two subalterns, as many sergeants, four corporals, two drummers and forty-two private men, under the orders of a captain of the day (to whom all reports were made) daily mounted for the public security, with such directions to use force, in case of necessity, as left no room for those who were the object of the order but to remain peaceable or perish by the bayonet.

As the straggling of the convicts was not only a desertion from the public labour, but might be attended with ill consequences to the settlement in case of their meeting the natives, every care was taken to prevent it. The provost-martial with his men was ordered to patrol the country around, and the convicts informed that the severest punishment would be inflicted on transgressors. In spite, however, of all our precautions, they soon found the road to Botany Bay, in visits to the French, who would gladly have dispensed with their company.

But as severity alone was known to be inadequate at once to chastise and reform, no opportunity was omitted to assure the convicts that by their good behaviour and submissive deportment every claim to present distinction and future favour was to be earned. That this caution was not attended with all the good effects which were hoped from it I have only to lament. That it operated in some cases is indisputable; nor will a candid and humane mind fail to consider and allow for the situation these unfortunate beings so peculiarly stood in. While they were on board ship the two sexes had been kept most rigorously apart, but when landed their separation became impracticable, and would have been, perhaps, wrong. Licentiousness was the unavoidable consequence, and their old habits of depravity were beginning to recur. What was to be attempted? To prevent their intercourse was impossible, and to palliate its evils only remained. Marriage was recommended, and such advantages held out to those who aimed at reformation as have greatly contributed to the tranquillity of the settlement.

On the Sunday after our landing divine service was performed under a great tree by the Rev. Mr Johnson, chaplain of the settlement, in the presence of the troops and convicts, whose behaviour on the occasion was equally regular and attentive. In the course of our passage this had been repeated every Sunday while the ships were in port, and in addition to it Mr Johnson had furnished them with books at once tending to promote instruction and piety.

The Indians, for a little while after our arrival, paid us frequent visits, but in a few days they were observed to be more shy of our company. From what cause their distaste arose we never could trace, as we had made it our study on these occasions to treat them with kindness and load them with presents. No quarrel had happened and we had flattered ourselves, from Governor Phillip's first reception among them, that such a connection might be established as would tend to the interest of both parties. It seems that on that occasion they not only received our people with great cordiality, but so far acknowledged their authority as to submit that a boundary, during their first interview, might be drawn on the sand, which they attempted not to infringe and appeared to be satisfied with.

10

The reading of the commissions, and taking possession of the settlement in form, with an account of the courts of law, and mode of administering public justice in this country

OWING to the multiplicity of pressing business necessary to be performed immediately after landing, it was found impossible to read the public commissions and take possession of the colony in form until the 7th of February. On that day all the officers of guard took post in the marine battalion which was drawn up and marched off the parade, with music playing and colours flying, to an adjoining ground which had been cleared for the occasion, whereon the convicts were assembled to hear His Majesty's commission read, appointing His Excellency Arthur Phillip, Esq. governor and captain-general in and over the territory of New South Wales and its dependencies; together with the act of parliament for establishing trials by law within the same; and the patents under the Great Seal of Great Britain for holding the civil and criminal courts of judicature, by which all cases of life and death, as well as matters of property, were to be decided.

When the judge advocate had finished reading, His Excellency addressed himself to the convicts in a pointed and judicious speech, informing them of his future intentions, which were invariably to cherish and render happy those who showed a disposition to amendment, and to let the rigour of the law take its course against such as might dare to transgress the bounds prescribed. At the close three volleys were fired in honour of the occasion and the battalion marched back to their parade, where they were reviewed by the governor, who was received with all the honours due to his rank. His Excellency was afterwards pleased to thank them, in public orders, for their behaviour from the time of their embarkation; and to ask the officers to partake of a cold collation, at which it is scarce necessary to observe that many loyal and public toasts were drank in commemoration of the day.

In the governor's commission the extent of this authority is defined to reach from the latitude of 43° 49′ south to the latitude of 10° 37′ south, being the northern and southern extremities of the continent of New Holland. It commences again at 135th degree of longitude east of Greenwich and, proceeding in an easterly direction, includes all islands within the limits of the above specified latitudes in the Pacific Ocean. By this partition it may be fairly presumed that every source of future litigation between the Dutch and us will be forever cut off, as the discoveries of English navigators alone are comprised in this territory.

Nor have government been more backward in arming Mr Phillip with plenitude of power than extent of dominion. No mention is made of a council to be appointed, so that he is left to act entirely from his own judgment. And as no stated time of assembling the courts of justice is pointed out, similar to the assizes and gaol deliveries of England, the duration of imprisonment is altogether in his hands. The power of summoning general courts martial to meet he is also invested with, but the insertion in the marine mutiny act of a smaller number of officers than thirteen being able to compose such a tribunal, has been neglected; so that a military court, should detachments be made from headquarters or sickness prevail, may not always be found practicable to be obtained, unless the number of officers at present in the settlement shall be increased.

Should the governor see cause, he is enabled to grant pardons to offenders convicted 'in all cases whatever, treason and wilful murder excepted', and even in these has authority to stay the execution of the law, until the King's pleasure shall be signified. In case of the governor's death the lieutenant-governor takes his place; and on his demise, the senior officer on the spot is authorised to assume the reins of power.

Notwithstanding the promises made on one side and the forbearance shown on the other, joined to the impending rod of justice, it was with infinite regret that everyone saw, in four days afterwards, the necessity of assembling a criminal court, which was accordingly convened by a warrant from the governor and consisted of the judge advocate (who presided), three naval and three marine officers.

As the constitution of this court is altogether new in the British annals I hope my reader will not think me prolix in the description I am about to give of it. The number of members, including the judge advocate, is limited by act of parliament to seven, who are expressly ordered to be officers either of His Majesty's sea or land forces. The court being met, completely arrayed and armed as at a military tribunal, the judge advocate proceeds to administer the usual oath taken by jurymen in England to each member, one of whom afterwards swears him in a like manner. This ceremony being adjusted, the crime laid to the prisoner's charge is read to him and the question of guilty or not guilty put. No law officer on the side of the crown being appointed (for I presume the head of the court ought hardly to consider himself in that light, notwithstanding the title he bears), to prosecute the criminal is left entirely to the party at whose suit he is tried. All the witnesses are examined on oath and the decision is directed to be given according to the laws of England, 'or as nearly as may be, allowing for the circumstances and situation of the settlement', by a majority of votes, beginning with the youngest member and ending with the president of the court.

In cases, however, of a capital nature, no verdict can be given unless five, at least, of the seven members present concur therein. The evidence on both sides being finished, and the prisoner's defence heard, the court is cleared and on the judgment being settled, is thrown open again and sentence pronounced. During the time the court sits, the place in which it is assembled is directed to be surrounded by a guard under arms, and admission to everyone who may choose to enter it granted. Of late, however, our colonists are supposed to be in such a train of subordination as to make the presence of so large a military force unnecessary, and two sentinels (in addition to the provost-martial) are considered as sufficient.

It would be as needless as impertinent to anticipate the reflections which will arise in reading the above account, wherein a regard to accuracy only has been consulted. By comparing it with the mode of administering justice in the English courts of law, it will be found to differ in many points very essentially. And if we turn our eyes to the usage of military tribunals, it no less departs from the customs observed in them. Let not the novelty of it, however, prejudice anyone so far as to dispute its efficacy and the necessity of the case which gave it birth.

The court, whose meeting is already spoken of, proceeded to the trial of three convicts, one of whom was convicted of having struck a marine with a cooper's adze and otherwise behaving in a very riotous and scandalous manner, for which he was sentenced to receive one hundred and fifty lashes, being a smaller punishment than a soldier in a like case would have suffered from the judgment of a court martial. A second, for having committed a petty theft, was sent to a small barren island and kept there on bread and water only, for a week.† And the third was sentenced to receive fifty lashes, but was recommended by the court to the governor, and forgiven.

Hitherto, however, (February) nothing of a very atrocious nature had appeared. But the day was at hand on which the violation of public security could no longer be restrained by the infliction of temporary punishment. A set of desperate and hardened villains leaguered themselves for the purposes of depredation and, as it generally happens, had art enough to persuade some others less deeply versed in iniquity to be the instruments for carrying it on. Fortunately the progress of these miscreants was not of long duration. They were detected in stealing a large quantity of provisions at the time of issuing them. And on being apprehended one of the tools of the superiors impeached the rest and disclosed the scheme. The trial came on the 28th of the month, and of four who were

† Probably Pinchgut in Sydney Harbour.

arraigned for the offence, three were condemned to die and the fourth to receive a very severe corporal punishment. In hopes that his lenity would not be abused, His Excellency was, however, pleased to order one only for execution, which took place a little before sunset the same day. The name of the unhappy wretch was Thomas Barret, an old and desperate offender who died with that hardy spirit which too often is found in the worst and most abandoned class of men. During the execution the battalion of marines was under arms and the whole of the convicts obliged to be present. The two associates of the sufferer were ordered to be kept close prisoners until an eligible place to banish them to could be fixed on, as were also two more who on the following day were condemned to die for a similar offence.

Besides the criminal court there is an inferior one, composed of the judge advocate and one or more justices of the peace, for the trial of small misdemeanours. This court is likewise empowered to decide all law suits and its verdict is final, except where the sum in dispute amounts to more than £300, in which case an appeal to England can be made from its decree. Should necessity warrant it, an Admiralty court, of which Lieutenant-Governor Ross is judge, can also be summoned for the trial of offences committed on the high seas.

From being unwilling to break the thread of my narrative I omitted to note in its proper place the sailing of the *Supply*, Lieut. Ball, on the 15th of the month, for Norfolk Island, which the governor had instructions from the ministry to take possession of. Lieut. King of the *Sirius* was sent as superintendent and commandant of this place and carried with him a surgeon, a midshipman, a sawyer, a weaver, two marines and sixteen convicts, of whom six were women. He was also supplied with a certain number of live animals to stock the island, besides garden seeds, grain and other requisites.

11

A description of the natives of New South Wales, and our transactions with them

I doubt not my readers will be as glad as I feel myself to conclude the dull detail of the last chapter. If they please they may turn from the subtle intricacies of the law to contemplate the simple undisguised workings of nature in her most artless colouring.

I have already said we had been but very few days at Port Jackson when an alteration in the behaviour of the natives was perceptible; and I wish I could add that a longer residence in their neighbourhood had introduced a greater degree of cordiality and intermixture between the old and new lords of the soil than, at the day on which this publication is dated, subsists.

From their easy reception of us in the beginning, many were induced to call in question the accounts which Mr Cook had given of this people. That celebrated navigator, we were willing to believe, had somehow by his conduct offended them, which prevented the intercourse that would otherwise have taken place. The result, however, of our repeated endeavours to induce them to come among us has been such as to confirm me in an opinion that they either fear or despise us too much to be anxious for a closer connection. And I beg leave at once to apprise the reader that all I can here, or in any future part of this work, relate with fidelity of the natives of New South Wales must be made up of detached observations, taken at different times, and not from a regular series of knowledge of the customs and manners of a people with whom opportunities of communication are so scarce as to have been seldom obtained.

In their persons, they are far from being a stout race of men, though nimble, sprightly, and vigorous. The deficiency of one of the fore teeth of the upper jaw, mentioned by Dampier, we have seen in almost the whole of the men. But their organs of sight, so far from being defective, as that author mentions those of the inhabitants of the western side of the continent to be, are remarkably quick and piercing. Their colour Mr Cook is inclined to think rather a deep chocolate than an absolute black, though he confesses they have the appearance of the latter, which he attributes to the greasy filth their skins are loaded with. Of their want of cleanliness we have had sufficient proofs but, I am of opinion, all the washing in the world would not render them two degrees less black than an African Negro. At some of our first interviews we had several droll instances of their mistaking the Africans we brought with us for their own countrymen.

Notwithstanding the disregard they have invariably shown for all the finery we could deck them with, they are fond of adorning themselves with scars, which increase their natural hideousness. It is hardly possible to see anything in human shape more ugly than one of these savages thus scarified, and farther ornamented with a fish bone struck through the gristle of the nose. The custom of daubing themselves with white earth is also frequent among both sexes, but unlike the inhabitants of the islands in the Pacific Ocean they reject the beautiful feathers which the birds of their country afford.

Exclusive of their weapons of offence and a few stone hatchets very rudely fashioned, their ingenuity is confined to manufacturing small nets in which they put the fish they catch, and to fish-hooks made of bone, neither of which are unskilfully executed. On many of the rocks are also to be found delineations of the figures of men and birds, very poorly cut.

Of the use or benefit of clothing these people appear to have no comprehension, though their sufferings from the climate they live in strongly point out the necessity of a covering from the rigour of the seasons. Both sexes, and those of all ages, are invariably found naked. But it must not be inferred from this that custom so inures them to the changes of the elements as to make them bear with indifference the extremes of heat and cold, for we have had visible and repeated proofs that the latter affects them severely, when they are seen shivering and huddling themselves up in heaps in their huts or the caverns of the rocks, until a fire can be kindled.

Than these huts nothing more rude in construction or deficient in conveniency can be imagined. They consist only of pieces of bark laid together in the form of an oven, open at one end and very low, though long enough for a man to lie at full length in. There is reason, however, to believe that they depend less on them for shelter than on the caverns with which the rocks abound.

To cultivation of the ground they are utter strangers, and wholly depend for food on the few fruits they gather, the roots they dig up in the swamps, and the fish they pick up along shore or contrive to strike from their canoes with spears. Fishing, indeed, seems to engross nearly the whole of their time, probably from its forming the chief part of a subsistence which, observation has convinced us, nothing short of the most painful labour and unwearied assiduity can procure. When fish are scarce, which frequently happens, they often watch the moment of our hauling the seine, and have more than once been known to plunder its contents, in spite of the opposition of those on the spot to guard it; and this even after having received a part of what had been caught. The only resource at these times is to show a musket, and if the bare sight is not sufficient, to fire it over their heads, which has seldom failed of dispersing them hitherto, but how long the terror which it excites may continue is doubtful.

The canoes in which they fish are as despicable as their huts, being nothing more than a large piece of bark tied up at both ends with vines. Their dexterous management of them, added to the swiftness with which they paddle and the boldness that leads them several miles in the open sea are, nevertheless, highly deserving of admiration. A canoe is seldom seen without a fire in it, to dress the fish by as soon as caught. Fire they procure by attrition.

From their manner of disposing of those who die, which will be mentioned hereafter, as well as from every other observation, there seems no reason to suppose these people cannibals. Nor do they ever eat animal substances in a raw state, unless pressed by extreme hunger, but indiscriminately broil them and their vegetables on a fire, which renders these last an innocent food, though in their raw state many of them are of a poisonous quality, as a poor convict who unguardedly eat of them experienced, by falling a sacrifice in twenty-four hours afterwards. If bread be given to the Indians they chew and spit it out again, seldom choosing to swallow it. Salt beef and pork they like rather better, but spirits they never could be brought to taste a second time.

The only domestic animal they have is the dog, which in their language is called *dingo*, and a good deal resembles the fox dog of England.† These animals are equally shy of us and attached to the natives. One of them is now in the possession of the governor, and tolerably well reconciled to his new master. As the Indians see the dislike of the dogs to us, they are sometimes mischievous enough to set them on single persons whom they chance to meet in the woods. A surly fellow was one day out shooting when the natives attempted to divert themselves in this manner at his expense. The man bore the teasing and gnawing of the dog at his heels for some time, but apprehending at length that his patience might embolden them to use still farther liberties, he turned round and shot poor dingo dead on the spot. The owners of him set off with the utmost expedition.

There is no part of the behaviour of these people that has puzzled us more than that which relates to their women. Comparatively speaking we have seen but few of them, and those have been sometimes kept back with every symptom of jealous sensibility; and sometimes offered with every appearance of courteous familiarity. Cautious, however, of alarming the feelings of the men on so tender a point, we have constantly made a rule of treating the females with that distance and reserve which we judged most likely to remove any impression they might have received of our intending aught which could

† This is the first recorded use of the word 'dingo' in English.

give offence on so delicate a subject. And so successful have our endeavours been that a quarrel on this head has in no instance, that I know of, happened. The tone of voice of the women, which is pleasingly soft and feminine, forms a striking contrast to the rough guttural pronunciation of the men. Of the other charms of the ladies I shall be silent, though justice obliges me to mention that in the opinion of some amongst us they show a degree of timidity and bashfulness which are, perhaps, inseparable from the female character in its rudest state. It is not a little singular that the custom of cutting off the two lower joints of the little finger of the left hand, observed in the Society Islands [Tahiti], is found here among the women, who have for the most part undergone this amputation. Hitherto we have not been able to trace out the cause of this usage. At first we supposed it to be peculiar to the married women or those who had borne children; but this conclusion must have been erroneous, as we have no right to believe that celibacy prevails in any instance; and some of the oldest of the women are without this distinction, and girls of a very tender age are marked by it.

On first setting foot in the country we were inclined to hold the spears of the natives very cheap. Fatal experience has, however, convinced us that the wound inflicted by this weapon is not a trivial one, and that the skill of the Indians in throwing it is far from despicable. Besides more than a dozen convicts who have unaccountably disappeared, we know that two who were employed as rush cutters up the harbour, were (from what cause we are yet ignorant) most dreadfully mangled and butchered by the natives. A spear had passed entirely through the thickest part of the body of one of them, though a very robust man, and the skull of the other was beaten in. Their tools were taken away, but some provisions which they had with them at the time of the murder, and their clothes, were left untouched. In addition to this misfortune, two more convicts, who were peaceably engaged in picking of greens on a spot very remote from that where their comrades suffered, were unawares attacked by a party of Indians, and before they could effect their escape one of them was pierced by a spear in the hip, after which they knocked him down and plundered his clothes. The poor wretch, though dreadfully wounded, made shift to crawl off, but his companion was carried away by these barbarians, and his fate doubtful until a soldier, a few days afterwards, picked up his jacket and hat in a native's hut, the latter pierced through by a spear.

We have found that these spears are not made invariably alike, some of them being barbed like a fish gig and others simply pointed. In repairing them they are no less dexterous than in throwing them. A broken one being given by a gentleman to an Indian, he instantly snatched up an oyster-shell and converted it with his teeth into a tool, with which he presently fashioned the spear and rendered it fit for use. In performing this operation the sole of his foot served him as a workboard. Nor are their weapons of offence confined to the spear only, for they have besides long wooden swords shaped like a sabre, capable of inflicting a mortal wound, and clubs of an immense size. Small targets, made of the bark of trees, are likewise now and then to be seen among them.†

From circumstances which have been observed, we have sometimes been inclined to believe these people at war with each other. They have more than once been seen assembled as if bent on an expedition. An officer one day met fourteen of them marching along in a regular Indian file through the woods, each man armed with a spear in his right hand and a large stone in his left. At their head appeared a chief, who was distinguished by being painted. Though in the proportion of five to one of our people they passed peaceably on.

That their skill in throwing the spear sometimes enables them to kill the kangaroo we have no right to doubt, as a long splinter of this weapon was taken out of the thigh of one of these animals, over which the flesh had completely closed; but

† These are shields.

we have never discovered that they have any method of ensnaring them, or that they know any other beasts but the kangaroo and dog. Whatever animal is shown them, a dog excepted, they call *kangaroo*: a strong presumption that the wild animals of the country are very few. †

Soon after our arrival at Port Jackson I was walking out near a place where I observed a party of Indians busily employed in looking at some sheep in an enclosure, and repeatedly crying out 'kangaroo, kangaroo'! As this seemed to afford them pleasure, I was willing to increase it by pointing out the horses and cows, which were at no great distance. But unluckily, at the moment, some female convicts employed near the place made their appearance, and all my endeavours to divert their attention from the ladies became fruitless. They attempted not, however, to offer them the least degree of violence or injury, but stood at the distance of several paces, expressing very significantly the manner they were attracted.

It would be trespassing on the reader's indulgence were I to impose on him an account of any civil regulations or ordinances which may possibly exist among this people. I declare to him that I know not of any, and that excepting a little tributary respect which the younger part appear to pay those more advanced in years, I never could observe any degrees of subordination among them. To their religious rites and opinions I am equally a stranger. Had an opportunity offered of seeing the ceremonies observed at disposing of the dead, perhaps, some insight might have been gained, but all that we at present know with certainty is that they burn the corpse and afterwards heap up the earth around it, somewhat in the

† The word 'kangaroo' was introduced to the Sydney area by members of the First Fleet. Sydney Aborigines knew the Eastern grey kangaroo (*Macropus giganteus*) as *patagorang*. It seems likely that they assumed that the word 'kangaroo' denoted something like 'large animal' to the Europeans, and used it in this context, hoping the strangers would understand.

manner of the small tumuli found in many counties of England.

I have already hinted that the country is more populous than it was generally believed to be in Europe at the time of our sailing. But this remark is not meant to be extended to the interior parts of the continent, which there is every reason to conclude, from our researches as well as from the manner of living practised by the natives, to be uninhabited. It appears as if some of the Indian families confine their society and connections within their own pale; but that this cannot always be the case we know, for on the north-west arm of Botany Bay stands a village which contains more than a dozen houses and perhaps five times that number of people, being the most considerable establishment that we are acquainted with in the country. As a striking proof, besides, of the numerousness of the natives, I beg leave to state that Governor Phillip, when on an excursion between the head of this harbour and that of Botany Bay, once fell in with a party which consisted of more than three hundred persons, 212 of whom were men. This happened only on the day following the murder of the two convict rush cutters, (before noticed) and His Excellency was at the very time in search of the murderers, on whom, could they have been found, he intended to inflict a memorable and exemplary punishment. The meeting was unexpected to both parties, and considering the critical situation of affairs perhaps not very pleasing to our side, which consisted but of twelve persons, until the peaceful disposition of the Indians was manifest. After the strictest search the governor was obliged to return without having gained any information. The laudable perseverance of His Excellency to throw every light on this unhappy and mysterious business did not, however, stop here, for he instituted the most rigorous inquiry to find out, if possible, whether the convicts had at any time ill treated or killed any of the natives; and farther, issued a proclamation offering the most tempting of all rewards, a state of freedom, to him who should point out the murderer, in case such an one existed.

I have thus impartially stated the situation of matters, as they stand while I write, between the natives and us. That greater progress in attaching them to us has not been made I have only to regret, but that all ranks of men have tried to effect it by every reasonable effort from which success might have been expected I can testify. Nor can I omit saying that in the higher stations this has been eminently conspicuous. The public orders of Governor Phillip have invariably tended to promote such a behaviour on our side as was most likely to produce this much wished-for event. To what cause then are we to attribute the distance which the accomplishment of it appears at? I answer, to the fickle, jealous, wavering disposition of the people we have to deal with, who, like all other savages, are either too indolent, too indifferent or too fearful to form an attachment on easy terms with those who differ in habits and manners so widely from themselves. Before I close the subject I cannot, however, omit to relate the following ludicrous adventure, which possibly may be of greater use in effecting what we have so much at heart than all our endeavours.

Some young gentlemen belonging to the *Sirius* one day met a native, an old man, in the woods. He had a beard of considerable length, which his new acquaintance gave him to understand, by signals, they would rid him of, if he pleased. Stroking their chins and showing him the smoothness of them at the same time, at length the old Indian consented, and one of the youngsters, taking a penknife from his pocket and making use of the best substitute for lather he could find, performed the operation with great success and, as it proved, much to the liking of the old man, who in a few days after reposed a confidence in us of which we had hitherto known no example, by paddling alongside the *Sirius* in his canoe and pointing to his beard. Various arts were ineffectually tried to induce him to enter the ship, but as he continued to decline the invitation a barber was sent down into the boat alongside the canoe, from whence, leaning over the gunnel, he complied with the wish of the old beau, to his infinite satisfaction. In addition to the consequences which our sanguine hopes led us to expect from this dawning of cordiality, it affords proof that the beard is considered by this people more as an encumbrance than a mark of dignity.

12

The departure of the French from Botany Bay, and the return of the Supply *from Norfolk Island, with a discovery made by Lieutenant Ball on his passage to it*

ABOUT the middle of the month our good friends the French departed from Botany Bay, in prosecution of their voyage. During their stay in that port the officers of the two nations had frequent opportunities of testifying their mutual regard by visits and every interchange of friendship and esteem. These ships sailed from France by order of the King on the 1st of August 1785, under the command of Monsieur La Perouse, an officer whose eminent qualifications, we had reason to think, entitle him to fill the highest stations. In England, particularly, he ought long to be remembered with admiration and gratitude for the humanity which marked his conduct when ordered to destroy our settlement at Hudsons's Bay in the last war. His second in command was the Chevalier Clonard, an officer also of distinguished merit.

In the course of the voyage these ships had been so unfortunate as to lose a boat, with many men and officers in her, off the west of California; and afterwards met with an accident still more to be regretted at an island in the Pacific Ocean, discovered by Monsieur Bougainville, in the latitude of 14° 19′ south, longitude 173° 3′20″ east of Paris. Here they had the misfortune to have no less than thirteen of their crews, among whom was the officer at that time second in command, cut off by the natives, and many more desperately wounded. To what cause this cruel event was to be attributed they knew not, as they were about to quit the island after having lived with the Indians in the greatest harmony for several weeks; and exchanged, during the time, their European commodities for the produce of the place, which they describe as filled with a race of people remarkable for beauty and comeliness; and abounding in refreshments of all kinds.

It was no less gratifying to an English ear than honourable to Monsieur La Perouse to witness the feeling manner in which he always mentioned the name and talents of Captain Cook. That illustrious circumnavigator had, he said, left nothing to those who might follow in his track to describe or fill up. As I found in the course of conversation that the French ships had touched at the Sandwich Islands,† I asked M. La Perouse what reception he had met with there. His answer deserves to be known: 'During the whole of our voyage in the South Seas, the people of the Sandwich Islands were the only Indians who never gave us cause of complaint. They furnished us liberally with provisions and administered cheerfully to all our wants.' It may not be improper to remark that Owhyee†† was not one of the islands visited by this gentleman.

In the short stay made by these ships at Botany Bay, an Abbe, one of the naturalists on board, died and was buried on the north shore. The French had hardly departed when the natives pulled down a small board which had been placed over the spot where the corpse was interred, and defaced everything around. On being informed of it, the governor sent a party over with orders to affix a plate of copper on a tree near the place, with the following inscription on it, which is a copy of what was written on the board:

Hic jacet L. RECEVEUR,

E. F. F. minnibus Galliae, Sacerdos, Physicus, in circumnavigatione mundi, Duce De La Perrouse.

Obiit die 17 Februarii, anno 1788.†††

† The Hawaiian Islands. †† Hawaii.

††† 'Here lies L. Receveur the Minorite, priest, physician, who died on

This mark of respectful attention was more particularly due from M. La Perouse having, when at Kamchatka, paid a similar tribute of gratitude to the memory of Captain Clarke, whose tomb was found in nearly as ruinous a state as that of the Abbe.

Like ourselves, the French found it necessary, more than once, to chastise a spirit of rapine and intrusion which prevailed among the Indians around the bay. The menace of pointing a musket to them was frequently used, and in one or two instances it was fired off, though without being attended with fatal consequences. Indeed the French commandant, both from a regard to the orders of his court, as well as to our quiet and security, showed a moderation and forbearance on this head highly becoming.

On the 20th of March the *Supply* arrived from Norfolk Island, after having safely landed Lieutenant King and his little garrison. The pine trees growing there are described to be of a growth and height superior, perhaps, to any in the world. But the difficulty of bringing them away will not be easily surmounted, from the badness and danger of the landing place. After the most exact search, not a single plant of the New Zealand flax could be found, though we had been taught to believe it abounded there.

Lieutenant Ball, in returning to Port Jackson, touched at a small island in latitude 31° 36′ south, longitude 159° 4′ east of Greenwich, which he had been fortunate enough to discover on his passage to Norfolk and to which he gave the name of Lord Howe's Island. It is entirely without inhabitants, or any traces of any having ever been there. But it happily abounds in what will be of infinitely more importance to the settlers on New South Wales. Green turtle of the finest kind frequent it in the summer season. Of this Mr Ball gave us some very handsome and acceptable specimens on his return. Besides turtle, the island is well stocked with birds, many of them so tame as

17 February 1788 while circumnavigating the globe under the leadership of La Perouse.'

to be knocked down by the seamen with sticks. At the distance of four leagues from Lord Howe's Island and in latitude 31° 30′ south, longitude 159° 8′ east, stands a remarkable rock of considerable height, to which Mr Ball gave the name of Ball's Pyramid, from the shape it bears.

While the *Supply* was absent Governor Phillip made an excursion to Broken Bay, a few leagues to the northward of Port Jackson, in order to explore it. As a harbour it almost equals the latter, but the adjacent country was found so rocky and bare as to preclude all possibility of turning it to account. Some rivulets of fresh water fall into the head of the bay, forming a very picturesque scene. The Indians who live on its banks are numerous and behaved attentively in a variety of instances while our people remained among them.

13

Transactions at Port Jackson in the months of April and May 1788

As winter was fast approaching it became necessary to secure ourselves in quarters which might shield us from the cold we were taught to expect in this hemisphere, though in so low a latitude. The erection of barracks for the soldiers was projected, and the private men of each company undertook to build for themselves two wooden houses, of sixty-eight feet in length and twenty-three in breadth. To forward the design, several sawpits were immediately set to work, and four ship carpenters attached to the battalion for the purpose of directing and completing this necessary undertaking. In prosecuting it, however, so many difficulties occurred that we were fain to circumscribe our original intentions and, instead of eight houses, content ourselves with four. And even these, from the badness of the timber, the scarcity of artificers and other impediments are, at the day on which I write, so little advanced that it will be well if at the close of the year 1788 we shall be established in them. In the meanwhile the married people, by proceeding on a more contracted scale, were soon under comfortable shelter. Nor were the convicts forgotten; and, as leisure was frequently afforded them for the purpose, little edifices quickly multiplied on the ground allotted them to build upon.

But as these habitations were intended by Governor Phillip to answer only the exigency of the moment, the plan of a town was drawn and the ground on which it is hereafter to stand surveyed and marked out. To proceed on a narrow, confined scale, in a country of the extensive limits we possess, would be unpardonable. Extent of empire demands grandeur of design. That this has been our view will be readily believed when I tell the reader that the principal street in our projected city will be, when completed agreeable to the plan laid down, two hundred feet in breadth, and all the rest of a corresponding proportion. How far this will be accompanied with adequate dispatch is another question, as the incredulous among us are sometimes hardy enough to declare that ten times our strength would not be able to finish it in as many years.

Invariably intent on exploring a country from which curiosity promises so many gratifications, His Excellency about this time undertook an expedition into the interior parts of the continent. His party consisted of eleven persons who, after being conveyed by water to the head of the harbour, proceeded in a westerly direction, to reach a chain of mountains which in clear weather are discernible, though at an immense distance, from some heights near our encampment.† With unwearied industry they continued to penetrate the country for four days but, at the end of that time, finding the base of the mountain to be yet at the distance of more than twenty miles and provisions growing scarce, it was judged prudent to return without having accomplished the end for which the expedition had been undertaken. To reward their toils our adventurers had, however, the pleasure of discovering and traversing an extensive tract of ground which they had reason to believe, from the

† The Blue Mountains.

observations they were enabled to make, capable of producing everything which a happy soil and genial climate can bring forth. In addition to this flattering appearance, the face of the country is such as to promise success whenever it shall be cultivated, the trees being at a considerable distance from each other and the intermediate space filled, not with underwood, but a thick rich grass growing in the utmost luxuriancy. I must not, however, conceal that in this long march our gentlemen found not a single rivulet, but were under a necessity of supplying themselves with water from standing pools which they met with in the valleys, supposed to be formed by the rains that fall at particular seasons of the year. Nor had they the good fortune to see any quadrupeds worth notice, except a few kangaroos. To their great surprise they observed indisputable tracks of the natives having been lately there, though in their whole route none of them were to be seen; nor any means to be traced by which they could procure subsistence so far from the sea shore.

On the 6th of May the *Supply* sailed for Lord Howe Island to take on board turtle for the settlement, but after waiting there several days was obliged to return without having seen one, owing we apprehended to the advanced season of the year. Three of the transports also, which were engaged by the East India Company to proceed to China to take on board a lading of tea, sailed about this time for Canton.

The unsuccessful return of the *Supply* cast a general damp on our spirits, for by this time fresh provisions were become scarcer than in a blockaded town. The little livestock, which with so heavy an expense and through so many difficulties, we had brought on shore, prudence forbade us to use; and fish, which on our arrival and for a short time after had been tolerable plenty, were become so scarce as to be rarely seen at the tables of the first among us. Had it not been for a stray kangaroo, which fortune now and then threw in our way, we should have been utter strangers to the taste of fresh food.

Thus situated, the scurvy began its usual ravages and extended its baneful influence, more or less through all descriptions of persons. Unfortunately the esculent vegetable productions of the country are neither plentiful nor tend very effectually to remove this disease. And the ground we had turned up and planted with garden seeds, either from the nature of the soil, or which is more probable, the lateness of the season, yielded but a scanty and insufficient supply of what we stood so greatly in need of.

During the period I am describing, few enormous offences were perpetrated by the convicts. A petty theft was now and then heard of and a spirit of refractory sullenness broke out at times in some individuals. One execution only, however, took place. The sufferer, who was a very young man, was convicted of a burglary, and met his fate with a hardiness and insensibility which the grossest ignorance and most deplorable want of feeling alone could supply.

14

From the beginning of June, to the departure of the ships for Europe

HOURS of festivity, which under happier skies pass away unregarded and are soon consigned to oblivion, acquire in this forlorn and distant circle a superior degree of acceptable importance.

On the anniversary of the King's birthday all the officers not on duty, both of the garrison and His Majesty's ships, dined with the governor. On so joyful an occasion, the first too ever celebrated in our new settlement, it were needless to say that loyal conviviality dictated every sentiment and inspired every guest. Among other public toasts drunk was prosperity to Sydney Cove, in Cumberland county, now named so by authority. At daylight in the morning the ships of war had fired twenty-one guns each, which was repeated at noon and answered by three volleys from the battalion of marines.

Nor were the officers alone partakers of the general relaxation. The four unhappy wretches labouring under the sentence of banishment were freed from their fetters to rejoin their former society; and three days given as holidays to every convict in the colony. Hospitality, too, which ever acquires a double relish by being extended, was not forgotten on the 4th of June, when each prisoner, male and female, received an allowance of grog; and every non-commissioned officer and private soldier had the honour of drinking prosperity to his royal master, in a pint of porter served out at the flagstaff, in addition to the customary allowance of spirits. Bonfires concluded the evening and I am happy to say that excepting a single instance which shall be taken notice of hereafter, no bad consequence or unpleasant remembrance flowed from an indulgence so amply bestowed.

About this time (June) an accident happened which I record with much regret. The whole of our black cattle, consisting of five cows and a bull, either from not being properly secured or from the negligence of those appointed to take care of them, strayed into the woods and in spite of all the search we have been able to make, are not yet found. As a convict of the name of Corbett, who was accused of a theft, eloped nearly at the same time, it was at first believed that he had taken the desperate measure of driving off the cattle in order to subsist on them as long as possible, or perhaps to deliver them to the natives. In this uncertainty, parties to search were sent out in different directions and the fugitive declared an outlaw, in case of not returning by a fixed day. After much anxiety and fatigue, those who had undertaken the task returned without finding the cattle. But on the 21st of the month Corbett made his appearance near a farm belonging to the governor, and entreated a convict who happened to be on the spot to give him some food, as he was perishing for hunger. The man applied to, under pretence of fetching what he asked for, went away and immediately gave the necessary information, in consequence of which a party under arms was sent out and apprehended him. When the poor wretch was brought in he was greatly emaciated and almost famished. But on proper restoratives being administered he was so far recovered by the 24th as to be able to stand his trial, when he pleaded guilty to the robbery with which he stood charged, and received sentence of death. In the course of repeated examinations it plainly appeared he was an utter stranger to the place where the cattle might be, and was in no shape concerned in having driven them off.

Samuel Peyton, convict, for having on the evening of the King's birthday broke open an officer's marquee with an intent to commit robbery, of which he was fully convicted, had sentence of death passed on him at the same time as Corbett; and on the following day they were both executed, confessing the justness of their fate and imploring the forgiveness of those whom they had injured. Peyton at the time of his suffering was but twenty years of age, the greatest part of which had been invariably passed in the commission of crimes that at length terminated in his ignominious end. The following letter, written by a fellow convict to the sufferer's unhappy mother, I shall make no apology for presenting to the reader. It affords a melancholy proof that not the ignorant and untaught only have provoked the justice of their country to banish them to this remote region.

Sydney Cove, Port Jackson,
New South Wales, 24th June, 1788.

My dear and honoured mother!

With a heart oppressed by the keenest sense of anguish, and too much agitated by the idea of my very melancholy condition, to express my own sentiments, I have prevailed on the goodness of a commiserating friend to do me the last sad office of acquainting you with the dreadful fate that awaits me.

My dear mother! with what agony of soul do I dedicate the few last moments of my life to bid you an eternal adieu: my doom being irrevocably fixed, and ere this hour tomorrow I shall have quitted this vale of wretchedness to enter into an unknown and endless eternity. I will not distress your tender maternal feelings by any long comment on the cause of my present misfortune. Let it therefore suffice to say that impelled by that strong propensity to evil, which neither the virtuous precepts nor example of the best of parents could eradicate, I have at length fallen an unhappy, though just, victim to my own follies.

Too late I regret my inattention to your admonitions, and feel myself sensibly affected by the remembrance of the many anxious moments you have passed on my account. For these and all my other transgressions, however great, I supplicate the Divine forgiveness; and encouraged by the promises of that Saviour who died for us all, I trust to receive that mercy in the world to come, which my offences have deprived me of all hope, or expectation of, in this. The affliction which this will cost you, I hope the Almighty will enable you to bear. Banish from your memory all my former indiscretions, and let the cheering hope of a happy meeting hereafter console you for my loss. Sincerely penitent for my sins; sensible of the justice of my conviction and sentence, and firmly relying on the merits of a Blessed Redeemer, I am at perfect peace with all mankind, and trust I shall yet experience that peace which this world cannot give. Commend my soul to the Divine mercy. I bid you an eternal farewell.

Your unhappy dying Son,
Samuel Peyton.

After this nothing occurred with which I think it necessary to trouble the reader. The contents of the following chapters could not, I conceive, be so properly interwoven in the body of the work. I have, therefore, assigned them a place by themselves with a view that the conclusions adopted in them may be more strongly enforced on the minds of those to whom they are more particularly addressed.

15

The face of the country, its productions, climate, etc.

To the geographical knowledge of this country supplied by Captain Cook and Captain Furneaux we were able to add nothing. The latter explored the coast from Van Diemen's

Land to the latitude of 39° south; and Cook from Point Hicks, which lies in 37° 58′, to Endeavour Straits. The intermediate space between the end of Furneaux's discovery and Point Hicks is therefore the only part of the south-east coast unknown, and it so happened on our passage thither, owing to the weather, which forbade any part of the ships engaging with the shore, that we are unable to pronounce whether or not a strait intersects the continent hereabouts: though I beg to say that I have been informed by a naval friend that, when the fleet was off this part of the coast, a strong set offshore was plainly felt.

At the distance of sixty miles inland, a prodigious chain of lofty mountains runs nearly in a north and south direction further than the eye can trace them. Should nothing intervene to prevent it, the governor intends shortly to explore their summits, and I think there can be little doubt that his curiosity will not go unrewarded. If large rivers do exist in the country, which some of us are almost sceptical enough to doubt, their sources must arise amidst these hills; and the direction they run in, for a considerable distance, must be either due north or due south. For it is strikingly singular that three such noble harbours as Botany Bay, Port Jackson and Broken Bay alike end in shallows and swamps filled with mangroves.†

The general face of the country is certainly pleasing, being diversified with gentle ascents, and little winding valleys, covered for the most part with large spreading trees which afford a succession of leaves in all seasons. In those places where trees are scarce a variety of flowering shrubs abound, most of them entirely new to an European and surpassing in beauty, fragrance and number, all I ever saw in an uncultivated state. Among these, a tall shrub bearing an elegant white flower which smells like English May is particularly delightful, and perfumes the air around to a great distance.†† The species of trees are few and, I am concerned to add, the wood universally

† The mouth of the Hawkesbury was not yet discovered.

†† Tench was encountering of course the distinctive and diverse

of so bad a grain as almost to preclude a possibility of using it. The increase of labour occasioned by this in our buildings has been such as nearly to exceed belief. These trees yield a profusion of thick red gum (not unlike the *sanguis draconis*) which is found serviceable in medicine, particularly in dysenteric complaints, where it has sometimes succeeded when all other preparations have failed. To blunt its acrid qualities, it is usual to combine it with opiates.

The nature of the soil is various. That immediately round Sydney Cove is sandy, with here and there a stratum of clay. From the sand we have yet been able to draw very little, but there seems no reason to doubt that many large tracts of land around us will bring to perfection whatever shall be sown in them. To give this matter a fair trial some practical farmers capable of such an undertaking should be sent out; for the spots we have chosen for experiments in agriculture, in which we can scarce be supposed adepts, have hitherto but ill repaid our toil, which may be imputable to our having chosen such as are unfavourable for our purpose.

Except from the size of the trees, the difficulties of clearing the land are not numerous, underwood being rarely found, though the country is not absolutely without it. Of the natural meadows which Mr Cook mentions near Botany Bay, we can give no account. None such exist about Port Jackson. Grass, however, grows in every place but the swamps with the greatest vigour and luxuriancy, though it is not of the finest quality and it is found to agree better with horses and cows than sheep. A few wild fruits are sometimes procured, among which is the small purple apple mentioned by Cook, and a fruit which has the appearance of a grape, though in taste more like a green gooseberry, being excessively sour.† Probably were it

heathland flora of the Sydney Sandstone. The shrub with white flowers is probably tea-tree or melaleuca.

† The former was probably a lilly pilly *Syzygium*, and the latter possibly a geebung *Persoonia*.

meliorated by cultivation it would become more palatable.

Fresh water, as I have said before, is found but in inconsiderable quantities. For the common purposes of life there is generally enough, but we know of no stream in the country capable of turning a mill; and the remarks made by Mr Anderson, of the dryness of the country round Adventure Bay,† extends without exception to every part of it which we have penetrated.

Previous to leaving England I remember to have frequently heard it asserted that the discovery of mines was one of the secondary objects of the expedition. Perhaps there are mines, but as no person competent to form a decision is to be found among us, I wish no one to adopt an idea that I mean to impress him with such a belief when I state that individuals, whose judgments are not despicable, are willing to think favourably of this conjecture, from specimens of ore seen in many of the stones picked up here. I cannot quit this subject without regretting that someone capable of throwing a better light on it is not in the colony. Nor can I help being equally concerned that an experienced botanist was not sent out, for the purpose of collecting and describing the rare and beautiful plants with which the country abounds. Indeed, we flattered ourselves when at the Cape of Good Hope that Mason, the King's botanical gardener (who was employed there in collecting for the royal nursery at Kew) would have joined us, but it seems his orders and engagements prevented him from quitting that beaten track to enter on this scene of novelty and variety.

To the naturalist this country holds out many invitations. Birds, though not remarkably numerous, are in great variety and of the most exquisite beauty of plumage, among which are the cockatoo, lory, and parakeet; but the bird which principally claims attention is a species of ostrich, approaching nearer to the emu of South America than any other we know of.†† One

† In Tasmania.

†† The South American emu is a rhea.

of them was shot at a considerable distance with a single ball by a convict employed for that purpose by the governor. Its weight, when complete, was seventy pounds, and its length from the end of the toe to the tip of the beak, seven feet two inches, though there was reason to believe it had not attained its full growth. On dissection many anatomical singularities were observed. The gall-bladder was remarkably large, the liver not bigger than that of a barn-door fowl, and after the strictest search no gizzard could be found. The legs, which were of a vast length, were covered with thick, strong scales, plainly indicating the animal to be formed for living amidst deserts, and the foot differed from an ostrich's by forming a triangle instead of being cloven.†

Goldsmith, whose account of the emu is the only one I can refer to, says, 'that it is covered from the back and rump with long feathers, which fall backward and cover the anus. These feathers are grey on the back and white on the belly.' The wings are so small as hardly to deserve the name, and are unfurnished with those beautiful ornaments which adorn the wings of the ostrich. All the feathers are extremely coarse, but the construction of them deserves notice—they grow in pairs from a single shaft, a singularity which the author I have quoted has omitted to remark. It may be presumed that these birds are not very scarce as several have been seen, some of them immensely large, but they are so wild as to make shooting them a matter of great difficulty. Though incapable of flying, they run with such swiftness that our fleetest greyhounds are left far behind in every attempt to catch them. The flesh was eaten, and tasted like beef.

Besides the emu, many birds of prodigious size have been seen, which promise to increase the number of those described by naturalists, whenever we shall be fortunate enough to obtain them; but among these the bat of the Endeavour River is not to be found. In the woods are various little songsters,

† The foot was three rather than two-toed.

whose notes are equally sweet and plaintive.

Of quadrupeds, except the kangaroo, I have little to say. The few met with are almost invariably of the opossum tribe, but even these do not abound. To beasts of prey we are utter strangers, nor have we yet any cause to believe that they exist in the country. And happy it is for us that they do not, as their presence would deprive us of the only fresh meals the settlement affords, the flesh of the kangaroo. This singular animal is already known in Europe by the drawing and description of Mr Cook. To the drawing nothing can be objected but the position of the claws of the hinder leg, which are mixed together like those of a dog, whereas no such indistinctness is to be found in the animal I am describing. It was the Chevalier La Perouse who pointed out this to me, while we were comparing a kangaroo with the plate, which, as he justly observed, is correct enough to give the world in general a good idea of the animal, but not sufficiently accurate for the man of science.

Of the natural history of the kangaroo we are still very ignorant. We may, however, venture to pronounce this animal a new species of opossum, the female being furnished with a bag in which the young is contained, and in which the teats are found. These last are only two in number, a strong presumptive proof, had we no other evidence, that the kangaroo brings forth rarely more than one at a birth. But this is settled beyond a doubt from more than a dozen females having been killed, which had invariably but one formed in the pouch. Notwithstanding this, the animal may be looked on as prolific from the early age it begins to breed at, kangaroos with young having been taken of not more than thirty pounds weight; and there is room to believe that when at their utmost growth they weigh not less than 150 pounds. A male of 130 pounds weight has been killed, whose dimensions were as follows:

	Feet	Inches
Extreme length	7	3
Ditto of the tail	3	4½
Ditto of the hinder legs	3	2
Ditto of the forepaws	1	7½
Circumference of the tail at the root	1	5

After this perhaps I shall hardly be credited when I affirm that the kangaroo, on being brought forth, is not larger than an English mouse. It is, however, in my power to speak positively on this head, as I have seen more than one instance of it.

In running, this animal confines himself entirely to his hinder legs, which are possessed with an extraordinary muscular power. Their speed is very great, though not in general quite equal to that of a greyhound; but when the greyhounds are so fortunate as to seize them they are incapable of retaining their hold, from the amazing struggles of the animal. The bound of the kangaroo, when not hard pressed, has been measured and found to exceed twenty feet.

At what time of the year they copulate, and in what manner, we know not. The testicles of the male are placed contrary to the usual order of nature.†

When young, the kangaroo eats tender and well flavoured, tasting like veal, but the old ones are more tough and stringy than bull-beef. They are not carnivorous and subsist altogether on particular flowers and grass. Their bleat is mournful and very different from that of any other animal. It is, however, seldom heard but in the young ones.

Fish, which our sanguine hopes led us to expect in great quantities, do not abound. In summer they are tolerably plentiful, but for some months past very few have been taken. Botany Bay in this respect exceeds Port Jackson. The French once caught near two thousand fish in one day, of a

† The testicles are placed in front of the penis in all marsupials.

species of grouper, to which, from the form of a bone in the head resembling a helmet, we have given the name of light horseman.† To this may be added bass, mullets, skate, soles, leather-jackets and many other species, all so good in their kind as to double our regret at their not being more numerous. Sharks of an enormous size are found here. One of these was caught by the people on board the *Sirius*, which measured at the shoulders six feet and a half in circumference. His liver yielded twenty-four gallons of oil, and in his stomach was found the head of a shark which had been thrown overboard from the same ship. The Indians, probably from having felt the effects of their voracious fury, testify the utmost horror on seeing these terrible fish.

Venomous animals and reptiles are rarely seen. Large snakes beautifully variegated have been killed, but of the effect of their bites we are happily ignorant.†† Insects, though numerous, are by no means, even in summer, so troublesome as I have found them in America, the West Indies and other countries.

The climate is undoubtedly very desirable to live in. In summer the heats are usually moderated by the sea breeze, which sets in early, and in winter the degree of cold is so slight as to occasion no inconvenience. Once or twice we have had hoar frosts and hail, but no appearance of snow. The thermometer has never risen beyond 84, nor fallen lower than 35. In general it stood in the beginning of February at between 78 and 74 at noon. Nor is the temperature of the air less healthy than pleasant. Those dreadful putrid fevers by which new countries are so often ravaged are unknown to us and, excepting a slight diarrhoea which prevailed soon after we had landed, and was fatal in very few instances, we are strangers to epidemic diseases.

On the whole (thunderstorms in the hot months excepted) I know not any climate equal to this I write in. Ere we had been a fortnight on shore we experienced some storms of thunder

† Snapper.

†† Diamond python, *Morelia spilotes*.

accompanied with rain, than which nothing can be conceived more violent and tremendous, and their repetition for several days, joined to the damage they did by killing several of our sheep, led us to draw presages of an unpleasant nature. Happily, however, for many months we have escaped any similar visitations.

16

The progress made in the settlement, and the situation of affairs at the time of the ship, which conveys this account, sailing for England

FOR the purpose of expediting the public work the male convicts have been divided into gangs, over each of which a person, selected from among themselves, is placed. It is to be regretted that government did not take this matter into consideration before we left England and appoint proper persons with reasonable salaries to execute the office of overseers, as the consequence of our present imperfect plan is such as to defeat in a great measure the purposes for which the prisoners were sent out. The female convicts have hitherto lived in a state of total idleness, except a few who are kept to work in making pegs for tiles and picking up shells for burning into lime. For the last time I repeat that the behaviour of all classes of these people since our arrival in the settlement has been better than could, I think, have been expected from them.

Temporary wooden storehouses covered with thatch or shingles, in which the cargoes of all the ships have been lodged, are completed; and an hospital is erected. Barracks for the military are considerably advanced and little huts to serve until something more permanent can be finished have been raised on all sides. Notwithstanding this the encampments of the marines and convicts are still kept up, and to secure their owners from the coldness of the nights are covered in with bushes and thatched over.

The plan of a town I have already said is marked out. And as freestone of an excellent quality abounds, one requisite towards the completion of it is attained. Only two houses of stone are yet begun, which are intended for the governor and lieutenant-governor. One of the greatest impediments we meet with is a want of limestone, of which no signs appear. Clay for making bricks is in plenty, and a considerable quantity of them burned and ready for use.

In enumerating the public buildings I find I have been so remiss as to omit an observatory which is erected at a small distance from the encampments. It is nearly completed, and when fitted up with the telescopes and other astronomical instruments sent out by the Board of Longitude, will afford a desirable retreat from the listlessness of a camp evening at Port Jackson. One of the principal reasons which induced the board to grant this apparatus was for the purpose of enabling Lieutenant Dawes of the marines (to whose care it is entrusted) to make observations on a comet which is shortly expected to appear in the southern hemisphere. The latitude of the observatory, from the result of more than three hundred observations, is fixed at 33° 52′ 30″ south, and the longitude at 151° 16′ 30″ east of Greenwich. The latitude of the south head which forms the entrance of the harbour, 33° 51′, and that of the north head opposite to it at 33° 49′ 45″ south.

Since landing here our military force has suffered a diminution of only three persons, a sergeant and two privates. Of the convicts fifty-four have perished, including the executions. Amidst the causes of this mortality, excessive toil and a scarcity of food are not to be numbered, as the reader will easily conceive when informed that they have the same allowance of provisions as every officer and soldier in the garrison, and are indulged by being exempted from labour every Saturday afternoon and Sunday. On the latter of those days they are expected to attend divine service, which is performed either within one of the storehouses or under a great tree in the open air, until a church can be built.

Amidst our public labours, that no fortified post or place of security is yet begun may be a matter of surprise. Were an emergency in the night to happen, it is not easy to say what might not take place before troops, scattered about in an extensive encampment, could be formed so as to act. An event that happened a few evenings since may, perhaps, be the means of forwarding this necessary work. In the dead of night the sentinels on the eastern side of the cove were alarmed by the voices of the Indians talking near their posts. The soldiers on this occasion acted with their usual firmness, and without creating a disturbance acquainted the officer of the guard with the circumstance, who immediately took every precaution to prevent an attack, and at the same time gave orders that no molestation, while they continued peaceable, should be offered them. From the darkness of the night and the distance they kept at, it was not easy to ascertain their number, but from the sound of the voices and other circumstances, it was calculated at near thirty. To their intentions in honouring us with this visit (the only one we have had from them in the last five months) we are strangers, though most probably it was either with a view to pilfer or to ascertain in what security we slept, and the precautions we used in the night. When the bells of the ships in the harbour struck the hour of the night and the sentinels called out on their posts 'All's well', they observed a dead silence, and continued it for some minutes, though talking with the greatest earnestness and vociferation but the moment before. After having remained a considerable time they departed without interchanging a syllable with our people.

17

Some thoughts on the advantages which may arise to the mother country from forming the colony

THE author of these sheets would subject himself to the charge of presumption were he to aim at developing the intentions of government in forming this settlement. But without giving offence, or incurring reproach, he hopes his opinion on the probability of advantage to be drawn from hence by Great Britain may be fairly made known.

If only a receptacle for convicts be intended, this place stands unequalled from the situation, extent, and nature of the country. When viewed in a commercial light, I fear its insignificance will appear very striking. The New Zealand hemp, of which so many sanguine expectations were formed, is not a native of the soil; and Norfolk Island, where we made sure to find this article, is also without it. So that the scheme of being able to assist the East Indies with naval stores, in case of a war, must fall to the ground, both from this deficiency and the quality of the timber growing here. Were it indeed possible to transport that of Norfolk Island, its value would be found very great, but the difficulty, from the surf, I am well informed, is so insuperable as to forbid the attempt. Lord Howe Island, discovered by Lieut. Ball, though an inestimable acquisition to our colony, produces little else than the mountain cabbage tree.†

Should a sufficient military force be sent out to those employed in cultivating the ground, I see no room to doubt that in the course of a few years the country will be able to yield grain enough for the support of its new possessors. But to effect this our present limits must be greatly extended, which will require detachments of troops not to be spared from the present establishment. And, admitting the position, the parent country will still have to supply us for a much longer time with every other necessary of life. For after what we have seen, the idea of being soon able to breed cattle sufficient for our consumption must appear chimerical and absurd. From all which it is evident that should Great Britain neglect to send out regular supplies, the most fatal consequences will ensue.

Speculators who may feel inclined to try their fortunes here will do well to weigh what I have said. If golden dreams of

† *Kentia* palm.

commerce and wealth flatter their imaginations, disappointment will follow. The remoteness of situation, productions of the country and want of connection with other parts of the world justify me in the assertion. But to men of small property, unambitious of trade, and wishing for retirement, I think the continent of New South Wales not without inducements. One of this description, with letters of recommendation and a sufficient capital (after having provided for his passage hither) to furnish him with an assortment of tools for clearing land, agricultural and domestic purposes, possessed also of a few household utensils, a cow, a few sheep and breeding sows, would, I am of opinion, with proper protection and encouragement, succeed in obtaining a comfortable livelihood, were he well assured before he quitted his native country that a provision for him until he might be settled should be secured, and that a grant of land on his arrival should be allotted him.

That this adventurer, if of a persevering character and competent knowledge, might in the course of ten years bring matters into such a train as to render himself comfortable and independent, I think highly probable. The superfluities of his farm would enable him to purchase European commodities from the masters of ships, which will arrive on government account, sufficient to supply his wants. But beyond this he ought not to reckon, for admitting that he might meet with success in raising tobacco, rice, indigo, or vineyards (for which last I think the soil and climate admirably adapted), the distance of a mart to vend them at would make the expense of transportation so excessive as to cut off all hopes of a reasonable profit. Nor can there be consumers enough here to take them off his hands, for so great a length of time to come as I shall not be at the trouble of computing.

Should then anyone, induced by this account, emigrate hither, let him, before he quits England, provide all his wearing apparel for himself, family and servants, his furniture, tools of every kind and implements of husbandry (among which a plough need not be included, as we make use of the hoe), for he will touch at no place where they can be purchased to advantage. If his sheep and hogs are English also, it will be better. For wines, spirits, tobacco, sugar, coffee, tea, rice, poultry and many other articles, he may venture to rely on at Tenerife or Madeira, the Brazils and Cape of Good Hope. It will not be his interest to draw bills on his voyage out, as the exchange of money will be found invariably against him and a large discount also deducted. Drafts on the place he is to touch at, or cash (dollars if possible) will best answer his end.

To men of desperate fortune and the lowest classes of the people, unless they can procure a passage as indented servants, similar to the custom practised of emigrating to America, this part of the world offers no temptation: for it can hardly be supposed that government will be fond of maintaining them here until they can be settled, and without such support they must starve.

Of the governor's instructions and intentions relative to the disposal of the convicts, when the term of their transportation shall be expired, I am ignorant. They will then be free men and at liberty, I apprehend, either to settle in the country or to return to Europe. The former will be attended with some public expense, and the latter, except in particular cases, will be difficult to accomplish from the numberless causes which prevent a frequent communication between England and this continent.

Postscript

Sydney Cove, Port Jackson, New South Wales.

October 1st, 1788. Little material has occurred in this colony since the departure of the ships for England on the 14th of July last. On the 20th of that month His Majesty's ship Supply, Captain Ball, sailed for Norfolk Island, and returned on 26th August. Our accounts from thence are more favourable than were expected. The soil proves admirably adapted to produce all kinds of grain and European vegetables. But the discovery that constitutes its value is the New Zealand flax, plants of which are found growing in every part of the island in the utmost luxuriancy and abundance. This will, beyond doubt, appear strange to the reader after what has been related in the former part of my work: and in future, let the credit of the testimony be as high as it may, I shall never without diffidence and hesitation presume to contradict the narrations of Mr Cook. The truth is that those sent to settle and explore the island knew not the form in which the plant grows, and were unfurnished with every particular which could lead to a knowledge of it. Unaccountable as this may sound, it is, nevertheless, incontestably true. Captain Ball brought away with him several specimens for inspection, and, on trial, by some flax-dressers among us, the threads produced from them, though coarse, are pronounced to be stronger, more likely to be durable, and fitter for every purpose of manufacturing cordage than any ever before dressed.

Every research has been made by those on the island to find a landing place whence it might be practicable to ship off the timber growing there, but hitherto none has been discovered. A plan, however, for making one has been laid before the governor, and it is at present under consideration, though (in the opinion of many here) it is not such an one as will be found to answer the end proposed.

Lieut. King and his little garrison were well when the *Supply* left them but I am sorry to add that, from casualties, their number is already five less than it originally was. A ship from hence is ready to sail with an increase in force, besides many convicts for the purpose of sawing up timber, and turning the flax-plant to advantage.

So much for Norfolk. In Port Jackson all is quiet and stupid as could be wished. We generally hear the lie of day as soon as the beating of the reveille announces the return of it; find it contradicted by breakfast time; and pursue a second through all its varieties, until night, welcome as to a lover, gives us to sleep and dream ourselves transported to happier climes.

Let me not, however, neglect telling you the little news which presents itself. All descriptions of men enjoy the highest state of health and the convicts continue to behave extremely well. A gang of one hundred of them, guarded by a captain, two subalterns and twenty marines, is about to be sent up to the head of the harbour, at the distance of three leagues in a westerly direction from Sydney Cove, for the purpose of establishing a settlement there. The convicts are to be employed in putting the land around into cultivation, as it appears to be of a more promising nature than that near the encampment. Indeed this last hitherto succeeds but very indifferently, though I do not yet despair that when good seeds can be procured, our toil will be better rewarded. But as this is an event at a distance, and in itself very precarious, Governor Phillip has determined on procuring a supply of flour and other necessaries from the Cape of Good Hope, as our stock on hand is found to be, on examination, not quite so ample as has been reckoned upon. To execute this purpose His Excellency has ordered the *Sirius* to prepare for the voyage, by which conveyance the opportunity of writing to you is afforded me. It was at first intended to dispatch the *Sirius* to some of the neighbouring islands (the Friendly or Society) in the Pacific Ocean to procure stock there, but the uselessness of the scheme, joined to the situation of matters here, has, happily for us, prevented its being put into execution.

Book Two:
A Complete Account of the Settlement at Port Jackson

WHEN it is recollected how much has been written to describe the settlement of New South Wales, it seems necessary, if not to offer an apology, yet to assign a reason for an additional publication.

The author embarked in the fleet which sailed to found the establishment at Botany Bay. He shortly after published a narrative of the proceedings and state of the colony, brought up to the beginning of July 1788, which was well received and passed through three editions. This could not but inspire both confidence and gratitude; but gratitude would be badly manifested were he, on the presumption of former favour, to lay claim to present indulgence. He resumes the subject in the humble hope of communicating information and increasing knowledge of the country which he describes.

He resided at Port Jackson nearly four years, from the 20th of January 1788 until the 18th of December 1791. To an active and contemplative mind a new country is an inexhaustible source of curiosity and speculation. It was the author's custom not only to note daily occurrences and to inspect and record the progression of improvement; but also, when not prevented by military duties, to penetrate the surrounding country in different directions in order to examine its nature and ascertain its relative geographical situations.

The greatest part of the work is inevitably composed of those materials which a journal supplies; but wherever reflections could be introduced without fastidiousness and parade he has not scrupled to indulge them, in common with every other deviation which the strictness of narrative would allow.

When this publication was nearly ready for the press, and when many of the opinions which it records had been declared, fresh accounts from Port Jackson were received. To the state of a country where so many anxious trying hours of his life have passed the author cannot feel indifferent. If by any sudden revolution of the laws of nature, or by any fortunate discovery of those on the spot, it has really become that fertile and prosperous land which some represent it to be, he begs permission to add his voice to the general congratulation. He rejoices at its success; but it is only justice to himself and those with whom he acted to declare that they feel no cause of reproach that so complete and happy an alteration did not take place at an earlier period.

1

A retrospect of the state of the colony of Port Jackson on the date of my former narrative in July 1788

PREVIOUS to commencing any farther account of the subject which I am about to treat, such a retrospection of the circumstances and situation of the settlement at the conclusion of my former narrative, as shall lay its state before the reader, seems necessary in order to connect the present with the past.

The departure of the first fleet of ships for Europe on the 14th of July 1788 had been long impatiently expected, and had filled us with anxiety to communicate to our friends an account of our situation, describing the progress of improvement and the probability of success or failure in our enterprise. That men should judge very oppositely on so doubtful and precarious an event will hardly surprise.

Such relations could contain little besides the sanguineness of hope and the enumeration of hardships and difficulties which former accounts had not led us to expect. Since our disembarkation in the preceding January, the efforts of everyone had been unremittingly exerted to deposit the public stores in a state of shelter and security and to erect habitations for ourselves. We were eager to escape from tents where a fold of canvas, only, interposed to check the vertic beams of the sun in summer and the chilling blasts of the south in winter. A marquee pitched in our finest season on an English lawn, or a transient view of those gay camps near the metropolis which so many remember, naturally draws forth careless and unmeaning exclamations of rapture which attach ideas of pleasure only to this part of a soldier's life. But an encampment amidst the rocks and wilds of a new country, aggravated by the miseries of bad diet and incessant toil, will find few admirers.

Nor were our exertions less unsuccessful than they were laborious. Under wretched covers of thatch lay our provisions and stores, exposed to destruction from every flash of lightning and every spark of fire. A few of the convicts had got into huts, but almost all the officers and the whole of the soldiery were still in tents.

In such a situation, where knowledge of the mechanic arts afforded the surest recommendation to notice, it may be easily conceived that attention to the parade duty of the troops gradually diminished. Now were to be seen officers and soldiers not 'trailing the puissant pike',† but felling the ponderous gum-tree or breaking the stubborn clod. And though 'the broad falchion did not in a ploughshare end',†† the possession of a spade, a wheelbarrow or a dunghill was more coveted than the most refulgent arms in which heroism ever dazzled. Those hours, which in other countries are devoted to martial acquirements, were here consumed in the labours of the sawpit, the forge and the quarry.*

† William Shakespeare, *Henry V*, iv, i, 40: 'Trail'st thou the puissant pike?'

†† Alexander Pope, 'Messiah—A sacred eclogue, in imitation of Virgil's *Pollio*': 'And the broad Faulchion in a Plow-share end.'

* 'The Swedish prisoners, taken at the battle of Pultowa, were transported

Of the two ships of war, the *Sirius* and *Supply*, the latter was incessantly employed in transporting troops, convicts and stores to Norfolk Island, and the *Sirius* in preparing for a voyage to some port where provisions for our use might be purchased, the expected supply from England not having arrived. It is but justice to the officers and men of both these ships to add that, on all occasions, they fully shared every hardship and fatigue with those on shore.

On the convicts the burden fell yet heavier. Necessity compelled us to allot to them the most slavish and laborious employments. Those operations, which in other countries are performed by the brute creation, were here effected by the exertions of men; but this ought not be considered a grievance because they had always been taught to expect it as the inevitable consequence of their offences against society. Severity was rarely exercised on them and justice was administered without partiality or discrimination. Their ration of provisions, except in being debarred from an allowance of spirits, was equal to that which the marines received. Under these circumstances I record with pleasure that they behaved better than had been predicted of them—to have expected sudden and complete reformation of conduct were romantic and chimerical.

Our cultivation of the land was yet in its infancy. We had hitherto tried only the country contiguous to Sydney. Here the governor had established a government farm, at the head of which a competent person of his own household was placed, with convicts to work under him. Almost the whole of the officers likewise accepted of small tracts of ground for the purpose of raising grain and vegetables, but experience proved to us

by the Czar Peter to the most remote parts of Siberia with a view to civilise the natives of the country and teach them the arts the Swedes possessed. In this hopeless situation all traces of discipline and subordination between the different ranks were quickly obliterated. The soldiers, who were husbandmen and artificers, found out their superiority, and assumed it; the officers became their servants.' Voltaire.

that the soil would produce neither without manure and, as this was not to be procured, our vigour soon slackened and most of the farms (among which was the one belonging to government) were successively abandoned.

With the natives we were very little more acquainted than on our arrival in the country. Our intercourse with them was neither frequent or cordial. They seemed studiously to avoid us, either from fear, jealousy or hatred. When they met with unarmed stragglers they sometimes killed and sometimes wounded them. I confess that, in common with many others, I was inclined to attribute this conduct to a spirit of malignant levity. But a farther acquaintance with them, founded on several instances of their humanity and generosity (which shall be noticed in their proper places), has entirely reversed my opinion and led me to conclude that the unprovoked outrages committed upon them by unprincipled individuals among us caused the evils we had experienced. To prevent them from being plundered of their fishing-tackle and weapons of war, a proclamation was issued forbidding their sale among us, but it was not attended with the good effect which was hoped for from it.

During this period, notwithstanding the want of fresh provisions and vegetables and almost constant exposure to the vicissitudes of a variable climate, disease rarely attacked us and the number of deaths was too inconsiderable to deserve mention.

Norfolk Island had been taken possession of by a party detached for that purpose early after our arrival. Few accounts of it had yet reached us and here I beg leave to observe that as I can speak of this island only from the relations of others (never having myself been there), I shall in every part of this work mention it as sparingly as possible. And this more especially as it seems probable that some of those gentlemen, who from accurate knowledge and long residence on it are qualified to write its history, will oblige the world with such a publication.

2

Transactions of the colony from the sailing of the first fleet in July 1788 to the close of that year

IT was impossible to behold without emotion the departure of the ships. On their speedy arrival in England perhaps hinged our fate, by hastening our supplies to us.

On the 20th of July, the *Supply* sailed for Norfolk Island and returned to us on the 26th of August, bringing no material news except that the soil was found to suit grain and other seeds, which had been sown in it, and that a species of flax plant was discovered to grow spontaneously on the island.

A survey of the harbour of Port Jackson was now undertaken in order to compute the number of canoes and inhabitants which it might contain. Sixty-seven canoes and 147 people were counted. No estimate, however, of even tolerable accuracy can be drawn from so imperfect a datum, though it was perhaps the best in our power to acquire.

In July and August we experienced more inclement, tempestuous weather than had been observed at any former period of equal duration. And yet it deserves to be remarked, in honour of the climate, that although our number of people exceeded 900, not a single death happened in the latter month.

The dread of want in a country destitute of natural resource is ever peculiarly terrible. We had long turned our eyes with impatience towards the sea, cheered by the hope of seeing supplies from England approach. But, none arriving, on the 2nd of October the *Sirius* sailed for the Cape of Good Hope, with directions to purchase provisions there for the use of our garrison.

A new settlement, named by the governor Rose Hill, sixteen miles inland, was established on the 3rd of November, the soil here being judged better than that around Sydney. A small redoubt was thrown up and a captain's detachment posted in it to protect the convicts who were employed to cultivate the ground.

The two last of the transports left us for England on the 19th of November, intending to make their passage by Cape Horn. There now remained with us only the *Supply*. Sequestered and cut off as we were from the rest of civilised nature, their absence carried the effect of desolation.

About this time a convict of the name of Daly was hanged, for a burglary. This culprit, who was a notorious thief and impostor, was the author of a discovery of a gold mine a few months before. A composition resembling ore mingled with earth, which he pretended to have brought from it, he produced. After a number of attendant circumstances too ludicrous and contemptible to relate, which befell a party who were sent under his guidance to explore this second Peru, he at last confessed that he had broken up an old pair of buckles and mixed the pieces with sand and stone. On essaying the composition, the brass was detected. The fate of this fellow I should not deem worth recording did it not lead to the following observation, that the utmost circumspection is necessary to prevent imposition in those who give accounts of what they see in unknown countries. We found the convicts particularly happy in fertility of invention and exaggerated descriptions. Hence large freshwater rivers, valuable ores, and quarries of limestone, chalk and marble were daily proclaimed soon after we had landed. At first we hearkened with avidity to such accounts, but perpetual disappointments taught us to listen with caution and to believe from demonstration only.

Unabated animosity continued to prevail between the natives and us. In addition to former losses, a soldier and several convicts suddenly disappeared and were never afterwards heard of. Three convicts were also wounded and one killed by them, near Botany Bay. Similar to the vindictive spirit which Mr Cook found to exist among their countrymen at Endeavour River, they more than once attempted to set fire to combustible matter in order to annoy us.

Early on the morning of the 18th of December, word was brought that they were assembled in force near the brick-kilns, which stand but a mile from the town of Sydney. The terror of those who brought the first intelligence magnified the number to two thousand. A second messenger diminished it to four hundred. A detachment under the command of an officer was ordered to march immediately and reconnoitre them. The officer soon returned and reported that about fifty Indians had appeared at the brick-kilns; but upon the convicts, who were at work there, pointing their spades and shovels at them, in the manner of guns, they had fled into the woods.

Tired of this state of petty warfare and endless uncertainty, the governor at length determined to adopt a decisive measure by capturing some of them and retaining them by force, which we supposed would either inflame the rest to signal vengeance (in which case we should know the worst, and provide accordingly) or else it would induce an intercourse, by the report which our prisoners would make of the mildness and indulgence with which we used them. And farther, it promised to unveil the cause of their mysterious conduct, by putting us in possession of their reasons for harassing and destroying our people in the manner I have related. Boats were accordingly ordered to be got ready and every preparation made which could lead to the attainment of our object.

But as this subject deserves to be particularly detailed, I shall, notwithstanding its being just within the period of time which this chapter professes to comprise, allot it a separate place in the beginning of the next.

Nor can I close this part of my work without congratulating both the reader and the author. New matter now presents itself. A considerable part of the foregoing chapters had been related before, either by others or myself. I was however, unavoidably compelled to insert it in order to preserve unbroken that chain of detail and perspicuity of arrangement at which books professing to convey information should especially aim.

3

Transactions of the colony from the commencement of the year 1789 until the end of March

PURSUANT to his resolution, the governor on the 31st of December sent two boats, under the command of Lieutenant Ball of the *Supply* and Lieutenant George Johnston of the marines, down the harbour with directions to those officers to seize and carry off some of the natives. The boats proceeded to Manly Cove, where several Indians were seen standing on the beach, who were enticed by courteous behaviour and a few presents to enter into conversation. A proper opportunity being presented, our people rushed in among them, and seized two men. The rest fled, but the cries of the captives soon brought them back, with many others, to their rescue, and so desperate were their struggles that in spite of every effort on our side, only one of them was secured; the other effected his escape. The boats put off without delay and an attack from the shore instantly commenced. They threw spears, stones, firebrands, and whatever else presented itself at the boats; nor did they retreat, agreeable to their former custom, until many muskets were fired over them.

The prisoner was now fastened by ropes to the thwarts of the boat and, when he saw himself irretrievably disparted from his countrymen, set up the most piercing and lamentable cries of distress. His grief, however, soon diminished. He accepted and ate of some broiled fish which was given to him and sullenly submitted to his destiny.

When the news of his arrival at Sydney was announced I went with every other person to see him. He appeared to be about thirty years old, not tall, but robustly made; and of a countenance which, under happier circumstances, I thought would display manliness and sensibility. His agitation was excessive and the clamorous crowds who flocked around him did not contribute to lessen it. Curiosity and observation seemed, nevertheless, not to have wholly deserted him. He showed the effect of novelty upon ignorance, he wondered at all he saw. Though broken and interrupted with dismay, his voice was soft and musical, when its natural tone could be heard; and he readily pronounced with tolerable accuracy the names of things which were taught him. To our ladies he quickly became extraordinarily courteous, a sure sign that his terror was wearing off.

Every blandishment was used to soothe him, and it had its effect. As he was entering the governor's house someone touched a small bell which hung over the door. He started with horror and astonishment, but in a moment after was reconciled to the noise and laughed at the cause of his perturbation. When pictures were shown to him, he knew directly those which represented the human figure. Among others, a very large handsome print of Her Royal Highness the Duchess of Cumberland being produced, he called out 'woman', a name by which we had just before taught him to call the female convicts. Plates of birds and beasts were also laid before him and many people were led to believe that such as he spoke about and pointed to were known to him. But this must have been an erroneous conjecture, for the elephant, rhinoceros, and several others which we must have discovered, did they exist in the country, were of the number. Again, on the other hand, those he did not point out were equally unknown to him.

His curiosity here being satiated, we took him to a large brick house, which was building for the governor's residence. Being about to enter, he cast up his eyes, and seeing some people leaning out of a window on the first storey, he exclaimed aloud and testified the most extravagant surprise. Nothing here was observed to fix his attention so strongly as some tame fowls who were feeding near him. Our dogs also he particularly noticed, but seemed more fearful than fond of them.

He dined at a side-table at the governor's and ate heartily of fish and ducks, which he first cooled. Bread and salt meat he smelled at, but would not taste; all our liquors he treated in the same manner, and could drink nothing but water. On being shown that he was not to wipe his hands on the chair which he sat upon, he used a towel which was gave to him with great cleanliness and decency.

In the afternoon his hair was closely cut, his head combed and his beard shaved; but he would not submit to these operations until he had seen them performed on another person, when he readily acquiesced. His hair, as might be supposed, was filled with vermin whose destruction seemed to afford him great triumph; nay, either revenge or pleasure prompted him to eat them! But on our expressing disgust and abhorrence he left it off.

To this succeeded his immersion in a tub of water and soap, where he was completely washed and scrubbed from head to foot; after which a shirt, a jacket and a pair of trousers were put upon him. Some part of this ablution I had the honour to perform, in order that I might ascertain the real colour of the skin of these people. My observation then was (and it has since been confirmed in a thousand other instances) that they are as black as the lighter cast of the African Negroes.

Many unsuccessful attempts were made to learn his name. The governor therefore called him Manly, from the cove in which he was captured. This cove had received its name from the manly, undaunted behaviour of a party of natives seen there, on our taking possession of the country.

To prevent his escape, a handcuff with a rope attached to it was fastened around his left wrist, which at first highly delighted him. He called it '*bengàdee*' (or ornament), but his delight changed to rage and hatred when he discovered its use. His supper he cooked himself. Some fish were given to him for this purpose, which, without any previous preparation whatever, he threw carelessly on the fire, and when they became warm took them up, and first rubbed off the scales, peeled the outside with his teeth, and ate it. Afterwards he gutted them and, laying them again on the fire, completed the dressing and ate them.

A convict was selected to sleep with him and to attend him wherever he might go. When he went with his keeper into his apartment he appeared very restless and uneasy while a light was kept in, but on its extinction he immediately lay down and composed himself.

Sullenness and dejection strongly marked his countenance on the following morning. To amuse him he was taken around the camp and to the observatory. Casting his eyes to the opposite shore from the point where he stood, and seeing the smoke of fire lighted by his countrymen, he looked earnestly at it and, sighing deeply two or three times, uttered the word '*gweeun*' (fire).

His loss of spirits had not, however, the effect of impairing his appetite. Eight fish, each weighing about a pound, constituted his breakfast, which he dressed as before. When he had finished his repast he turned his back to the fire in a musing posture, and crept so close to it that his shirt was caught by the flame. Luckily his keeper soon extinguished it, but he was so terrified at the accident that he was with difficulty persuaded to put on a second.

1st January 1789. Today being New Year's Day, most of the officers were invited to the governor's table. Manly dined heartily on fish and roasted pork. He was seated on a chest near a window, out of which, when he had done eating, he would have thrown his plate had he not been prevented. During dinner time a band of music played in an adjoining apartment and, after the cloth was removed, one of the company sang in a very soft and superior style; but the powers of melody were lost on Manly, which disappointed our expectations, as he had before shown pleasure and readiness in imitating our tunes. Stretched out on his chest, and putting his hat under his head, he fell asleep.

To convince his countrymen that he had received no injury from us, the governor took him in a boat down the harbour, that they might see and converse with him. When the boat arrived and lay at a little distance from the beach, several Indians who had retired at her approach, on seeing Manly, returned. He was greatly affected, and shed tears. At length they began to converse. Our ignorance of the language prevented us from knowing much of what passed. It was, however, easily understood that his friends asked him why he did not jump overboard and rejoin them. He only sighed and pointed to the fetter on his leg, by which he was bound.

In going down the harbour he had described the names by which they distinguish its numerous creeks and headlands. He was now often heard to repeat that of *Weèrong*,† which was doubtless to inform his countrymen of the place of his captivity and perhaps to invite them to rescue him. By this time his gloom was chased away and he parted from his friends without testifying reluctance. His vivacity and good humour continued all the evening and produced so good an effect on his appetite that he ate for supper two kangaroo rats, each of the size of a moderate rabbit, and in addition not less than three pounds of fish.

Two days after, he was taken on a similar excursion; but to our surprise the natives kept aloof and would neither approach the shore or discourse with their countryman. We could get no explanation of this difficulty, which seemed to affect us more than it did him. Uncourteous as they were, he performed to them an act of attentive benevolence. Seeing a basket made of bark used by them to carry water, he conveyed into it two hawks and another bird which the people in the boat had shot and, carefully covering them over, left them as a present to his old friends. But indeed the gentleness and humanity of his disposition frequently displayed themselves. When our children, stimulated by wanton curiosity, used to flock around him, he never failed to fondle them and, if he were eating at the time, constantly offered them the choicest part of his fare.

February 1789. His reserve, from want of confidence in us, continued gradually to wear away. He told us his name, and Manly gave place to Arabanoo. Bread he began to relish and tea he drank with avidity. Strong liquors he would never taste, turning from them with disgust and abhorrence. Our dogs and

† Sydney Cove.

cats had ceased to be objects of fear and were become his greatest pets and constant companions at table. One of our chief amusements, after the cloth was removed, was to make him repeat the names of things in his language, which he never hesitated to do with the utmost alacrity, correcting our pronunciation when erroneous. Much information relating to the customs and manners of his country was also gained from him; but as this subject will be separately and amply treated, I shall not anticipate myself by partially touching on it here.

On the 2nd of February died Captain John Shea of the marines, after a lingering illness. He was interred on the following day with the customary military honours amidst the regret of all who knew him. In consequence of his decease, appointments for the promotion of the oldest officer of each subordinate rank were signed by the major commandant of the marine battalion, until the pleasure of the lords of the admiralty should be notified.*

On the 17th of February the *Supply* again sailed for Norfolk Island. The governor went down the harbour in her and carried Arabanoo with him, who was observed to go on board with distrust and reluctance. When he found she was under sail, every effort was tried without success to exhilarate him. At length, an opportunity being presented, he plunged overboard and struck out for the nearest shore. Believing that those who were left behind would fire at him, he attempted to dive, at which he was known to be very expert, but this was attended with a difficulty which he had not foreseen. His clothes proved so buoyant that he was unable to get more than his head under water. A boat was immediately dispatched after him and picked him up, though not without struggles and resistance on his side. When brought on board, he appeared neither afraid or ashamed of what he had done, but sat apart, melancholy and dispirited, and continued so until he saw the governor and his other friends descend into a boat and heard himself called upon

* These appointments were confirmed by the admiralty.

to accompany them. He sprang forward and his cheerfulness and alacrity of temper immediately returned and lasted during the remainder of the day. The dread of being carried away, on an element of whose boundary he could form no conception, joined to the uncertainty of our intention towards him, unquestionably caused him to act as he did.

One of the principal effects which we had supposed the seizure and captivity of Arabanoo would produce seemed yet at as great a distance as ever. The natives neither manifested signs of increased hostility on his account, or attempted to ask any explanation of our conduct through the medium of their countryman who was in our possession, and who they knew was treated with no farther harshness than in being detained among us. Their forbearance of open and determined attack upon us can be accounted for only by recollecting their knowledge of our numbers and their dread of our firearms. That they wanted not sufficient provocation to do so will appear from what I am about to relate.

March 1789. Sixteen convicts left their work at the brick-kilns without leave and marched to Botany Bay, with a design to attack the natives and to plunder them of their fishing tackle and spears. They had armed themselves with their working tools and large clubs. When they arrived near the bay, a body of Indians, who had probably seen them set out and had penetrated their intention from experience, suddenly fell upon them. Our heroes were immediately routed, and separately endeavoured to effect their escape by any means which were left. In their flight one was killed and seven were wounded, for the most part very severely. Those who had the good fortune to outstrip their comrades and arrive in camp first gave the alarm, and a detachment of marines, under an officer, was ordered to march to their relief. The officer arrived too late to repel the Indians, but he brought in the body of the man that was killed and put an end to the pursuit. The governor was justly incensed at what had happened and instituted the most rigorous scrutiny into the cause which had produced it. At first the convicts were unanimous in affirming that they were quietly picking sweet-tea,* when they were without provocation assaulted by the natives, with whom they had no wish to quarrel. Some of them, however, more irresolute than the rest, at last disclosed the purpose for which the expedition had been undertaken; and the whole were ordered to be severely flogged. Arabanoo was present at the infliction of the punishment, and was made to comprehend the cause and the necessity of it, but he displayed on the occasion symptoms of disgust and terror only.

On the 24th instant the *Supply* arrived from Norfolk Island and Lord Howe Island, bringing from the latter place three turtles.

An awful and terrible example of justice took place towards the close of this month, which I record with regret, but which it would be disingenuous to suppress. Six marines, the flower of our battalion, were hanged by the public executioner, on the sentence of a criminal court composed entirely of their own officers, for having at various times robbed the public stores of flour, meat, spirits, tobacco and many other articles.

4

Transactions of the colony in April and May 1789

AN extraordinary calamity was now observed among the natives. Repeated accounts, brought by our boats, of finding bodies of the Indians in all the coves and inlets of the harbour, caused the gentlemen of our hospital to procure some of them for the purposes of examination and anatomy. On inspection, it appeared that all the parties had died a natural death. Pustules, similar to those occasioned by the smallpox, were thickly

* A vegetable creeper found growing on the rocks which yields, on infusion in hot water, a sweet astringent taste whence it derives its name. To its virtues the healthy state of the soldiery and convicts may be greatly attributed. It was drank universally.

spread on the bodies; but how a disease to which our former observations had led us to suppose them strangers could at once have introduced itself, and have spread so widely, seemed inexplicable.* Whatever might be the cause, the existence of the malady could no longer be doubted. Intelligence was brought that an Indian family lay sick in a neighbouring cove. The governor, attended by Arabanoo and a surgeon, went in a boat immediately to the spot. Here they found an old man stretched before a few lighted sticks and a boy of nine or ten years old pouring water on his head from a shell which he held in his hand. Near them lay a female child dead, and a little farther off, its unfortunate mother. The body of the woman showed that famine, superadded to disease, had occasioned her death. Eruptions covered the poor boy from head to foot, and the old man was so reduced that he was with difficulty got into the boat. Their situation rendered them incapable of escape and they quietly submitted to be led away. Arabanoo, contrary to his usual character, seemed at first unwilling to render them any assistance, but his shyness soon wore off, and he treated them with the kindest attention. Nor would he leave the place until he had buried the corpse of the child. That of the woman he did not see from its situation and as his countrymen did not point it out the governor ordered that it should not be shown to him. He scooped a grave in the sand with his hands, of no peculiarity of shape, which he lined completely with grass, and put the body into it, covering it also with grass; and then he filled up the hole and raised over it a small mound with the earth which had been removed. Here the ceremony ended, unaccompanied by any invocation to a superior being, or any

* No solution of this difficulty had been given when I left the country in December 1791. I can, therefore, only propose queries for the ingenuity of others to exercise itself upon: is it a disease indigenous to the country? Did the French ships under Monsieur La Perouse introduce it? Let it be remembered that they had now been departed more than a year and we had never heard of its existence on board of them. Had it travelled across

attendant circumstance whence an inference of their religious opinions could be deduced.

An uninhabited house near the hospital was allotted for their reception and a cradle prepared for each of them. By the encouragement of Arabanoo, who assured them of protection, and the soothing behaviour of our medical gentlemen, they became at once reconciled to us and looked happy and grateful at the change of their situation. Sickness and hunger had, however, so much exhausted the old man that little hope was entertained of his recovery. As he pointed frequently to his throat, at the instance of Arabanoo he tried to wash it with a gargle which was given to him; but the obstructed, tender state of the part rendered it impracticable. *Bàdo, bàdo* (water) was his cry. When brought to him he drank largely at intervals of it. He was equally importunate for fire, being seized with shivering fits, and one was kindled. Fish were produced to tempt him to eat, but he turned away his head with signs of loathing. Nanbaree (the boy), on the contrary, no sooner saw them than he leaped from his cradle and eagerly seizing them, began to cook them. A warm bath being prepared, they were immersed in it; and after being thoroughly cleansed they had clean shirts put on them and were again laid in bed.

The old man lived but a few hours. He bore the pangs of dissolution with patient composure and, though he was sensible to the last moment, expired almost without a groan. Nanbaree appeared quite unmoved at the event and surveyed the corpse of his father without emotion, simply exclaiming, *bòee* (dead). This surprised us, as the tenderness and anxiety of

the continent from its western shore, where Dampier and other European voyagers had formerly landed? Was it introduced by Mr Cook? Did we give it birth here? No person among us had been afflicted with the disorder since we had quitted the Cape of Good Hope, seventeen months before. It is true that our surgeons had brought out variolous matter in bottles, but to infer that it was produced from this cause were a supposition so wild as to be unworthy of consideration.

the old man about the boy had been very moving. Although barely able to raise his head, while so much strength was left to him, he kept looking into his child's cradle. He patted him gently on the bosom and, with dying eyes, seemed to recommend him to our humanity and protection. Nanbaree was adopted by Mr White, surgeon-general of the settlement, and became henceforth one of his family.

Arabanoo had no sooner heard of the death of his countryman than he hastened to inter him. I was present at the ceremony, in company with the governor, Captain Ball and two or three other persons. It differed, by the accounts of those who were present at the funeral of the girl, in no respect from what had passed there in the morning, except that the grave was dug by a convict. But I was informed that when intelligence of the death reached Arabanoo, he expressed himself with doubt whether he should bury or burn the body, and seemed solicitous to ascertain which ceremony would be most gratifying to the governor.

Indeed, Arabanoo's behaviour during the whole of the transactions of this day was so strongly marked by affection to his countryman and by confidence in us that the governor resolved to free him from all farther restraint and at once to trust to his generosity, and the impression which our treatment of him might have made, for his future residence among us. The fetter was accordingly taken off his leg.

In the evening, Captain Ball and I crossed the harbour, and buried the corpse of the woman before mentioned.

Distress continued to drive them in upon us. Two more natives, one of them a young man and the other his sister (a girl of fourteen years old), were brought in by the governor's boat in a most deplorable state of wretchedness from the smallpox. The sympathy and affection of Arabanoo, which had appeared languid in the instance of Nanbaree and his father, here manifested themselves immediately. We conjectured that a difference of the tribes to which they belonged might cause the preference, but nothing afterwards happened to strengthen or confirm such a supposition. The young man died at the end of three days. The girl recovered and was received as an inmate, with great kindness, in the family of Mrs Johnson, the clergyman's wife. Her name was Bòoron, but from our mistake of pronunciation she acquired that of Abaròo, by which she was generally known, and by which she will always be called in this work. She showed at the death of her brother more feeling than Nanbaree had witnessed for the loss of his father. When she found him dying, she crept to his side and lay by him until forced by the cold to retire. No exclamation or other sign of grief, however, escaped her for what had happened.

May 1789. At sunset, on the evening of the 2nd instant, the arrival of the *Sirius*, Captain Hunter, from the Cape of Good Hope, was proclaimed, and diffused universal joy and congratulation. The day of famine was at least procrastinated by the supply of flour and salt provisions she brought us.

The *Sirius* had made her passage to the Cape of Good Hope by the route of Cape Horn in exactly thirteen weeks. Her highest latitude was 57° 10′ south, where the weather proved intolerably cold. Ice in great quantity was seen for many days, and in the middle of December (which is correspondent to the middle of June in our hemisphere) water froze in open casks upon deck in the moderate latitude of 44°.

They were very kindly treated by the Dutch governor and amply supplied by the merchants at the Cape, where they remained seven weeks. Their passage back was effected by Van Diemen's Land, near which, and close under Tasman's Head, they were in the utmost peril of being wrecked.

In this long run, which had extended round the circle, they had always determined their longitude, to the greatest nicety, by distances taken between the sun and moon, or between the moon and a star. But it falls to the lot of very few ships to possess such indefatigable and accurate observers as Captain Hunter and Mr (now Captain) Bradley, the first lieutenant of the *Sirius*.

I feel assured that I have no reader who will not join in

regretting the premature loss of Arabanoo, who died of the smallpox on the 18th instant, after languishing in it six days. From some imperfect marks and indents on his face we were inclined to believe that he had passed this dreaded disorder. Even when the first symptoms of sickness seized him, we continued willing to hope that they proceeded from a different cause. But at length the disease burst forth with irresistible fury. It were superfluous to say that nothing which medical skill and unremitting attention could perform were left unexerted to mitigate his sufferings, and prolong a life which humanity and affectionate concern towards his sick compatriots unfortunately shortened.

During his sickness he reposed entire confidence in us. Although a stranger to medicine and nauseating the taste of it, he swallowed with patient submission innumerable drugs,* which the hope of relief induced us to administer to him. The governor, who particularly regarded him,** caused him to be buried in his own garden and attended the funeral in person.

The character of Arabanoo, as far as we had developed it,

* Very different had been his conduct on a former occasion of a similar kind. Soon after he was brought among us he was seized with a diarrhoea, for which he could by no persuasion be induced to swallow any of our prescriptions. After many ineffectual trials to deceive or overcome him, it was at length determined to let him pursue his own course and to watch if he should apply for relief to any of the productions of the country. He was in consequence observed to dig fern-root and to chew it. Whether the disorder had passed its crisis, or whether the fern-root effected a cure, I know not; but it is certain that he became speedily well.

** The regard was reciprocal. His Excellency had been ill but a short time before, when Arabanoo had testified the utmost solicitude for his ease and recovery. It is probable that he acquired, on this occasion, just notions of the benefit to be derived from medical assistance. A doctor is, among them, a person of consequence. It is certain that he latterly estimated our professional gentlemen very highly.

was distinguished by a portion of gravity and steadiness which our subsequent acquaintance with his countrymen by no means led us to conclude a national characteristic. In that daring, enterprising frame of mind which, when combined with genius, constitutes the leader of a horde of savages, or the ruler of a people, boasting the power of discrimination and the resistance of ambition, he was certainly surpassed by some of his successors who afterwards lived among us. His countenance was thoughtful but not animated. His fidelity and gratitude, particularly to his friend the governor, were constant and undeviating and deserve to be recorded. Although of a gentle and placable temper, we early discovered that he was impatient of indignity and allowed of no superiority on our part. He knew that he was in our power, but the independence of his mind never forsook him. If the slightest insult were offered to him, he would return it with interest. At retaliation of merriment he was often happy, and frequently turned the laugh against his antagonist. He did not want docility, but either from the difficulty of acquiring our language, from the unskilfulness of his teachers, or from some natural defect, his progress in learning it was not equal to what we had expected. For the last three or four weeks of his life, hardly any restraint was laid upon his inclinations, so that had he meditated escape, he might easily have effected it. He was, perhaps, the only native who was ever attached to us from choice, and who did not prefer a precarious subsistence among wilds and precipices to the comforts of a civilised system.

By his death, the scheme which had invited his capture was utterly defeated. Of five natives who had been brought among us, three had perished from a cause which, though unavoidable, it was impossible to explain to a people who would condescend to enter into no intercourse with us. The same suspicious dread of our approach, and the same scenes of vengeance acted on unfortunate stragglers, continued to prevail.

5

Transactions of the colony until the close of the year 1789

THE anniversary of His Majesty's birthday was celebrated, as heretofore, at the government house, with loyal festivity. In the evening, the play of *The Recruiting Officer* was performed by a party of convicts, and honoured by the presence of His Excellency and the officers of the garrison.† That every opportunity of escape from the dreariness and dejection of our situation should be eagerly embraced will not be wondered at. The exhilarating effect of a splendid theatre is well known; and I am not ashamed to confess that the proper distribution of three or four yards of stained paper, and a dozen farthing candles stuck around the mud walls of a convict hut, failed not to diffuse general complacency on the countenances of sixty persons of various descriptions who were assembled to applaud the representation. Some of the actors acquitted themselves with great spirit and received the praises of the audience. A prologue and an epilogue, written by one of the performers, were also spoken on the occasion; which, although not worth inserting here, contained some tolerable allusions to the situation of the parties, and the novelty of a stage representation in New South Wales.

Broken Bay, which was supposed to be completely explored, became again an object of research. On the sixth instant, the governor, accompanied by a large party in two boats, proceeded thither. Here they again wandered over piles of misshapen desolation, contemplating scenes of wild solitude whose unvarying appearance renders them incapable of affording either novelty or gratification. But when they had given over the hope of farther discovery, by pursuing the windings of an inlet which, from its appearance, was supposed to be a short creek, they suddenly found themselves at the entrance of a

† Written in 1706 by the Irish playwright George Farquhar, *The Recruiting Officer* was the first play staged in the colony.

freshwater river, up which they proceeded twenty miles in a westerly direction; and would have farther prosecuted their research had not a failure of provisions obliged them to return. This river they described to be of considerable breadth and of great depth, but its banks had hitherto presented nothing better than a counterpart of the rocks and precipices which surround Broken Bay.

June 1789. A second expedition, to ascertain its course, was undertaken by His Excellency, who now penetrated (measuring by the bed of the river) between sixty and seventy miles, when the farther progress of the boats was stopped by a fall. The water in every part was found to be fresh and good. Of the adjoining country, the opinions of those who had inspected it (of which number I was not) were so various that I shall decline to record them. Some saw a rich and beautiful country, and others were so unfortunate as to discover little else than large tracts of low land covered with reeds, and rank with the inundations of the stream by which they had been recently covered. All parties, however, agreed that the rocky, impenetrable country seen on the first excursion had ended nearly about the place whence the boats had then turned back. Close to the fall stands a very beautiful hill which our adventurers mounted, and enjoyed from it an extensive prospect. Potatoes, maize and garden seeds of various kinds were put into the earth by the governor's order, on different parts of Richmond Hill, which was announced to be its name. The latitude of Richmond Hill, as observed by Captain Hunter, was settled at 33° 36′ south.

Here also the river received the name of Hawkesbury, in honour of the noble lord who bears that title.

Natives were found on the banks in several parts, many of whom were labouring under the smallpox. They did not attempt to commit hostilities against the boats, but on the contrary showed every sign of welcome and friendship to the strangers.

At this period, I was unluckily invested with the command of the outpost at Rose Hill, which prevented me from being in the list of discoverers of the Hawkesbury. Stimulated, however, by a desire of acquiring a further knowledge of the country, on the 26th instant, accompanied by Mr Arndell, assistant surgeon of the settlement, Mr Lowes, surgeon's mate of the *Sirius*, two marines and a convict, I left the redoubt at daybreak, pointing our march to a hill distant five miles in a westerly or inland direction, which commands a view of the great chain of mountains called Caermarthen Hills, extending from north to south farther than the eye can reach.† Here we paused, surveying 'the wild abyss; pondering our voyage'.†† Before us lay the trackless immeasurable desert, in awful silence. At length, after consultation, we determined to steer west and by north, by compass, the make of the land in that quarter indicating the existence of a river. We continued to march all day through a country untrodden before by an European foot. Save that a melancholy crow now and then flew croaking overhead, or a kangaroo was seen to bound at a distance, the picture of solitude was complete and undisturbed. At four o'clock in the afternoon we halted near a small pond of water where we took up our residence for the night, lighted a fire, and prepared to cook our supper: that was, to broil over a couple of ramrods a few slices of salt pork and a crow which we had shot.

At daylight we renewed our peregrination and in an hour after we found ourselves on the banks of a river nearly as broad as the Thames at Putney and apparently of great depth, the current running very slowly in a northerly direction. Vast flocks of wild ducks were swimming in the stream, but after being once fired at, they grew so shy that we could not get near them a second time. Nothing is more certain than that the sound of a gun had never before been heard within many miles of this spot.

We proceeded upwards by a slow pace, through reeds,

† The Blue Mountains.
†† John Milton, *Paradise Lost*, II, 917: 'Into this wild abyss the wary fiend / Stood on the brink of Hell and looked a while / Pondering his voyage...'

thickets and a thousand other obstacles which impeded our progress, over coarse sandy ground which had been recently inundated, though full forty feet above the present level of the river. Traces of the natives appeared at every step; sometimes in their hunting-huts, which consist of nothing more than a large piece of bark, bent in the middle and open at both ends, exactly resembling two cards set up to form an acute angle; sometimes in marks on trees which they had climbed; or in squirrel-traps;* or, which surprised us more from being new, in decoys for the purpose of ensnaring birds. These are formed of underwood and reeds, long and narrow, shaped like a mound raised over a grave, with a small aperture at one end for admission of the prey and a grate made of sticks at the other. The bird enters at the aperture, seeing before him the light of the grate, between the bars of which he vainly endeavours to thrust himself, until taken. Most of these decoys were full of feathers, chiefly those of quails, which showed their utility. We also met with two old damaged canoes hauled up on the beach, which differed in no wise from those found on the sea coast.

Having remained out three days, we returned to our quarters at Rose Hill with the pleasing intelligence of our discovery. The country we had passed through we found tolerably plain and little encumbered with underwood, except near the riverside. It is entirely covered with the same sorts of trees as grow near Sydney and in some places grass springs up luxuriantly;

* A squirrel-trap is a cavity of considerable depth, formed by art, in the body of a tree. When the Indians in their hunting parties set fire to the surrounding country (which is a very common custom) the squirrels, opossums, and other animals who live in trees, flee for refuge into these holes, whence they are easily dislodged and taken. The natives always pitch on a part of a tree for this purpose which has been perforated by a worm, which indicates that the wood is in an unsound state and will readily yield to their efforts. If the rudeness and imperfection of the tools with which they work be considered, it must be confessed to be an operation of great toil and difficulty.

other places are quite bare of it. The soil is various, in many parts a stiff arid clay covered with small pebbles; in other places of a soft loamy nature; but invariably, in every part near the river, it is a coarse sterile sand. Our observations on it (particularly mine, from carrying the compass by which we steered) were not so numerous as might have been wished. But certainly, if the qualities of it be such as to deserve future cultivation, no impediment of surface but that of cutting down and burning the trees exists to prevent its being tilled.

To this river the governor gave the name of Nepean. The distance of the part of the river which we first hit upon from the sea coast is about thirty-nine miles, in a direct line almost due west.

A survey of Botany Bay took place in September. I was of the party, with several other officers. We continued nine days in the bay, during which time the relative position of every part of it, to the extent of more than thirty miles following the windings of the shore was ascertained, and laid down on paper by Captain Hunter.

So complete an opportunity of forming a judgment enables me to speak decisively of a place which has often engaged conversation and excited reflection. Variety of opinions here disappeared. I shall, therefore, transcribe literally what I wrote in my journal, on my return from the expedition. 'We were unanimously of opinion, that had not the nautical part of Mr Cook's description, in which we include the latitude and longitude of the bay, been so accurately laid down, there would exist the utmost reason to believe that those who have described the contiguous country had never seen it. On the sides of the harbour, a line of sea coast more than thirty miles long, we did not find 200 acres which could be cultivated.'

September 1789. But all our attention was not directed to explore inlets and toil for discovery. Our internal tranquillity was still more important. To repress the inroads of depredation, and to secure to honest industry the reward of its labour, had become a matter of the most serious consideration, hardly a night passing without the commission of robbery. Many expedients were devised, and the governor at length determined to select from the convicts a certain number of persons, who were meant to be of the fairest character, for the purpose of being formed into a nightly watch for the preservation of public and private property under the following regulations which, as the first system of police in a colony, so peculiarly constituted as ours, may perhaps prove not uninteresting.

I. A night-watch, consisting of twelve persons divided into four parties, is appointed and fully authorised to patrol at all hours in the night; and to visit such places as may be deemed necessary for the discovery of any felony, trespass or misdemeanour; and for the apprehending and securing for examination any person or persons who may appear to them concerned therein, either by entrance into any suspected hut or dwelling or by such other measure as may seem to them expedient.

II. Those parts in which the convicts reside are to be divided and numbered in the following manner. The convict huts on the eastern side of the stream and the public farm are to be the first division. Those at the brick-kilns and the detached parties in the different private farms in that district are to be the second division. Those on the western side of the stream, as far as the line which separates the district of the women from the men, to be the third division. The huts occupied from that line to the hospital, and from there to the observatory, to be the fourth division.

III. Each of these districts or divisions is to be under the particular inspection of one person, who may be judged qualified to inform himself of the actual residence of each individual in his district, as well as of his business, connections and acquaintances.

IV. Cognisance is to be taken of such convicts as may sell or barter their slops or provisions, and also of such as are addicted to gaming for either of the aforesaid articles, who are to be reported to the judge advocate.

V. Any soldier or seaman found straggling after the beating of the tattoo, or who may be found in a convict's hut, is to be detained and information of him immediately given to the nearest guard.

VI. Any person who may be robbed during the night is to give immediate information thereof to the watch of his district who, on the instant of application being made, shall use the most effectual means to trace out the offender or offenders, so that he, she, or they may be brought to justice.

VII. The watch of each district is to be under the direction of one person, who will be named for that purpose. All the patrols are placed under the immediate inspection of Herbert Keeling. They are never to receive any fee, gratuity or reward from any individual whatever to engage their exertions in the execution of the above trust. Nor will they receive any stipulated encouragement for the conviction of any offender. But their diligence and good behaviour will be rewarded by the governor. And for this purpose their conduct will be strictly attended to by those who are placed in authority over them.

VIII. The night-watch is to go out as soon as the tattoo ceases beating, to return to their huts when the working drum beats in the morning, and are to make their report to the judge advocate, through Herbert Keeling, of all robberies and misdemeanours which may have been committed. Any assistance the patrols may require will be given to them on applying to the officer commanding the nearest guard, and by the civil power, if necessary; for which last, application is to be made to the provost martial.

IX. Any negligence on the part of those who shall be employed on this duty will be punished with the utmost rigour of the law.

X. The night-watch is to consist of twelve persons.

Every political code, either from a defect of its constitution or from the corruptness of those who are entrusted to execute it, will be found less perfect in practice than speculation had promised itself. It were, however, prejudice to deny that for some time following the institution of this patrol, nightly depredations became less frequent and alarming. The petty villains, at least, were restrained by it. And to keep even a garden unravaged was now become a subject of the deepest concern.

For in October our weekly allowance of provisions, which had hitherto been eight pounds of flour, five pounds of salt pork, three pints of peas, six ounces of butter, was reduced to five pounds five ounces of flour, three pounds five ounces of pork, and two pints of peas.

In order to lessen the consumption from the public stores, the *Supply* was ordered to touch at Lord Howe Island in her way from Norfolk Island to try if turtle could be procured for the purpose of being publicly served in lieu of salt provisions. But she brought back only three turtles, which were distributed in the garrison.

December 1789. At the request of His Excellency, Lieutenant Dawes of the marines, accompanied by Lieutenant Johnston and Mr Lowes, about this time undertook the attempt to cross the Nepean River and to penetrate to Carmarthen mountains. Having discovered a ford in the river, they passed it and proceeded in a westerly direction. But they found the country so rugged and the difficulty of walking so excessive that in three days they were able to penetrate only fifteen miles, and were therefore obliged to relinquish their object. This party, at the time they turned back, were farther inland than any other persons ever were before or since, being fifty-four miles in a direct line from the sea coast when on the summit of Mount Twiss, a hill so named by them, and which bounded their peregrination.

Intercourse with the natives, for the purpose of knowing whether or not the country possessed any resources by which life might be prolonged,* as well as on other accounts, becoming every day more desirable, the governor resolved to make prisoners of two more of them.

Boats properly provided, under the command of Lieutenant

* One of the convicts, a Negro, had twice eloped with an intention of establishing himself in the society of the natives, with a wish to adopt their customs and to live with them, but he was always repulsed by them, and compelled to return to us from hunger and wretchedness.

Bradley of the *Sirius*, were accordingly dispatched on this service and completely succeeded in trepanning and carrying off, without opposition, two fine young men, who were safely landed among us at Sydney.

Nanbaree and Abaroo welcomed them on shore, calling them immediately by their names, Bàneelon and Còlbee.† But they seemed little disposed to receive the congratulations or repose confidence in the assurances of their friends. The same scenes of awkward wonder and impatient constraint, which had attended the introduction of Arabanoo, succeeded. Baneelon we judged to be about twenty-six years old, of good stature and stoutly made, with a bold intrepid countenance which bespoke defiance and revenge. Colbee was perhaps near thirty, of a less sullen aspect than his comrade, considerably shorter and not so robustly framed, though better fitted for purposes of activity. They had both evidently had the smallpox; indeed Colbee's face was very thickly imprinted with the marks of it.

Positive orders were issued by the governor to treat them indulgently and guard them strictly; notwithstanding which, Colbee contrived to effect his escape in about a week, with a small iron ring round his leg. Had those appointed to watch them been a moment later, his companion would have contrived to accompany him.

But Baneelon, though haughty, knew how to temporise. He quickly threw off all reserve, and pretended, nay, at particular moments, perhaps felt satisfaction in his new state. Unlike poor Arabanoo, he became at once fond of our viands and would drink the strongest liquors, not simply without reluctance but with eager marks of delight and enjoyment. He was the only native we ever knew who immediately showed a fondness for spirits; Colbee would not at first touch them. Nor was the effect of wine or brandy upon him more perceptible than an

† Baneelon we know of course as Bennelong, who gave his name to the point where the Sydney Opera House now stands, the site of his house in the settlement.

equal quantity would have produced upon one of us, although fermented liquor was new to him.

In his eating, he was alike compliant. When a turtle was shown to Arabanoo he would not allow it to be a fish and could not be induced to eat of it. Baneelon also denied it to be a fish, but no common councilman in Europe could do more justice than he did to a very fine one that the *Supply* had brought from Lord Howe Island, and which was served up at the governor's table on Christmas Day.

His powers of mind were certainly far above mediocrity. He acquired knowledge, both of our manners and language, faster than his predecessor had done. He willingly communicated information, sang, danced and capered, told us all the customs of his country and all the details of his family economy. Love and war seemed his favourite pursuits, in both of which he had suffered severely. His head was disfigured by several scars; a spear had passed through his arm and another through his leg. Half of one of his thumbs was carried away, and the mark of a wound appeared on the back of his hand. The cause and attendant circumstances of all these disasters, except one, he related to us.

'But the wound on the back of your hand, Baneelon! How did you get that?'

He laughed, and owned that it was received in carrying off a lady of another tribe by force. 'I was dragging her away. She cried aloud, and stuck her teeth in me.'

'And what did you do then?'

'I knocked her down, and beat her till she was insensible, and covered with blood. Then...'

Whenever he recounted his battles, 'poised his lance, and showed how fields were won',† the most violent exclamations of rage and vengeance against his competitors in arms, those of the tribe called Cameragal in particular, would burst from him.

† Tench is thinking of Oliver Goldsmith's *The Deserted Village*: 'Shouldered his crutch, and showed how fields were won.'

And he never failed at such times to solicit the governor to accompany him, with a body of soldiers, in order that he might exterminate this hated name.

Although I call him only Baneelon, he had besides several appellations, and for a while he chose to be distinguished by that of Wolarawàree. Again, as a mark of affection and respect to the governor, he conferred on him the name of Wolarawaree and sometimes called him *Beenèna* (father), adopting to himself the name of governor. This interchange we found is a constant symbol of friendship among them.* In a word, his temper seemed pliant, and his relish of our society so great that hardly anyone judged he would attempt to quit us were the means of escape put within his reach. Nevertheless it was thought proper to continue a watch over him.

6

Transactions of the colony, from the beginning of the year 1790 until the end of May following

OUR impatience of news from Europe strongly marked the commencement of the year. We had now been two years in the country, and thirty-two months from England, in which long period no supplies except what had been procured at the Cape of Good Hope by the *Sirius* had reached us. From intelligence of our friends and connections we had been entirely cut off, no communication whatever having passed with our native country since the 13th of May 1787, the day of our departure from Portsmouth. Famine besides was approaching with gigantic strides, and gloom and dejection overspread every countenance. Men abandoned themselves to the most desponding reflections and adopted the most extravagant conjectures.

* It is observable that this custom prevails as a pledge of friendship and kindness all over Asia, and has also been mentioned by Captain Cook to exist among the natives in the South Sea Islands.

Still we were on the tiptoe of expectation. If thunder broke at a distance, or a fowling-piece of louder than ordinary report resounded in the woods, 'a gun from a ship', was echoed on every side and nothing but hurry and agitation prevailed. For eighteen months after we had landed in the country, a party of marines used to go weekly to Botany Bay to see whether any vessel, ignorant of our removal to Port Jackson, might be arrived there. But a better plan was now devised on the suggestion of Captain Hunter. A party of seamen were fixed on a high bluff, called the South Head, at the entrance of the harbour, on which a flag was ordered to be hoisted whenever a ship might appear, which should serve as a direction to her, and as a signal of approach to us. Every officer stepped forward to volunteer a service which promised to be so replete with beneficial consequences. But the zeal and alacrity of Captain Hunter and our brethren of the *Sirius* rendered superfluous all assistance or co-operation.

Here on the summit of the hill, every morning from daylight until the sun sunk, did we sweep the horizon in hope of seeing a sail. At every fleeting speck which arose from the bosom of the sea, the heart bounded and the telescope was lifted to the eye. If a ship appeared here, we knew she must be bound to us; for on the shores of this vast ocean (the largest in the world) we were the only community which possessed the art of navigation, and languished for intercourse with civilised society.

To say that we were disappointed and shocked would very inadequately describe our sensations. But the misery and horror of such a situation cannot be imparted, even by those who have suffered under it.

March 1790. Vigorous measures were become indispensable. The governor therefore, early in February, ordered the *Sirius* to prepare for a voyage to China; and a farther retrenchment of our ration, we were given to understand, would take place on her sailing.

But the *Sirius* was destined not to reach China. Previously to her intended departure on that voyage, she was ordered, in concert with the *Supply*, to convey Major Ross, with a large detachment of marines and more than two hundred convicts, to Norfolk Island, it being hoped that such a division of our numbers would increase the means of subsistence, by diversified exertions. She sailed on the 6th of March, and on the 27th of the same month, the following order was issued from headquarters.

Parole—Honour
Counter sign—Example

The expected supply of provisions not having arrived, makes it necessary to reduce the present ration. And the commissary is directed to issue, from the 1st of April, the undermentioned allowance, to every person in the settlement without distinction.

Four pounds of flour, two pounds and a half of salt pork, and one pound and a half of rice, per week.

On the 5th of April news was brought that the flag on the South Head was hoisted. Less emotion was created by the news than might be expected. Everyone coldly said to his neighbour, 'the *Sirius* and *Supply* are returned from Norfolk Island.' To satisfy myself that the flag was really flying, I went to the observatory and looked for it through the large astronomical telescope, when I plainly saw it. But I was immediately convinced that it was not to announce the arrival of ships from England; for I could see nobody near the flagstaff except one solitary being, who kept strolling around, unmoved by what he saw. I well knew how different an effect the sight of strange ships would produce.

April 1790. The governor, however, determined to go down the harbour and I begged permission to accompany him. Having turned a point about halfway down, we were surprised to see a boat which was known to belong to the *Supply* rowing towards us. On nearer approach I saw Captain Ball make an extraordinary motion with his hand, which too plainly indicated that something disastrous had happened; and I could not help turning to the governor, near whom I sat, and saying, 'Sir, prepare yourself for bad news.' A few minutes changed doubt into certainty; and to our unspeakable consternation we learned that the *Sirius* had been wrecked on Norfolk Island on the 19th of February. Happily, however, Captain Hunter and every other person belonging to her were saved.

Dismay was painted on every countenance when the tidings were proclaimed at Sydney. The most distracting apprehensions were entertained. All hopes were now concentred in the little *Supply*.

At six o'clock in the evening all the officers of the garrison, both civil and military, were summoned to meet the governor in council, when the nature of our situation was fully discussed and an account of the provisions yet remaining in store laid before the council by the commissary. This account stated that on the present ration* the public stores contained salt meat sufficient to serve until the 2nd of July, flour until the 20th of August and rice, or peas in lieu of it, until the 1st of October.

Several regulations for the more effectual preservation of gardens and other private property were proposed and adopted, and after some interchange of opinion the following ration was decreed to commence immediately, a vigorous exertion to prolong existence, or the chance of relief, being all now left to us.

> Two pounds of pork, two pounds and a half of flour, two pounds of rice, or a quart of peas, per week, to every grown person, and to every child of more than eighteen months old.
>
> To every child under eighteen months old, the same quantity of rice and flour, and one pound of pork.**

* See the ration of the 27th of March, a few pages back.

** When the age of this provision is recollected, its inadequacy will more strikingly appear. The pork and rice were brought with us from England. The pork had been salted between three and four years, and every grain of rice was a moving body from the inhabitants lodged within it. We

The immediate departure of the *Supply*, for Batavia, was also determined.†

Nor did our zeal stop here. The governor being resolved to employ all the boats, public and private, in procuring fish—which was intended to be served in lieu of salt malt—all the officers, civil and military, including the clergyman and the surgeons of the hospital, made the voluntary offer, in addition to their other duties, to go alternately every night in these boats in order to see that every exertion was made, and that all the fish which might be caught was deposited with the commissary.

The best marksmen of the marines and convicts were also selected and put under the command of a trusty sergeant, with directions to range the woods in search of kangaroos, which were ordered, when brought in, to be delivered to the commissary.

And as it was judged that the inevitable fatigues of shooting and fishing could not be supported on the common ration, a small additional quantity of flour and pork was appropriated to the use of the gamekeepers; and each fisherman who had been out during the preceding night had, on his return in the morning, a pound of uncleaned fish allowed for his breakfast.

On the 17th instant, the *Supply*, Captain Ball, sailed for Batavia. We followed her with anxious eyes until she was no longer visible. Truly did we say to her '*In te omnis domus inclinata recumbit.*'†† We were, however, consoled by reflecting that everything which zeal, fortitude and seamanship

soon left off boiling the pork as it had become so old and dry that it shrunk one half in its dimensions when so dressed. Our usual method of cooking it was to cut off the daily morsel and toast it on a fork before the fire, catching the drops which fell on a slice of bread, or in a saucer of rice. Our flour was the remnant of what was brought from the Cape by the *Sirius*, and was good. Instead of baking it, the soldiers and convicts used to boil it up with greens.

† Batavia: modern Jakarta.

†† Virgil, *Aeneid*, XII, 59: 'Our frail state depends utterly on you.'

could produce was concentred in her commander.

Our bosoms consequently became less perturbed, and all other labour and attention were turned on one object—the procuring of food. 'Pride, pomp, and circumstance of glorious war' were no more.†

The distress of the lower classes for clothes was almost equal to their other wants. The stores had been long exhausted and winter was at hand. Nothing more ludicrous can be conceived than the expedients of substituting, shifting and patching which ingenuity devised to eke out wretchedness and preserve the remains of decency. The superior dexterity of the women was particularly conspicuous. Many a guard have I seen mount, in which the number of soldiers without shoes exceeded that which had yet preserved remnants of leather.

Nor was another part of our domestic economy less whimsical. If a lucky man who had knocked down a dinner with his gun, or caught a fish by angling from the rocks, invited a neighbour to dine with him, the invitation always ran, 'bring your own bread.' Even at the governor's table this custom was constantly observed. Every man when he sat down pulled his bread out of his pocket and laid it by his plate.

The insufficiency of our ration soon diminished our execution of labour. Both soldiers and convicts pleaded such loss of strength as to find themselves unable to perform their accustomed tasks. The hours of public work were accordingly shortened or, rather, every man was ordered to do as much as his strength would permit, and every other possible indulgence was granted.

May 1790. In proportion, however, as lenity and mitigation were extended to inability and helplessness, inasmuch was the most rigorous justice executed on disturbers of the public tranquillity. Persons detected in robbing gardens or pilfering provisions were never screened because, as every man could possess, by his utmost exertions, but a bare sufficiency to

† Shakespeare, *Othello*, III, iii, 351.

preserve life,* he, who deprived his neighbour of that little, drove him to desperation. No new laws for the punishment of theft were enacted, but persons of all descriptions were publicly warned that the severest penalties, which the existing law in its greatest latitude would authorise, should be inflicted on offenders. The following sentence of a court of justice, of which I was a member, on a convict detected in a garden stealing potatoes, will illustrate the subject. He was ordered to receive three hundred lashes immediately, to be chained for six months to two other criminals who were thus fettered for former offences, and to have his allowance of flour stopped for six months. So that during the operation of the sentence, two pounds of pork and two pounds of rice (or, in lieu of the latter, a quart of peas) per week, constituted his whole subsistence. Such was the melancholy length to which we were compelled to stretch our penal system.

Farther to contribute to the detection of villainy, a proclamation offering a reward of sixty pounds of flour, more tempting than the ore of Peru or Potosi, was promised to anyone who should apprehend and bring to justice a robber of garden ground.

Our friend Baneelon, during this season of scarcity, was as well taken care of as our desperate circumstances would allow. We knew not how to keep him and yet were unwilling to part with him. Had he penetrated our state, perhaps he might have given his countrymen such a description of our diminished

* Its preservation in some cases was found impracticable. Three or four instances of persons who perished from want have been related to me. One only, however, fell within my own observation. I was passing the provision store when a man with a wild haggard countenance who had just received his daily pittance to carry home came out. His faltering gait and eager devouring eye led me to watch him, and he had not proceeded ten steps before he fell. I ordered him to be carried to the hospital where, when he arrived, he was found dead. On opening the body, the cause of death was pronounced to be inanition.

numbers and diminished strength as would have emboldened them to become more troublesome. Every expedient was used to keep him in ignorance. His allowance was regularly received by the governor's servant, like that of any other person, but the ration of a week was insufficient to have kept him for a day. The deficiency was supplied by fish whenever it could be procured, and a little Indian corn which had been reserved was ground and appropriated to his use. In spite of all these aids, want of food has been known to make him furious and often melancholy.

There is reason to believe that he had long meditated his escape, which he effected in the night of the 3rd instant. About two o'clock in the morning he pretended illness and, awaking the servant who lay in the room with him, begged to go downstairs. The other attended him without suspicion of his design and Baneelon no sooner found himself in a backyard than he nimbly leaped over a slight paling and bade us adieu.

The following public order was issued within the date of this chapter, and is too pleasing a proof that universal depravity did not prevail among the convicts to be omitted.

> The governor, in consequence of the unremitted good behaviour and meritorious conduct of John Irving, is pleased to remit the remainder of the term for which he was sentenced to transportation. He is therefore to be considered as restored to all those rights and privileges which had been suspended in consequence of the sentence of the law. And, as such, he is hereby appointed to act as an assistant to the surgeon at Norfolk Island.

7

Transactions of the colony in June, July and August 1790

At length the clouds of misfortune began to separate and on the evening of the 3rd of June the joyful cry of 'the flag's up', resounded in every direction.

I was sitting in my hut, musing on our fate, when a confused clamour in the street drew my attention. I opened my door and saw several women with children in their arms running to and fro with distracted looks, congratulating each other and kissing their infants with the most passionate and extravagant marks of fondness. I needed no more, but instantly started out and ran to a hill where, by the assistance of a pocket-glass, my hopes were realised. My next door neighbour, a brother officer, was with me, but we could not speak. We wrung each other by the hand, with eyes and hearts overflowing.

Finding that the governor intended to go immediately in his boat down the harbour, I begged to be of his party.

As we proceeded, the object of our hopes soon appeared: a large ship with English colours flying, working in between the heads which form the entrance of the harbour. The tumultuous state of our minds represented her in danger and we were in agony. Soon after, the governor, having ascertained what she was, left us and stepped into a fishing boat to return to Sydney. The weather was wet and tempestuous but the body is delicate only when the soul is at ease. We pushed through wind and rain, the anxiety of our sensations every moment redoubling. At last we read the word *London* on her stern. 'Pull away, my lads! She is from Old England! A few strokes more and we shall be aboard! Hurrah for a bellyfull, and news from our friends!' Such were our exhortations to the boat's crew.

A few minutes completed our wishes and we found ourselves on board the *Lady Juliana* transport, with 225 of our country-women whom crime or misfortune had condemned to exile. We learned that they had been almost eleven months on their passage, having left Plymouth, into which port they had put, in July 1789. We continued to ask a thousand questions on a breath. Stimulated by curiosity, they inquired in turn; but the right of being first answered, we thought, lay on our side. 'Letters, letters!' was the cry. They were produced, and torn open in trembling agitation. News burst upon us like meridian splendour on a blind man. We were overwhelmed with it: public, private, general and particular. Nor was it until some days had elapsed that we were able to methodise it or reduce it into form. We now heard for the first time of our sovereign's illness and his happy restoration to health.† The French revolution of 1789, with all the attendant circumstances of that wonderful and unexpected event, succeeded to amaze us.* Now too, the disaster which had befallen the *Guardian*, and the liberal and enlarged plan on which she had been stored and fitted out by government for our use, was promulged. It served also, in some measure, to account why we had not sooner heard from England. For had not the *Guardian* struck on an island of ice she would probably have reached us three months before, and in this case have prevented the loss of the *Sirius*, although she had sailed from England three months after the *Lady Juliana*.

A general thanksgiving to Almighty God, for His Majesty's recovery and happy restoration to his family and subjects, was ordered to be offered up on the following Wednesday, when all

† The madness of King George III.

* These words bring to my mind an anecdote which, though rather out of place, I shall offer no apology for introducing. Among other inquiries, we were anxious to learn whether Monsieur La Perouse, with the two ships under his command bound on a voyage of discovery, had arrived in France. We heard with concern that no accounts of them had been received since they had left Botany Bay in March 1788. I remember, when they were at that place, one day conversing with Monsieur La Perouse about the best method of treating savage people. 'Sir,' said he, 'I have sometimes been compelled to commit hostilities upon them, but never without suffering the most poignant regret; for, independent of my own feelings on the occasion, His Majesty's (Louis XVI) last words to me, *de sa propre bouche* [from his own mouth] when I took leave of him at Versailles, were: 'It is my express injunction that you always treat the Indian nations with kindness and humanity. Gratify their wishes and never, but in a case of the last necessity, when self-defence requires it, shed human blood.' Are these the sentiments of a tyrant, of a sanguinary and perfidious man?

public labour was suspended. Every person in the settlement attended at church where a sermon, suited to an occasion at once so full of gratitude and solemnity, was preached by the Reverend Richard Johnson, chaplain of the colony.

All the officers were afterwards entertained at dinner by the governor. And in the evening an address to His Excellency, expressive of congratulation and loyalty, was agreed upon, and two days after was presented and very graciously received.

The following invitation to the non-commissioned officers and private soldiers of the marine battalion was also about this time published.

> In consequence of the assurance that was given to the non-commissioned officers and men belonging to the battalion of marines, on their embarking for the service of this country, that such of them as should behave well, would be allowed to quit the service on their return to England; or be discharged abroad upon the relief taking place, and permitted to settle in the country—His Majesty has been graciously pleased to direct the following encouragement to be held up to such non-commissioned officers and privates, as may be disposed to become settlers in this country, or in any of the islands comprised within the government of the continent of New South Wales, on the arrival of the corps raised and intended for the service of this colony, and for their relief, *viz*:
>
> To every non-commissioned officer, an allotment of one hundred and thirty acres of land, if single; and of one hundred and fifty acres, if married. To every private soldier, an allotment of eighty acres, if single, and of one hundred acres, if married; and also an allotment of ten acres for every child, whether of a non-commissioned officer, or of a private soldier. These allotments will be free of all fines, taxes, quit-rents and other acknowledgments for the space of ten years; but after the expiration of that period will be subject to an annual quit-rent of one shilling for every fifty acres.
>
> His Majesty has likewise been farther pleased to signify his royal will and pleasure, that a bounty of three pounds be offered to each non-commissioned officer and soldier who

may be disposed to continue in this country, and enlist in the corps appointed for the service of New South Wales; with a farther assurance, that in case of a proper demeanour on their part, they shall, after a farther service of five years, be entitled to double the former portion of land, provided they then choose to become settlers in the country, free of all taxes, fines, and quit-rents, for the space of fifteen years; but after that time, to be subject to the beforementioned annual quit-rent of one shilling for every fifty acres.

And as a farther encouragement to those men who may be desirous to become settlers and continue in the country, His Majesty has been likewise pleased to direct that every man shall, on being discharged, receive out of the public store a portion of clothing and provisions sufficient for his support for one year; together with a suitable quantity of seeds, grain, &c. for the tillage of the land; and a portion of tools and implements of agriculture, proper for their use. And whenever any man, who may become a settler, can maintain, feed, and clothe, such number of convicts as may be judged necessary by the governor, for the time being, to assist him in clearing and cultivating the land, the service of such convicts shall be assigned to him.

We were joyfully surprised on the 20th of the month to see another sail enter the harbour. She proved to be the Justinian transport, commanded by Captain Maitland, and our rapture was doubled on finding that she was laden entirely with provisions for our use. Full allowance, and general congratulation, immediately took place. This ship had left Falmouth on the preceding 20th of January and completed her passage exactly in five months.* She had stayed at Madeira one day and four at

* Accident only prevented her from making it in eighteen days less, for she was then in sight of the harbour's mouth, when an unpropitious gale of wind blew her off. Otherwise she would have reached us one day sooner than the *Lady Juliana*. It is a curious circumstance that these two ships had sailed together from the River Thames, one bound to Port Jackson and the other bound to Jamaica. The *Justinian* carried her cargo to the

Sao Tiago, from which last place she had steered directly for New South Wales, neglecting Rio de Janeiro on her right and the Cape of Good Hope on her left; and, notwithstanding the immense tract of ocean she had passed, brought her crew without sickness into harbour. When the novelty and boldness of such an attempt shall be recollected, too much praise on the spirit and activity of Mr Maitland cannot be bestowed.

Good fortune continued to befriend us. Before the end of the month, three more transports, having on board two companies of the New South Wales corps, arrived to add to our society. These ships also brought out a large body of convicts, whose state and sufferings will be best estimated by the following return.

Names of the ships	Number of people embarked	Number of persons who died on the passage	Number landed sick at Port Jackson
Neptune	530	163	269
Surprise	252	42	121
Scarborough	256	68	96
	1038	273	486

N.B. Of those landed sick, 124 died in the hospital at Sydney.

On our passage from England, which had lasted more than eight months, and with nearly an equal number of persons,

last mentioned place, landed it and loaded afresh with sugars, which she returned with and delivered in London. She was then hired as a transport, reladen, and sailed for New South Wales. Let it be remembered that no material accident had happened to either vessel. But what will not zeal and diligence accomplish!

only twenty-four had died and not thirty were landed sick. The difference can be accounted for only by comparing the manner in which each fleet was fitted out and conducted. With us, the provisions served on board were laid in by a contractor who sent a deputy to serve them out, and it became a part of duty for the officers of the troops to inspect their quality and to order that everyone received his just proportion. Whereas in the fleet now arrived, the distribution of provisions rested entirely with the masters of the merchantmen, and the officers were expressly forbidden to interfere in any shape farther about the convicts than to prevent their escape.

Seventeen pounds, in full of all expense, was the sum paid by the public for the passage of each person. And this sum was certainly competent to afford fair profit to the merchant who contracted. But there is reason to believe that some of those who were employed to act for him violated every principle of justice, and rioted on the spoils of misery, for want of a controlling power to check their enormities. No doubt can be entertained that a humane and liberal government will interpose its authority to prevent the repetition of such flagitious conduct.

Although the convicts had landed from these ships with every mark of meagre misery, yet it was soon seen that a want of room in which more conveniences might have been stowed for their use had not caused it. Several of the masters of the transports immediately opened stores, and exposed large quantities of goods to sale which, though at most extortionate prices, were eagerly bought up.

Such was the weakly state of the newcomers that for several weeks little real benefit to the colony was derived from so great a nominal addition to our number. However, as fast as they recovered, employment was immediately assigned to them. The old hours of labour, which had been reduced in our distress, were re-established, and the most vigorous measures adopted to give prosperity to the settlement. New buildings were immediately planned, and large tracts of ground at Rose

Hill ordered to be cleared and prepared for cultivation. Some superintendents who had arrived in the fleet, and were hired by government for the purpose of overlooking and directing the convicts, were found extremely serviceable in accelerating the progress of improvement.

July 1790. This month was marked by nothing worth communication, except a melancholy accident which befell a young gentleman of amiable character (one of the midshipmen lately belonging to the *Sirius*) and two marines. He was in a small boat, with three marines, in the harbour, when a whale was seen near them. Sensible of their danger, they used every effort to avoid the cause of it, by rowing in a contrary direction from that which the fish seemed to take, but the monster suddenly arose close to them and nearly filled the boat with water. By exerting themselves, they baled her out and again steered from it. For some time it was not seen, and they conceived themselves safe when, rising immediately under the boat, it lifted her to the height of many yards on its back, whence slipping off, she dropped as from a precipice and immediately filled and sunk. The midshipman and one of the marines were sucked into the vortex which the whale had made, and disappeared at once. The two other marines swam for the nearest shore, but one only reached it to recount the fate of his companions.

August 1790. In the beginning of this month, in company with Mr Dawes and Mr Worgan, late surgeon of the *Sirius*, I undertook an expedition to the southward and westward of Rose Hill, where the country had never been explored. We remained out seven days and penetrated to a considerable distance in a SSW direction, bounding our course at a remarkable hill, to which, from its conical shape, we gave the name of Pyramid Hill.† Except the discovery of a river (which is unquestionably the Nepean near its source) to which we gave the name of the Worgan, in honour of one of our party, nothing very interesting was remarked.

† Mt Prudhoe, Razorback Range.

Towards the end of the month we made a second excursion to the north-west of Rose Hill, when we again fell in with the Nepean and traced it to the spot where it had been first discovered by the party of which I was a member fourteen months before, examining the country as we went along. Little doubt now subsisted that the Hawkesbury and Nepean were one river.

We undertook a third expedition soon after to Broken Bay, which place we found had not been exaggerated in description, whether its capacious harbour or its desolate incultivable shores be considered. On all these excursions we brought away, in small bags, as many specimens of the soil of the country we had passed through as could be conveniently carried, in order that by analysis its qualities might be ascertained.

8

Transactions of the colony in the beginning of September 1790

THE tremendous monster who had occasioned the unhappy catastrophe just recorded was fated to be the cause of farther mischief to us.

On the 7th instant, Captain Nepean of the New South Wales corps, and Mr White, accompanied by little Nanbaree and a party of men, went in a boat to Manly Cove, intending to land there and walk on to Broken Bay. On drawing near the shore, a dead whale in the most disgusting state of putrefaction was seen lying on the beach, and at least two hundred Indians surrounding it, broiling the flesh on different fires and feasting on it with the most extravagant marks of greediness and rapture. As the boat continued to approach they were observed to fall into confusion and to pick up their spears, on which our people lay upon their oars and Nanbaree, stepping forward, harangued them for some time assuring them that we were friends.

Mr White now called for Baneelon who, on hearing his

name, came forth and entered into conversation. He was greatly emaciated, and so far disfigured by a long beard that our people not without difficulty recognised their old acquaintance. His answering in broken English, and inquiring for the governor, however, soon corrected their doubts. He seemed quite friendly. And soon after Colbee came up, pointing to his leg to show that he had freed himself from the fetter which was upon him when he had escaped from us.

When Baneelon was told that the governor was not far off, he expressed great joy and declared that he would immediately go in search of him, and if he found him not, would follow him to Sydney. 'Have you brought any hatchets with you?' cried he. Unluckily they had not any which they chose to spare; but two or three shirts, some handkerchiefs, knives and other trifles were given to them, and seemed to satisfy. Baneelon, willing to instruct his countrymen, tried to put on a shirt, but managed it so awkwardly that a man of the name of McEntire, the governor's gamekeeper, was directed by Mr White to assist him. This man, who was well known to him, he positively forbade to approach, eyeing him ferociously and with every mark of horror and resentment. He was in consequence left to himself, and the conversation proceeded as before. The length of his beard seemed to annoy him much, and he expressed eager wishes to be shaved, asking repeatedly for a razor. A pair of scissors was given to him, and he showed he had not forgotten how to use such an instrument, for he forthwith began to clip his hair with it.

During this time, the women and children, to the number of more than fifty, stood at a distance and refused all invitations which could be conveyed by signs and gestures to approach nearer. 'Which of them is your old favourite, Barangaroo, of whom you used to speak so often?'

'Oh,' said he, 'she is become the wife of Colbee! But I have got *bulla murree deein* (two large women) to compensate for her loss.'

It was observed that he had received two wounds in addition

to his former numerous ones since he had left us; one of them from a spear, which had passed through the fleshy part of his arm; and the other displayed itself in a large scar above his left eye. They were both healed, and probably were acquired in the conflict wherein he had asserted his pretensions to the two ladies.

Nanbaree, all this while, though he continued to interrogate his countrymen, and to interpret on both sides, showed little desire to return to their society, and stuck very close to his new friends. On being asked the cause of their present meeting, Baneelon pointed to the whale, which stunk immoderately, and Colbee made signals that it was common among them to eat until the stomach was so overladen as to occasion sickness.

Their demand of hatchets being reiterated, notwithstanding our refusal, they were asked why they had not brought with them some of their own. They excused themselves by saying that on an occasion of the present sort they always left them at home, and cut up the whale with the shell which is affixed to the end of the throwing-stick.

Our party now thought it time to proceed on their original expedition, and having taken leave of their sable friends, rowed to some distance, where they landed and set out for Broken Bay, ordering the coxswain of the boat in which they had come down to go immediately and acquaint the governor of all that had passed. When the natives saw that the boat was about to depart, they crowded around her, and brought down, by way of present, three or four great junks of the whale, and put them on board of her, the largest of which Baneelon expressly requested might be offered, in his name, to the governor.†

It happened that His Excellency had this day gone to a landmark, which was building on the South Head, near the flagstaff, to serve as a direction to ships at sea, and the boat met him on his return to Sydney. Immediately on receiving the

† Sailors were in the habit of calling the salt meat they ate on long voyages 'junks', but the word was also used synonymously with 'chunks'.

intelligence he hastened back to the South Head, and having procured all the firearms which could be mustered there, consisting of four muskets and a pistol, set out attended by Mr Collins and Lieutenant Waterhouse of the navy.

When the boat reached Manly Cove the natives were found still busily employed around the whale. As they expressed not any consternation on seeing us row to the beach, Governor Phillip stepped out unarmed and attended by one seaman only, and called for Baneelon, who appeared but, notwithstanding his former eagerness, would not suffer the other to approach him for several minutes. Gradually, however, he warmed into friendship and frankness and, presently after, Colbee came up. They discoursed for some time, Baneelon expressing pleasure to see his old acquaintance, and inquiring by name for every person whom he could recollect at Sydney; and among others for a French cook, one of the governor's servants, whom he had constantly made the butt of his ridicule by mimicking his voice, gait, and other peculiarities, all of which he again went through with his wonted exactness and drollery. He asked also particularly for a lady from whom he had once ventured to snatch a kiss and, on being told that she was well, by way of proving that the token was fresh in his remembrance, he kissed Lieutenant Waterhouse, and laughed aloud. On his wounds being noticed, he coldly said that he had received them at Botany Bay, but went no farther into their history.

Hatchets still continued to be called for with redoubled eagerness, which rather surprised us, as formerly they had always been accepted with indifference. But Baneelon had probably demonstrated to them their superiority over those of their own manufacturing. To appease their importunity, the governor gave them a knife, some bread, pork and other articles; and promised that in two days he would return hither and bring with him hatchets to be distributed among them, which appeared to diffuse general satisfaction.

Baneelon's love of wine has been mentioned; and the governor, to try whether it still subsisted, uncorked a bottle and poured out a glass of it, which the other drank off with his former marks of relish and good humour, giving for a toast, as he had been taught, 'The King'.

Our party now advanced from the beach but, perceiving many of the Indians filing off to the right and left, so as in some measure to surround them, they retreated gently to their old situation, which produced neither alarm or offence. The others by degrees also resumed their former position. A very fine barbed spear of uncommon size being seen by the governor, he asked for it. But Baneelon, instead of complying with the request, took it away and laid it at some distance, and brought back a throwing-stick which he presented to His Excellency.

Matters had proceeded in this friendly train for more than half an hour, when a native with a spear in his hand came forward, and stopped at the distance of between twenty and thirty yards from the place where the governor, Mr Collins, Lieutenant Waterhouse and a seaman stood. His Excellency held out his hand and called to him, advancing towards him at the same time, Mr Collins following close behind. He appeared to be a man of middle age, short of stature, sturdy and well set, seemingly a stranger and but little acquainted with Baneelon and Colbee. The nearer the governor approached, the greater became the terror and agitation of the Indian. To remove his fear, Governor Phillip threw down a dirk, which he wore at his side.† The other, alarmed at the rattle of the dirk, and probably misconstruing the action, instantly fixed his lance in his throwing-stick.*

To retreat His Excellency now thought would be more dangerous than to advance. He therefore cried out to the man, *weèree, weèree* (bad; you are doing wrong), displaying at

† A dirk was a kind of dagger.

* Such preparation is equal to what cocking a gun, and directing it at its object, would be with us. To launch the spear, or to touch the trigger, only remains.

the same time every token of amity and confidence. The words had, however, hardly gone forth when the Indian, stepping back with one foot, aimed his lance with such force and dexterity that, striking* the governor's right shoulder just above the collarbone, the point glancing downward, came out at his back, having made a wound of many inches long. The man was observed to keep his eye steadily fixed on the lance until it struck its object, when he directly dashed into the woods and was seen no more.

Instant confusion on both sides took place. Baneelon and Colbee disappeared and several spears were thrown from different quarters, though without effect. Our party retreated as fast as they could, calling to those who were left in the boat to hasten up with firearms. A situation more distressing than that of the governor, during the time that this lasted, cannot readily be conceived: the pole of the spear, not less than ten feet in length, sticking out before him and impeding his flight, the butt frequently striking the ground and lacerating the wound. In vain did Mr Waterhouse try to break it; and the barb which appeared on the other side forbade extraction until that could be performed. At length it was broken, and His Excellency reached the boat, by which time the seamen with the muskets had got up and were endeavouring to fire them, but one only would go off, and there is no room to believe that it was attended with any execution.

When the governor got home, the wound was examined. It had bled a good deal in the boat and it was doubtful whether the subclavian artery might not be divided. On moving the spear, it was found, however, that it might be safely extracted, which was accordingly performed.

Apprehension for the safety of the party who had gone to Broken Bay now took place. Lieutenant Long, with a detachment of marines, was immediately sent to escort them back,

* His Excellency described the shock to me as similar to a violent blow, with such energy was the weapon thrown.

lest any ambush might be laid by the natives to cut them off. When Mr Long reached Manly Cove the sun had set; however, he pursued his way in the dark, scrambling over rocks and thickets as well as he could, until two o'clock on the following morning, when he overtook them at a place where they had halted to sleep, about halfway between the two harbours.

At daybreak they all returned, and were surprised to find tracks in the sand of the feet of the Indians, almost the whole way from the place where they had slept to the cove. By this it should seem as if these last had secretly followed them, probably with hostile intentions but, on discovering their strength, and that they were on their guard, had abandoned their design.

On reaching Manly Cove, three Indians were observed standing on a rock, with whom they entered into conversation. The Indians informed them that the man who had wounded the governor belonged to a tribe residing at Broken Bay, and they seemed highly to condemn what he had done. Our gentlemen asked them for a spear, which they immediately gave. The boat's crew said that Baneelon and Colbee had just departed, after a friendly intercourse. Like the others, they had pretended highly to disapprove the conduct of the man who had thrown the spear, vowing to execute vengeance upon him.

From this time until the 14th, no communication passed between the natives and us. On that day, the chaplain and Lieutenant Dawes, having Abaroo with them in a boat, learned from two Indians that Wileemarin was the name of the person who had wounded the governor. These two people inquired kindly how His Excellency did, and seemed pleased to hear that he was likely to recover. They said that they were inhabitants of Rose Hill, and expressed great dissatisfaction at the number of white men who had settled in their former territories. In consequence of which declaration, the detachment at that post was reinforced on the following day.

A hazardous enterprise (but when liberty is the stake, what enterprise is too hazardous for its attainment!) was undertaken in this month by five convicts at Rose Hill who, in the night, seized a small punt there and proceeded in her to the South Head, whence they seized and carried off a boat, appropriated to the use of the lookout house, and put to sea in her, doubtless with a view of reaching any port they could arrive at and asserting their freedom. They had all come out in the last fleet, and for some time previous to their elopement had been collecting fishing tackle and hoarding up provisions, to enable them to put their scheme into execution.*

9

Transactions of the colony in part of September and October 1790

FROM so unfavourable an omen as I have just related, who could prognosticate that an intercourse with the natives was about to commence! That the foundation of what neither entreaty, munificence or humanity could induce, should be laid by a deed which threatened to accumulate scenes of bloodshed and horror was a consequence which neither speculation could predict, or hope expect to see accomplished.

On the 15th, a fire being seen on the north shore of the harbour, a party of our people went thither, accompanied by Nanbaree and Abaroo. They found there Baneelon and several other natives, and much civility passed, which was cemented by a mutual promise to meet in the afternoon at the same place. Both sides were punctual to their engagement, and no objection being made to our landing, a party of us went ashore to them unarmed. Several little presents, which had been purposely brought, were distributed among them; and to Baneelon were given a hatchet and a fish. At a distance

* They have never since been heard of. Before they went away they tried in vain to procure firearms. If they were not swallowed by the sea, probably they were cut off by the natives on some part of the coast where their necessities obliged them to land.

stood some children who, though at first timorous and unwilling to approach, were soon persuaded to advance and join the men.

A bottle of wine was produced, and Baneelon immediately prepared for the charge. Bread and beef he called loudly for, which were given to him, and he began to eat, offering a part of his fare to his countrymen, two of whom tasted the beef, but none of them would touch the bread. Having finished his repast, he made a motion to be shaved and, a barber being present, his request was complied with, to the great admiration of his countrymen, who laughed and exclaimed at the operation. They would not, however, consent to undergo it, but suffered their beards to be clipped with a pair of scissors.

On being asked where their women were, they pointed to the spot, but seemed not desirous that we should approach it. However, in a few minutes, a female appeared not far off, and Abaroo was dispatched to her. Baneelon now joined with Abaroo to persuade her to come to us, telling us she was Barangaroo, and his wife, notwithstanding he had so lately pretended that she had left him for Colbee. At length she yielded, and Abaroo, having first put a *petticoat* on her, brought her to us. But this was the prudery of the wilderness, which her husband joined us to ridicule, and we soon laughed her out of it. The petticoat was dropped with hesitation, and Barangaroo stood 'armed cap-a-pee in nakedness'. At the request of Baneelon, we combed and cut her hair, and she seemed pleased with the operation. Wine she would not taste, but turned from it with disgust, though heartily invited to drink by the example and persuasion of Baneelon. In short, she behaved so well, and assumed the character of gentleness and timidity to such advantage that, had our acquaintance ended here, a very moderate share of the spirit of travelling would have sufficed to record that amidst a horde of roaming savages in the desert wastes of New South Wales might be found as much feminine innocence, softness and modesty (allowing for inevitable difference of education) as the most finished system could bestow, or the most polished circle produce. So little fitted are we to judge of human nature at once! And yet on such grounds have countries been described and nations characterised. Hence have arisen those speculative and laborious compositions on the advantages and superiority of a state of nature. But to resume my subject.

Supposing that by a private conversation she might be induced to visit Sydney, which would be the means of drawing her husband and others thither, Abaroo was instructed to take her aside and try if she could persuade her to comply with our wish. They wandered away together accordingly, but it was soon seen that Barangaroo's arguments to induce Abaroo to rejoin their society were more powerful than those of the latter to prevail upon her to come among us; for it was not without manifest reluctance, and often repeated injunctions, that Abaroo would quit her countrywomen; and when she had done so she sat in the boat in sullen silence, evidently occupied by reflection on the scene she had left behind, and returning inclination to her former habits of life.

Nor was a circumstance which had happened in the morning interview, perhaps, wholly unremembered by the girl. We had hinted to Baneelon to provide a husband for her, who should be at liberty to pass and repass to and from Sydney as he might choose. There was, at the time, a slender fine-looking youth in company called Imeerawanyee, about sixteen years old. The lad, on being invited, came immediately up to her and offered many blandishments, which proved that he had assumed the *toga virilis*. But Abaroo disclaimed his advances, repeating the name of another person who we knew was her favourite. The young lover was not, however, easily repulsed, but renewed his suit on our return in the afternoon with such warmth of solicitation as to cause an evident alteration in the sentiments of the lady.

To heighten the good humour which pervaded both parties we began to play and romp with them. Feats of bodily strength were tried, and their inferiority was glaring. One of our party lifted with ease two of them from the ground, in spite of their efforts to prevent him, whereas in return no one of them could move him. They called him *mùrree mùlla* (a large strong man). Compared with our English labourers their muscular power would appear very feeble and inadequate.†

Before we parted, Baneelon informed us that his countrymen had lately been plundered of fish-gigs, spears, a sword and many other articles by some of our people, and expressed a wish that they should be restored, promising that if they were, the governor's dirk should be produced and returned to us tomorrow, if we would meet him there.

Accordingly on the following day we rowed to the spot, carrying with us the stolen property. We found here several natives, but not Baneelon. We asked for him and were told that he was gone down the harbour with Barangaroo to fish. Although disappointed at his breach of promise, we went on shore and mingled without distrust among those we found, acquainting them that we had brought with us the articles of which they had been plundered. On hearing this account they expressed great joy, and Imeerawanyee, darting forward, claimed the sword. It was given to him, and he had no sooner grasped it than he hastened to convince his mistress that his prowess in war was not inferior to his skill in courtship. Singling out a yellow gum-tree for the foe, he attacked it with great fierceness, calling to us to look on, and accompanying his onset with all the gestures and vociferation which they use in battle.†† Having conquered his enemy, he laid aside his fighting face and joined us with a countenance which carried in it every mark of youth and good nature.

Whether Abaroo's coyness and preference of another had displeased him, or it was owing to natural fickleness, he paid her no farther attention, but seemed more delighted with us.

† The Aborigines of the Sydney area were slight of stature, possibly the result of living in such a nutrient-poor environment.

†† Imeerawanyee was doing battle with a grass tree (*Xanthorrhoea*).

He had no beard, but was highly gratified in being combed and having his hair clipped.

All the stolen property being brought on shore, an old man came up and claimed one of the fish-gigs, singling it from the bundle, and taking only his own; and this honesty, within the circle of their society, seemed to characterise them all.

During this time it was observed that one of the Indians, instead of mixing with the rest, stood aloof, in a musing posture, contemplating what passed. When we offered to approach him, he shunned us not, and willingly shook hands with all who chose to do so. He seemed to be between thirty and forty years old, was jolly, and had a thoughtful countenance, much marked by the smallpox. He wore a string of bits of dried reed round his neck, which I asked him to exchange for a black stock. He smiled at the proposal, but made no offer of what I wanted; which our young friend, Imeerawanyee, observing, flew to him and, taking off the necklace, directly fixed it about my neck. I feared he would be enraged, but he bore it with serenity, and suffered a gentleman present to fasten his black stock upon him, with which he appeared to be pleased. To increase his satisfaction, some other trifle was given to him.

Having remained here an hour we went in quest of Baneelon, agreeably to the directions which his companions pointed out. We found him and Barangaroo shivering over a few lighted sticks, by which they were dressing small fish, and their canoe hauled up on the beach near them. On first seeing the boat they ran into the woods, but on being called by name they came back, and consented to our landing. We carried on shore with us the remaining part of the fish-gigs and spears which had been stolen, and restored them to Baneelon. Among other things was a net full of fishing lines and other tackle, which Barangaroo said was her property and, immediately on receiving it, she slung it around her neck.

Baneelon inquired, with solicitude, about the state of the governor's wound, but he made no offer of restoring the dirk, and when he was asked for it he pretended to know nothing of it, changing the conversation with great art, and asking for wine, which was given to him.

At parting, we pressed him to appoint a day on which he should come to Sydney, assuring him that he would be well received and kindly treated. Doubtful, however, of being permitted to return, he evaded our request, and declared that the governor must first come and see him, which we promised should be done.

The governor did not hesitate to execute the engagement which we had contracted for him. But Baneelon still resisted coming among us, and matters continued in this fluctuating state until the 8th of October when a fire, which they had agreed to light as a signal for us to visit them, was observed. The eager desire by which we were stimulated to carry our point of effecting an intercourse had appeared. Various parties accordingly set out to meet them, provided with different articles which we thought would prove acceptable to them. We found assembled Baneelon, Barangaroo and another young woman, and six men, all of whom received us with welcome except the grave looking gentleman beforementioned, who stood aloof in his former musing posture. When they saw that we had brought hatchets and other articles with us, they produced spears, fish-gigs and lines for the purpose of barter,* which immediately commenced to the satisfaction of both parties. I had brought with me an old blunted spear which wanted repair. An Indian immediately undertook to perform the task and, carrying it to a fire, tore with his teeth a piece of bone from a fish-gig which he fastened on the spear with yellow gum, rendered flexible by heat.

October 1790. Many of them now consented to be shaved by a barber whom we had purposely brought over. As I thought he who could perform an operation of such importance must be

* It had long been our wish to establish a commerce of this sort. It is a painful consideration that every previous addition to the cabinet of the virtuosi from this country had wrung a tear from the plundered Indian.

deemed by them an eminent personage, I bade him ask one of them for a fine barbed spear which he held in his hand; but all the barber's eloquence was wasted on the Indian, who plainly gave him to understand that he meant not to part with his spear without receiving an equivalent. Unfortunately, his price was a hatchet, and the only one which I had brought with me was already disposed of to the man who had pointed my spear. In vain did I tempt him with a knife, a handkerchief, and a hat; nothing but a hatchet seemed to be regarded. '*Bùlla mògo parrabùgò*' (two hatchets tomorrow), I repeatedly cried; but having probably experienced our insincerity, he rejected the proposal with disdain. Finding him inflexible, and longing to possess the spear, I told him at length that I would go to Sydney and fetch what he required. This seemed to satisfy and he accompanied me to my boat, in which I went away, and as quickly as possible procured what was necessary to conclude the bargain. On my return, I was surprised to see all our boats rowing towards home, and with them a canoe in which sat two Indians paddling. I pulled to them and found that Baneelon and another Indian were in one of the boats, and that the whole formed a party going over to visit the governor. I now learned that during my absence the governor had passed in a boat, on his return from Rose Hill, near the place where they were standing; and that finding he would not come to them, although they had called to him to do so, they had at once determined to venture themselves unreservedly among us. One of the men in the canoe was the person to whom I was to give the hatchet I had been to fetch; and directly as he saw me, he held up his spear, and the exchange took place, with which, and perhaps to reward me for the trouble I had taken, he was so delighted that he presented me with a throwing-stick *gratis*.

Not seeing Barangaroo of the party, I asked for her, and was informed that she had violently opposed Baneelon's departure. When she found persuasion vain, she had recourse to tears, scolding and threats, stamping the ground and tearing her hair.

But Baneelon continuing determined, she snatched up in her rage one of his fish-gigs, and dashed it with such fury on the rocks that it broke. To quiet her apprehensions on the score of her husband's safety, Mr Johnson, attended by Abaroo, agreed to remain as a hostage until Baneelon should return.

We landed our four friends opposite the hospital and set out for the governor's house. On hearing of their arrival, such numbers flocked to view them that we were apprehensive the crowd of persons would alarm them, but they had left their fears behind, and marched on with boldness and unconcern. When we reached the governor's house, Baneelon expressed honest joy to see his old friend, and appeared pleased to find that he had recovered of his wound. The governor asked for Wileemarin, and they said he was at Broken Bay. Some bread and beef were distributed among them but unluckily no fish was to be procured, which we were sorry for, as a promise of it had been one of the leading temptations by which they had been allured over. A hatchet apiece was, however, given to them, and a couple of petticoats and some fishing tackle sent for Barangaroo and the other woman.

The ceremony of introduction being finished, Baneelon seemed to consider himself quite at home, running from room to room with his companions and introducing them to his old friends, the domestics, in the most familiar manner. Among these last, he particularly distinguished the governor's orderly sergeant, whom he kissed with great affection, and a woman who attended in the kitchen; but the gamekeeper, McEntire,* he continued to hold in abhorrence, and would not suffer his approach.

Nor was his importance to his countrymen less conspicuous in other respects. He undertook to explain the use and nature of those things which were new to them. Some of his explanations were whimsical enough. Seeing, for instance, a pair of

* Look at the account of the governor being wounded, when his detestation of this man burst forth.

snuffers, he told them that they were '*Nuffer*[*] *for candle*'—which the others not comprehending, he opened the snuffers and, holding up the fore-finger of his left hand, to represent a candle, made the motion of snuffing it. Finding that even this sagacious interpretation failed, he threw down the snuffers in a rage and, reproaching their stupidity, walked away.

It was observed that a soft gentle tone of voice, which we had taught him to use, was forgotten, and his native vociferation returned in full force. But the tenderness which (like Abaroo) he had always manifested to children he still retained, as appeared by his behaviour to those who were presented to him.

The first wish they expressed to return was complied with, in order to banish all appearance of constraint, the party who had conducted them to Sydney returning with them. When we reached the opposite shore we found Abaroo and the other woman fishing in a canoe, and Mr Johnson and Barangaroo sitting at the fire, the latter employed in manufacturing fish-hooks. At a little distance, on an adjoining eminence, sat an Indian with his spear in his hand, as if sentinel over the hostages, for the security of his countrymen's return.

During our absence, Barangaroo had never ceased whining and reproaching her husband. Now that he was returned, she met him with unconcern, and seemed intent on her work only, but this state of repose did not long continue. Baneelon, eyeing the broken fish-gig, cast at her a look of savage fury and began to interrogate her, and it seemed more than probable that the remaining part would be demolished about her head had we not interposed to pacify him. Nor would we quit the place until his forgiveness was complete and his good humour restored. No sooner, however, did she find her husband's rage subsided than her hour of triumph commenced. The alarm and

* The S is a letter which they cannot pronounce, having no sound in their language similar to it. When bidden to pronounce *sun*, they always say *tun*; *salt*, *talt*, and so of all words wherein it occurs.

trepidation she had manifested disappeared. Elated at his condescension, and emboldened by our presence and the finery in which we had decked her, she in turn assumed a haughty demeanour, refused to answer his caresses, and viewed him with a reproaching eye. Although long absence from female society had somewhat blunted our recollection, the conduct of Barangaroo did not appear quite novel to us, nor was our surprise very violent at finding that it succeeded in subduing Baneelon who, when we parted, seemed anxious only to please her.

Thus ended a day, the events of which served to complete what an unhappy accident had begun. From this time our intercourse with the natives, though partially interrupted, was never broken off. We gradually continued, henceforth, to gain knowledge of their customs and policy, the only knowledge which can lead to a just estimate of national character.

10

The arrival of the Supply *from Batavia; the state of the colony in November 1790*

JOY sparkled in every countenance to see our old friend the *Supply* (I hope no reader will be so captious as to quarrel with the phrase) enter the harbour from Batavia on the 19th of October. We had witnessed her departure with tears; we hailed her return with transport.

Captain Ball was rather more than six months in making this voyage, and is the first person who ever circumnavigated the continent of New Holland. On his passage to Batavia he had discovered several islands which he gave names to and, after fighting his way against adverse elements and through unexplored dangers, safely reached his destined port. He had well stored his little bark with every necessary and conveniency which he judged we should first want, leaving a cargo of rice and salt provisions to be brought on by a Dutch snow which he had hired and freighted for the use of the settlement.† While at Batavia, the *Supply* had lost many of her people by sickness, and left several others in the general hospital at that place.

As the arrival of the *Supply* naturally leads the attention from other subjects to the state of the colony, I shall here take a review of it by transcribing a statement drawn from actual observation soon after, exactly as I find it written in my journal.

November 1790. Cultivation, on a public scale, has for some time past been given up here (Sydney), the crop of last year being so miserable as to deter from farther experiment, in consequence of which the government farm is abandoned, and the people who were fixed on it have been removed. Necessary public buildings advance fast; an excellent storehouse of large dimensions, built of bricks and covered with tiles, is just completed; and another planned which will shortly be begun. Other buildings, among which I heard the governor mention an hospital and permanent barracks for the troops, may also be expected to arise soon. Works of this nature are more expeditiously performed than heretofore, owing, I apprehend, to the superintendents lately arrived, who are placed over the convicts and compel them to labour. The first difficulties of a new country being subdued may also contribute to this comparative facility.

Vegetables are scarce, although the summer is so far advanced, owing to want of rain. I do not think that all the showers of the last four months, put together, would make twenty-four hours rain. Our farms, what with this and a poor soil, are in wretched condition. My winter crop of potatoes, which I planted in days of despair (March and April last), turned out very badly when I dug them about two months back. Wheat returned so poorly last harvest that very little, besides Indian corn, has been sown this year. The governor's wound is quite healed, and he feels no inconveniency whatever from it. With the natives we are hand and glove. They throng

† A snow was a small brig-like sailing vessel.

the camp every day, and sometimes by their clamour and importunity for bread and meat (of which they now all eat greedily) are become very troublesome. God knows, we have little enough for ourselves! Full allowance (if eight pounds of flour, and either seven pounds of beef or four pounds of pork, served alternately, per week, without either pease, oatmeal, spirits, butter or cheese can be called so) is yet kept up; but if the Dutch snow does not arrive soon it must be shortened, as the casks in the storehouse, I observed yesterday, are woefully decreased.

The convicts continue to behave pretty well; three only have been hanged since the arrival of the last fleet, in the latter end of June, all of whom were newcomers. The number of convicts here diminishes every day; our principal efforts being wisely made at Rose Hill, where the land is unquestionably better than about this place. Except building, sawing and brickmaking, nothing of consequence is now carried on here. The account which I received a few days ago from the brickmakers of their labours was as follows. Wheeler (one of the master brickmakers), with two tile stools and one brick stool, was tasked to make and burn ready for use 30,000 tiles and bricks per month. He had twenty-one hands to assist him, who performed everything; cut wood, dug clay, etc. This continued (during the days of distress excepted, when they did what they could) until June last. From June, with one brick and two tile stools he has been tasked to make 40,000 bricks and tiles monthly (as many of each sort as may be), having twenty-two men and two boys to assist him, on the same terms of procuring materials as before. They fetch the clay of which the tiles are made two hundred yards; that for bricks is close at hand. He says that the bricks are such as would be called in England moderately good, and he judges they would have fetched about 24 shillings per thousand at Kingston-upon-Thames (where he resided) in the year 1784. Their greatest fault is being too brittle. The tiles he thinks not so good as those made about London. The stuff has a rotten quality, and besides wants the advantage of being ground, in lieu of which they tread it.

King (another master bricklayer) last year, with the assistance of sixteen men and two boys, made 11,000 bricks weekly, with two stools. During short allowance did what he could. Resumed his old task when put again on full allowance, and had his number of assistants augmented to twenty men and two boys on account of the increased distance of carrying wood for the kilns. He worked at Hammersmith for Mr Scot of that place. He thinks the bricks made here as good as those made near London, and says that in the year 1784 they would have sold for a guinea per thousand and to have picked the kiln at 30 shillings.

Such is my Sydney detail dated the 12th of November 1790. Four days after I went to Rose Hill and wrote the subjoined remarks.

November 16th. Got to Rose Hill in the evening. Next morning walked round the whole of the cleared and cultivated land, with the Rev. Mr Johnson, who is the best farmer in the country. Edward Dod, one of the governor's household, who conducts everything here in the agricultural line, accompanied us part of the way, and afforded all the information he could. He estimates the quantity of cleared and cultivated land at 200 acres. Of these, fifty-five are in wheat, barley, and a little oats, thirty in maize, and the remainder is either just cleared of wood, or is occupied by buildings, gardens, etc. Four enclosures of twenty acres each are planned for the reception of cattle which may arrive in the colony, and two of these are already fenced in. In the centre of them is to be erected a house for a person who will be fixed upon to take care of the cattle. All these enclosures are supplied with water; and only a part of the trees which grew in them being cut down, gives to them a very park-like and beautiful appearance.

'Our survey commenced on the north side of the river. Dod says he expects this year's crop of wheat and barley from the fifty-five acres to yield full 400 bushels. Appearances hitherto hardly indicate so much. He says he finds the beginning of May the best time to sow barley,* but that it may continue to be sown until August. That sown in May is reaped in December; that of August in January. He sowed his wheat, part in June and part in July. He thinks June the best time, and says that he invariably finds that which is deepest sown grows strongest and best; even as deep as three inches he has put it in, and found it to answer. The wheat sown in June is now turning yellow; that of July is more backward. He has used only the broad-cast husbandry, and sowed two bushels per acre. The plough has never yet been tried here; all the ground is hoed and (as Dod confesses) very incompetently turned up. Each convict labourer was obliged to hoe sixteen rods a day, so that in some places the earth was but just scratched over.† The ground was left open for some months, to receive benefit from the sun and air; and on that newly cleared the trees were burnt and the ashes dug in. I do not find that a succession of crops has yet been attempted; surely it would help to meliorate and improve the soil. Dod recommends strongly the culture of potatoes on a large scale, and says that were they planted even as late as January they would answer, but this I doubt. He is more than ever of opinion that without a large supply of cattle nothing can be done. They have not at this time either horse, cow or sheep here. I asked him how the stock they had was coming on. The fowls he said multiplied exceedingly, but the hogs neither thrived or increased in number, for want of food. He pointed out to us his best wheat, which looks tolerable, and may perhaps yield thirteen or fourteen bushels per acre.** Next came the oats which are in ear, though no more than six inches high: they will

* The best crop of barley ever produced in New South Wales was sown by a private individual, in February 1790, and reaped in the following October.

† A rod is five metres long.

** As all the trees on our cleared ground were cut down, and not grubbed up, the roots and stumps remain, on which account a tenth part of surface in every acre must be deducted. This is slovenly husbandry; but in a not return as much seed as was sown. The barley, except one patch in a corner of a field, little better than the oats. Crossed the river and inspected the south side. Found the little patch of wheat at the bottom of the crescent very bad. Proceeded and examined the large field on the ascent to the westward: here are about twenty-five acres of wheat, which from its appearance we guessed would produce perhaps seven bushels an acre. The next patch to this is in maize, which looks not unpromising; some of the stems are stout, and beginning to throw out large broad leaves, the surest sign of vigour. The view from the top of the wheat field takes in, except a narrow slip, the whole of the cleared land at Rose Hill. From not having before seen an opening of such extent for the last three years, this struck us as grand and capacious. The beautiful diversity of the ground (gentle hill and dale) would certainly be reckoned pretty in any country. Continued our walk, and crossed the old field which is intended to form part of the main street of the projected town. The wheat in this field is rather better, but not much, than in the large field before mentioned. The next field is maize, inferior to what we have seen, but not despicable. An acre of maize, at the bottom of the marine garden, is equal in luxuriancy of promise to any I ever saw in any country.

The main street of the new town is already begun. It is to be a mile long, and of such breadth as will make Pall Mall and Portland Place 'hide their diminished heads'.† It contains at present thirty-two houses completed, of twenty-four feet

country where immediate subsistence is wanted it is perhaps necessary. None of these stumps, when I left Port Jackson, showed any symptoms of decay, though some of the trees had been cut down four years. To the different qualities of the wood of Norfolk Island and New South Wales, perhaps the difference of soil may in some measure be traced. That of Norfolk Island is light and porous: it rots and turns into mould in two years. Besides its hardness that of Port Jackson abounds with red corrosive gum, which contributes its share of mischief.

† Milton, *Paradise Lost*, IV, 34.

by twelve each, on a ground floor only, built of wattles plastered with clay, and thatched. Each house is divided into two rooms, in one of which is a fireplace and a brick chimney. These houses are designed for men only; and ten is the number of inhabitants allotted to each; but some of them now contain twelve or fourteen, for want of better accommodation. More are building. In a cross street stand nine houses for unmarried women; and exclusive of all these are several small huts where convict families of good character are allowed to reside. Of public buildings, besides the old wooden barrack and store, there is a house of lath and plaster, forty-four feet long by sixteen wide, for the governor, on a ground floor only, with excellent outhouses and appurtenances attached to it. A new brick storehouse, covered with tiles, 100 feet long by twenty-four wide, is nearly completed; and a house for the storekeeper. The first stone of a barrack, 100 feet long by twenty-four wide, to which are intended to be added wings for the officers, was laid today. The situation of the barrack is judicious, being close to the storehouse, and within 150 yards of the wharf, where all boats from Sydney unload. To what I have already enumerated must be added an excellent barn, a granary, an enclosed yard to rear stock in, a commodious blacksmith's shop, and a most wretched hospital, totally destitute of every conveniency. Luckily for the gentleman who superintends this hospital, and still more luckily for those who are doomed in case of sickness to enter it, the air of Rose Hill has hitherto been generally healthy. A tendency to produce slight inflammatory disorders, from the rapid changes* of the temperature of the air, is most to be dreaded.

The hours of labour for the convicts are the same here as at Sydney. On Saturdays after ten o'clock in the morning they are allowed to work in their own gardens. These gardens are at

* In the close of the year 1788, when this settlement was established, the thermometer has been known to stand at 50° a little before sunrise, and between one and two o'clock in the afternoon at above 100°.

present, from the long drought and other causes, in a most deplorable state. Potatoes, I think, thrive better than any other vegetable in them. For the public conveniency a baker is established here in a good bakehouse, who exchanges with every person bread for flour, on stipulated terms, but no compulsion exists for anyone to take his bread; it is left entirely to everybody's own option to consume his flour as he pleases. Divine service is performed here, morning and afternoon, one Sunday in every month, when all the convicts are obliged to attend church, under penalty of having a part of their allowance of provisions stopped, which is done by the chaplain, who is a justice of the peace.

For the punishment of offenders, where a criminal court is not judged necessary, two or more justices occasionally assemble, and order the infliction of slight corporal punishment, or short confinement in a strong room built for this purpose. The military present here consists of two subalterns, two sergeants, three corporals, a drummer, and twenty-one privates. These have been occasionally augmented and reduced, as circumstances have been thought to render it necessary.

Brick-kilns are now erected here, and bricks manufactured by a convict of the name of Becket, who came out in the last fleet, and has fifty-two people to work under him. He makes 25,000 bricks weekly. He says that they are very good, and would sell at Birmingham, where he worked about eighteen months ago, at more than 30 shillings per thousand.

Nothing farther of public nature remaining to examine, I next visited a humble adventurer, who is trying his fortune here. James Ruse, convict, was cast for seven years at Bodmin assizes in August 1782. He lay five years in prison and on board the *Dunkirk* hulk at Plymouth, and then was sent to this country. When his term of punishment expired, in August 1789, he claimed his freedom, and was permitted by the governor, on promising to settle in the country, to take, in December following, an uncleaned piece of ground with an assurance that, if he would cultivate it, it should not be taken from him. Some assistance was given him to fell the timber, and he accordingly began. His present account to me was as follows:

> I was bred a husbandman, near Launcester in Cornwall. I cleared my land as well as I could, with the help afforded me. The exact limit of what ground I am to have, I do not yet know; but a certain direction has been pointed out to me, in which I may proceed as fast as I can cultivate. I have now an acre and a half in bearded wheat, half an acre in maize, and a small kitchen garden. On my wheat land I sowed three bushels of seed, the produce of this country, broad cast. I expect to reap about twelve or thirteen bushels. I know nothing of the cultivation of maize, and cannot therefore guess so well at what I am likely to gather. I sowed part of my wheat in May, and part in June. That sown in May has thriven best. My maize I planted in the latter end of August, and the beginning of September. My land I prepared thus: having burnt the fallen timber off the ground, I dug in the ashes, and then hoed it up, never doing more than eight, or perhaps nine, rods in a day; by which means it was not like the government farm, just scratched over, but properly done. Then I clod-moulded it, and dug in the grass and weeds. This I think almost equal to ploughing. I then let it lie as long as I could, exposed to air and sun; and, just before I sowed my seed, turned it all up afresh. When I shall have reaped my crop, I purpose to hoe it again, and harrow it fine, and then sow it with turnip seed, which will mellow and prepare it for next year. My straw I mean to bury in pits, and throw in with it everything which I think will rot and turn to manure. I have no person to help me at present but my wife, whom I married in this country; she is industrious. The governor, for some time, gave me the help of a convict man, but he is taken away. Both my wife and myself receive our provisions regularly at the store, like all other people. My opinion of the soil of my farm is that it is middling; neither good or bad. I will be bound to make it do with the aid of manure, but without cattle it will fail. The greatest check upon me is the dishonesty of the convicts who, in spite of all my vigilance, rob me almost every night.

The annexed return will show the number of persons of all descriptions at Rose Hill, at this period. On the morning of the 17th, I went down to Sydney.

Here terminates the transcription of my diary. It were vain to suppose that it can prove either agreeable or interesting to a majority of readers but as this work is intended not only for amusement, but information, I considered it right to present this detail unaltered, either in its style or arrangement.

A return of the number of persons employed at Rose Hill, November 16th, 1790.

How employed	Troops	Civil department	Troops		Convicts		
			Wives	Children	Men	Women	Children
Storekeeper	—	1	—	—	—	—	—
Surgeon	—	1	—	—	—	—	—
Carpenters	—	—	—	—	24	—	—
Blacksmiths	—	—	—	—	5	—	—
Master Bricklayer	—	—	—	—	1	—	—
Bricklayers	—	—	—	—	28	—	—
Master Brickmaker	—	—	—	—	1	—	—
Brickmakers	—	—	—	—	52	—	—
Labourers	—	—	—	—	326*	—	—
Assistants to the provision store	—	—	—	—	4	—	—
Assistants to the hospital	—	—	—	—	3	—	—
Officers' servants	—	—	—	—	6	—	—
Making clothing	—	—	—	—	—	50	—
Superintendents	—	4	—	—	—	—	—
Total number of persons 552	29	6	1	3	450	50	13

* Of these labourers, 16 are sawyers. The rest are variously employed in clearing fresh land, in dragging brick and timber carts; and a great number in making a road of a mile long, through the main street, to the governor's house.

11

Farther transactions of the colony in November 1790

DURING the intervals of duty our greatest source of entertainment now lay in cultivating the acquaintance of our new friends, the natives. Ever liberal of communication, no difficulty but of understanding each other subsisted between us. Inexplicable contradictions arose to bewilder our researches which no ingenuity could unravel and no credulity reconcile.

Baneelon, from being accustomed to our manners and understanding a little English, was the person through whom we wished to prosecute inquiry, but he had lately become a man of so much dignity and consequence that it was not always easy to obtain his company. Clothes had been given to him at various times, but he did not always condescend to wear them. One day he would appear in them, and the next day he was to be seen carrying them in a net slung around his neck. Farther to please him, a brick house of twelve feet square was built for his use, and for that of such of his countrymen as might choose to reside in it, on a point of land fixed upon by himself.† A shield, double cased with tin, to ward off the spears of his enemies, was also presented to him by the governor.

Elated by these marks of favour, and sensible that his importance with his countrymen arose in proportion to our patronage of him, he warmly attached himself to our society. But the gratitude of a savage is ever a precarious tenure. That of Baneelon was fated to suffer suspension, and had well nigh been obliterated by the following singular circumstance.

One day the natives were observed to assemble in more than an ordinary number at their house on the point, and to be full of bustle and agitation, repeatedly calling on the name of Baneelon and that of *deein* (a woman). Between twelve and one o'clock Baneelon, unattended, came to the governor at his house, and told him that he was going to put to death a woman

† Bennelong Point, the site of the Sydney Opera House.

immediately, whom he had brought from Botany Bay. Having communicated his intention, he was preparing to go away, seeming not to wish that the governor should be present at the performance of the ceremony. But His Excellency was so struck with the fierce gestures and wild demeanour of the other, who held in his hand one of our hatchets and frequently tried the sharpness of it, that he determined to accompany him, taking with him Mr Collins and his orderly sergeant. On the road, Baneelon continued to talk wildly and incoherently of what he would do, and manifested such extravagant marks of fury and revenge that his hatchet was taken away from him, and a walking-stick substituted for it.

When they reached the house, they found several natives of both sexes lying promiscuously before the fire, and among them a young woman, not more than sixteen years old who, at sight of Baneelon, started, and raised herself half up. He no sooner saw her than, snatching a sword of the country, he ran at her, and gave her two severe wounds on the head and one on the shoulder, before interference in behalf of the poor wretch could be made. Our people now rushed in and seized him; but the other Indians continued quiet spectators of what was passing, either awed by Baneelon's superiority or deeming it a common case, unworthy of notice and interposition. In vain did the governor by turns soothe and threaten him. In vain did the sergeant point his musket at him. He seemed dead to every passion but revenge; forgot his affection to his old friends and, instead of complying with the request they made, furiously brandished his sword at the governor, and called aloud for his hatchet to dispatch the unhappy victim of his barbarity. Matters now wore a serious aspect. The other Indians appeared under the control of Baneelon and had begun to arm and prepare their spears, as if determined to support him in his violence.

Farther delay might have been attended with danger. The *Supply* was therefore immediately hailed, and an armed boat ordered to be sent on shore. Luckily, those on board the ship had already observed the commotion and a boat was ready, into which Captain Ball with several of his people stepped, armed with muskets, and put off. It was reasonable to believe that so powerful a reinforcement would restore tranquillity, but Baneelon stood unintimidated at disparity of numbers and boldly demanded his prisoner, whose life, he told the governor, he was determined to sacrifice, and afterwards to cut off her head. Everyone was eager to know what could be the cause of such inveterate inhumanity. Undaunted, he replied that her father was his enemy, from whom he had received the wound in his forehead beforementioned; and that when he was down in battle, and under the lance of his antagonist, this woman had contributed to assail him. 'She is now,' added he, 'my property: I have ravished her by force from her tribe: and I will part with her to no person whatever, until my vengeance shall be glutted.'

Farther remonstrance would have been wasted. His Excellency therefore ordered the woman to be taken to the hospital in order that her wounds might be dressed. While this was doing, one of the natives, a young man named Boladèree, came up and supplicated to be taken into the boat also, saying that he was her husband, which she confirmed and begged that he might be admitted. He was a fine, well grown lad, of nineteen or twenty years old, and was one of the persons who had been in the house in the scene just described, which he had in no wise endeavoured to prevent, or to afford assistance to the poor creature who had a right to his protection.

All our people now quitted the place, leaving the exasperated Baneelon and his associates to meditate farther schemes of vengeance. Before they parted he gave them, however, to understand that he would follow the object of his resentment to the hospital, and kill her there, a threat which the governor assured him if he offered to carry into execution he should be immediately shot. Even this menace he treated with disdain.

To place the refugees in security, a sentinel was ordered to take post at the door of the house in which they were lodged. Nevertheless they attempted to get away in the night, either from fear that we were not able to protect them, or some apprehension of being restrained from future liberty. When questioned where they proposed to find shelter, they said they would go to the Cameragal tribe, with whom they should be safe. On the following morning, Imeerawanyee* joined them, and expressed strong fears of Baneelon's resentment. Soon after a party of natives, known to consist of Baneelon's chosen friends, with a man of the name of Bìgon, at their head, boldly entered the hospital garden and tried to carry off all three by force. They were driven back and threatened, to which their leader only replied by contemptuous insolence.

Baneelon, finding he could not succeed, withdrew himself for two days. At length he made his appearance, attended only by his wife. Unmindful of what had so recently happened, he marched singly up to the governor's house and, on being refused admittance, though unarmed, attempted to force the sentinel. The soldier spared him, but the guard was instantly sent for and drawn up in front of the house; not that their co-operation was necessary, but that their appearance might terrify. His ardour now cooled, and he seemed willing, by submission, to atone for his misconduct. His intrepid disregard of personal risk, nay of life, could not, however, but gain admiration; though it led us to predict that this Baneelon,

* This good-tempered lively lad was become a great favourite with us, and almost constantly lived at the governor's house. He had clothes made up for him and, to amuse his mind, he was taught to wait at table. One day a lady, Mrs McArthur, wife of an officer of the garrison, dined there, as did Nanbaree. This latter, anxious that his countryman should appear to advantage in his new office, gave him many instructions, strictly charging him, among other things, to take away the lady's plate whenever she should cross her knife and fork, and to give her a clean one. This Imeerawanyee executed, not only to Mrs McArthur, but to several of the other guests. At last Nanbaree crossed his knife and fork with great gravity, casting a glance at the other, who looked for a moment with cool indifference at what he had done, and then turned his head another way. Stung at this supercilious treatment, he called in rage to know why he was

whom imagination had fondly pictured like a second Omai, the gaze of a court and the scrutiny of the curious, would perish untimely, the victim of his own temerity.†

To encourage his present disposition of mind, and to try if feelings of compassion towards an enemy could be exerted by an Indian warrior, the governor ordered him to be taken to the hospital that he might see the victim of his ferocity. He complied in sullen silence. When about to enter the room in which she lay, he appeared to have a momentary struggle with himself, which ended his resentment. He spoke to her with kindness, and professed sorrow for what he had done, and promised her future protection. Barangaroo, who had accompanied him, now took the alarm: and as in shunning one extreme we are ever likely to rush into another, she thought him perhaps too courteous and tender. Accordingly she began to revile them both with great bitterness, threw stones at the girl and attempted to beat her with a club.

Here terminated this curious history, which I leave to the reader's speculation. Whether human sacrifices of prisoners be common among them is a point which all our future inquiry never completely determined. It is certain that no second instance of this sort was ever witnessed by us.

12

Transactions of the colony in part of December 1790

ON the 9th of the month, a sergeant of marines, with three convicts, among whom was McEntire, the governor's

not attended to as well as the rest of the company. But Imeerawanyee only laughed; nor could all the anger and reproaches of the other prevail upon him to do that for one of his countrymen which he cheerfully continued to perform to every other person.

† Omai was a Tahitian who travelled to London with James Cook, played chess well, and met Dr Johnson.

gamekeeper (the person of whom Baneelon had, on former occasions, shown so much dread and hatred) went out on a shooting party. Having passed the north arm of Botany Bay, they proceeded to a hut formed of boughs which had been lately erected on this peninsula for the accommodation of sportsmen who wished to continue by night in the woods; for, as the kangaroos in the daytime chiefly keep in the cover, it is customary on these parties to sleep until near sunset, and watch for the game during the night and in the early part of the morning. Accordingly, having lighted a fire, they lay down, without distrust or suspicion.

About one o'clock, the sergeant was awakened by a rustling noise in the bushes near him and, supposing it to proceed from a kangaroo, called to his comrades, who instantly jumped up. On looking about more narrowly, they saw two natives with spears in their hands, creeping towards them, and three others a little farther behind. As this naturally created alarm, McEntire said, 'Don't be afraid, I know them,' and immediately laying down his gun, stepped forward and spoke to them in their own language. The Indians, finding they were discovered, kept slowly retreating, and McEntire accompanied them about a hundred yards, talking familiarly all the while.

One of them now jumped on a fallen tree and, without giving the least warning of his intention, launched his spear at McEntire and lodged it in his left side. The person who committed this wanton act was described as a young man with a speck or blemish on his left eye. That he had been lately among us was evident from his being newly shaved.

The wounded man immediately drew back and, joining his party, cried, 'I am a dead man.' While one broke off the end of the spear, the other two set out with their guns in pursuit of the natives; but their swiftness of foot soon convinced our people of the impossibility of reaching them. It was now determined to attempt to carry McEntire home, as his death was apprehended to be near, and he expressed a longing desire not be left to expire in the woods. Being an uncommonly robust muscular man, notwithstanding a great effusion of blood, he was able, with the assistance of his comrades, to creep slowly along, and reached Sydney about two o'clock the next morning. On the wound being examined by the surgeons, it was pronounced mortal. The poor wretch now began to utter the most dreadful exclamations, and to accuse himself of the commission of crimes of the deepest dye, accompanied with such expressions of his despair of God's mercy as are too terrible to repeat.

In the course of the day, Colbee and several more natives came in, and were taken to the bed where the wounded man lay. Their behaviour indicated that they had already heard of the accident, as they repeated twice or thrice the name of the murderer Pimelwì, saying that he lived at Botany Bay. To gain knowledge of their treatment of similar wounds, one of the surgeons made signs of extracting the spear, but this they violently opposed and said, if it were done, death would instantly follow.

On the 12th, the extraction of the spear was, however, judged practicable, and was accordingly performed. That part of it which had penetrated the body measured seven inches and a half long, having on it a wooden barb, and several smaller ones of stone fastened on with yellow gum, most of which, owing to the force necessary in extraction, were torn off and lodged in the patient. The spear had passed between two ribs and had wounded the left lobe of the lungs. He lingered* until the 20th of January, and then expired. On opening the corpse, it was found that the left lung had perished from suppuration,

* From the aversion uniformly shown by all the natives to this unhappy man, he had long been suspected by us of having in his excursions shot and injured them. To gain information on this head from him, the moment of contrition was seized. On being questioned with great seriousness, he, however, declared that he had never fired but once on a native, and then had not killed but severely wounded him, and this in his own defence. Notwithstanding this death-bed confession, most people doubted the truth of the relation, from his general character and other circumstances.

its remains adhering to the ribs. Some pieces of stone which had dropped from the spear were seen, but no barb of wood.

The governor was at Rose Hill when this accident happened. On the day after he returned to Sydney, the following order was issued:

> Several tribes of the natives still continuing to throw spears at any man they meet unarmed, by which several have been killed or dangerously wounded, the governor, in order to deter the natives from such practices in future, has ordered out a party to search for the man who wounded the convict McEntire in so dangerous a manner on Friday last, though no offence was offered on his part, in order to make a signal example of that tribe. At the same time, the governor strictly forbids, under penalty of the severest punishment, any soldier, or other person, not expressly ordered out for that purpose, ever to fire on any native except in his own defence; or to molest him in any shape, or to bring away any spears, or other articles, which they may find belonging to those people. The natives will be made severe examples of whenever any man is wounded by them; but this will be done in a manner which may satisfy them that it is a punishment inflicted on them for their own bad conduct, and of which they cannot be made sensible if they are not treated with kindness while they continue peaceable and quiet.
>
> A party, consisting of two captains, two subalterns, and forty privates, with a proper number of non-commissioned officers from the garrison, with three days provisions &c., are to be ready to march tomorrow morning at daylight, in order to bring in six of those natives who reside near the head of Botany Bay; or, if that should be found impracticable, to put that number to death.

Just previous to this order being issued, the author of this publication received a direction to attend the governor at headquarters immediately. I went, and His Excellency informed me that he had pitched upon me to execute the foregoing command. He added that the two subalterns who were to be drawn from the marine corps should be chosen by myself; that the sergeant and the two convicts who were with McEntire should attend as guides; that we were to proceed to the peninsula at the head of Botany Bay; and thence, or from any part of the north arm of the bay, we were, if practicable, to bring away two natives as prisoners; and to put to death ten; that we were to destroy all weapons of war, but nothing else; that no hut was to be burned; that all women and children were to remain uninjured, not being comprehended within the scope of the order; that our operations were to be directed either by surprise or open force; that after we had made any prisoners, all communication, even with those natives with whom we were in habits of intercourse, was to be avoided, and none of them suffered to approach us. That we were to cut off and bring in the heads of the slain; for which purpose hatchets and bags would be furnished. And finally, that no signal of amity or invitation should be used in order to allure them to us; or if made on their part, to be answered by us: for that such conduct would be not only present treachery, but give them reason to distrust every future mark of peace and friendship on our part.

His Excellency was now pleased to enter into the reasons which had induced him to adopt measures of such severity. He said that since our arrival in the country no less than seventeen of our people had either been killed or wounded by the natives; that he looked upon the tribe known by the name of Bideegàl, living on the beforementioned peninsula, and chiefly on the north arm of Botany Bay, to be the principal aggressors; that against this tribe he was determined to strike a decisive blow, in order at once to convince them of our superiority and to infuse an universal terror, which might operate to prevent farther mischief. That his observations on the natives had led him to conclude that although they did not fear death individually, yet that the relative weight and importance of the different tribes appeared to be the highest object of their estimation, as each tribe deemed its strength and security to consist wholly in its powers, aggregately considered. That his motive for having so long delayed to use violent measures had arisen from believing that in every former instance of hostility, they had acted either from having received injury, or from misapprehension.

'To the latter of these causes,' added he, 'I attribute my own wound, but in this business of McEntire, I am fully persuaded that they were unprovoked, and the barbarity of their conduct admits of no extenuation; for I have separately examined the sergeant, of whose veracity I have the highest opinion, and the two convicts; and their story is short, simple, and alike. I have in vain tried to stimulate Baneelon, Colbee, and the other natives who live among us, to bring in the aggressor. Yesterday, indeed, they promised me to do it and actually went away as if bent on such a design; but Baneelon, instead of directing his steps to Botany Bay, crossed the harbour in his canoe in order to draw the foreteeth of some of the young men; and Colbee, in the room of fulfilling his engagement, is loitering about the lookout house. Nay, so far from wishing even to describe faithfully the person of the man who has thrown the spear, they pretended that he has a distorted foot, which is a palpable falsehood. So that we have our efforts only to depend upon; and I am resolved to execute the prisoners who may be brought in, in the most public and exemplary manner, in the presence of as many of their countrymen as can be collected, after having explained the cause of such a punishment; and my fixed determination to repeat it, whenever any future breach of good conduct on their side shall render it necessary.'

Here the governor stopped and, addressing himself to me, said if I could propose any alteration of the orders under which I was to act, he would patiently listen to me. Encouraged by this condescension, I begged leave to offer for consideration whether, instead of destroying ten persons, the capture of six would not better answer all the purposes for which the expedition was to be undertaken; as out of this number, a part might be set aside for retaliation; and the rest, at a proper time, liberated, after having seen the fate of their comrades and being made sensible of the cause of their own detention.

This scheme, His Excellency was pleased instantly to adopt,

adding. 'If six cannot be taken, let this number be shot. Should you, however, find it practicable to take so many, I will hang two and send the rest to Norfolk Island for a certain period, which will cause their countrymen to believe that we have dispatched them secretly.' The order was accordingly altered to its present form; and I took my leave to prepare, after being again cautioned not to deceive by holding signals of amity.

At four o'clock on the morning of the 14th we marched. The detachment consisted, besides myself, of Captain Hill of the New South Wales corps, lieutenants Poulden and Dawes of the marines, Mr Worgan and Mr Lowes, surgeons, three sergeants, three corporals and forty private soldiers, provided with three days provisions, ropes to bind our prisoners with, and hatchets and bags to cut off and contain the heads of the slain. By nine o'clock this terrific procession reached the peninsula at the head of Botany Bay, but after having walked in various directions until four o'clock in the afternoon, without seeing a native, we halted for the night.

At daylight on the following morning our search recommenced. We marched in an easterly direction, intending to fall in with the south-west arm of the bay, about three miles above its mouth, which we determined to scour and thence passing along the head of the peninsula, to proceed to the north arm and complete our search. However, by a mistake of our guides, at half past seven o'clock, instead of finding ourselves on the south-west arm, we came suddenly upon the sea shore at the head of the peninsula, about midway between the two arms. Here we saw five Indians on the beach, whom we attempted to surround; but they penetrated our design, and before we could get near enough to effect our purpose, ran off. We pursued; but a contest between heavy-armed Europeans fettered by ligatures, and naked unencumbered Indians, was too unequal to last long. They darted into the wood and disappeared.

The alarm being given, we were sensible that no hope of success remained but by a rapid movement to a little village (if five huts deserve the name) which we knew stood on the nearest point of the north arm, where possibly someone unapprised of our approach might yet be found. Thither we hastened, but before we could reach it three canoes filled with Indians were seen paddling over in the utmost hurry and trepidation to the opposite shore, where universal alarm prevailed. All we could now do was to search the huts for weapons of war; but we found nothing except fish gigs, which we left untouched.

On our return to our baggage (which we had left behind under a small guard near the place were the pursuit had begun) we observed a native fishing in shallow water not higher than his waist, at the distance of 300 yards from the land. In such a situation it would not have been easily practicable either to shoot or seize him. I therefore determined to pass without noticing him, as he seemed either from consciousness of his own security, or from some other cause, quite unintimidated at our appearance. At length he called to several of us by name, and in spite of our formidable array, drew nearer with unbounded confidence. Surprised at his behaviour, I ordered a halt that he might overtake us, fully resolved, whoever he might be, that he should be suffered to come to us and leave us uninjured. Presently we found it to be our friend Colbee, and he joined us at once with his wonted familiarity and unconcern. We asked him were Pimelwi was, and found that he perfectly comprehended the nature of our errand, for he described him to have fled to the southward, and to be at such a distance as, had we known the account to be true, would have prevented our going in search of him without a fresh supply of provisions.

When we arrived at our baggage, Colbee sat down, ate, drank, and slept with us, from ten o'clock until past noon. We asked him several questions about Sydney, which he had left on the preceding day;* and told us he had been present at

* He had, it seems, visited the governor about noon, after having gained information from Nanbaree of our march, and for what purpose it was undertaken. This he did not scruple to tell to the governor, proclaiming

an operation performed at the hospital, where Mr White had cut off a woman's leg. The agony and cries of the poor sufferer he depicted in a most lively manner.

At one o'clock we renewed our march, and at three halted near a freshwater swamp, where we resolved to remain until morning; that is, after a day of severe fatigue, to pass a night of restless inquietude, when weariness is denied repose by swarms of mosquitoes and sandflies, which in the summer months bite and sting the traveller without measure or intermission.

Next morning we bent our steps homeward and, after wading breast-high through two arms of the sea as broad as the Thames at Westminster, were glad to find ourselves at Sydney, between one and two o'clock in the afternoon.

The few remarks which I was able to make on the country through which we had passed were such as will not tempt adventurers to visit it on the score of pleasure or advantage. The soil of every part of the peninsula which we had traversed is shallow and sandy, and its productions meagre and wretched. When forced to quit the sand, we were condemned to drag through morasses or to clamber over rocks unrefreshed by streams and unmarked by diversity. Of the soil I brought away several specimens.

Our first expedition having so totally failed, the gov–ernor resolved to try the fate of a second, and the 'painful

at the same time a resolution of going to Botany Bay, which His Excellency endeavoured to dissuade him from by every argument he could devise: a blanket, a hatchet, a jacket, or aught else he would ask for, was offered to him in vain, if he would not go. At last it was determined to try to *eat him down*, by setting before him his favourite food, of which it was hoped he would feed so voraciously as to render him incapable of executing his intention. A large dish of fish was accordingly set before him. But after devouring a light horseman [snapper] and at least five pounds of beef and bread, even until the sight of food became disgusting to him, he set out on his journey with such lightness and gaiety as plainly showed him to be a stranger to the horrors of indigestion.

pre-eminence' again devolved on me.

The orders under which I was commanded to act differing in no respect from the last, I resolved to try once more to surprise the village beforementioned. And in order to deceive the natives and prevent them from again frustrating our design by promulging it, we feigned that our preparations were directed against Broken Bay; and that the man who had wounded the governor was the object of punishment. It was now also determined, being full moon, that our operations should be carried on in the night, both for the sake of secrecy and for avoiding the extreme heat of the day.

A little before sunset on the evening of the 22nd, we marched. Lieutenant Abbot and Ensign Prentice of the New South Wales corps were the two officers under my command, and with three sergeants, three corporals and thirty privates, completed the detachment.

We proceeded directly to the fords of the north arm of Botany Bay, which we had crossed in our last expedition, on the banks of which we were compelled to wait until a quarter past two in the morning, for the ebb of the tide. As these passing-places consist only of narrow slips of ground, on each side of which are dangerous holes, and as fording rivers in the night is at all times an unpleasant task, I determined before we entered the water to disburthen the men as much as possible; that in case of stepping wrong everyone might be as ready as circumstances would admit to recover himself. The firelock and cartouche-box were all that we carried, the latter tied fast on the top of the head to prevent it from being wetted. The knapsacks, &c. I left in charge of a sergeant and six men, who from their low stature and other causes were most likely to impede our march, the success of which I knew hinged on our ability, by a rapid movement, to surprise the village before daybreak.

The two rivers were crossed without any material accident, and in pursuit of my resolution, I ordered the guides to conduct us by the nearest route, without heeding difficulty or impediment of road. Having continued to push along the river-bank very briskly for three-quarters of an hour, we were suddenly stopped by a creek about sixty yards wide, which extended to our right and appeared dry from the tide being out. I asked if it could be passed, or whether it would be better to wheel round the head of it. Our guides answered that it was bad to cross, but might be got over, which would save us more than a quarter of a mile. Knowing the value of time, I directly bade them to push through, and everyone began to follow as well as he could. They who were foremost had not, however, got above half over when the difficulty of progress was sensibly experienced. We were immersed nearly to the waist in mud so thick and tenacious that it was not without the most vigorous exertion of every muscle of the body that the legs could be disengaged. When we had reached the middle, our distress became not only more pressing but serious, and each succeeding step buried us deeper. At length a sergeant of grenadiers stuck fast, and declared himself incapable of moving either forward or backward; and just after, Ensign Prentice and I felt ourselves in a similar predicament, close together. 'I find it impossible to move; I am sinking' resounded on every side. What to do I knew not. Every moment brought increase of perplexity and augmented danger, as those who could not proceed kept gradually subsiding. From our misfortunes, however, those in the rear profited. Warned by what they saw and heard, they inclined to the right towards the head of the creek, and thereby contrived to pass over.

Our distress would have terminated fatally had not a soldier cried out to those on shore to cut boughs of trees* and throw them to us—a lucky thought which certainly saved many of us from perishing miserably; and even with this assistance, had we been burdened by our knapsacks, we could not have emerged; for it employed us near half an hour to disentangle some of our

* I had often read of this contrivance to facilitate the passage of a morass. But I confess that in my confusion I had entirely forgotten it, and probably should have continued to do so until too late to be of use.

number. The sergeant of grenadiers, in particular, was sunk to his breast-bone, and so firmly fixed in that the efforts of many men were required to extricate him, which was effected in the moment after I had ordered one of the ropes, destined to bind the captive Indians, to be fastened under his arms.

Having congratulated each other on our escape from this 'Serbonian Bog', and wiped our arms (half of which were rendered unserviceable by the mud) we once more pushed forward to our object, within a few hundred yards of which we found ourselves about half an hour before sunrise. Here I formed the detachment into three divisions, and having enjoined the most perfect silence, in order, if possible, to deceive Indian vigilance, each division was directed to take a different route, so as to meet at the village at the same moment.

We rushed rapidly on, and nothing could succeed more exactly than the arrival of the several detachments. To our astonishment, however, we found not a single native at the huts; nor was a canoe to be seen on any part of the bay. I was at first inclined to attribute this to our arriving half an hour too late, from the numberless impediments we had encountered. But on closer examination there appeared room to believe that many days had elapsed since an Indian had been on the spot, as no mark of fresh fires or fish-bones was to be found.

Disappointed and fatigued, we would willingly have profited by the advantage of being near water, and have halted to refresh. But on consultation it was found that unless we reached in an hour the rivers we had so lately passed, it would be impossible, on account of the tide, to cross to our baggage, in which case we should be without food until evening. We therefore pushed back, and by dint of alternately running and walking, arrived at the fords, time enough to pass with ease and safety. So excessive, however, had been our efforts, and so laborious our progress, that several of the soldiers, in the course of the last two miles, gave up and confessed themselves unable to proceed farther. All that I could do for these poor fellows was to order their comrades to carry their muskets, and to leave with them a small party of those men who were least exhausted, to assist them and hurry them on. In three-quarters of an hour after we had crossed the water, they arrived at it, just time enough to effect a passage.

The necessity of repose, joined to the succeeding heat of the day, induced us to prolong our halt until four o'clock in the afternoon, when we recommenced our operations on the opposite side of the north arm to that we had acted upon in the morning. Our march ended at sunset, without our seeing a single native. We had passed through the country which the discoverers of Botany Bay extol as 'some of the finest meadows in the world'.* These meadows, instead of grass, are covered with high coarse rushes, growing in a rotten spongy bog, into which we were plunged knee-deep at every step.

Our final effort was made at half past one o'clock next morning; and after four hours toil, ended as those preceding it had done, in disappointment and vexation. At nine o'clock we returned to Sydney to report our fruitless peregrination.

But if we could not retaliate on the murderer of McEntire, we found no difficulty in punishing offences committed within our own observation. Two natives, about this time, were detected in robbing a potato garden. When seen, they ran away, and a sergeant and a party of soldiers were dispatched in pursuit of them. Unluckily it was dark when they overtook them, with some women at a fire; and the ardour of the soldiers transported them so far that, instead of capturing the offenders, they fired in among them. The women were taken, but the two men escaped.

On the following day, blood was traced from the fireplace to the sea-side, where it seemed probable that those who had lost

* The words which are quoted may be found in Mr Cook's first voyage, and form part of his description of Botany Bay. It has often fallen to my lot to traverse these fabled plains; and many a bitter execration have I heard poured on those travellers, who could so faithlessly relate what they saw.

it had embarked. The natives were observed to become immediately shy; but an exact knowledge of the mischief which had been committed was not gained until the end of two days, when they said that a man of the name of Bangai (who was known to be one of the pilferers) was wounded and dead. Imeerawanyee, however, whispered that though he was wounded, he was not dead. A hope now existed that his life might be saved; and Mr White, taking Imeerawanyee, Nanbaree, and a woman with him, set out for the spot where he was reported to be. But, on their reaching it, they were told by some people who were there that the man was dead, and that the corpse was deposited in a bay about a mile off. Thither they accordingly repaired, and found it as described, covered—except one leg, which seemed to be designedly left bare—with green boughs, and a fire burning near it. Those who had performed the funeral obsequies seemed to have been particularly solicitous for the protection of the face, which was covered with a thick branch, interwoven with grass and fern so as to form a complete screen. Around the neck was a strip of the bark of which they make fishing lines, and a young straight stick growing near was stripped of its bark and bent down so as to form an arch over the body, in which position it was confined by a forked branch stuck into the earth.

On examining the corpse, it was found to be warm. Through the shoulder had passed a musket ball, which had divided the subclavian artery and caused death by loss of blood. No mark of any remedy having been applied could be discovered. Possibly the nature of the wound, which even among us would baffle cure without amputation of the arm at the shoulder, was deemed so fatal that they despaired of success, and therefore left it to itself. Had Mr White found the man alive, there is little room to think that he could have been of any use to him; for that an Indian would submit to so formidable and alarming an operation seems hardly probable.

None of the natives who had come in the boat would touch the body, or even go near it, saying the *mawn* would come; that is literally, 'the spirit of the deceased would seize them'. Of the people who died among us, they had expressed no such apprehension. But how far the difference of a natural death, and one effected by violence, may operate on their fears to induce superstition; and why those who had performed the rites of sepulture should not experience similar fears and reluctance, I leave to be determined. Certain it is (as I shall insist upon more hereafter), that they believe the spirit of the dead not to be extinct with the body.

Baneelon took an odd method of revenging the death of his countryman. At the head of several of his tribe, he robbed one of the private boats of fish, threatening the people, who were unarmed, that in case they resisted he would spear them. On being taxed by the governor with this outrage, he at first stoutly denied it; but on being confronted with the people who were in the boat, he changed his language and, without deigning even to palliate his offence, burst into fury and demanded who had killed Bangai.

13

The transactions of the colony continued to the end of May 1791

December 1790. The Dutch snow from Batavia arrived on the 17th of the month, after a passage of twelve weeks, in which she had lost sixteen of her people. But death, to a man who has resided at Batavia, is too familiar an object to excite either terror or regret. All the people of the *Supply* who were left there sick, except one midshipman, had also perished in that fatal climate.

The cargo of the snow consisted chiefly of rice, with a small quantity of beef, pork and flour.

A letter was received by this vessel, written by the *Shebander* at Batavia, to Governor Phillip, acquainting him that war had commenced between England and Spain. As this letter was written in the Dutch language we did not find it easy of translation. It filled us, however, with anxious perturbation, and with wishes as impotent as they were eager, in the cause of our country. Though far beyond the din of arms, we longed to contribute to her glory, and to share in her triumphs.

Placed out of the reach of attack, both by remoteness and insignificancy, our only dread lay lest those supplies intended for our consumption should be captured. Not, however, to be found totally unprovided in case an enemy should appear, a battery was planned near the entrance of Sydney Cove, and other formidable preparations set on foot.

The commencement of the year 1791, though marked by no circumstances particularly favourable, beamed far less inauspicious than that of 1790 had done.

January 1791. No circumstance, however apparently trivial, which can tend to throw light on a new country, either in respect of its present situation or its future promise, should pass unregarded. On the 24th of January, two bunches of grapes were cut in the governor's garden, from cuttings of vines brought three years before from the Cape of Good Hope. The bunches were handsome, the fruit of a moderate size but well filled out and the flavour high and delicious.

The first step after unloading the Dutch snow was to dispatch the *Supply* to Norfolk Island for Captain Hunter, and the crew of the *Sirius* who had remained there ever since the loss of that ship. It had always been the governor's wish to hire the Dutchman, for the purpose of transporting them to England. But the frantic extravagant behaviour of the master of her, for a long time frustrated the conclusion of a contract. He was so totally lost to a sense of reason and propriety as to ask *eleven pounds* per ton, monthly, for her use, until she should arrive *from England, at Batavia*. This was treated with proper contempt; and he was at last induced to accept *twenty shillings* a ton, per month (rating her at three hundred tons) until she should arrive *in England*—being about the twenty-fifth part of his original demand. And even at this price she was, perhaps, the dearest vessel ever hired on a similar service, being totally destitute of every accommodation and every good quality which could promise to render so long a voyage either comfortable or expeditious.

February 1791. On the 26th, Captain Hunter, his officers and ship's company joined us; and on the 28th of March the snow sailed with them for England, intending to make a northern passage by Timor and Batavia, the season being too far advanced to render the southern route by Cape Horn practicable.*

Six days previous to the departure of Captain Hunter, the indefatigable Supply again sailed for Norfolk Island, carrying thither Captain Hill and a detachment of the New South Wales corps. A little native boy named Bòndel, who had long particularly attached himself to Captain Hill, accompanied him, at his own earnest request. His father had been killed in battle and his mother bitten in two by a shark: so that he was an orphan, dependent on the humanity of his tribe for protection.** His disappearance seemed to make no impression on the rest of his countrymen, who were apprised of his resolution to go. On the return of the Supply they inquired eagerly for him, and on being told that the place he was gone to afforded plenty of birds and other good fare, innumerable volunteers presented themselves to follow him, so great was their confidence in us and so little hold of them had the amor patriae.†

March 1791. The snow had but just sailed when a very daring manoeuvre was carried into execution, with complete success, by a set of convicts, eleven in number, including a woman, wife of one of the party, and two little children. They seized the governor's cutter and putting into her a seine, fishing-lines and hooks, firearms, a quadrant, compass and some provisions, boldly pushed out to sea, determined to brave every danger and combat every hardship, rather than remain longer

* They did not arrive in England until April 1792.

** I am of opinion that such protection is always extended to children who may be left destitute.

† 'Love of one's homeland.'

in a captive state. Most of these people had been brought out in the first fleet, and the terms of transportation of some of them were expired. Among them were a fisherman, a carpenter and some competent navigators, so that little doubt was entertained that a scheme so admirably planned would be adequately executed.* When their elopement was discovered, a pursuit was ordered by the governor. But the fugitives had made too good an use of the intermediate time to be even seen by their pursuers. After the escape of Captain Bligh, which was well known to us, no length of passage or hazard of navigation seemed above human accomplishment. However, to prevent future attempts of a like nature, the governor directed that boats only of stated dimensions should be built. Indeed, an order of this sort had been issued on the escape of the first party, and it was now repeated with additional restrictions.

April 1791. Notwithstanding the supplies which had recently arrived from Batavia, short allowance was again proclaimed

* It was my fate to fall in again with part of this little band of adventurers. In March 1792, when I arrived in the *Gorgon* at the Cape of Good Hope, six of these people, including the woman and one child, were put on board of us to be carried to England. Four had died, and one had jumped overboard at Batavia. The particulars of their voyage were briefly as follows. They coasted the shore of New Holland, putting occasionally into different harbours which they found in going along. One of these harbours, in the latitude of 30° south, they described to be of superior excellence and capacity. Here they hauled their bark ashore, paid her seams with tallow, and repaired her. But it was with difficulty they could keep off the attacks of the Indians. These people continued to harass them so much that they quitted the mainland and retreated to a small island in the harbour, where they completed their design. Between the latitude of 26° and 27°, they were driven by a current thirty leagues from the shore, among some islands, where they found plenty of large turtles. Soon after they closed again with the continent, when the boat got entangled in the surf and was driven on shore, and they had all well nigh perished. They passed through the straits of Endeavour and, beyond the

on the 2nd of April, on which day we were reduced to the following ration:

Three pounds of rice, three pounds of flour and three pounds of pork per week.

It was singularly unfortunate that these retrenchments should always happen when the gardens were most destitute of vegetables. A long drought had nearly exhausted them. The hardships which we in consequence suffered were great, but not comparable to what had been formerly experienced. Besides, now we made sure of ships arriving soon to dispel our distress. Whereas, heretofore, from having never heard from England, the hearts of men sunk and many had begun to doubt whether it had not been resolved to try how long misery might be endured with resignation.

Notwithstanding the incompetency of so diminished a pittance, the daily task of the soldier and convict continued unaltered. I never contemplated the labours of these men without finding abundant cause of reflection on the miseries which our nature can overcome. Let me for a moment quit the cold track of narrative. Let me not fritter away by servile adaptation those reflections and the feelings they gave birth to. Let me transcribe them fresh as they arose, ardent and generous,

gulf of Carpentaria, found a large freshwater river, which they entered, and filled from it their empty casks.

Until they reached the gulf of Carpentaria, they saw no natives or canoes differing from those about Port Jackson. But now they were chased by large canoes, fitted with sails and fighting stages, and capable of holding thirty men each. They escaped by dint of rowing to windward. On the 5th of June 1791 they reached Timor, and pretended that they had belonged to a ship which, on her passage from Port Jackson to India, had foundered; and that they only had escaped. The Dutch received them with kindness and treated them with hospitality. But their behaviour giving rise to suspicion, they were watched; and one of them at last, in a moment of intoxication, betrayed the secret. They were immediately secured and committed to prison. Soon after Captain Edwards of the though hopeless and romantic. I every day see wretches pale with disease and wasted with famine, struggle against the horrors of their situation. How striking is the effect of subordination; how dreadful is the fear of punishment! The allotted task is still performed, even on the present reduced subsistence. The blacksmith sweats at the sultry forge, the sawyer labours pent-up in his pit and the husbandman turns up the sterile glebe. Shall I again hear arguments multiplied to violate truth, and insult humanity! Shall I again be told that the sufferings of the wretched Africans are indispensable for the culture of our sugar colonies; that white men are incapable of sustaining the heat of the climate! I have been in the West Indies. I have lived there. I know that it is a rare instance for the mercury in the thermometer to mount there above 90°; and here I scarcely pass a week in summer without seeing it rise to 100°; sometimes to 105°; nay, beyond even that burning altitude.

But toil cannot be long supported without adequate refreshment. The first step in every community which wishes to preserve honesty should be to set the people above want. The throes of hunger will ever prove too powerful for integrity to withstand. Hence arose a repetition of petty delinquencies,

Pandora, who had been wrecked near Endeavour straits, arrived at Timor, and they were delivered up to him, by which means they became passengers in the Gorgon.

I confess that I never looked at these people without pity and astonishment. They had miscarried in a heroic struggle for liberty after having combated every hardship and conquered every difficulty.

The woman, and one of the men, had gone out to Port Jackson in the ship which had transported me thither. They had both of them been always distinguished for good behaviour. And I could not but reflect with admiration at the strange combination of circumstances which had again brought us together, to baffle human foresight and confound human speculation. [The woman in the story Tench tells was Mary Bryant who was defended in court by James Boswell, and finally pardoned in 1793.]

which no vigilance could detect, and no justice reach. Gardens were plundered, provisions pilfered, and the Indian corn stolen from the fields where it grew for public use. Various were the measures adopted to check this depredatory spirit. Criminal courts, either from the tediousness of their process, or from the frequent escape of culprits from their decision, were seldomer convened than formerly. The governor ordered convict-offenders either to be chained together, or to wear singly a large iron collar with two spikes projecting from it, which effectually hindered the party from concealing it under his shirt; and thus shackled, they were compelled to perform their quota of work.

May 1791. Had their marauding career terminated here, humanity would have been anxious to plead in their defence; but the natives continued to complain of being robbed of spears and fishing tackle. A convict was at length taken in the fact of stealing fishing-tackle from Darìnga, the wife of Colbee. The governor ordered that he should be severely flogged in the presence of as many natives as could be assembled, to whom the cause of punishment should be explained. Many of them, of both sexes, accordingly attended. Arabanoo's aversion to a similar sight has been noticed; and if the behaviour of those now collected be found to correspond with it, it is, I think, fair to conclude that these people are not of a sanguinary and implacable temper. Quick indeed of resentment, but not unforgiving of injury. There was not one of them that did not testify strong abhorrence of the punishment and equal sympathy with the sufferer. The women were particularly affected; Daringa shed tears, and Barangaroo, kindling into anger, snatched a stick and menaced the executioner. The conduct of these women, on this occasion, was exactly descriptive of their characters. The former was ever meek and feminine, the latter fierce and unsubmissive.

On the first of May many allotments of ground were parcelled out by the governor to convicts whose periods of transportation were expired, and who voluntarily offered to become settlers in the country. The terms on which they settled, and their progress in agriculture, will be hereafter set forth.

14

Travelling diaries in New South Wales

FROM among my numerous travelling journals into the interior parts of the country, I select the following to present to the reader, as equally important in their object, and more amusing in their detail, than any other.

In April 1791 an expedition was undertaken in order to ascertain whether or not the Hawkesbury and the Nepean were the same river. With this view, we proposed to fall in a little above Richmond Hill,* and trace down to it; and if the weather should prove fine to cross at the ford, and go a short distance westward, then to repass the river and trace it upward until we should either arrive at some spot which we knew to be the Nepean, or should determine by its course that the Hawkesbury was a different stream.

Our party was strong and numerous. It consisted of twenty-one persons, *viz.*, the governor, Mr Collins and his servant, Mr White, Mr Dawes, the author, three gamekeepers, two sergeants, eight privates and our friends Colbee and Boladeree. These two last were volunteers on the occasion, on being assured that we should not stay out many days and that we should carry plenty of provisions. Baneelon wished to go, but his wife would not permit it. Colbee, on the other hand, would listen to no objections. He only stipulated (with great care and consideration) that, during his absence, his wife and child should remain at Sydney under our protection, and be supplied with provisions.

But before we set out, let me describe our equipment, and

* Look at the map for the situation of this place.

try to convey to those who have rolled along on turnpike roads only, an account of those preparations which are required in traversing the wilderness. Every man (the governor excepted) carried his own knapsack, which contained provisions for ten days. If to this be added a gun, a blanket and a canteen, the weight will fall nothing short of forty pounds. Slung to the knapsack are the cooking kettle and the hatchet, with which the wood to kindle the nightly fire and build the nightly hut is to be cut down. Garbed to drag through morasses, tear through thickets, ford rivers and scale rocks, our autumnal heroes, who annually seek the hills in pursuit of grouse and black game, afford but an imperfect representation of the picture.

Thus encumbered, the march begins at sunrise, and with occasional halts continues until about an hour and a half before sunset. It is necessary to stop thus early to prepare for passing the night, for toil here ends not with the march. Instead of the cheering blaze, the welcoming landlord, and the long bill of fare, the traveller has now to collect his fuel, to erect his wigwam, to fetch water, and to broil his morsel of salt pork. Let him then lie down and, it if be summer, try whether the effect of fatigue is sufficiently powerful to overcome the bites and stings of the myriads of sandflies and mosquitoes which buzz around him.

Monday, April 11th, 1791. At twenty minutes before seven o'clock, we started from the governor's house at Rose Hill and steered* for a short time nearly in a north-east direction, after which we turned to north 34° west, and steadily pursued that course until a quarter before four o'clock, when we halted for the night. The country for the first two miles, while we walked

* Our method, on these expeditions, was to steer by compass, noting the different courses as we proceeded; and, counting the number of paces, of which two thousand two hundred, on good ground, were allowed to be a mile. At night when we halted, all these courses were separately cast up, and worked by a traverse table, in the manner a ship's reckoning is kept, so that by observing this precaution we always knew exactly where we

to the north-east, was good, full of grass and without rock or underwood. Afterwards it grew very bad, being full of steep, barren rocks, over which we were compelled to clamber for seven miles, when it changed to a plain country apparently very sterile, and with very little grass in it, which rendered walking easy. Our fatigue in the morning had, however, been so oppressive that one of the party knocked up. And had not a soldier, as strong as a pack-horse, undertaken to carry his knapsack in addition to his own, we must either have sent him back, or have stopped at a place for the night which did not afford water. Our two natives carried each his pack, but its weight was inconsiderable, most of their provisions being in the knapsacks of the soldiers and gamekeepers. We expected to have derived from them much information relating to the country, as no one doubted that they were acquainted with every part of it between the sea coast and the river Hawkesbury. We hoped also to have witnessed their manner of living in the woods, and the resources they rely upon in their journeys. Nothing, however, of this sort had yet occurred, except their examining some trees to see if they could discover on the bark any marks of the claws of squirrels and opossums, which they said would show whether any of those animals were hidden among the leaves and branches.† They walked stoutly, appeared but little fatigued, and maintained their spirits admirably, laughing to excess when any of us either tripped or stumbled, misfortunes which much seldomer fell to their lot than to ours.

At a very short distance from Rose Hill, we found that they were in a country unknown to them, so that the farther they

were, and how far from home: an unspeakable advantage in a new country, where one hill, and one tree, is so like another that fatal wanderings would ensue without it. This arduous task was always allotted to Mr Dawes who, from habit and superior skill, performed it almost without a stop, or an interruption of conversation: to any other man, on such terms, it would have been impracticable.

† Sugar-gliders, and ringtail and brushtail possums.

went the more dependent on us they became, being absolute strangers inland. To convey to their understandings the intention of our journey was impossible. For, perhaps, no words could unfold to an Indian the motives of curiosity which induce men to encounter labour, fatigue and pain, when they might remain in repose at home, with a sufficiency of food. We asked Colbee the name of the people who live inland, and he called them Boòrooberongal; and said they were bad, whence we conjectured that they sometimes war with those on the sea coast, by whom they were undoubtedly driven up the country from the fishing ground, that it might not be overstocked; the weaker here, as in every other country, giving way to the stronger.

We asked how they lived. He said, on birds and animals, having no fish. Their laziness appeared strongly when we halted, for they refused to draw water or to cleave wood to make a fire; but as soon as it was kindled (having first well stuffed themselves), they lay down before it and fell asleep. About an hour after sunset, as we were chatting by the fireside and preparing to go to rest, we heard voices at a little distance in the wood. Our natives catched the sound instantaneously and, bidding us be silent, listened attentively to the quarter whence it had proceeded. In a few minutes we heard the voices plainly; and, wishing exceedingly to open a communication with this tribe, we begged our natives to call to them, and bid them to come to us, to assure them of good treatment, and that they should have something given them to eat. Colbee no longer hesitated, but gave them the signal of invitation, in a loud hollow cry. After some whooping and shouting on both sides, a man with a lighted stick in his hand advanced near enough to converse with us. The first words which we could distinctly understand were, 'I am Colbee, of the tribe of Càdigal.' The stranger replied, 'I am Bèreewan, of the tribe of Boorooberongal.' Boladeree informed him also of his name and that we were white men and friends, who would give him something to eat. Still he seemed irresolute. Colbee therefore advanced to him, took him by the hand and led him to us. By the light of the moon, we were introduced to this gentleman, all our names being repeated in form by our two masters of the ceremonies, who said that we were Englishmen and *budyeree* (good), that we came from the sea coast, and that we were travelling inland.

Bereewan seemed to be a man about thirty years old, differing in no respect from his countrymen with whom we were acquainted. He came to us unarmed, having left his spears at a little distance. After a long conversation with his country–men, and having received some provisions, he departed highly satisfied.

Tuesday, April 12th, 1791. Started this morning at half past six o'clock, and in two hours reached the river. The whole of the country we passed was poor, and the soil within a mile of the river changed to a coarse deep sand, which I have invariably found to compose its banks in every part without exception that I ever saw. The stream at this place is about 350 feet wide; the water pure and excellent to the taste. The banks are about twenty feet high and covered with trees, many of which had been evidently bent by the force of the current in the direction which it runs, and some of them contained rubbish and drift wood in their branches at least forty-five feet above the level of the stream. We saw many ducks, and killed one, which Colbee swam for. No new production among the shrubs growing here was found. We were acquainted with them all. Our natives had evidently never seen this river before. They started at it with surprise, and talked to each other. Their total ignorance of the country, and of the direction in which they had walked, appeared when they asked which way Rose Hill lay; for they pointed almost oppositely to it. Of our compass they had taken early notice, and had talked much to each other about it. They comprehended its use, and called it '*naa-mòro*', literally, 'to see the way'; a more significant or expressive term cannot be found.

Supposing ourselves to be higher on the stream than Richmond Hill, we agreed to trace downward, or to the right hand. In tracing, we kept as close to the bank of the river as the innumerable impediments to walking which grow upon it would allow. We found the country low and swampy; came to a native fireplace, at which were some small fish bones; soon after we saw a native, but he ran away immediately. Having walked nearly three miles we were stopped by a creek which we could neither ford or fall a tree across. We were therefore obliged to coast it, in hope to find a passing place or to reach its head. At four o'clock we halted for the night on the bank of the creek. Our natives continued to hold out stoutly. The hindrances to walking by the river side which plagued and entangled us so much seemed not to be heeded by them, and they wound through them with ease; but to us they were intolerably tiresome. Our perplexities afforded them an inexhaustible fund of merriment and derision. Did the sufferer, stung at once with nettles and ridicule, and shaken nigh to death by his fall, use any angry expression to them, they retorted in a moment by calling him by every opprobrious name* which their language affords.

Boladeree destroyed a native hut today very wantonly before we could prevent him. On being asked why he did so, he answered that the inhabitants inland were bad; though no longer since than last night, when Bereewan had departed, they were loud in their praise. But now they had reverted to their first opinion; so fickle and transient are their motives of love and hatred.

Wednesday, April 13th, 1791. We did not set out this morning until past seven o'clock, when we continued to trace the creek. The country which we passed through yesterday was good and desirable to what was now presented to us. It was in general high and universally rocky. 'Toiling our

* Their general favourite term of reproach is *gonin-patta*, which signifies, 'an eater of human excrement.' Our language would admit a very concise and familiar translation. They have, besides this, innumerable others which they often salute their enemies with.

uncouth way', we mounted a hill, and surveyed the contiguous country.† To the northward and eastward, the ground was still higher than that we were upon; but in a south-west direction we saw about four miles. The view consisted of nothing but trees growing on precipices; not an acre of it could be cultivated. Saw a tree on fire here, and several other vestiges of the natives. To comprehend the reasons which induce an Indian to perform many of the offices of life is difficult; to pronounce that which could lead him to wander amidst these dreary wilds baffles penetration. About two o'clock we reached the head of the creek, passed it and scrambled with infinite toil and difficulty to the top of a neighbouring mountain, whence we saw the adjacent country in almost every direction, for many miles. I record with regret that this extended view presented not a single gleam of change which could encourage hope or stimulate industry to attempt its culture. We had, however, the satisfaction to discover plainly the object of our pursuit, Richmond Hill, distant about eight miles, in a *contrary* direction from what we had been proceeding upon. It was readily known to those who had been up the Hawkesbury in the boats, by a remarkable cleft or notch which distinguishes it. It was now determined that we should go back to the head of the creek and pass the night there; and in the morning cut across the country to that part of the river which we had first hit upon yesterday, and thence to trace upward, or to the left. But before I descend, I must not forget to relate that to this pile of desolation on which, like the fallen angel on the top of Niphates, we stood contemplating our nether Eden, His Excellency was pleased to give the name of *Tench's Prospect Mount*.

Our fatigue today had been excessive; but our two sable companions seemed rather enlivened than exhausted by it. We had not sooner halted and given them something to eat than they began to play ten thousand tricks and gambols. They imitated the leaping of the kangaroo; sang, danced, poised the

† Another reminiscence of Milton, *Paradise Lost*, X, 475.

spear and met in mock encounter. But their principal source of merriment was again derived from our misfortunes, in tumbling amidst nettles, and sliding down precipices, which they mimicked with inimitable drollery. They had become, however, very urgent in their inquiries about the time of our return, and we pacified them as well as we could by saying it would be soon, but avoided naming how many days.

Their method of testifying dislike to any place is singular: they point to the spot they are upon, and all around it, crying *weèree, weèree* (bad), and immediately after mention the name of any other place to which they are attached (Rose Hill or Sydney for instance), adding to it, *budyeree, budyeree* (good). Nor was their preference in the present case the result of caprice, for they assigned very substantial reasons for such predilection. 'At Rose Hill,' said they, 'are potatoes, cabbages, pumpkins, turnips, fish and wine; here are nothing but rocks and water.' These comparisons constantly ended with the question of 'Where's Rose Hill? Where?' on which they would throw up their hands and utter a sound to denote distance, which it is impossible to convey an idea of upon paper.

Thursday, April 14th, 1791. We started early and reached the river in about two hours and a half. The intermediate country, except for the last half mile, was a continued bed of stones, which were in some places so thick and close together that they looked like a pavement formed by art. When we got off the stones, we came upon the coarse river sand beforementioned.

Here we began to trace upward. We had not proceeded far when we saw several canoes on the river. Our natives made us immediately lie down among the reeds, while they gave their countrymen the signal of approach. After much calling, finding that they did not come, we continued our progress until it was again interrupted by a creek, over which we threw a tree and passed upon it. While this was doing, a native, from his canoe, entered into conversation with us, and immediately after paddled to us with a frankness and confidence which surprised everyone. He was a man of middle age, with an open cheerful countenance, marked with the smallpox, and distinguished by a nose of uncommon magnitude and dignity. He seemed to be neither astonished or terrified at our appearance and number. Two stone hatchets and two spears he took from his canoe, and presented to the governor, who in return for his courteous generosity, gave him two of our hatchets and some bread, which was new to him, for he knew not its use, but kept looking at it, until Colbee showed him what to do, when he ate it without hesitation. We pursued our course and, to accommodate us, our new acquaintance pointed out a path and walked at the head of us. A canoe, also with a man and a boy in it, kept gently paddling up abreast of us. We halted for the night at our usual hour, on the bank of the river. Immediately that we had stopped, our friend (who had already told us his name) Gombeèree, introduced the man and the boy from the canoe to us. The former was named Yèllomundee, the latter Dèeimba. The ease with which these people behaved among strangers was as conspicuous as unexpected. They seated themselves at our fire, partook of our biscuit and pork, drank from our canteens, and heard our guns going off around them without betraying any symptom of fear, distrust or surprise. On the opposite bank of the river they had left their wives and several children, with whom they frequently discoursed; and we observed that these last manifested neither suspicion or uneasiness of our designs towards their friends.

Having refreshed ourselves, we found leisure to enter into conversation with them. It could not be expected that they should differ materially from the tribes with whom we were acquainted. The same manners and pursuits, the same amusements, the same levity and fickleness, undoubtedly characterised them. What we were able to learn from them was that they depend but little on fish, as the river yields only mullets, and that their principal support is derived from small animals which they kill, and some roots (a species of wild yam chiefly) which they dig out of the earth. If we rightly understood them, each man possesses two wives. Whence can arise this superabundance of females? Neither of the men had suffered the extraction of a front tooth. We were eager to know whether or not this custom obtained among them. But neither Colbee nor Boladeree would put the question for us; and, on the contrary, showed every desire to waive the subject. The uneasiness which they testified, whenever we renewed it, rather served to confirm a suspicion which we had long entertained, that this is a mark of subjection imposed by the tribe of Cameragal (who are certainly the most powerful community in the country) on the weaker tribes around them.† Whether the women cut off a joint of one of the little fingers, like those on the sea coast, we had no opportunity of observing. These are petty remarks. But one variety struck us more forcibly. Although our natives and the strangers conversed on a par and understood each other perfectly, yet they spoke different dialects of the same language; many of the most common and necessary words used in life bearing no similitude, and others being slightly different.

English	Name on the sea coast	Name at the Hawkesbury
The Moon	Yèn-ee-da	Con-dò-en
The Ear	Goo-reè	Bèn-na
The Forehead	Nùl-lo	Nar-ràn
The Belly	Bar-an`g	Bin`-dee
The Navel	Mùn-ee-ro	Boom-bon`g
The Buttocks	Boong	Bay-leè
The Neck	Càl-ang	Gan-gà
The Thigh	Tàr-a	Dàr-a
The Hair	Deè-war-a	Keè-war-a

† Tooth evulsion is part of some Aboriginal initiation ceremonies, whose secret nature may have made Colbee and Boldaree reluctant to discuss the practice. It is also interesting to note that Governor Phillip was missing a foretooth. Did this predispose the Aborigines to accept him?

That these diversities arise from want of intercourse with the people on the coast can hardly be imagined, as the distance inland is but thirty-eight miles; and from Rose Hill not more than twenty, where the dialect of the sea-coast is spoken. It deserves notice that all the different terms seemed to be familiar to both parties, though each in speaking preferred its own.*

Stretched out at ease before our fire, all sides continued to chat and entertain each other. Gombeeree showed us the mark of a wound which he had received in his side from a spear. It was large, appeared to have passed to a considerable depth, and must certainly have been attended with imminent danger. By whom it had been inflicted, and on what occasion, he explained to Colbee; and afterwards (as we understood) he entered into a detail of the wars and, as effects lead to causes, probably of the gallantries of the district, for the word which signifies a woman

* How easily people, unused to speak the same language, mistake each other, everyone knows. We had lived almost three years at Port Jackson (for more than half of which period natives had resided with us) before we knew that the word *bèeal*, signified 'no', and not 'good', in which latter sense we had always used it without suspecting that we were wrong; and even without being corrected by those with whom we talked daily. The cause of our error was this. The epithet *weeree*, signifying 'bad' we knew; and as the use of this word and its opposite afford the most simple form of denoting consent or disapprobation to uninstructed Indians, in order to find out their word for 'good', when Arabanoo was first brought among us, we used jokingly to say that any thing which he liked was *weeree*, in order to provoke him to tell us that it was good. When we said *weeree*, he answered *beeal*, which we translated and adopted for 'good'; whereas he meant no more than simply to deny our inference, and say, 'no—it is not bad.' After this, it cannot be thought extraordinary that the little vocabulary inserted in Mr Cook's account of this part of the world should appear defective—even were we not to take in the great probability of the dialects at Endeavour River and Van Diemen's Land differing from that spoken at Port Jackson. And it remains to be proved that the animal called here *Patagaram* is not there called *Kangaroo*.

was often repeated. Colbee, in return for his communication, informed him who we were; of our numbers at Sydney and Rose Hill, of the stores we possessed and, above all, of the good things which were to be found among us, enumerating potatoes, cabbages, turnips, pumpkins and many other names which were perfectly unintelligible to the person who heard them, but which he nevertheless listened to with profound attention.

Perhaps the relation given by Gombeeree, of the cure of his wound, now gave rise to the following superstitious ceremony. While they were talking, Colbee turned suddenly round and asked for some water. I gave him a cupful, which he presented with great seriousness to Yellomundee, as I supposed to drink. This last indeed took the cup and filled his mouth with water, but instead of swallowing it, threw his head into Colbee's bosom, spit the water upon him and, immediately after, began to suck strongly at his breast, just below the nipple. I concluded that the man was sick; and called to the governor to observe the strange place which he had chosen to exonerate his stomach. The silent attention observed by the other natives, however, soon convinced us that something more than merely the accommodation of Yellomundee was intended. The ceremony was again performed; and, after having sucked the part for a considerable time, the operator pretended to receive something in his mouth, which was drawn from the breast. With this he retired a few paces, put his hand to his lips and threw into the river a stone, which I had observed him to pick up slyly and secrete. When he returned to the fireside, Colbee assured us that he had received signal benefit from the operation; and that this second *Machaon*† had extracted from his breast two splinters of a spear by which he had been formerly wounded. We examined the part, but it was smooth and whole, so that to the force of imagination alone must be imputed both the wound and its cure. Colbee himself seemed nevertheless

† A doctor to the Greeks in the Trojan war.

firmly persuaded that he had received relief, and assured us that Yellomundee was a *Cáradyee*, or 'doctor of renown.' And Boladeree added that not only he but all the rest of his tribe were *Cáradyee* of especial note and skill.

The doctors remained with us all night, sleeping before the fire in the fullness of good faith and security. The little boy slept in his father's arms, and we observed that whenever the man was inclined to shift his position, he first put over the child, with great care, and then turned round to him.

Friday, April 15th, 1791. The return of light aroused us to the repetition of toil. Our friends breakfasted with us, and previous to starting Gombeeree gave a specimen of their manner of climbing trees in quest of animals. He asked for a hatchet and one of ours was offered to him, but he preferred one of their own making. With this tool he cut a small notch in the tree he intended to climb, about two feet and a half above the ground, in which he fixed the great toe of his left foot, and sprung upwards, at the same time embracing the tree with his left arm. In an instant he had cut a second notch for his right toe on the other side of the tree, into which he sprung, and thus, alternately cutting on each side, he mounted to the height of twenty feet in nearly as short a space as if he had ascended by a ladder, although the bark of the tree was quite smooth and slippery and the trunk four feet in diameter and perfectly straight. To us it was a matter of astonishment, but to him it was sport; for while employed thus he kept talking to those below and laughing immoderately. He descended with as much ease and agility as he had raised himself. Even our natives allowed that he was a capital performer, against whom they dared not enter the lists; for as they subsist chiefly by fishing they are less expert at climbing on the coast than those who daily practise it.

Soon after they bade us adieu, in unabated friendship and good humour. Colbee and Boladeree parted from them with a slight nod of the head, the usual salutation of the country; and we shook them by the hand, which they returned lustily.

At the time we started the tide was flowing up the river, a decisive proof that we were below Richmond Hill. We had continued our march but a short time when we were again stopped by a creek, which baffled all our endeavours to cross it, and seemed to predict that the object of our attainment, though but a very few miles distant, would take us yet a considerable time to reach, which threw a damp on our hopes. We traced the creek until four o'clock, when we halted for the night. The country, on both sides, we thought in general unpromising; but it is certainly very superior to that which we had seen on the former creek. In many places it might be cultivated, provided the inundations of the stream can be repelled.

In passing along we shot some ducks, which Boladeree refused to swim for when requested, and told us in a surly tone that they swam for what was killed, and had the trouble of fetching it ashore, only for the white men to eat it. This reproof was, I fear, too justly founded; for of the few ducks we had been so fortunate as to procure, little had fallen to their share except the offals, and now and then a half-picked bone. True, indeed, all the crows and hawks which had been shot were given to them; but they plainly told us that the taste of ducks was more agreeable to their palates, and begged they might hereafter partake of them. We observed that they were thoroughly sick of the journey, and wished heartily for its conclusion: the exclamation of 'Where's Rose Hill, where?' was incessantly repeated, with many inquiries about when we should return to it.

Saturday, April 16th, 1791. It was this morning resolved to abandon our pursuit and to return home; at hearing of which our natives expressed great joy. We started early and reached Rose Hill about three o'clock, just as a boat was about to be sent down to Sydney. Colbee and Boladeree would not wait for us until the following morning, but insisted on going down immediately to communicate to Baneelon and the rest of their countrymen the novelties they had seen.

The country we passed through was, for the most part, very indifferent, according to our universal opinion. It is in general badly watered. For eight miles and a half on one line we did not find a drop of water.

RICHMOND HILL

Having eluded our last search, Mr Dawes and myself, accompanied by a sergeant of marines and a private soldier, determined on another attempt, to ascertain whether it lay on the Hawkesbury or Nepean. We set out on this expedition on the 24th of May 1791; and having reached the opposite side of the mouth of the creek which had in our last journey prevented our progress, we proceeded from there up to Richmond Hill by the river side; mounted it; slept at its foot; and on the following day penetrated some miles westward or inland of it until we were stopped by a mountainous country, which our scarcity of provisions, joined to the terror of a river at our back, whose sudden rising is almost beyond computation, hindered us from exploring. To the elevation which bounded our research we gave the name of Knight Hill, in honour of the trusty sergeant who had been the faithful indefatigable companion of all our travels.

This excursion completely settled the long contested point about the Hawkesbury and Nepean. We found them to be *one river*. Without knowing it, Mr Dawes and myself had passed Richmond Hill almost a year before (in August 1790), and from there walked on the bank of the river to the spot where my discovery of the Nepean happened, in June 1789. Our ignorance arose from having never before seen the hill, and from the erroneous position assigned to it by those who had been in the boats up the river.

Except the behaviour of some natives whom we met on the river, which it would be ingratitude to pass in silence, nothing particularly worthy of notice occurred on this expedition.

When we had reached within two miles of Richmond Hill, we heard a native call. We directly answered him and conversed across the river for some time. At length he launched his canoe and crossed to us without distrust or hesitation. We had never seen him before; but he appeared to know our friend Gombeeree, of whom he often spoke. He said his name was Deedòra. He presented us with two spears and a throwing-stick, and in return we gave him some bread and beef. Finding that our route lay up the river, he offered to accompany us and, getting into his canoe, paddled up abreast of us. When we arrived at Richmond Hill it became necessary to cross the river; but the question was, how this should be effected? Deedora immediately offered his canoe. We accepted of it and, Mr Dawes and the soldier putting their clothes into it, pushed it before them, and by alternately wading and swimming, soon passed. On the opposite shore sat several natives, to whom Deedora called, by which precaution the arrival of the strangers produced no alarm. On the contrary, they received them with every mark of benevolence. Deedora, in the meanwhile, sat talking with the sergeant and me. Soon after, another native, named Morùnga, brought back the canoe, and now came our turn to cross. The sergeant (from a foolish trick which had been played upon him when he was a boy) was excessively timorous of water, and could not swim. Morunga offered to conduct him, and they got into the canoe together; but, his fears returning, he jumped out and refused to proceed. I endeavoured to animate him, and Morunga ridiculed his apprehensions, making signs of the ease and dispatch with which he would land him; but he resolved to paddle over by himself which, by dint of good management and keeping his position very steadily, he performed. It was now become necessary to bring over the canoe a third time for my accommodation, which was instantly done, and I entered it with Deedora. But, like the sergeant, I was so disordered at seeing the water within a hair's breadth of the level of our skiff (which brought to my remembrance a former disaster I had experienced on this river) that I jumped out, about knee-deep, and determined to swim over, which I effected. My clothes, half our knapsacks, and three of our guns yet remained to be transported across. These I recommended to the care of our grim ferrymen, who instantaneously loaded their boat with them and delivered them on the opposite bank, without damage or diminution.

During this long trial of their patience and courtesy—in the latter part of which I was entirely in their power, from their having possession of our arms—they had manifested no ungenerous sign of taking advantage of the helplessness and dependence of our situation; no rude curiosity to pry into the packages with which they were entrusted; or no sordid desire to possess the contents of them; although among them were articles exposed to view, of which it afterwards appeared they knew the use, and longed for the benefit. Let the banks of the rivers, 'known to song', let him whose travels have lain among polished nations produce me a brighter example of disinterested urbanity than was shown by these denizens of a barbarous clime to a set of destitute wanderers on the side of the Hawkesbury.

On the top of Richmond Hill we shot a hawk, which fell in a tree. Deedora offered to climb for it and we lent him a hatchet, the effect of which delighted him so much that he begged for it. As it was required to chop wood for our evening fire, it could not be conveniently spared; but we promised him that if he would visit us on the following morning, it should be given to him. Not a murmur was heard; no suspicion of our insincerity; no mention of benefits conferred; no reproach of ingratitude. His good humour and cheerfulness were not clouded for a moment. Punctual to our appointment, he came to us at daylight next morning and the hatchet was given to him, the only token of gratitude and respect in our power to bestow. Neither of these men had lost his front tooth.

The last expedition which I ever undertook in the country I am describing was in July 1791, when Mr Dawes and myself went in search of a large river which was said to exist a few miles to the southward of Rose Hill. We went to the place described, and found this second Nile or Ganges to be nothing but a saltwater creek communicating with Botany Bay, on whose banks we passed a miserable night from want of a drop of water to quench our thirst, for as we believed that we were going to a river we thought it needless to march with full canteens.

On this expedition we carried with us a thermometer which (in unison with our feelings) showed so extraordinary a degree of cold for the latitude of the place that I think myself bound to transcribe it.

Monday, 18th July, 1791. The sun arose in unclouded splendour and presented to our sight a novel and picturesque view. The contiguous country, as white as if covered with snow, contrasted with the foliage of trees flourishing in the verdure of tropical luxuriancy.* Even the exhalation which steamed from the lake beneath contributed to heighten the beauty of the scene. Wind SSW. Thermometer at sunrise 25°. The following night was still colder. At sunset the thermometer stood at 45°; at a quarter before four in the morning, it was at 26°; at a quarter before six at 24°; at a quarter before seven at 23°; at seven o'clock, 22.7°; at sunrise, 23°; after which it continued gradually to mount, and between one and two o'clock, stood at 59.6° in the shade. Wind SSW. The horizon perfectly clear all day, not the smallest speck to be seen. Nothing but demonstration could have convinced me that so severe a degree of cold ever existed in this low latitude. Drops of water on a tin pot, not altogether out of the influence of the fire, were frozen into solid ice in less than twelve minutes. Part of a leg of kangaroo which we had roasted for supper was frozen quite hard, all the juices of it being converted into ice. On those ponds which were near the surface of the earth, the covering of ice was very

* All the trees of New South Wales, may, I apprehend, be termed evergreen. For after such weather as this journal records, I did not observe either that the leaves had dropped off, or that they had assumed that sickly autumnal tint which marks English trees in corresponding circumstances.

thick; but on those which were lower down it was found to be less so, in proportion to their depression; and wherever the water was twelve feet below the surface (which happened to be the case close to us) it was uncongealed. It remains to be observed that the cold of both these nights, at Rose Hill and Sydney, was judged to be greater than had ever before been felt.

15

Transactions of the colony to the end of November 1791

THE extreme dryness of the preceding summer has been noticed. It had operated so far in the beginning of June that we dreaded a want of water for common consumption, most of the little reservoirs in the neighbourhood of Sydney being dried up. The small stream near the town was so nearly exhausted (being only the drain of a morass) that a ship could not have watered at it, and the *Supply* was preparing to sink casks in a swamp when rain fell and banished our apprehensions.

June 1791. On the second instant, the name of the settlement at the head of the harbour (Rose Hill) was changed, by order of the governor, to that of Parramàtta, the native name of it. As Rose Hill has, however, occurred so often in this book, I beg leave, to avoid confusion, still to continue the appellation in all future mention of it.

Our travelling friend Boladeree, who makes so conspicuous a figure in the last chapter, about this time committed an offence which we were obliged to notice. He threw a spear at a convict in the woods, and wounded him. The truth was, some mischievous person belonging to us had wantonly destroyed his canoe, and he revenged the injury on the first of our people whom he met unarmed. He now seemed to think the matter adjusted; and probably such is the custom they observe in their own society in similar cases. Hearing, however, that an order was issued to seize him, or in case that could not be effected, to shoot him, he prudently dropped all connection with us and was for a long time not seen.

But, if they sometimes injured us, to compensate they were often of signal benefit to those who needed their assistance: two instances of which had recently occurred. A boat was overset in the harbour. Baneelon and some other natives, who saw the accident happen, immediately plunged in and saved all the people. When they had brought them on shore they undressed them, kindled a fire and dried their clothes, gave them fish to eat and conducted them to Sydney.

The other instance was of a soldier lost in the woods, when he met a party of natives. He at first knew not whether to flee from them or to implore their assistance. Seeing among them one whom he knew, he determined to communicate his distress to him and to rely on his generosity. The Indian told him that he had wandered a long way from home, but that he would conduct him thither, on the single condition of his delivering up a gun which he held in his hand, promising to carry it for him and to restore it to him at parting. The soldier felt little inclination to surrender his arms, by which he would be put entirely in their power. But seeing no alternative he at last consented; on which the whole party laid down their spears and faithfully escorted him to the nearest part of the settlement, where the gun was given up, and they took their leave without asking for any remuneration, or even seeming to expect it.

The distressful state of the colony for provisions continued gradually to augment until the 9th of July, when the *Mary Anne* transport arrived from England. This ship had sailed from the Downs so lately as the 25th of February, having been only four months and twelve days on her passage. She brought out convicts, by contract, at a specific sum for each person. But to demonstrate the effect of humanity and justice, of 144 female convicts embarked on board only three had died, and the rest were landed in perfect health, all loud in praise of their conductor. The master's name was Munro; and his ship, after fulfilling her engagement with government, was bound on the southern fishery. The reader must not conclude that I sacrifice to dull detail, when he finds such benevolent conduct minutely narrated. The advocates of humanity are not yet become too numerous: but those who practise its divine precepts, however humble and unnoticed be their station, ought not to sink into obscurity, unrecorded and unpraised, with the vile monsters who deride misery and fatten on calamity.

July 1791. If, however, the good people of this ship delighted us with their benevolence, here gratification ended. I was of a party who had rowed in a boat six miles out to sea, beyond the harbour's mouth, to meet them; and what was our disappointment, on getting aboard, to find that they had not brought a letter (a few official ones for the governor excepted) to any person in the colony! Nor had they a single newspaper or magazine in their possession; nor could they conceive that any person wished to hear news; being as ignorant of everything which had passed in Europe for the last two years as ourselves, at the distance of half the circle. 'No war—the fleet's dismantled,' was the whole that we could learn. When I asked whether a new parliament had been called they stared at me in stupid wonder, not seeming to comprehend that such a body either suffered renovation or needed it.

'Have the French settled their government?'

'As to that matter I can't say; I never heard; but, damn them, they were ready enough to join the Spaniards against us.'

'Are Russia and Turkey at peace?'

'That you see does not lie in my way; I have heard talk about it, but don't remember what passed.'

'For heaven's sake, why did you not bring out a bundle of newspapers? You might have procured a file at any coffee house, which would have amused you and instructed us.'

'Why, really, I never thought about the matter until we were off the Cape of Good Hope, when we spoke with a man of war, who asked us the same question, and then I wished I had.'

To have prosecuted inquiry farther would have only served to increase disappointment and chagrin. We therefore quitted the ship, wondering and lamenting that so large a portion of plain undisguised honesty should be so totally unconnected with a common share of intelligence, and acquaintance with the feelings and habits of other men.

By the governor's letters we learned that a large fleet of transports, with convicts on board, and His Majesty's ship *Gorgon* (Captain Parker), might soon be expected to arrive. The following intelligence which they contained was also made public.

> That such convicts as had served their period of transportation were not to be compelled to remain in the colony; but that no temptation should be offered to induce them to quit it, as there existed but too much reason to believe that they would return to former practices; that those who might choose to settle in the country should have portions of land, subject to stipulated restrictions, and a portion of provisions assigned to them on signifying their inclinations; and that it was expected that those convicts, who might be possessed of means to transport themselves from the country, would leave it free of all encumbrances of a public nature.

The rest of the fleet continued to drop in, in this and the two succeeding months. The state of the convicts whom they brought out, though infinitely preferable to what the fleet of last year had landed, was not unexceptionable. Three of the ships had naval agents on board to control them. Consequently, if complaint had existed there, it would have been immediately redressed. Exclusive of these, the *Salamander* (Captain Nichols), who, of 155 men lost only five; and the *William and Anne* (Captain Buncker), who of 187 men lost only seven, I find most worthy of honourable mention. In the list of convicts brought out was Barrington, of famous memory.†

Two of these ships also added to our geographic knowledge of the country. The *Atlantic*, under the direction of Lieutenant

† George Barrington was a celebrated pickpocket who became chief constable of Parramatta in 1796.

Bowen, a naval agent, ran into a harbour between Van Diemen's Land and Port Jackson, in latitude 35° 12′ south, longitude 151° east, to which, in honour of Sir John Jervis, Knight of the Bath, Mr Bowen gave the name of Port Jervis.† Here was found good anchoring ground with a fine depth of water, within a harbour about a mile and a quarter broad at its entrance, which afterwards opens into a basin five miles wide and of considerable length. They found no fresh water, but as their want of this article was not urgent, they did not make sufficient researches to pronounce that none existed there.* They saw, during the short time they stayed, two kangaroos and many traces of inhabitants. The country at a little distance to the southward of the harbour is hilly, but that contiguous to the sea is flat. On comparing what they had found here afterwards, with the native produce of Port Jackson, they saw no reason to think that they differed in any respect.

The second discovery was made by Captain Wetherhead, of the *Matilda* transport, which was obligingly described to me, as follows, by that gentleman, on my putting to him the underwritten questions.

'When did you make your discovery?'

'On the 27th of July 1791.'

'In what latitude and longitude does it lie?'

'In 42° 15′ south by observation, and in 148½ east by reckoning.'

'Is it on the mainland or is it an island?'

'It is an island, distant from the mainland about eight miles.'

'Did you anchor?'

'Yes, and found good anchorage in a bay open about six points.'

'Did you see any other harbour or bay in the island?'

'None.'

† Jervis Bay.

* Just before I left the country, word was brought by a ship which had put into Port Jervis that a large freshwater brook was found there.

'Does the channel between the island and the main appear to afford good shelter for shipping?'

'Yes, like Spithead.'

'Did you find any water on the island?'

'Yes, in plenty.'

'Of what size does the island appear to be?'

'It is narrow and long; I cannot say how long. Its breadth is inconsiderable.'

'Did you make any observations on the soil?'

'It is sandy; and many places are full of craggy rocks.'

'Do you judge the productions which you saw on the island to be similar to those around Port Jackson?'

'I do not think they differ in any respect.'

'Did you see any animals?'

'I saw three kangaroos.'

'Did you see any natives, or any marks of them?'

'I saw no natives, but I saw a fire, and several huts like those at Port Jackson, in one of which lay a spear.'

'What name did you give to your discovery?'

'I called it, in honour of my ship, Matilda Bay.'†

November 1791. A very extraordinary instance of folly stimulated to desperation occurred in the beginning of this month among the convicts at Rose Hill. Twenty men and a pregnant woman, part of those who had arrived in the last fleet, suddenly disappeared with their clothes, working tools, bedding, and their provisions for the ensuing week, which had just been issued to them. The first intelligence heard of them was from some convict settlers, who said they had seen them pass and had enquired whither they were bound. To which they had received for answer, 'to *China*'. The extravagance and infatuation of such an attempt was explained to them by the settlers; but neither derision nor demonstration could avert them from pursuing their purpose. It was observed by those who brought

† Probably Wine Glass Bay on the Freycinet Peninsula which Captain Wetherhead mistook for an island.

in the account that they had general idea enough of the point of the compass in which China lies from Port Jackson, to keep in a northerly direction.

An officer with a detachment of troops was sent in pursuit of them; but after a harassing march returned without success. In the course of a week the greatest part of them were either brought back by different parties who had fallen in with them, or were driven in by famine. Upon being questioned about the cause of their elopement, those whom hunger had forced back did not hesitate to confess that they had been so grossly deceived as to believe that China might easily be reached, being not more than 100 miles distant and separated only by a river. The others, however, ashamed of the merriment excited at their expense, said that their reason for running away was on account of being overworked and harshly treated, and that they preferred a solitary and precarious existence in the woods to a return to the misery they were compelled to undergo. One or two of the party had certainly perished by the hands of the natives, who had also wounded several others.

I trust that no man would feel more reluctant than myself to cast an illiberal national reflection, particularly on a people whom I regard in an aggregate sense as brethren and fellow-citizens; and among whom I have the honour to number many of the most cordial and endearing intimacies which a life passed on service could generate. But it is certain that all these people were *Irish*.

16

Transactions of the colony until the 18th of December 1791, when I quitted it, with an account of its state at that time

THE *Gorgon* had arrived on the 21st of September, and the hour of departure to England, for the marine battalion, drew nigh. If I be allowed to speak from my own feelings on the occasion, I will not say that we contemplated its approach with mingled sensations: we hailed it with rapture and exultation.

The *Supply*, ever the harbinger of welcome and glad tidings, proclaimed by her own departure that ours was at hand. On the 26th of November she sailed for England. It was impossible to view our separation with insensibility: the little ship which had so often agitated our hopes and fears, which from long acquaintance we had learned to regard as part of ourselves, whose doors of hospitality had been ever thrown open to relieve our accumulated wants, and chase our solitary gloom!

In consequence of the offers made to the non-commissioned officers and privates of the marine battalion to remain in the country as settlers or to enter into the New South Wales corps, three corporals, one drummer and 59 privates accepted of grants of land, to settle at Norfolk Island and Rose Hill. Of these men, several were undoubtedly possessed of sufficient skill and industry, by the assistance of the pay which was due to them (from the date of their embarkation, in the beginning of the year 1787, to the day on which they were discharged), to set out with reasonable hopes of being able to procure a maintenance. But the only apparent reason to which the behaviour of a majority of them could be ascribed was from infatuated affection to female convicts, whose characters and habits of life, I am sorry to say, promise from a connection neither honour nor tranquillity.

The narrative part of this work will, I conceive, be best brought to a termination by a description of the existing state of the colony, as taken by myself a few days previous to my embarkation in the *Gorgon*, to sail for England.

December 2nd, 1791. Went up to Rose Hill. Public buildings here have not greatly multiplied since my last survey. The storehouse and barrack have been long completed; also apartments for the chaplain of the regiment, and for the judge-advocate, in which last, criminal courts, when necessary, are held; but these are petty erections. In a colony which contains only a few hundred hovels built of twigs and mud, we feel consequential enough already to talk of a treasury, an admiralty, a public library and many other similar edifices, which are to form part of a magnificent square. The great road from near the landing place to the governor's house is finished, and a very noble one it is, being of great breadth, and a mile long, in a straight line. In many places it is carried over gullies of considerable depth, which have been filled up with trunks of trees covered with earth. All the sawyers, carpenters and blacksmiths will soon be concentred under the direction of a very adequate person of the governor's household. This plan is already so far advanced as to contain nine covered sawpits which change of weather cannot disturb the operations of, an excellent workshed for the carpenters and a large new shop for the blacksmiths. It certainly promises to be of great public benefit. A new hospital has been talked of for the last two years, but is not yet begun. Two long sheds, built in the form of a tent and thatched, are however finished, and capable of holding 200 patients. The sick list of today contains 382 names. Rose Hill is less healthy than it used to be. The prevailing disorder is a dysentery, which often terminates fatally. There was lately one very violent putrid fever which, by timely removal of the patient, was prevented from spreading. Twenty-five men and two children died here in the month of November.

When at the hospital I saw and conversed with some of the *Chinese travellers*; four of them lay here, wounded by the natives. I asked these men if they really supposed it possible to reach China. They answered that they were certainly made to believe (they knew not how) that at a considerable distance to the northward existed a large river, which separated this country from the back part of China; and that when it should be crossed (which was practicable) they would find themselves among a copper-coloured people, who would receive and treat them kindly. They added that on the third day of their elopement, one of the party died of fatigue; another they saw butchered by the natives who, finding them unarmed, attacked them and put them to flight. This happened near Broken Bay, which harbour stopped their progress to the northward and forced them to turn to the right hand, by which means they soon after found themselves on the sea shore, where they wandered about in a destitute condition, picking up shellfish to allay hunger. Deeming the farther prosecution of their scheme impracticable, several of them agreed to return to Rose Hill, which with difficulty they accomplished, arriving almost famished. On their road back they met six fresh adventurers sallying forth to join them, to whom they related what had passed and persuaded them to relinquish their intention. There are at this time not less than thirty-eight convict men missing, who live in the woods by day, and at night enter the different farms and plunder for subsistence.

December 3rd, 1791. Began my survey of the cultivated land belonging to the public. The harvest has commenced. They are reaping both wheat and barley. The field between the barrack and the governor's house contains wheat and maize, both very bad, but the former particularly so. In passing through the main street I was pleased to observe the gardens of the convicts look better than I had expected to find them. The vegetables in general are but mean, but the stalks of maize, with which they are interspersed, appear green and flourishing. The semi-circular hill which sweeps from the overseer of the cattle's house to the governor's house, is planted with maize, which, I am told, is the best here. It certainly looks in most parts very good—stout thick stalks with large spreading leaves—but I am surprised to find it so backward. It is at least a month later than that in the gardens at Sydney. Behind the maize is a field of wheat, which looks tolerably for this part of the world. It will, I reckon, yield about twelve bushels an acre. Continued my walk and looked at a little patch of wheat in the governor's garden, which was sown in drills, the ground being first mixed with a clay which its discoverers pretended was marle. Whatever it be, this experiment bespeaks not much in favour of its enriching qualities; for the corn looks miserably, and is far exceeded by some neighbouring spots on which no such advantage has been bestowed. Went round the crescent at the bottom of the garden, which certainly in beauty of form and situation is unrivalled in New South Wales. Here are eight thousand vines planted, all of which in another season are expected to bear grapes. Besides the vines are several small fruit trees, which were brought in the *Gorgon* from the Cape, and look lively; on one of them are half a dozen apples as big as nutmegs. Although the soil of the crescent be poor, its aspect and circular figure, so advantageous for receiving and retaining the rays of the sun, eminently fit it for a vineyard. Passed the rivulet and looked at the corn land on its northern side. On the western side of Clarke's* house the wheat and maize are bad, but on the eastern side is a field supposed to be the best in the colony. I thought it of good height, and the ears well filled, but it is far from thick.

While I was looking at it, Clarke came up. I told him I thought he would reap fifteen or sixteen bushels an acre; he seemed to think seventeen or eighteen. I have now inspected all the European corn. A man of so little experience of these matters as myself cannot speak with much confidence. Perhaps the produce may average ten bushels an acre, or twelve at the outside. Allowance should, however, be made in estimating the quality of the soil, for the space occupied by roots of trees, for inadequate culture, and in some measure to want of rain. Less has fallen than was wished, but this spring was by no means so dry as the last. I find that the wheat grown at Rose Hill last year weighed fifty-seven pounds and a half per bushel. My next visit was to the cattle, which consists of two stallions, six mares, and two colts; besides sixteen cows, two cow-calves, and one bull-calf, which were brought out by the *Gorgon*. Two bulls

* Dod, who is mentioned in my former journal of this place, had died some months ago. And Mr Clarke, who was put in his room, is one of the superintendents sent out by government, on a salary of forty pounds per annum. He was bred to husbandry, under his father at Lewes in Sussex; and is, I conceive, competent to his office of principal conductor of the agriculture of Rose Hill.

which were on board died on the passage, so that on the young gentleman just mentioned depends the stocking of the colony.

The period of the inhabitants of New South Wales being supplied with animal food of their own raising is too remote for a prudent man to calculate. The cattle look in good condition, and I was surprised to hear that neither corn nor fodder is given to them. The enclosures in which they are confined furnish hardly a blade of grass at present. There are people appointed to tend them who have been used to this way of life, and who seem to execute it very well.

Sunday, December 4th, 1791. Divine service is now performed here every Sunday, either by the chaplain of the settlement or the chaplain of the regiment. I went to church today. Several hundred convicts were present, the majority of whom I thought looked the most miserable beings in the shape of humanity I ever beheld. They appeared to be worn down with fatigue.

December 5th. Made excursions this day to view the public settlements. Reached the first, which is about a mile in a northwest direction from the governor's house. This settlement contains, by admeasurement, 134 acres, a part of which is planted with maize, very backward, but in general tolerably good, and beautifully green. Thirteen large huts, built in the form of a tent, are erected for the convicts who work here; but I could not learn the number of these last, being unable to find a superintendent or any person who could give me information. Ponds of water here are sufficient to supply a thousand persons.

Walked on to the second settlement, about two miles farther, through an uncleared country. Here met Daveney, the person who planned and now superintends all the operations carried on here. He told me that he estimated the quantity of cleared ground here at 300 acres. He certainly over-rates it one-third, by the judgment of every other person. Six weeks ago this was a forest. It has been cleared, and the wood nearly burnt off the ground, by 500 men, in the before-mentioned period, or rather in thirty days, for only that number have the convicts worked. He said it was too late to plant maize, and therefore he should sow turnips, which would help to meliorate and prepare it for next year. On examining the soil, I thought it in general light, though in some places loamy to the touch. He means to try the Rose Hill *marle* upon it, with which he thinks it will incorporate well. I hope it will succeed better than the experiment in the governor's garden. I wished to know whether he had chosen this ground simply from the conveniency of its situation to Rose Hill, and its easy form for tillage, and having water, or from any marks which he had thought indicated good soil. He said that what I had mentioned no doubt weighed with him, and that he judged the soil to be good, from the limbs of many of the trees growing on it being *covered with mo*ss.

'Are,' said I, 'your 500 men still complete?'

'No; this day's muster gave only 460. The rest are either sick and removed to the hospital, or are run away in the woods.'

'How much is each labourer's daily task?'

'Seven rods. It was eight, but on their representing to the governor that it was beyond their strength to execute, he took off one.'

Thirteen large huts, similar to those beforementioned, contain all the people here. To every hut are appointed two men as hutkeepers, whose only employment is to watch the huts in working hours to prevent them from being robbed. This has somewhat checked depredations, and those endless complaints of the convicts that they could not work because they had nothing to eat, their allowance being stolen. The working hours at this season (summer) are from five o'clock in the morning until ten; rest from ten to two; return to work at two; and continue till sunset. This surely cannot be called very severe toil; but on the other hand must be remembered the inadequacy of a ration of salt provisions, with few vegetables, and unassisted by any liquor but water.

Here finished my remarks on everything of a public nature

at Rose Hill. But having sufficient time, I determined to visit all the private settlers to inspect their labours, and learn from them their schemes, their hopes and expectations.

In pursuance of my resolution, I crossed the country to Prospect Hill, at the bottom of which live the following thirteen convicts, who have accepted allotments of ground, and are become settlers.

Men's names	Trades	Number of acres in each allotment	Number of acres in cultivation
John Silverthorne	Weaver	40	1¾
Thomas Martin	"	40	1½
John Nichols	Gardener	40	2
William Butler, and his wife	Seaman	50 }	4*
———Lisk	Watchmaker	40 }	
William Parish, wife, and a child	Seaman	60	2¾
William Kilby, and his wife	Husbandman	60	1¼
Edward Pugh, wife and two children	Carpenter	70	2½
Samuel Griffith	Butcher	40	1½
John Herbert **			
James Castle	Husbandman	40	2
Joseph Marlow***			
John Williams, and his wife	Carpenter	50	1

* In partnership
** Not out of his time; but allowed to work here at his leisure hours, as he has declared his intention of settling.
*** In a similar predicament with Herbert.

The terms on which these allotments have been granted are: that the estates shall be fully ceded forever to all who shall continue to cultivate for five years, or more; that they shall be free of all taxes for the first ten years; but after that period to pay an annual quit-rent of one shilling. The penalty on non-performance of any of these articles is forfeiture of the estate, and all the labour which may have been bestowed upon it.

These people are to receive provisions (the same quantity as the working convicts), clothes, and medicinal assistance, for eighteen months from the day on which they settled.

To clear and cultivate the land, a hatchet, a tomahawk, two hoes, a spade and a shovel are given to each person, whether man or woman; and a certain number of cross-cut saws among the whole. To stock their farms, two sow pigs were promised to each settler, but they almost all say they have not yet received any, of which they complain loudly. They all received grain to sow and plant for the first year. They settled here in July and August last. Most of them were obliged to build their own houses; and wretched hovels three-fourths of them are. Should any of them fall sick, the rest are bound to assist the sick person two days in a month, provided the sickness lasts not longer than two months; four days labour in each year, from every person, being all that he is entitled to. To give protection to this settlement, a corporal and two soldiers are encamped in the centre of the farms, as the natives once attacked the settlers and burnt one of their houses. These guards are, however, inevitably at such a distance from some of the farms as to be unable to afford them any assistance in case of another attack.

With all these people I conversed and inspected their labours. Some I found tranquil and determined to persevere, provided encouragement should be given. Others were in a state of despondency, and predicted that they should starve unless the period of eighteen months, during which they are to be clothed and fed, should be extended to three years. Their cultivation is yet in its infancy, and therefore opinions should not be hastily formed of what it may arrive at, with moderate skill and industry. They have at present little in the ground besides maize, and that looks not very promising. Some small patches of wheat which I saw are miserable indeed. The greatest part of the land I think but indifferent, being light and stony. Of the thirteen farms ten are unprovided with water; and at some of them they are obliged to fetch this necessary article from the distance of a mile and a half. All the settlers complain sadly of being frequently robbed by the runaway convicts, who plunder them incessantly.

December 6th. Visited the settlements to the northward of the rivulet. The nearest of them lies about a mile due north of Mr Clarke's house. Here are only the undernamed five settlers.

Men's names	Trades	Number of acres in each allotment	Number of acres in cultivation
Thomas Brown, wife, and child	—	60	
William Bradbury	—	30	3½*
William Mold	—	30	
Simon Burne, and wife	Hosier	50	3
———Parr, and wife	Merchant's clerk	50	3½

* These three cultivate in partnership.

These settlers are placed on the same footing in every respect which concerns their tenure and the assistance to be granted to them as those at Prospect Hill. Near them is water. Parr and Burne are men of great industry. They have both good houses which they hired people to build for them. Parr told me that he had expended thirteen guineas on his land, which nevertheless he does not seem pleased with. Of the three poor fellows who work in partnership, one (Bradbury) is run away. This man had been allowed to settle, on a belief, from his own assurance, that his term of transportation was expired; but it was afterwards discovered that he had been cast for life. Hereupon he grew desperate, and declared he would rather perish at once than remain as a convict. He disappeared a week ago and has never since been heard of. Were I compelled to settle in New South Wales, I should fix my residence here, both from the appearance of the soil, and its proximity to Rose Hill. A corporal and two privates are encamped here to guard this settlement, as at Prospect.

Proceeded to the settlement called the *Ponds*, a name which I suppose it derived from several ponds of water which are near the farms. Here reside the fourteen following settlers.

Men's names	Trades	Number of acres in each allotment	Number of acres in cultivation
Thomas Kelly	Servant	30	1½
William Hubbard, and wife	Plasterer	50	2¼
Curtis Brand, and wife	Carpenter	50	3
John Ramsay, and wife	Seaman	50	3½
William Field	—	30	2½
John Richards	Stone-cutter	30	4½*
John Summers	Husbandman	30	
——Varnell	—	30	1
Anthony Rope, and wife, and two children	Bricklayer	70	1**
Joseph Bishop, and wife	None	50	1½
Mathew Everingham, and wife	Attorney's clerk	50	2
John Anderson, and wife	—	50	2
Edward Elliot	Husbandman	30	2***
Joseph Marshall	Weaver	30	

* They cultivate in partnership.

** A convict who means to settle here, and is permitted to work in his leisure hours.

*** They cultivate in partnership.

The Prospect Hill terms of settlement extend to this place. My private remarks were not many. Some spots which I passed over I thought desirable, particularly Ramsay's farm; and he deserves a good spot, for he is a civil, sober, industrious man. Besides his corn land, he has a well laid-out little garden, in which I found him and his wife busily at work. He praised her industry to me; and said he did not doubt of succeeding. It is not often seen that sailors make good farmers; but this man I think bids fair to contradict the observation. The gentleman of no trade (his own words to me) will, I apprehend, at the conclusion of the time when victualling from the store is to cease, have the honour of returning to drag a timber or brick cart for his maintenance. The little maize he has planted is done in so slovenly a style as to promise a very poor crop. He who looks forward to eat grapes from his own vine, and to sit under the shade of his own fig-tree, must labour in every country. Here he must exert more than ordinary activity. The attorney's clerk I also thought out of his province. I dare believe that he finds cultivating his own land not half so easy a task as he formerly found that of stringing together volumes of tautology to encumber, or convey away, that of his neighbour. Hubbard's farm, and Kelly's also, deserve regard, from being better managed than most of the others. The people here complain sadly of a destructive grub which destroys the young plants of maize. Many of the settlers have been obliged to plant twice, nay thrice, on the same land, from the depredations of these reptiles. There is the same guard here as at the other settlements.

Nothing now remains for inspection but the farms on the river side.

December 7th. Went to Scheffer's farm. I found him at home, conversed with him, and walked with him over all his cultivated ground. He had 140 acres granted to him, fourteen of which are in cultivation, twelve in maize, one in wheat and one in vines and tobacco. He has besides twenty-three acres on which the trees are cut down but not burnt off the land. He resigned his appointment and began his farm last May, and had at first five convicts to assist him; he has now four. All his maize, except three acres, is mean. This he thinks may be attributed to three causes: a middling soil; too dry a spring; and from the ground not being sufficiently pulverised before the seed was put into it. The wheat is thin and poor: he does not reckon its produce at more than eight or nine bushels. His vines, 900 in number, are flourishing, and will, he supposes, bear fruit next year. His tobacco plants are not very luxuriant: to these two last articles he means principally to direct his exertions. He says (and truly) that they will always be saleable and profitable. On one of the boundaries of his land is plenty of water. A very good brick house is nearly completed for his use, by the governor; and in the meantime he lives in a very decent one, which was built for him on his settling here. He is to be supplied with provisions from the public store, and with medical assistance for eighteen months, reckoning from last May. At the expiration of this period he is bound to support himself and the four convicts are to be withdrawn. But if he shall then, or at any future period, declare himself able to maintain a moderate number of these people for their labour, they will be assigned to him.

Mr Scheffer is a man of industry and respectable character. He came out to this country as a superintendent of convicts, at a salary of forty pounds per annum, and brought with him a daughter of twelve years old. He is by birth a Hessian, and served in America, in a corps of Yaghers, with the rank of lieutenant. He never was professionally, in any part of life, a farmer, but he told me that his father owned a small estate on the banks of the Rhine, on which he resided, and that he had always been fond of looking at and assisting in his labours, particularly in the vineyard. In walking along, he more than once shook his head and made some mortifying observations on the soil of his present domain, compared with the banks of his native stream. He assured me that (exclusive of the sacrifice of his salary) he has expended more than forty pounds in advancing his ground to the state in which I saw it. Of the probability of success in his undertaking, he spoke with moderation and good sense. Sometimes he said he had almost despaired, and had often balanced about relinquishing it; but had as often been checked by recollecting that hardly any difficulty can arise which vigour and perseverance will not overcome. I asked him what was the tenure on which he held his estate. He offered to show the written document, saying that it was exactly the same as Ruse's. I therefore declined to trouble him, and took my leave with wishes for his success and prosperity.

Near Mr Scheffer's farm is a small patch of land cleared by Lieutenant Townson of the New South Wales corps, about two acres of which are in maize and wheat, both looking very bad.

Proceeded to the farm of Mr Arndell, one of the assistant surgeons. This gentleman has six acres in cultivation as follows: rather more than four in maize, one in wheat, and the remainder in oats and barley. The wheat looks tolerably good, rather thin, but of a good height, and the ears well filled. His farming servant guesses the produce will be twelve bushels,* and I do not think he over-rates it. The maize he guesses at thirty bushels, which from appearances it may yield, but not more. The oats and barley are not contemptible. This ground has been turned up but once. The aspect of it is nearly south, on a declivity of the river, or arm of the sea, on which Rose Hill stands. It was cleared of wood about nine months ago, and sown this year for the first time.

December 8th. Went this morning to the farm of Christopher Magee, a convict settler, nearly opposite to that of Mr Scheffer. The situation of this farm is very eligible, provided the river in floods does not inundate it, which I think doubtful. This man was bred to husbandry, and lived eight years in America; he has no less than eight acres in cultivation, five and a half in maize, one in wheat, and one and a half in tobacco. From the wheat he does not expect more than ten bushels, but he is extravagant enough to rate the produce of maize at 100 bushels (perhaps he may get fifty); on tobacco he means to go largely hereafter. He began to clear this ground in April, but did not settle until last July. I asked by what means

* I have received a letter from Port Jackson dated in April 1792, which states that the crop of wheat turned out fifteen bushels, and the maize rather more than forty bushels.

he had been able to accomplish so much. He answered, 'By industry, and by hiring all the convicts I could get to work in their leisure hours, besides some little assistance which the governor has occasionally thrown in.' His greatest impediment is want of water, being obliged to fetch all he uses more than half a mile. He sunk a well, and found water, but it was brackish and not fit to drink. If this man shall continue in habits of industry and sobriety, I think him sure of succeeding.

Reached Ruse's farm,* and begged to look at his grant, the material part of which runs thus: 'A lot of thirty acres, to be called Experiment Farm; the said lot to be holden, free of all taxes, quit-rents, &c. for ten years, provided that the occupier, his heirs or assigns, shall reside within the same, and proceed to the improvement thereof; reserving, however, for the use of the crown, all timber now growing, or which thereafter shall grow, fit for naval purposes. At the expiration of ten years, an annual quit-rent of one shilling shall be paid by the occupier in acknowledgment.'

Ruse now lives in a comfortable brick house, built for him by the governor. He has eleven acres and a half in cultivation, and several more which have been cleared by convicts in their leisure hours, on condition of receiving the first year's crop. He means to cultivate little besides maize; wheat is so much less productive. Of the culture of vineyards and tobacco he is ignorant; and, with great good sense, he declared that he would not quit the patch he knew, for an uncertainty. His livestock consists of four breeding sows and thirty fowls. He has been taking from the store (that is, has supplied himself with provisions) for some months past; and his wife is to be taken off at Christmas, at which time, if he deems himself able to maintain a convict labourer, one is to be given to him.

Crossed the river in a boat to Robert Webb's farm. This man was one of the seamen of the *Sirius*, and has taken, in

* See the state of this farm in my former Rose Hill journal of November 1790, thirteen months before.

conjunction with his brother (also a seaman of the same ship) a grant of sixty acres, on the same terms as Ruse, save that the annual quit-rent is to commence at the expiration of five years, instead of ten. The brother is gone to England to receive the wages due to them both for their services, which money is to be expended by him in whatever he judges will be most conducive to the success of their plan. Webb expects to do well; talks as a man should talk who has just set out on a doubtful enterprise which he is bound to pursue. He is sanguine in hope, and looks only at the bright side of the prospect. He has received great encouragement and assistance from the governor. He has five acres cleared and planted with maize, which looks thriving, and promises to yield a decent crop. His house and a small one adjoining for pigs and poultry were built for him by the governor, who also gave him two sows and seven fowls, to which he adds a little stock of his own acquiring.

Near Webb is placed William Read, another seaman of the *Sirius*, on the same terms, and to whom equal encouragement has been granted.

My survey of Rose Hill is now closed. I have inspected every piece of ground in cultivation here, both public and private, and have written from actual examination only.

But before I bade adieu to Rose Hill, in all probability for the last time of my life, it struck me that there yet remained one object of consideration not to be slighted: Barrington had been in the settlement between two and three months, and I had not seen him.

I saw him with curiosity. He is tall, approaching to six feet, slender, and his gait and manner bespeak liveliness and activity. Of that elegance and fashion with which my imagination had decked him (I know not why), I could distinguish no trace. Great allowance should, however, be made for depression and unavoidable deficiency of dress. His face is thoughtful and intelligent; to a strong cast of countenance he adds a penetrating eye, and a prominent forehead. His whole demeanour is humble, not servile. Both on his passage from England, and since his arrival here, his conduct has been irreproachable. He is appointed high-constable of the settlement of Rose Hill, a post of some respectability, and certainly one of importance to those who live here. His knowledge of men, particularly of that part of them into whose morals, manners and behaviour he is ordered especially to inspect, eminent fit him for the office.

I cannot quit him without bearing my testimony that his talents promise to be directed in future to make reparation to society for the offences he has heretofore committed against it.

The number of persons of all descriptions at Rose Hill at this period will be seen in the following return.

A return of the number of persons at Rose Hill,
3rd of December 1791.

Quality	Men	Women	Children		
			of 10 years	of 2 years	under 2 years
Convicts*	1336	133	—	9	17
Troops	94	9	1	5	2
Civil Department	7	—	—	—	—
Seamen Settlers	3	—	—	—	—
Free Persons	—	7	2	1	2
Total number of persons 1628	1440	149	3	15	21

Of my Sydney journal, I find no part sufficiently interesting to be worth extraction. This place had long been considered only as a depot for stores. It exhibited nothing but a few old scattered huts and some sterile gardens. Cultivation of the ground was abandoned, and all our strength transferred to Rose Hill. Sydney, nevertheless, continued to be the place of the governor's residence, and consequently the headquarters of

* The convicts who are become settlers are included in this number.

the colony. No public building of note, except a storehouse, had been erected since my last statement. The barracks, so long talked of, so long promised, for the accommodation and discipline of the troops, were not even begun when I left the country; and instead of a new hospital, the old one was patched up and, with the assistance of one brought ready-framed from England, served to contain the sick.

The employment of the male convicts here, as at Rose Hill, was the public labour. Of the women, the majority were compelled to make shirts, trousers and other necessary parts of dress for the men, from materials delivered to them from the stores, into which they returned every Saturday night the produce of their labour, a stipulated weekly task being assigned to them. In a more early stage, government sent out all articles of clothing ready made; but, by adopting the present judicious plan, not only a public saving is effected, but employment of a suitable nature created for those who would otherwise consume leisure in idle pursuits only.

On the 26th of November 1791, the number of persons, of all descriptions, at Sydney, was 1259, to which, if 1628 at Rose Hill and 1172 at Norfolk Island be added, the total number of persons in New South Wales and its dependency will be found to amount to 4059.*

On the 13th of December 1791, the marine battalion embarked on board His Majesty's ship *Gorgon*, and on the 18th sailed for England.

* A very considerable addition to this number has been made since I quitted the settlement, by fresh troops and convicts sent thither from England.

17

Miscellaneous remarks on the country. On its vegetable productions. On its climate. On its animal productions. On its natives, etc.

THE journals contained in the body of this publication, illustrated by the map which accompanies it, are, I conceive, so descriptive of every part of the country known to us that little remains to be added beyond a few general observations.

The first impression made on a stranger is certainly favourable. He sees gently swelling hills connected by vales which possess every beauty that verdure of trees, and form, simply considered in itself, can produce; but he looks in vain for those murmuring rills and refreshing springs which fructify and embellish more happy lands. Nothing like those tributary streams which feed rivers in other countries are here seen; for when I speak of the stream at Sydney, I mean only the drain of a morass; and the river at Rose Hill is a creek of the harbour, which above high water mark would not in England be called even a brook. Whence the Hawkesbury, the only freshwater river known to exist in the country, derives its supplies, would puzzle a transient observer. He sees nothing but torpid unmeaning ponds (often stagnant and always still, unless agitated by heavy rains) which communicate with it. Doubtless the springs which arise in Caermarthen mountains† may be said to constitute its source. To cultivate its banks within many miles of the bed of the stream (except on some elevated detached spots) will be found impracticable, unless some method be devised of erecting a mound, sufficient to repel the encroachments of a torrent which sometimes rises fifty feet above its ordinary level, inundating the surrounding country in every direction.

The country between the Hawkesbury and Rose Hill is that which I have hitherto spoken of. When the river is crossed, this prospect soon gives place to a very different one. The green

† Blue Mountains.

vales and moderate hills disappear at the distance of about three miles from the river side, and from Knight Hill†, and Mount Twiss,* the limits which terminate our researches, nothing but precipices, wilds and deserts are to be seen. Even these steeps fail to produce streams. The difficulty of penetrating this country, joined to the dread of a sudden rise of the Hawkesbury, forbidding all return, has hitherto prevented our reaching Caermarthen mountains.

Let the reader now cast his eye on the relative situation of Port Jackson. He will see it cut off from communication with the northward by Broken Bay, and with the southward by Botany Bay; and what is worse, the whole space of intervening country yet explored (except a narrow strip called the Kangaroo Ground) in both directions, is so bad as to preclude cultivation.

The course of the Hawkesbury will next attract his attention. To the southward of every part of Botany Bay we have traced this river; but how much farther in that line it extends we know not. Hence its channel takes a northerly direction and finishes its course in Broken Bay, running at the back of Port Jackson in such a manner as to form the latter into a peninsula.

The principal question then remaining is, what is the distance between the head of Botany Bay and the part of the Hawkesbury nearest to it? And is the intermediate country a good one, or does it lead to one which appearances indicate to be good? To future adventurers who shall meet with more encouragement to persevere and discover than I and my fellow wanderer[s] did, I resign the answer. In the meantime the reader is desired to look at the remarks on the map, which were made in the beginning of August 1790, from Pyramid Hill, which bounded our progress on the southern expedition; when, and when only, this part of the country has been seen.

It then follows that from Rose Hill to within such a distance

† Kurrajong Heights.

* Look at the Map.

of the Hawkesbury as is protected from its inundations, is the only tract of land we yet know of in which cultivation can be carried on for many years to come. To aim at forming a computation of the distance of time, of the labour and of the expense, which would attend forming distinct convict settlements, beyond the bounds I have delineated; or of the difficulty which would attend a system of communication between such establishments and Port Jackson, is not intended here.

Until that period shall arrive, the progress of cultivation, when it shall have once passed Prospect Hill, will probably steal along to the southward, in preference to the northward, from the superior nature of the country in that direction, as the remarks inserted in the map will testify.†

Such is my statement of a plan which I deem inevitably entailed on the settlement at Port Jackson. In sketching this outline of it let it not be objected that I suppose the reader as well acquainted with the respective names and boundaries of the country as long residence and unwearying journeying among them have made the author. To have subjoined perpetual explanations would have been tedious and disgusting. Familiarity with the relative positions of a country can neither be imparted, or acquired, but by constant recurrence to geographic delineations.

On the policy of settling, with convicts only, a country at once so remote and extensive, I shall offer no remarks. Whenever I have heard this question agitated since my return to England, the cry of, 'What can we do with them! Where else can they be sent!' has always silenced me.

Of the soil, opinions have not differed widely. A spot eminently fruitful has never been discovered. That there are many spots cursed with everlasting and unconquerable sterility, no one who has seen the country will deny. At the same time I am decidedly of opinion that many large tracts of land between Rose Hill and the Hawkesbury, even now, are of a

† Tench was proven right in his summations.

nature sufficiently favourable to produce moderate crops of whatever may be sown in them. And provided a sufficient number of cattle* be imported to afford manure for dressing the ground, no doubt can exist that subsistence for a limited number of inhabitants may be drawn from it. To imperfect husbandry, and dry seasons, must indubitably be attributed part of the deficiency of former years. Hitherto all our endeavours to derive advantage from mixing the different soils have proved fruitless, though possibly only from want of skill on our side.

The spontaneous productions of the soil will be soon recounted. Every part of the country is a forest: of the quality of the wood take the following instance. The *Supply* wanted wood for a mast, and more than forty of the choicest young trees were cut down before as much wood as would make it could be procured, the trees being either rotten at the heart or riven by the gum which abounds in them. This gum runs not always in a longitudinal direction in the body of the tree, but is found in it in circles, like a scroll. There is however, a species of light wood which is found excellent for boat building, but it is scarce and hardly ever found of large size.

To find limestone many of our researches were directed. But after repeated assays with fire and chemical preparations on all the different sorts of stone to be picked up, it is still a *desideratum*. Nor did my experiments with a magnet induce me to think that any of the stones I tried contained iron. I have, however, heard other people report very differently on this head.

The list of esculent vegetables and wild fruits is too

* In my former narrative I have particularly noticed the sudden disappearance of the cattle which we had brought with us into the country. Not a trace of them has ever since been observed. Their fate is a riddle, so difficult of solution that I shall not attempt it. Surely had they strayed inland, in some of our numerous excursions, marks of them must have been found. It is equally impossible to believe that either the convicts or natives killed and ate them, without some sign of detection ensuing.

contemptible to deserve notice, if the *sweet tea*† whose virtues have been already recorded, and the common orchis root be excepted. That species of palm tree which produces the mountain cabbage is also found in most of the freshwater swamps, within six or seven miles of the coast.†† But it is rarely seen farther inland. Even the banks of the Hawkesbury are unprovided with it. The inner part of the trunk of this tree was greedily eaten by our hogs, and formed their principal support. The grass, as has been remarked in former publications, does not overspread the land in a continued sward, but arises in small detached tufts, growing every way about three inches apart, the intermediate space being bare; though the heads of the grass are often so luxuriant as to hide all deficiency on the surface. The rare and beautiful flowering shrubs, which abound in every part, deserve the highest admiration and panegyric.†††

Of the vegetable productions transplanted from other climes, maize flourishes beyond any other grain. And as it affords a strong and nutritive article of food, its propagation will, I think, altogether supersede that of wheat and barley.

Horticulture has been attended in some places with tolerable success. At Rose Hill I have seen gardens which, without the assistance of manure, have continued for a short time to produce well grown vegetables. But at Sydney, without constantly dressing the ground, it was in vain to expect them; and with it a supply of common vegetables might be procured by diligence in all seasons. Vines of every sort seem to flourish. Melons, cucumbers and pumpkins run with unbounded luxuriancy, and I am convinced that the grapes of New South Wales will, in a few years, equal those of any other country. 'That their juice will probably hereafter furnish an indispensable article of luxury at European tables', has already been predicted in the vehemence of speculation. Other fruits are yet in their

† Native sarsparilla, *Smilax slyciphylla*.

†† Cabbage tree palm, *Livistona australis*.

††† An apt description of the Sydney heath flora.

infancy; but oranges, lemons and figs (of which last indeed I have eaten very good ones) will, I dare believe, in a few years become plentiful. Apples and the fruits of colder climes also promise to gratify expectation. The banana-tree has been introduced from Norfolk Island, where it grows spontaneously.

Nor will this surprise, if the genial influence of the climate be considered. Placed in a latitude where the beams of the sun in the dreariest season are sufficiently powerful for many hours of the day to dispense warmth and nutrition, the progress of vegetation never is at a stand. The different temperatures of Rose Hill and Sydney, in winter, though only twelve miles apart, afford, however, curious matter of speculation. Of a well attested instance of ice being seen at the latter place, I never heard. At the former place its production is common, and once a few flakes of snow fell. The difference can be accounted for only by supposing that the woods stop the warm vapours of the sea from reaching Rose Hill, which is at the distance of sixteen miles inland; whereas Sydney is but four.* Again, the heats of summer are more violent at the former place than at the latter, and the variations incomparably quicker. The thermometer has been known to alter at Rose Hill, in the course of nine hours, more than 50°; standing a little before sunrise at 50°, and between one and two at more than 100°. To convey an idea of the climate in summer, I shall transcribe from my meteorological journal, accounts of two particular days which were the hottest we ever suffered under at Sydney.

December 27th 1790. Wind NNW; it felt like the blast of a heated oven, and in proportion as it increased the heat was found to be more intense, the sky hazy, the sun gleaming through at intervals.

* Look at the journal which describes the expedition in search of the river, said to exist to the southward of Rose Hill. At the time we felt that extraordinary degree of cold, we were not more than six miles south-west of Rose Hill, and about nineteen miles from the sea coast. When I mentioned this circumstance to Colonel Gordon, at the Cape of Good Hope,

At 9 a.m.	85°	By a large thermometer made by Ramsden, and graduated on Fahrenheit's scale.
At noon	104°	
Half past twelve	107½°	
From 1 p.m. until 20 minutes past two	108½°	
At 20 minutes past two	109°	
At sunset	89°	
At 11 p.m.	78½°	

December 28th		
At 8 a.m.	86°	At a quarter past one, it stood at only 89°, having, from a sudden shift of wind, fallen 13° in 15 minutes
10 a.m.	93°	
11 a.m.	101°	
At noon	103½°	
Half an hour past noon	104½°	
At 1 p.m.	102°	At 5p.m. 73°
		At sunset 69½°

My observations on this extreme heat, succeeded by so rapid a change, were that of all animals, man seemed to bear it best. Our dogs, pigs and fowls lay panting in the shade, or were rushing into the water. I remarked that a hen belonging to me, which had sat for a fortnight, frequently quitted her eggs and showed great uneasiness, but never remained from them many minutes at one absence; taught by instinct that the wonderful power in the animal body of generating cold in air heated beyond a certain degree, was best calculated for the production of her young. The gardens suffered considerably. All the plants which had not taken deep root were withered by the power of the sun. No lasting ill effects, however, arose to the human constitution. A temporary sickness at the stomach,

he wondered at it; and owned that, in his excursions into the interior parts of Africa, he had never experienced anything to match it: he attributed its production to large beds of nitre, which he said must exist in the neighbourhood.

accompanied with lassitude and headache, attacked many, but they were removed generally in twenty-four hours by an emetic, followed by an anodyne. During the time it lasted, we invariably found that the house was cooler than the open air, and that in proportion as the wind was excluded, was comfort augmented.

But even this heat was judged to be far exceeded in the latter end of the following February, when the north-west wind again set in, and blew with great violence for three days. At Sydney, it fell short by one degree of what I have just recorded: but at Rose Hill, it was allowed, by every person, to surpass all that they had before felt, either there or in any other part of the world. Unluckily they had no thermometer to ascertain its precise height. It must, however, have been intense, from the effects it produced. An immense flight of bats driven before the wind, covered all the trees around the settlement, whence they every moment dropped dead or in a dying state, unable longer to endure the burning state of the atmosphere.† Nor did the *perroquettes*, though tropical birds, bear it better.†† The ground was strewed with them in the same condition as the bats.

Were I asked the cause of this intolerable heat, I should not hesitate to pronounce that it was occasioned by the wind blowing over immense deserts, which, I doubt not, exist in a north-west direction from Port Jackson, *and not from fires kindled by the natives.* This remark I feel necessary, as there were methods used by some persons in the colony, both for estimating the degree of heat and for ascertaining the cause of its production, which I deem equally unfair and unphilosophical. The thermometer, whence my observations were constantly made, was hung in the open air, in a southern aspect, never reached by the rays of the sun, at the distance of several feet above the ground.

† Flying foxes, *Pteropus.*

†† Parrakeets.

My other remarks on the climate will be short. It is changeable beyond any other I ever heard of; but no phenomena sufficiently accurate to reckon upon, are found to indicate the approach of alteration. Indeed, for the first eighteen months that we lived in the country, changes were supposed to take place more commonly at the quartering of the moon than at other times. But lunar empire afterwards lost its credit. For the last two years and a half of our residing at Port Jackson, its influence was unperceived. Three days together seldom passed without a necessity occurring for lighting a fire in an evening. A *habit d'ete*, or a *habit de demi sáison*,† would be in the highest degree absurd. Clouds, storms and sunshine pass in rapid succession. Of rain, we found in general not a sufficiency, but torrents of water sometimes fall. Thunderstorms, in summer, are common and very tremendous, but they have ceased to alarm, from rarely causing mischief. Sometimes they happen in winter. I have often seen large hailstones fall. Frequent strong breezes from the westward purge the air. These are almost invariably attended with a hard clear sky. The easterly winds, by setting in from the sea, bring thick weather and rain, except in summer, when they become regular sea-breezes. The *aurora australis* is sometimes seen, but is not distinguished by superior brilliancy.

To sum up: notwithstanding the inconveniences which I have enumerated, I will venture to assert in few words that no climate hitherto known is more generally salubrious,* or affords more days on which those pleasures which depend on the state of the atmosphere can be enjoyed, than that of New South Wales. The winter season is particularly delightful.

The leading animal production is well known to be the

† 'Summer or light clothing.'

* To this cause, I ascribe the great number of births which happened, considering the age and other circumstances, of many of the mothers. Women who certainly would never have bred in any other climate here produced as fine children as ever were born.

kangaroo. The natural history of this animal will, probably, be written from observations made upon it in England, as several living ones of both sexes have been brought home. Until such an account shall appear, probably the following desultory observation may prove acceptable.

The genus in which the kangaroo is to be classed I leave to better naturalists than myself to determine. How it copulates, those who pretend to have seen disagree in their accounts: nor do we know how long the period of gestation lasts. Prolific it cannot be termed, bringing forth only one at a birth, which the dam carries in her pouch wherever she goes until the young one be enabled to provide for itself; and even then, in the moment of alarm, she will stop to receive and protect it. We have killed she-kangaroos whose pouches contained young ones completely covered with fur and of more than fifteen pounds weight, which had ceased to suck and afterwards were reared by us. In what space of time it reaches such a growth as to be abandoned entirely by the mother, we are ignorant. It is born blind, totally bald, the orifice of the ear closed and only just the centre of the mouth open, but a black score, denoting what is hereafter to form the dimension of the mouth, is marked very distinctly on each side of the opening. At its birth, the kangaroo (notwithstanding it weighs when full grown 200 pounds) is *not so large as a half-grown mouse*. I brought some with me to England even less, which I took from the pouches of the old ones. This phenomenon is so striking and so contrary to the general laws of nature, that an opinion has been started that the animal is brought forth not by the pudenda, but descends from the belly into the pouch by one of the teats which are there deposited. On this difficulty, as I can no throw no light, I shall hazard no conjecture. It may, however, be necessary to observe that the teats are several inches long and capable of great dilatation. And here I beg leave to correct an error which crept into my former publication wherein I asserted that, 'the teats of the kangaroo never exceed two in number.' They sometimes, though rarely, amount to four. There is great reason to believe that they are slow of growth and live many years. This animal has a clavicle, or collarbone, similar to that of the human body. The general colour of the kangaroo is very like that of the ass, but varieties exist. Its shape and figure are well known by the plates which have been given of it. The elegance of the ear is particularly deserving of admiration. This far exceeds the ear of the hare in quickness of sense and is so flexible as to admit of being turned by the animal nearly quite round the head, doubtless for the purpose of informing the creature of the approach of its enemies, as it is of a timid nature and poorly furnished with means of defence; though when compelled to resist, it tears furiously with its forepaws, and strikes *forward* very hard with its hind legs. Notwithstanding its unfavourable conformation for such a purpose, it swims strongly; but never takes to the water unless so hard pressed by its pursuers as to be left without all other refuge. The noise they make is a faint bleat, querulous, but not easy to describe. They are sociable animals and unite in droves, sometimes to the number of fifty or sixty together; when they are seen playful and feeding on grass, which alone forms their food. At such time they move gently about like all other quadrupeds, on all fours; but at the slightest noise they spring up on their hind legs and sit erect, listening to what it may proceed from, and if it increases they bound off on those legs only, the fore ones at the same time being carried close to the breast like the paws of a monkey; and the tail stretched out, acts as a rudder on a ship. In drinking, the kangaroo laps. It is remarkable that they are never found in a fat state, being invariably lean. Of the flesh we always eat with avidity, but in Europe it would not be reckoned a delicacy. A rank flavour forms the principal objection to it. The tail is accounted the most delicious part, when stewed.

Hitherto I have spoken only of the large, or grey kangaroo, to which the natives give the name of *patagaràn*.* But there are

* Kangaroo was a name unknown to them for any animal, until we introduced it. When I showed Colbee the cows brought out in the *Gorgon*, he asked me if they were kangaroos.

(besides the kangaroo-rat) two other sorts. One of them we called the red kangaroo, from the colour of its fur, which is like that of a hare, and sometimes is mingled with a large portion of black: the natives call it *bàgaray*.† It rarely attains to more than forty pounds weight. The third sort is very rare, and in the formation of its head resembles the opossum. The kangaroo-rat is a small animal, never reaching, at its utmost growth, more than fourteen or fifteen pounds, and its usual size is not above seven or eight pounds. It joins to the head and bristles of a rat the leading distinctions of a kangaroo, by running when pursued on its hind legs only, and the female having a pouch. Unlike the kangaroo, who appears to have no fixed place of residence, this little animal constructs for itself a nest of grass, on the ground, of a circular figure, about ten inches in diameter, with a hole on one side for the creature to enter at; the inside being lined with a finer sort of grass, very soft and downy. But its manner of carrying the materials with which it builds the nest is the greatest curiosity: by entwining its tail (which, like that of all the kangaroo tribe, is long, flexible and muscular) around whatever it wants to remove, and thus dragging along the load behind it. This animal is good to eat; but whether it be more prolific at a birth than the kangaroo, I know not.

The Indians sometimes kill the kangaroo; but their greatest destroyer is the wild dog,* who feeds on them. Immediately on hearing or seeing this formidable enemy, the kangaroo flies to the thickest cover, in which, if he can involve himself, he generally escapes. In running to the cover, they always, if possible, keep in paths of their own forming, to avoid the high grass and

† Swamp wallaby, *Wallabia bicolor*.

* I once found in the woods the greatest part of a kangaroo, just killed by the dogs, which afforded to three of us a most welcome repast. Marks of its turns and struggles on the ground were very visible. This happened in the evening, and the dogs probably had seen us approach and had run away. At daylight next morning they saluted us with most dreadful howling for the loss of their prey.

stumps of trees which might be sticking up among it to wound them and impede their course.

Our methods of killing them were but two; either we shot them, or hunted them with greyhounds. We were never able to ensnare them. Those sportsmen who relied on the gun seldom met with success, unless they slept near covers, into which the kangaroos were wont to retire at night, and watched with great caution and vigilance when the game, in the morning, sallied forth to feed. They were, however, sometimes stolen in upon in the daytime; and that fascination of the eye, which has been by some authors so much insisted upon, so far acts on the kangaroo that if he fix his eye upon anyone, and no other object move at the same time, he will often continue motionless, in stupid gaze, while the sportsman advances with measured step towards him, until within reach of his gun. The greyhounds for a long time were incapable of taking them; but with a brace of dogs, if not near cover a kangaroo almost always falls, since the greyhounds have acquired by practice the proper method of fastening upon them. Nevertheless the dogs are often miserably torn by them. The rough wiry greyhound suffers least in the conflict, and is most prized by the hunters.

Other quadrupeds, besides the wild dog, consist only of the flying squirrel, of three kinds of opossums and some minute animals, usually marked by the distinction which so peculiarly characterises the opossum tribe. The rats, soon after our landing, became not only numerous but formidable, from the destruction they occasioned in the stores. Latterly they had almost disappeared, though to account for their absence were not easy. The first time Colbee saw a monkey, he called *wurra* (a rat), but on examining its paws he exclaimed with astonishment and affright, *mulla* (a man).

At the head of the birds the cassowary, or emu, stands conspicuous. The print of it which has already been given to the public is so accurate for the most part, that it would be malignant criticism in a work of this kind to point out a few trifling defects.

Here again naturalists must look forward to that information which longer and more intimate knowledge of the feathered tribe than I can supply, shall appear. I have nevertheless had the good fortune to see what was never seen but once, in the country I am describing, by Europeans—a hatch, or flock, of young cassowaries with the old bird.† I counted ten, but others said there were twelve. We came suddenly upon them, and they ran up a hill exactly like a flock of turkeys, but so fast that we could not get a shot at them. The largest cassowary ever killed in the settlement, weighed ninety-four pounds. Three young ones, which had been by accident separated from the dam, were at once taken and presented to the governor. They were not larger than so many pullets, although at first sight they appeared to be so from the length of their necks and legs. They were very beautifully striped, and from their tender state were judged to be not more than three or four days old. They lived only a few days.

A single egg, the production of a cassowary, was picked up in a desert place, dropped on the sand, without covering or protection of any kind. Its form was nearly a perfect ellipsis; and the colour of the shell a dark green, full of little indents on its surface. It measured eleven inches and a half in circumference, five inches and a quarter in height, and weighed a pound and a quarter. Afterwards we had the good fortune to take a nest. It was found by a soldier in a sequestered solitary situation, made in a patch of lofty fern about three feet in diameter, rather of an oblong shape and composed of dry leaves and tops of fern stalks, very inartificially put together. The hollow in which lay the eggs, twelve in number, seemed made solely by the pressure of the bird. The eggs were regularly placed in the following position.

† Emus.

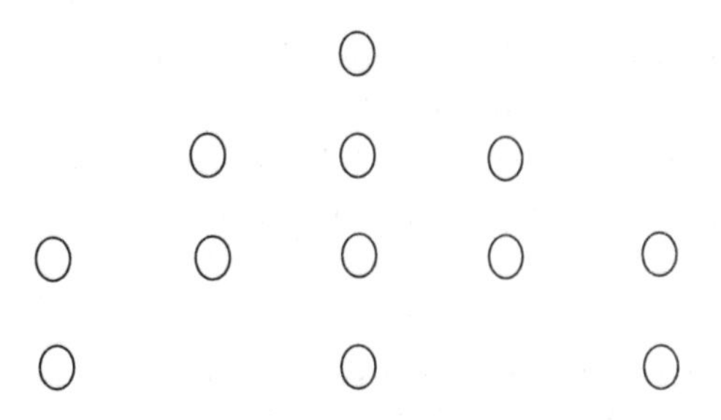

The soldier, instead of greedily plundering his prize, communicated the discovery to an officer, who immediately set out for the spot. When they had arrived there they continued for a long time to search in vain for their object, and the soldier was just about to be stigmatised with ignorance, credulity or imposture, when suddenly up started the old bird and the treasure was found at their feet.

The food of the cassowary is either grass, or a yellow bell-flower growing in the swamps. It deserves remark that the natives deny the cassowary to be a bird, because it does not fly.

Of other birds the varieties are very numerous. Of the parrot tribe alone I could, while I am writing, count up from memory fourteen different sorts. Hawks are very numerous, so are quails. A single snipe has been shot. Ducks, geese and other aquatic birds are often seen in large flocks, but are universally so shy that it is found difficult to shoot them. Some of the smaller birds are very beautiful, but they are not remarkable for either sweetness or variety of notes. To one of them, not bigger than a tomtit, we have given the name of coach-whip, from its note exactly resembling the smack of a whip.† The country, I am of opinion, would abound with birds did not the natives, by perpetually setting fire to the grass and bushes, destroy the greater part of the nests; a cause which also contributes to render small quadrupeds scarce. They are besides ravenously fond of eggs and eat them whenever they find them. They call the roe of a fish and a bird's egg by one name.

† Eastern whipbird, *Posphodes olivaceus.*

So much has been said of the abundance in which fish are found in the harbours of New South Wales that it looks like detraction to oppose a contradiction. Some share of knowledge may, however, be supposed to belong to experience. Many a night have I toiled (in the times of distress) on the public service, from four o'clock in the afternoon until eight o'clock next morning, hauling the seine in every part of the harbour of Port Jackson: and after a circuit of many miles and between twenty and thirty hauls, seldom more than a hundred pounds of fish were taken. However, it sometimes happens that a glut enters the harbour, and for a few days they sufficiently abound. But the universal voice of all professed fishermen is that they never fished in a country where success was so precarious and uncertain.

I shall not pretend to enumerate the variety of fish which are found. They are seen from a whale to a gudgeon. In the intermediate classes may be reckoned sharks of a monstrous size, skate, rock-cod, grey-mullet, bream, horse-mackerel, now and then a sole and john-dory, and innumerable others unknown in Europe, many of which are extremely delicious, and many highly beautiful. At the top of the list, as an article of food, stands a fish which we named light-horseman.† The relish of this excellent fish was increased by our natives, who pointed out to us its delicacies. No epicure in England could pick a head with more glee and dexterity than they do that of a light-horseman.

Reptiles in the swamps and covers are numerous. Of snakes there are two or three sorts: but whether the bite of any of them be mortal, or even venomous, is somewhat doubtful. I know but of one well attested instance of a bite being received from a snake. A soldier was bitten so as to draw blood, and the wound healed as a simple incision usually does without showing any symptom of malignity. A dog was *reported* to be bitten by a snake, and the animal swelled and died in great agony. But

† Snapper, *Crysophrys guttulatus.*

I will by no means affirm that the cause of his death was fairly ascertained. It is, however, certain that the natives show on all occasions the utmost horror of the snake, and will not eat it, although they esteem lizards, goannas and many other reptiles delicious fare. On this occasion they always observe that if the snake bites them, they become lame, but whether by this they mean temporary or lasting lameness I do not pretend to determine. I have often eaten snakes and always found them palatable and nutritive, though it was difficult to stew them to a tender state.

Summer here, as in all other countries, brings with it a long list of insects. In the neighbourhood of rivers and morasses, mosquitoes and sandflies are never wanting at any season, but at Sydney they are seldom numerous or troublesome. The most nauseous and destructive of all the insects is a fly which blows not eggs but large living maggots, and if the body of the fly be opened it is found full of them. Of ants there are several sorts, one of which bites very severely. The white ant is sometimes seen. Spiders are large and numerous. Their webs are not only the strongest, but the finest and most silky I ever felt. I have often thought their labour might be turned to advantage. It has, I believe, been proved that spiders, were it not for their quarrelsome disposition which irritates them to attack and destroy each other, might be employed more profitably than silk-worms.

The hardiness of some of the insects deserves to be mentioned. A beetle was immersed in proof spirits for four hours, and when taken out crawled away almost immediately. It was a second time immersed, and continued in a glass of rum for a day and a night, at the expiration of which period it still showed symptoms of life. Perhaps, however, what I from ignorance deem wonderful is common.

*

The last but the most important production yet remains to be considered. Whether plodding in London, reeking with human blood in Paris or wandering amidst the solitary wilds of New South Wales—Man is ever an object of interest, curiosity and reflection.

The natives around Port Jackson are in person rather more diminutive and slighter made, especially about the thighs and legs, than the Europeans. It is doubtful whether their society contained a person of six feet high. The tallest I ever measured reached five feet eleven inches, and men of his height were rarely seen. Baneelon, who towered above the majority of his countrymen, stood barely five feet eight inches high. His other principal dimensions were as follows:

Girth of the chest	Girth of the belly	Girth of the thigh	Girth of the leg at the calf	Girth of the leg at the small	Girth of the arm half way between the shoulder and the elbow
feet inches	feet inches	inches	inches	inches	inches
2 10	2 6½	18⅛	12⅛	10	9

Instances of natural deformity are scarce, nor did we ever see one of them left-handed. They are, indeed, nearly ambidexter; but the sword, the spear and the fish-gig are always used with the right hand. Their muscular force is not great; but the pliancy of their limbs renders them very active. 'Give to civilised man all his machines, and he is superior to the savage; but without these, how inferior is he found on opposition, even more so than the savage in the first instance.' These are the words of Rousseau, and like many more of his positions must be received with limitation. Were an unarmed Englishman and an unarmed New Hollander to engage, the latter, I think, would fall.

Mr Cook seems inclined to believe the covering of their heads to be wool. But this is erroneous. It is certainly hair, which when regularly combed becomes soon nearly as flexible and docile as our own. Their teeth are not so white and good as those generally found in Indian nations, except in the children, but the inferiority originates in themselves. They bite sticks, stones, shells and all other hard substances indiscriminately with them, which quickly destroys the enamel and gives them a jagged and uneven appearance. A high forehead, with prominent overhanging eyebrows, is their leading characteristic, and when it does not operate to destroy all openness of countenance gives an air of resolute dignity to the aspect, which recommends, in spite of a true Negro nose, thick lips, and a wide mouth. The prominent shin bone, so invariably found in the Africans, is not, however, seen. But in another particular they are more alike. The rank offensive smell which disgusts so much in the Negro, prevails strongly among them when they are in their native state, but it wears off in those who have resided with us and have been taught habits of cleanliness. Their hands and feet are small,* especially the former.

Their eyes are full, black and piercing, but the almost perpetual strain in which the optic nerve is kept, by looking out for prey, renders their sight weak at an earlier age than we in general find ours affected. These large black eyes are universally shaded by the long thick sweepy eyelash, so much prized in appreciating beauty, that perhaps hardly any face is so homely which this aid cannot in some degree render interesting; and hardly any so lovely which, without it, bears not some trace of insipidity. Their tone of voice is loud but not harsh. I have in some of them found it very pleasing.

Longevity, I think, is seldom attained by them. Unceasing agitation wears out the animal frame and is unfriendly to

* I mentioned this, among other circumstances, to Colonel Gordon when I was at the Cape, and he told me that it indicated poverty and inadequacy of living. He instanced to me the Hottentots and Caffres. The former fare poorly, and have small hands and feet. The Caffres, their neighbours, live plenteously and have very large ones. This remark cannot be applied to civilised nations, where so many factitious causes operate.

length of days. We have seen them grey with age, but not old; perhaps never beyond sixty years. But, it may be said, the American Indian, in his undebauched state, lives to an advanced period. True, but he has his seasons of repose. He reaps his little harvest of maize and continues in idleness while it lasts. He kills the roebuck or the moose-deer, which maintains him and his family for many days, during which cessation the muscles regain their spring and fit him for fresh toils. Whereas every sun awakes the native of New South Wales (unless a whale be thrown upon the coast) to a renewal of labour, to provide subsistence for the present day.

The women are proportionally smaller than the men. I never measured but two of them, who were both, I think, about the medium height. One of them, a sister of Baneelon, stood exactly five feet two inches high. The other, named Gooreedeeàna, was shorter by a quarter of an inch.

But I cannot break from Gooreedeeana so abruptly. She belonged to the tribe of Cameragal and rarely came among us. One day, however, she entered my house to complain of hunger. She excelled in beauty all their females I ever saw. Her age about eighteen, the firmness, the symmetry and the luxuriancy of her bosom might have tempted painting to copy its charms. Her mouth was small and her teeth, though exposed to all the destructive purposes to which they apply them, were white, sound and unbroken. Her countenance, though marked by some of the characteristics of her native land, was distinguished by a softness and sensibility unequalled in the rest of her countrywomen, and I was willing to believe that these traits indicated the disposition of her mind. I had never before seen this elegant timid female, of whom I had often heard; but the interest I took in her led me to question her about her husband and family. She answered me by repeating a name which I have now forgotten, and told me she had no children. I was seized with a strong propensity to learn whether the attractions of Gooreedeeana were sufficiently powerful to secure her from the brutal violence with which the women are treated, and as I found my question either ill-understood or reluctantly answered, I proceeded to examine her head, the part on which the husband's vengeance generally alights. With grief I found it covered by contusions and mangled by scars. The poor creature, grown by this time more confident from perceiving that I pitied her, pointed out a wound just above her left knee which she told me was received from a spear, thrown at her by a man who had lately dragged her by force from her home to gratify his lust. I afterwards observed that this wound had caused a slight lameness and that she limped in walking. I could only compassionate her wrongs and sympathise in her misfortunes. To alleviate her present sense of them, when she took her leave I gave her, however, all the bread and salt pork which my little stock afforded.

After this I never saw her but once, when I happened to be near the harbour's mouth in a boat with Captain Ball. We met her in a canoe with several more of her sex. She was painted for a ball, with broad stripes of white earth from head to foot, so that she no longer looked like the same Gooreedeeana. We offered her several presents, all of which she readily accepted; but finding our eagerness and solicitude to inspect her, she managed her canoe with such address as to elude our too near approach, and acted the coquet to admiration.

To return from this digression to my subject, I have only farther to observe that the estimation of female beauty among the natives (the men at least) is in this country the same as in most others. Were a New Hollander to portray his mistress, he would draw her the *Venus aux belles fesses*.† Whenever Baneelon described to us his favourite fair, he always painted her in this, and another particular, as eminently luxuriant.

Unsatisfied, however, with natural beauty (like the people of all other countries) they strive by adscititious embellishments to heighten attraction, and often with as little success. Hence the naked savage of New South Wales pierces the septum of his

† 'Venus of the beautiful buttocks'.

nose, through which he runs a stick or a bone, and scarifies his body, the charms of which increase in proportion to the number and magnitude of seams by which it is distinguished. The operation is performed by making two longitudinal incisions with a sharpened shell, and afterwards pinching up with the nails the intermediate space of skin and flesh, which thereby becomes considerably elevated and forms a prominence as thick as a man's finger. No doubt but pain must be severely felt until the wound be healed. But the love of ornament defies weaker considerations, and no English beau can bear more stoutly the extraction of his teeth to make room for a fresh set from a chimney sweeper, or a fair one suffer her tender ears to be perforated, with more heroism than the grisly nymphs on the banks of Port Jackson, submit their sable shoulders to the remorseless lancet.

That these scarifications are intended solely to increase personal allurement I will not, however, positively affirm. Similar, perhaps, to the cause of an excision of part of the little finger of the left hand in the women, and of a front tooth in the men;* or probably after all our conjectures, superstitious ceremonies by which they hope either to avert evil or to propagate good, are intended. The colours with which they besmear the bodies of both sexes possibly date from the same common origin. White paint is strictly appropriate to the dance. Red seems to be used

* It is to be observed that neither of these ceremonies is universal, but nearly so. Why there should exist exemptions I cannot resolve. The manner of executing them is as follows. The finger is taken off by means of a ligature (generally a sinew of a kangaroo) tied so tight as to stop the circulation of the blood, which induces mortification and the part drops off. I remember to have seen Colbee's child, when about a month old, on whom this operation had just been performed by her mother. The little wretch seemed in pain, and her hand was greatly swelled. But this was deemed too trifling a consideration to deserve regard in a case of so much importance.

The tooth intended to be taken out is loosened by the gum being on numberless occasions, and is considered as a colour of less consequence. It may be remarked that they translate the epithet white when they speak of us, not by the name which they assign to this white earth, but by that with which they distinguish the palms of their hands.

As this leads to an important subject I shall at once discuss it. 'Have these people any religion: any knowledge of, or believe in a deity?—any conception of the immortality of the soul?' are questions which have been often put to me since my arrival in England. I shall endeavour to answer them with candour and seriousness.

Until belief be enlightened by revelation and chastened by reason, religion and superstition are terms of equal import. One of our earliest impressions is the consciousness of a superior power. The various forms under which this impression has manifested itself are objects of the most curious speculation.

The native of New South Wales believes that particular aspects and appearances of the heavenly bodies predict good or evil consequences to himself and his friends. He oftentimes calls the sun and moon '*weeree*,' that is, malignant, pernicious. Should he see the leading fixed stars (many of which he can call by name) obscured by vapours, he sometimes disregards the omen, and sometimes draws from it the most dreary conclusions. I remember Abaroo running into a room where a company was assembled, and uttering frightful exclamations of impending mischiefs about to light on her and her countrymen. When questioned on the cause of such agitation she went

scarified on both sides with a sharp shell. The end of a stick is then applied to the tooth, which is struck gently several times with a stone, until it becomes easily moveable, when the *coup de grace* is given by a smart stroke. Notwithstanding these precautions, I have seen a considerable degree of swelling and inflammation follow the extraction. Imeerawanyee, I remember, suffered severely. But he boasted the firmness and hardihood with which he had endured it. It is seldom performed on those who are under sixteen years old.

to the door and pointed to the skies, saying that whenever the stars wore that appearance, misfortunes to the natives always followed. The night was cloudy and the air disturbed by meteors. I have heard many more of them testify similar apprehensions.

However involved in darkness and disfigured by error such a belief be, no one will, I presume, deny that it conveys a direct implication of superior agency; of a power independent of and uncontrolled by those who are the objects of its vengeance. But proof stops not here. When they hear the thunder roll and view the livid glare, they flee them not, but rush out and deprecate destruction. They have a dance and a song appropriated to this awful occasion, which consist of the wildest and most uncouth noises and gestures. Would they act such a ceremony did they not conceive that either the thunder itself, or he who directs the thunder, might be propitiated by its performance? That a living intellectual principle exists, capable of comprehending their petition and of either granting or denying it? They never address prayers to bodies which they know to be inanimate, either to implore their protection or avert their wrath. When the gum-tree in a tempest nods over them; or the rock overhanging the cavern in which they sleep threatens by its fall to crush them, they calculate (as far as their knowledge extends) on physical principles, like other men, the nearness and magnitude of the danger, and flee it accordingly. And yet there is reason to believe that from accidents of this nature they suffer more than from lightning. Baneelon once showed us a cave, the top of which had fallen in and buried under its ruins seven people who were sleeping under it.

To descend; is not even the ridiculous superstition of Colbee related in one of our journeys to the Hawkesbury? And again the following instance. Abaroo was sick. To cure her, one of her own sex slightly cut her on the forehead, in a perpendicular direction with an oyster shell, so as just to fetch blood. She then put one end of a string to the wound and, beginning to sing, held the other end to her own gums, which she rubbed until they bled copiously. This blood she contended was the blood of the patient, flowing through the string, and that she would thereby soon recover. Abaroo became well, and firmly believed that she owed her cure to the treatment she had received. Are not these, I say, links, subordinate ones indeed, of the same golden chain? He who believes in magic confesses supernatural agency, and a belief of this sort extends farther in many persons than they are willing to allow. There have lived men so inconsistent with their own principles as to deny the existence of a God, who have nevertheless turned pale at the tricks of a mountebank.

But not to multiply arguments on a subject where demonstration (at least to me) is incontestable, I shall close by expressing my firm belief that the Indians of New South Wales acknowledge the existence of a superintending deity. Of their ideas of the origin and duration of his existence; of his power and capacity; of his benignity or maleficence; or of their own emanation from him, I pretend not to speak. I have often, in common with others, tried to gain information from them on this head; but we were always repulsed by obstacles which we could neither pass by or surmount. Mr Dawes attempted to teach Abaroo some of our notions of religion, and hoped that she would thereby be induced to communicate hers in return. But her levity and love of play in a great measure defeated his efforts, although everything he did learn from her served to confirm what is here advanced. It may be remarked, that when they attended at church with us (which was a common practice) they always preserved profound silence and decency, as if conscious that some religious ceremony on our side was performing.

The question of whether they believe in the immortality of the soul will take up very little time to answer. They are universally fearful of spirits.* They call a spirit *mawn*. They often scruple to approach a corpse, saying that the *mawn* will

* 'It is remarkable,' says Cicero, 'that there is no nation, whether barbarous or civilised, that does not believe in the existence of spirits.'

seize them and that it fastens upon them in the night when asleep.* When asked where their deceased friends are they always point to the skies. To believe in after-existence is to confess the immortality of some part of being. To enquire whether they assign a *limited* period to such future state would be superfluous. This is one of the subtleties of speculation which a savage may be supposed not to have considered, without impeachment either of his sagacity or happiness.

Their manner of interring the dead has been amply described. It is certain that instead of burying they sometimes burn the corpse; but the cause of distinction we know not. A dead body, covered by a canoe, at whose side a sword and shield were placed in state, was once discovered. All that we could learn about this important personage was that he was a *Gweeagal* (one of the tribe of Gweea) and a celebrated warrior.

To appreciate their general powers of mind is difficult. Ignorance, prejudice, the force of habit, continually interfere to prevent dispassionate judgment. I have heard men so unreasonable as to exclaim at the stupidity of these people for not comprehending what a small share of reflection would have taught them they ought not to have expected. And others again I have heard so sanguine in their admiration as to extol for proofs of elevated genius what the commonest abilities were capable of executing.

If they be considered as a nation whose general advancement and acquisitions are to be weighed, they certainly rank very low, even in the scale of savages. They may perhaps dispute the right of precedency with the Hottentots or the shivering tribes who inhabit the shores of Magellan. But how inferior do they show when compared with the subtle African; the patient watchful American; or the elegant timid islander of the South Seas. Though suffering from the vicissitudes of their

* As they often eat to satiety, even to produce sickness, may not this be the effect of an overloaded stomach: the nightmare?

climate, strangers to clothing, though feeling the sharpness of hunger and knowing the precariousness of supply from that element on whose stores they principally depend, ignorant of cultivating the earth—a less enlightened state we shall exclaim can hardly exist.

But if from general view we descend to particular inspection, and examine individually the persons who compose this community, they will certainly rise in estimation. In the narrative part of this work I have endeavoured rather to detail information than to deduce conclusions, leaving to the reader the exercise of his own judgment. The behaviour of Arabanoo, of Baneelon, of Colbee and many others is copiously described, and assuredly he who shall make just allowance for uninstructed nature will hardly accuse any of those persons of stupidity or deficiency of apprehension.

To offer my own opinion on the subject, I do not hesitate to declare that the natives of New South Wales possess a considerable portion of that acumen, or sharpness of intellect, which bespeaks genius. All savages hate toil and place happiness in inaction, and neither the arts of civilised life can be practised or the advantages of it felt without application and labour. Hence they resist knowledge and the adoption of manners and customs differing from their own. The progress of reason is not only slow, but mechanical. '*De toutes les instructions propres à l'homme, celle qu'il acquiert le plus tard, et le plus difficilement, est la raison meme*.'† The tranquil indifference and unenquiring eye with which they surveyed our works of art have often, in my hearing, been stigmatised as proofs of stupidity and want of reflection. But surely we should discriminate between ignorance and defect of understanding. The truth was, they often neither comprehended the design nor conceived the utility of such works, but on subjects in any degree familiarised to their ideas, they generally testified not only acuteness of discernment

† 'The longest and most difficult thing for people to learn is how to reason.'

but a large portion of good sense. I have always thought that the distinctions they showed in their estimate of us, on first entering into our society, strongly displayed the latter quality. When they were led into our respective houses, at once to be astonished and awed by our superiority, their attention was directly turned to objects with which they were acquainted. They passed without rapture or emotion our numerous artifices and contrivances, but when they saw a collection of weapons of war or of the skins of animals and birds, they never failed to exclaim, and to confer with each other on the subject. The master of that house became the object of their regard, as they concluded he must be either a renowned warrior, or an expert hunter.

Our surgeons grew into their esteem from a like cause. In a very early stage of intercourse, several natives were present at the amputation of a leg. When they first penetrated the intention of the operator, they were confounded, not believing it possible that such an operation could be performed without loss of life, and they called aloud to him to desist; but when they saw the torrent of blood stopped, the vessels taken up and the stump dressed, their horror and alarm yielded to astonishment and admiration, which they expressed by the loudest tokens. If these instances bespeak not nature and good sense, I have yet to learn the meaning of the terms.

If it be asked why the same intelligent spirit which led them to contemplate and applaud the success of the sportsman and the skill of the surgeon, did not equally excite them to meditate on the labours of the builder and the ploughman, I can only answer, that what we see in its remote cause is always more feebly felt than that which presents to our immediate grasp both its origin and effect.

Their leading good and bad qualities I shall concisely touch upon. Of their intrepidity no doubt can exist. Their levity, their fickleness, their passionate extravagance of character, cannot be defended. They are indeed sudden and quick in quarrel; but if their resentment be easily roused, their thirst of revenge is not implacable. Their honesty, when tempted by novelty, is not unimpeachable; but in their own society there is good reason to believe that few breaches of it occur. It were well if similar praise could be given to their veracity: but truth they neither prize nor practice. When they wish to deceive they scruple not to utter the grossest and most hardened lies.* Their attachment and gratitude to those among us whom they have professed to love have always remained inviolable, unless effaced by resentment, from sudden provocation: then, like all other Indians, the impulse of the moment is alone regarded by them.

Some of their manufactures display ingenuity, when the rude tools with which they work and their celerity of execution are considered. The canoes, fish-gigs, swords, shields, spears, throwing-sticks, clubs and hatchets, are made by the men. To the women are committed the fishing-lines, hooks and nets. As very ample collections of all these articles are to be found in many museums in England, I shall only briefly describe the way in which the most remarkable of them are made. The fish-gigs and spears are commonly (but not universally) made of the long spiral shoot which arises from the top of the yellow gum-tree, and bears the flower. The former have several prongs, barbed with the bone of kangaroo. The latter are sometimes barbed with the same substance, or with the prickle of the stingray, or with stone or hardened gum, and sometimes simply pointed. Dexterity in throwing and parrying the spear is considered as the highest acquirement. The children of both sexes practise from the time that they are able to throw a rush; their first essay. It forms their constant recreation. They afterwards heave at each other with pointed twigs. He who acts on the defensive holds a piece of new soft bark in the left hand, to represent a shield, in which he receives the darts of the assailant, the points sticking in it. Now commences his turn. He extracts the twigs and darts them back at the first thrower, who catches

* This may serve to account for the contradictions of many of their accounts to us.

them similarly. In warding off the spear they never present their front, but always turn their side, their head at the same time just clear of the shield, to watch the flight of the weapon; and the body covered. If a spear drop from them when thus engaged, they do not stoop to pick it up, but hook it between the toes and so lift it until it meet the hand. Thus the eye is never diverted from its object, the foe. If they wish to break a spear or any wooden substance, they lay it not across the thigh or the body, but upon the head, and press down the ends until it snap. Their shields are of two sorts. That called *ileemon* is nothing but a piece of bark with a handle fixed in the inside of it. The other, dug out of solid wood, is called *aragoòn* and is made as follows, with great labour. On the bark of a tree they mark the size of the shield, then dig the outline as deep as possible in the wood with hatchets, and lastly flake it off as thick as they can, by driving in wedges. The sword is a large heavy piece of wood, shaped like a sabre, and capable of inflicting a mortal wound. In using it they do not strike with the convex side, but with the concave one, and strive to hook in their antagonists so as to have them under their blows. The fishing-lines are made of the bark of a shrub. The women roll shreds of this on the inside of the thigh, so as to twist it together, carefully inserting the ends of every fresh piece into the last made. They are not as strong as lines of equal size formed of hemp. The fish-hooks are chopped with a stone out of a particular shell, and afterwards rubbed until they become smooth. They are very much curved, and not barbed. Considering the quickness with which they are finished, the excellence of the work, if it be inspected, is admirable. In all these manufactures the sole of the foot is used both by men and women as a work-board. They chop a piece of wood, or aught else upon it, even with an iron tool, without hurting themselves. It is indeed nearly as hard as the hoof of an ox.

Their method of procuring fire is this. They take a reed and shave one side of the surface flat. In this they make a small incision to reach the pith, and introducing a stick, purposely blunted at the end, into it, turn it round between the hands (as chocolate is milled) as swiftly as possible, until flame be produced. As this operation is not only laborious, but the effect tedious, they frequently relieve each other at the exercise. And to avoid being often reduced to the necessity of putting it in practice, they always, if possible, carry a lighted stick with them, whether in their canoes or moving from place to place on land.

Their treatment of wounds must not be omitted. A doctor is, with them, a person of importance and esteem, but his province seems rather to charm away occult diseases than to act the surgeon's part, which, as a subordinate science, is exercised indiscriminately. Their excellent habit of body,* the effect of drinking water only, speedily heals wounds without an exterior application which with us would take weeks or months to close. They are, nevertheless, sadly tormented by a cutaneous eruption, but we never found it contagious. After receiving a contusion, if the part swell they fasten a ligature very tightly above it, so as to stop all circulation. Whether to this application, or to their undebauched habit, it be attributable, I know not, but it is certain that a disabled limb among them is rarely seen, although violent inflammations from bruises, which in us would bring on a gangrene, daily happen. If they get burned, either from rolling into the fire when asleep, or from the flame catching the grass on which they lie (both of which are common accidents) they cover the part with a thin paste of kneaded clay, which excludes the air and adheres to the wound until it be cured, and the eschar falls off.

Their form of government, and the detail of domestic life, yet remain untold. The former cannot occupy much space. Without distinctions of rank, except those which youth and

* Their native hardiness of constitution is great. I saw a woman on the day she was brought to bed, carry her newborn infant from Botany Bay to Port Jackson, a distance of six miles, and afterwards light a fire and dress fish.

vigour confer, there is strictly a system of *equality* attended with only one inconvenience—the strong triumph over the weak. Whether any laws exist among them for the punishment of offences committed against society; or whether the injured party in all cases seeks for relief in private revenge, I will not positively affirm; though I am strongly inclined to believe that only the latter method prevails. I have already said that they are divided into tribes; but what constitutes the right of being enrolled in a tribe, or where exclusion begins and ends, I am ignorant. The tribe of Cameragal is of all the most numerous and powerful. Their superiority probably arose from possessing the best fishing ground, and perhaps from their having suffered less from the ravages of the smallpox.

In their domestic detail there may be novelty, but variety is unattainable. One day must be very like another in the life of a savage. Summoned by the calls of hunger and the returning light, he starts from his beloved indolence, and snatching up the remaining brand of his fire, hastens with his wife to the strand to commence their daily task. In general the canoe is assigned to her, into which she puts the fire and pushes off into deep water, to fish with hook and line, this being the province of the women. If she have a child at the breast, she takes it with her. And thus in her skiff, a piece of bark tied at both ends with vines, and the edge of it but just above the surface of the water, she pushes out regardless of the elements, if they be but commonly agitated. While she paddles to the fishing-bank, and while employed there, the child is placed on her shoulders, entwining its little legs around her neck and closely grasping her hair with its hands. To its first cries she remains insensible, as she believes them to arise only from the inconveniency of a situation, to which she knows it must be inured. But if its plaints continue, and she supposes it to be in want of food, she ceases her fishing and clasps it to her breast. An European spectator is struck with horror and astonishment at their perilous situation, but accidents seldom happen. The management of the canoe alone appears a work of unsurmountable difficulty, its breadth is so inadequate to its length. The Indians, aware of its ticklish formation, practise from infancy to move in it without risk. Use only could reconcile them to the painful position in which they sit in it. They drop in the middle of the canoe upon their knees, and resting the buttocks on the heels, extend the knees to the sides, against which they press strongly so as to form a poise sufficient to retain the body in its situation, and relieve the weight which would otherwise fall wholly upon the toes. Either in this position or cautiously moving in the centre of the vessel, the mother tends her child, keeps up her fire (which is laid on a small patch of earth), paddles her boat, broils fish and provides in part the subsistence of the day. Their favourite bait for fish is a cockle.

The husband in the meantime warily moves to some rock, over which he can peep into unruffled water to look for fish. For this purpose he always chooses a weather shore, and the various windings of the numerous creeks and indents always afford one. Silent and watchful, he chews a cockle and spits it into the water. Allured by the bait, the fish appear from beneath the rock. He prepares his fish-gig, and pointing it downward, moves it gently towards the object, always trying to approach it as near as possible to the fish before the stroke be given. At last he deems himself sufficiently advanced and plunges it at his prey. If he has hit his mark, he continues his efforts and endeavours to transpierce it or so to entangle the barbs in the flesh as to prevent its escape. When he finds it secure he drops the instrument, and the fish, fastened on the prongs, rises to the surface, floated by the buoyancy of the staff. Nothing now remains to be done but to haul it to him, with either a long stick or another fish-gig (for an Indian, if he can help it, never goes into the water on these occasions) to disengage it, and to look out for fresh sport.

But sometimes the fish have either deserted the rocks for deeper water, or are too shy to suffer approach. He then launches his canoe, and leaving the shore behind, watches the rise of prey out of the water, and darts his gig at them to the distance of many yards. Large fish he seldom procures by this method; but among shoals of mullets, which are either pursued by enemies, or leap at objects on the surface, he is often successful. Baneelon has been seen to kill more than twenty fish by this method in an afternoon. The women sometimes use the gig, and always carry one in each canoe to strike large fish which may be hooked and thereby facilitate the capture. But generally speaking, this instrument is appropriate to the men, who are never seen fishing with the line, and would indeed consider it as a degradation of their pre-eminence.

When prevented by tempestuous weather or any other cause, from fishing, these people suffer severely. They have then no resource but to pick up shellfish, which may happen to cling to the rocks and be cast on the beach, to hunt particular reptiles and small animals, which are scarce, to dig fern root in the swamps or to gather a few berries, destitute of flavour and nutrition, which the woods afford. To alleviate the sensation of hunger, they tie a ligature tightly around the belly, as I have often seen our soldiers do from the same cause.

Let us, however, suppose them successful in procuring fish. The wife returns to land with her booty, and the husband quitting the rock joins his stock to hers, and they repair either to some neighbouring cavern or to their hut. This last is composed of pieces of bark, very rudely piled together, in shape as like a soldier's tent as any known image to which I can compare it: too low to admit the lord of it to stand upright, but long and wide enough to admit three or four persons to lie under it. 'Here shelters himself a being, born with all those powers which education expands, and all those sensations which culture refines.'† With a lighted stick brought from the canoe they now kindle a small fire at the mouth of the hut and prepare to dress their meal. They begin by throwing the fish, exactly in the state in which it came from the water, on the fire. When it has become a little warmed they take it off, rub away the scales, and then peel

† Source unidentified.

off with their teeth the surface, which they find done, and eat. Now, and not before, they gut it; but if the fish be a mullet or any other which has a fatty substance about the intestines, they carefully guard that part and esteem it a delicacy. The cooking is now completed by the remaining part being laid on the fire until it be sufficiently done. A bird, a lizard, a rat, or any other animal, they treat in the same manner. The feathers of the one and the fur of the other, they thus get rid of. *

Unless summoned away by irresistible necessity, sleep always follows the repast. They would gladly prolong it until the following day; but the canoe wants repair, the fish-gig must be barbed afresh, new lines must be twisted and new hooks chopped out. They depart to their respective tasks, which end only with the light.

Such is the general life of an Indian. But even he has his hours of relaxation, in seasons of success, when fish abounds. Wanton with plenty, he now meditates an attack upon the chastity of some neighbouring fair one; and watching his opportunity he seizes her and drags her way to complete his purpose. The signal of war is lighted; her lover, her father, her brothers, her tribe, assemble, and vow revenge on the spoiler. He tells his story to his tribe. They judge the case to be a common one and agree to support him. Battle ensues; they discharge their spears at each other, and legs and arms are transpierced. When the spears are expended the combatants close and every species of

* They broil indiscriminately all substances which they eat. Though they boil water in small quantities in oyster shells for particular purposes, they never conceived it possible until shown by us, to dress meat by this method, having no vessel capable of containing a fish or a bird which would stand fire. Two of them once stole twelve pounds of rice and carried it off. They knew how we cooked it, and by way of putting it in practice they spread the rice on the ground before a fire, and as it grew hot continued to throw water on it. Their ingenuity was however very ill rewarded, for the rice became so mingled with the dirt and sand on which it was laid, that even they could not eat it, and the whole was spoiled.

violence is practised. They seize their antagonist and snap like enraged dogs, they wield the sword and club, the bone shatters beneath their fall and they drop the prey of unsparing vengeance.

Too justly, as my observations teach me, has *Hobbes* defined a state of nature to be a state of war. In the method of waging it among these people, one thing should not, however, escape notice. Unlike all other Indians, they never carry on operations in the night, or seek to destroy by ambush and surprise. Their ardent fearless character seeks fair and open combat only.

But enmity has its moments of pause. Then they assemble to sing and dance. We always found their songs disagreeable from their monotony. They are numerous, and vary both in measure and time. They have songs of war, of hunting, of fishing, for the rise and set of the sun, for rain, for thunder and for many other occasions. One of these songs, which may be termed a speaking pantomime, recites the courtship between the sexes and is accompanied with acting highly expressive. I once heard and saw Nanbaree and Abaroo perform it. After a few preparatory motions she gently sunk on the ground, as if in a fainting fit. Nanbaree, applying his mouth to her ear, began to whisper in it, and baring her bosom, breathed on it several times. At length, the period of the swoon having expired, with returning animation she gradually raised herself. She now began to relate what she had seen in her vision, mentioning several of her countrymen by name, whom we knew to be dead; mixed with other strange incoherent matter, equally new and inexplicable, though all tending to one leading point—the sacrifice of her charms to her lover.

At their dances I have often been present; but I confess myself unable to convey in description an accurate account of them. Like their songs, they are conceived to represent the progress of the passions and the occupations of life. Full of seeming confusion, yet regular and systematic, their wild gesticulations and frantic distortions of body are calculated rather to terrify, than delight, a spectator. These dances consist of short parts, or acts, accompanied with frequent vociferations and a kind of hissing or whizzing noise. They commonly end with a loud rapid shout, and after a short respite are renewed. While the dance lasts, one of them (usually a person of note and estimation) beats time with a stick on a wooden instrument held in the left hand, accompanying the music with his voice; and the dancers sometimes sing in concert.

I have already mentioned that white is the colour appropriated to the dance, but the style of painting is left to everyone's fancy. Some are streaked with waving lines from head to foot; others marked by broad cross-bars, on the breast, back and thighs, or encircled with spiral lines, or regularly striped like a zebra. Of these ornaments, the face never wants its share, and it is hard to conceive anything in the shape of humanity more hideous and terrific than they appear to a stranger—seen, perhaps, through the livid gleam of a fire, the eyes surrounded by large white circles, in contrast with the black ground, the hair stuck full of pieces of bone and in the hand a grasped club, which they occasionally brandish with the greatest fierceness and agility. Some dances are performed by men only, some by women only, and in others the sexes mingle. In one of them I have seen the men drop on their hands and knees and kiss the earth with the greatest fervour, between the kisses looking up to Heaven. They also frequently throw up their arms, exactly in the manner in which the dancers of the Friendly Islands are depicted in one of the plates of Mr Cook's last voyage.[†]

Courtship here, as in other countries, is generally promoted by this exercise, where everyone tries to recommend himself to attention and applause. Dancing not only proves an incentive, but offers an opportunity in its intervals. The first advances are made by the men, who strive to render themselves agreeable to their favourites by presents of fishing-tackle and other articles which they know will prove acceptable. Generally speaking, a man has but one wife; but infidelity on the side of the husband,

† *Voyage to the Pacific Ocean*, plate 16.

with the unmarried girls, is very frequent. For the most part, perhaps, they intermarry in their respective tribes. This rule is not, however, constantly observed, and there is reason to think that a more than ordinary share of courtship and presents, on the part of the man, is required in this case. Such difficulty seldom operates to extinguish desire, and nothing is more common than for the unsuccessful suitor to ravish by force that which he cannot accomplish by entreaty. I do not believe that very near connexions by blood ever cohabit. We knew of no instance of it.

But indeed the women are in all respects treated with savage barbarity. Condemned not only to carry the children but all other burthens, they meet in return for submission only with blows, kicks and every other mark of brutality. When an Indian is provoked by a woman, he either spears her or knocks her down on the spot. On this occasion he always strikes on the head, using indiscriminately a hatchet, a club or any other weapon which may chance to be in his hand. The heads of the women are always consequently seen in the state which I found that of Gooreedeeana. Colbee, who was certainly in other respects a good tempered merry fellow, made no scruple of treating Daringa, who was a gentle creature, thus. Baneelon did the same to Barangaroo, but she was a scold and a vixen, and nobody pitied her. It must nevertheless be confessed that the women often artfully study to irritate and inflame the passions of the men, although sensible that the consequence will alight on themselves.

Many a matrimonial scene of this sort have I witnessed. Lady Mary Wortley Montague, in her sprightly letters from Turkey, longs for some of the advocates for passive obedience and unconditional submission then existing in England to be present at the sights exhibited in a despotic government. A thousand times, in like manner, have I wished that those European philosophers whose closest speculations exalt a state of nature above a state of civilisation, could survey the phantom which their heated imaginations have raised. Possibly they might then learn that a state of nature is, of all others, least adapted to promote the happiness of a being capable of sublime research and unending ratiocination. That a savage roaming for prey amidst his native deserts is a creature deformed by all those passions which afflict and degrade our nature, unsoftened by the influence of religion, philosophy and legal restriction: and that the more men unite their talents, the more closely the bands of society are drawn and civilisation advanced, inasmuch is human felicity augmented, and man fitted for his unalienable station in the universe.

Of the language of New South Wales I once hoped to have subjoined to this work such an exposition as should have attracted public notice and have excited public esteem. But the abrupt departure of Mr Dawes, who, stimulated equally by curiosity and philanthropy, had hardly set foot on his native country when he again quitted it to encounter new perils in the service of the Sierra Leona company, precludes me from executing this part of my original intention, in which he had promised to co-operate with me; and in which he had advanced his research beyond the reach of competition. The few remarks which I can offer shall be concisely detailed.

We were at first inclined to stigmatise this language as harsh and barbarous in its sounds. Their combinations of words in the manner they utter them frequently convey such an effect. But if not only their proper names of men and places, but many of their phrases and a majority of their words, be simply and unconnectedly considered, they will be found to abound with vowels and to produce sounds sometimes mellifluous, and sometimes sonorous. What ear can object to the names of *Còlbee* (pronounced exactly as Colby is with us), *Bèreewan*, *Bòndel*, *Imèerawanyee*, *Deedòra*, *Wòlarawaree*, or *Bàneelon*, among the men; or to *Wereewèea*, *Gòoreedeeana*, *Milba*,* or *Matilba*,

* Mrs Johnson, wife of the chaplain of the settlement, was so pleased with this name that she christened her little girl, born in Port Jackson, Milba Maria Johnson.

among the women. *Parramàtta*, *Gwèea*, *Càmeera*, *Càdi*, and *Memel*, are names of places. The tribes derive their appellations from the places they inhabit. Thus *Càmeragal* means the men who reside in the bay of Cameera; *Càdigal*, those who reside in the bay of Cadi; and so of the others. The women of the tribe are denoted by adding *eean* to any of the foregoing words. A *Cadigalèean* imports a woman living at Cadi, or of the tribe of Cadigal. These words, as the reader will observe, are accented either on the first syllable or the penultima. In general, however, they are partial to the emphasis being laid as near the beginning of the word as possible.

Of compound words they seem fond. Two very striking ones appear in the journal to the Hawkesbury. Their translations of our words into their language are always apposite, comprehensive, and drawn from images familiar to them. A gun for instance they call *goòroobeera*, that is, *a stick of fire*. Sometimes also, by a licence of language, they call those who carry guns by the same name. But the appellation by which they generally distinguished us was that of *bèreewolgal*, meaning *men come from afar*. When they salute any one they call him *damèeli*, or *namesake*, a term which not only implies courtesy and goodwill, but a certain degree of affection in the speaker. An interchange of names with anyone is also a symbol of friendship. Each person has several names; one of which, there is reason to believe, is always derived from the first fish or animal which the child, in accompanying its father to the chase or a fishing, may chance to kill.

Not only their combinations, but some of their simple sounds, were difficult of pronunciation to mouths purely English. Diphthongs often occur. One of the most common is that of 'ae', or perhaps, 'ai', pronounced not unlike those letters in the French verb *haïr*, to hate. The letter 'y' frequently follows 'd' in the same syllable. Thus the word which signifies a woman is *dyin*; although the structure of our language requires us to spell it *deein*.

But if they sometimes put us to difficulty, many of our

words were to them unutterable. The letters 's' and 'v' they never could pronounce. The latter became invariably 'w', and the former mocked all their efforts, which in the instance of Baneelon has been noticed; and a more unfortunate defect in learning our language could not easily be pointed out.

They use the ellipsis in speaking very freely; always omitting as many words as they possibly can, consistent with being understood. They inflect both their nouns and verbs regularly; and denote the cases of the former and the tenses of the latter, not like the English by auxiliary words, but like the Latins by change of termination. Their nouns, whether substantive or adjective, seem to admit of no plural. I have heard Mr Dawes hint his belief of their using a dual number, similar to the Greeks, but I confess that I never could remark aught to confirm it. The method by which they answer a question that they cannot resolve is similar to what we sometimes use. Let for example the following question be put: *Waw Colbee yagoono?*— Where is Colbee today? *Waw, baw!*—Where, *indeed!* would be the reply. They use a direct and positive negative, but express the affirmative by a nod of the head or an inclination of the body.

Opinions have greatly differed whether or not their language be copious. In one particular it is notoriously defective. They cannot count with precision more than *four*. However as far as ten, by holding up the fingers, they can both comprehend others and explain themselves. Beyond four every number is called great; and should it happen to be very large, *great great*, which is an Italian idiom also. This occasions their computations of time and space to be very confused and incorrect. Of the former they have no measure but the visible diurnal motion of the sun or the monthly revolution of the moon.

To conclude the history of a people for whom I cannot but feel some share of affection. Let those who have been born in more favoured lands and who have profited by more enlightened systems, compassionate, but not despise their destitute and obscure situation. Children of the same omniscient paternal care, let them recollect that by the fortuitous advantage of birth alone they possess superiority: that untaught, unaccommodated man is the same in Pall Mall as in the wilderness of New South Wales. And ultimately let them hope and trust that the progress of reason and the splendour of revelation will in their proper and allotted season be permitted to illumine and transfuse into these desert regions, knowledge, virtue and happiness.

18

Observations on the convicts

A short account of that class of men for whose disposal and advantage the colony was principally, if not totally, founded, seems necessary.

If it be recollected how large a body of these people are now congregated in the settlement of Port Jackson and at Norfolk Island, it will, I think, not only excite surprise but afford satisfaction, to learn that in a period of four years few crimes of a deep dye or of a hardened nature have been perpetrated. Murder and unnatural sins rank not hitherto in the catalogue of their enormities, and one suicide only has been committed.

To the honour of the female part of our community let it be recorded that only one woman has suffered capital punishment. On her condemnation she pleaded pregnancy, and a jury of venerable matrons was empanelled on the spot, to examine and pronounce her state, which the forewoman, a grave personage between sixty and seventy years old, did, by this short address to the court: 'Gentlemen! she is as much with child as I am.' Sentence was accordingly passed, and she was executed.

Besides the instance of Irving, two other male convicts, William Bloodsworth, of Kingston upon Thames, and John Arscott, of Truro in Cornwall, were both emancipated for their good conduct, in the years 1790 and 1791. Several men whose terms of transportation had expired, and against whom no legal impediment existed to prevent their departure, have been permitted to enter in merchant ships wanting hands: and as my Rose Hill journals testify, many others have had grants of land assigned to them, and are become settlers in the country.

In so numerous a community, many persons of perverted genius and of mechanical ingenuity could not but be assembled. Let me produce the following example. Frazer was an iron manufacturer, bred at Sheffield, of whose abilities as a workman we had witnessed many proofs. The governor had written to England for a set of locks to be sent out for the security of the public stores, which were to be so constructed as to be incapable of being picked. On their arrival His Excellency sent for Frazer and bade him examine them, telling him at the same time that they could not be picked. Frazer laughed and asked for a crooked nail only, to open them all. A nail was brought, and in an instant he verified his assertion. Astonished at his dexterity, a gentleman present determined to put it to farther proof. He was sent for in a hurry, some days after, to the hospital, where a lock of still superior intricacy and expense to the others had been provided. He was told that the key was lost and that the lock must be immediately picked. He examined it attentively, remarked that it was the production of a workman, and demanded ten minutes to make an instrument *to speak with it*. Without carrying the lock with him, he went directly to his shop, and at the expiration of his term returned, applied his instrument, and open flew the lock. But it was not only in this part of his business that he excelled. He executed every branch of it in superior style. Had not his villainy been still more notorious than his skill, he would have proved an invaluable possession to a new country. He had passed through innumerable scenes in life, and had played many parts. When too lazy to work at his trade he had turned thief in fifty different shapes, was a receiver of stolen goods, a soldier and a travelling conjurer. He once confessed to me that he had made a set of tools for a gang of coiners, every man of whom was hanged.

Were the nature of the subject worthy of farther illustration, many similar proofs of misapplied talents might be adduced.

Their love of the marvellous has been recorded in an early part of this work. The imposture of the gold finder, however prominent and glaring, nevertheless contributed to awaken attention and to create merriment. He enjoyed the reputation of a discoverer, until experiment detected the imposition. But others were less successful to acquire even momentary admiration. The execution of forgery seems to demand at least neatness of imitation and dexterity of address. On the arrival of the first fleet of ships from England, several convicts brought out recommendatory letters from different friends. Of these some were genuine, and many owed their birth to the ingenuity of the bearers. But these last were all such bungling performances as to produce only instant detection and succeeding contempt. One of them addressed to the governor, with the name of Baron Hotham affixed to it, began 'Honored Sir!'

A leading distinction, which marked the convicts on their outset in the colony, was an use of what is called the *flash*, or *kiddy* language. In some of our early courts of justice an interpreter was frequently necessary to translate the deposition of the witness and the defence of the prisoner. This language has many dialects. The sly dexterity of the pickpocket, the brutal ferocity of the footpad, the more elevated career of the highwayman and the deadly purpose of the midnight ruffian is each strictly appropriate in the terms which distinguish and characterise it. I have ever been of opinion that an abolition of this unnatural jargon would open the path to reformation. And my observations on these people have constantly instructed me that indulgence in this infatuating cant is more deeply associated with depravity and continuance in vice than is generally supposed. I recollect hardly one instance of a return to honest pursuits, and habits of industry, where this miserable perversion of our noblest and peculiar faculty was not previously conquered.

Those persons to whom the inspection and management of our numerous and extensive prisons in England are committed will perform a service to society by attending to the foregoing observation. Let us always keep in view, that punishment, when not directed to promote reformation, is arbitrary and unauthorised.

19

Facts relating to the probability of establishing a whale fishery on the coast of New South Wales, with thoughts on the same

In every former part of this publication I have studiously avoided mentioning a whale fishery, as the information relating to it will, I conceive, be more acceptably received in this form, by those to whom it is addressed, than if mingled with other matter.

Previous to entering on this detail, it must be observed that several of the last fleet of ships which had arrived from England with convicts, were fitted out with implements for whale fishing, and were intended to sail for the coast of Brazil to pursue the fishery, immediately on having landed the convicts.

On the 14th of October 1791, the *Britannia*, Captain Melville, one of these ships, arrived at Sydney. In her passage between Van Diemen's Land and Port Jackson, the master reported that he had seen a large shoal of spermaceti whales. His words were, 'I saw more whales at one time around my ship than in the whole of six years which I have fished on the coast of Brazil.'

This intelligence was no sooner communicated than all the whalers were eager to push to sea. Melville himself was among the most early; and on the 10th of November, returned to Port Jackson, more confident of success than before. He assured me that in the fourteen days which he had been out, he had seen more spermaceti whales than in all his former life. They amounted, he said, to many thousands, most of them of enormous magnitude; and had he not met with bad weather he could have killed as many as he pleased. Seven he did kill, but owing to the stormy agitated state of the water he could not get any of them aboard. In one however, which in a momentary interval of calm, was killed and secured by a ship in company, he shared. The oil and *head matter* of this fish, he extolled as of an extraordinary fine quality. He was of opinion the former would fetch ten pounds per ton more in London than that procured on the Brazil coast. He had not gone farther south than 37°; and described the latitude of 35° to be the place where the whales most abounded, just on the edge of soundings, which here extends about fifteen leagues from the shore; though perhaps on other parts of the coast the bank will be found to run hardly so far off.

On the following day (November 11th) the *Mary Anne*, Captain Munro, another of the whalers, returned into port, after having been out sixteen days. She had gone as far south as 41° but saw not a whale, and had met with tremendously bad weather, in which she had shipped a sea that had set her boiling coppers afloat and had nearly carried them overboard.

November 22nd. The *William and Anne*, Captain Buncker, returned after having been more than three weeks out, and putting into Broken Bay. This is the ship that had killed the fish in which Melville shared. Buncker had met with no farther success, owing, he said, entirely to gales of wind; for he had seen several immense shoals and was of opinion that he should have secured fifty tons of oil, had the weather been tolerably moderate. I asked him whether he thought the whales he had seen were fish of passage. 'No,' he answered, 'they were going on every point of the compass, and were evidently on feeding ground, which I saw no reason to doubt that they frequent.' Melville afterwards confirmed to me this observation. December 3rd, the *Mary Anne* and *Matilda* again returned. The former had gone to the southward, and off Port Jervis had fallen in with two shoals of whales, nine of which were killed, but owing to bad weather, part of five only were got on board. As much, the master computed, as would yield thirty barrels of oil. He said the whales were the least shy of any he had ever seen, 'not having been cut up'.† The latter had gone to the northward, and had seen no whales but a few fin-backs.

On the 5th of December, both these ships sailed again; and on the 16th or 17th of the month (just before the author sailed for England) they and the *Britannia* and *William and Anne* returned to Port Jackson without success, having experienced a continuation of the bad weather and seen very few fish. They all said that their intention was to give the coast one more trial, and if it miscarried to quit it and steer to the northward in search of less tempestuous seas.

The only remark which I have to offer to adventurers on the above subject, is not to suffer discouragement by concluding that bad weather only is to be found on the coast of New South Wales, where the whales have hitherto been seen. Tempests happen sometimes there, as in other seas, but let them feel assured that there are in every month of the year many days in which the whale fishery may be safely carried on. The evidence of the abundance in which spermaceti whales are sometimes seen is incontrovertible. That which speaks to their being *not fish of passage* is at least respectable and hitherto uncontradicted. The prospect merits attention—may it stimulate to enterprise.

The two discoveries of Port Jervis and Matilda Bay (which are to be found in the foregoing sheets) may yet be wanting in the maps of the coast. My account of their geographic situation, except possibly in the exact longitude of the latter (a point not very material) may be safely depended upon. A knowledge of Oyster Bay, discovered and laid down by the *Mercury* storeship in the year 1789, would also be desirable. But this I am incapable of furnishing.

Here terminates my subject. Content with the humble province of detailing facts and connecting events by undisturbed narration, I leave to others the task of anticipating

† A fisherman's phrase for 'harassed' or 'disturbed'.

glorious, or gloomy, consequences, from the establishment of a colony, which unquestionably demands serious investigation, ere either its prosecution or abandonment be determined.

But doubtless not only those who planned, but those who have been delegated to execute, an enterprise of such magnitude, have deeply revolved, that 'great national expense does not imply the necessity of national suffering. While revenue is employed with success to some valuable end, the profits of every adventure being more than sufficient to repay its costs, the public should gain, and its resources should continue to multiply. But an expense whether sustained at home or abroad; whether a waste of the present, or an anticipation of the future, revenue, if it bring no adequate return, is to be reckoned among the causes of national ruin.'*

* Ferguson's *Essay on the History of Civil Society*.

A LIST OF THE CIVIL AND MILITARY ESTABLISHMENTS IN NEW SOUTH WALES

Governor and Commander in Chief, His Excellency Arthur Phillip, Esq.
Lieutenant-Governor, Robert Ross, Esq.
Judge of the Admiralty Court, Robert Ross, Esq.
Chaplain of the settlement, the Rev. Richard Johnson.
Judge Advocate of the settlement, David Collins, Esq.
Secretary to the governor, David Collins, Esq.
Surveyor-General, Augustus Alt, Esq.
Commissary of stores and provisions, Andrew Miller, Esq.
Assistant Commissary, Mr Zechariah Clarke.
Provost-Martial, who acts as *Sheriff of Cumberland County*, Mr Henry Brewer.
Peace Officer, Mr James Smith.

MILITARY ESTABLISHMENTS

His Majesty's ship, *Sirius*, John Hunter, Esq. Commander.
Lieutenants, Bradley, King, Maxwell.
His Majesty's armed brig, *Supply*, Lieutenant Henry Lidgbird Ball, Commander.

FOUR COMPANIES OF MARINES

Major Robert Ross, Commandant.

CAPTAINS COMMANDING COMPANIES
James Campbell, John Shea,
Captain-Lieutenants, James Meredith, Watkin Tench.

FIRST LIEUTENANTS
George Johnson, John Johnson, John Creswell, James Maitland Shairp, Robert Nellow, Thomas Davey, James Furzer, Thomas Timins, John Poulden.

SECOND LIEUTENANTS
Ralph Clarke, John Long, William Dawes, William Feddy.
Adjutant, John Long.
Quarter Master, James Furzer
Aide de camp to the governor, George Johnson.
Officer of engineers and artillery, William Dawes.

HOSPITAL ESTABLISHMENT
Surgeon-General of the settlement, John White, Esq.
First Assistant, Mr Dennis Considen.
Second Assistant, Mr Thomas Arndell.
Third Assistant, Mr William Balmain.

Index

Life *and* Adventures
1776–1801

JOHN NICOL, *Mariner*

JOHN NICOL

Contents

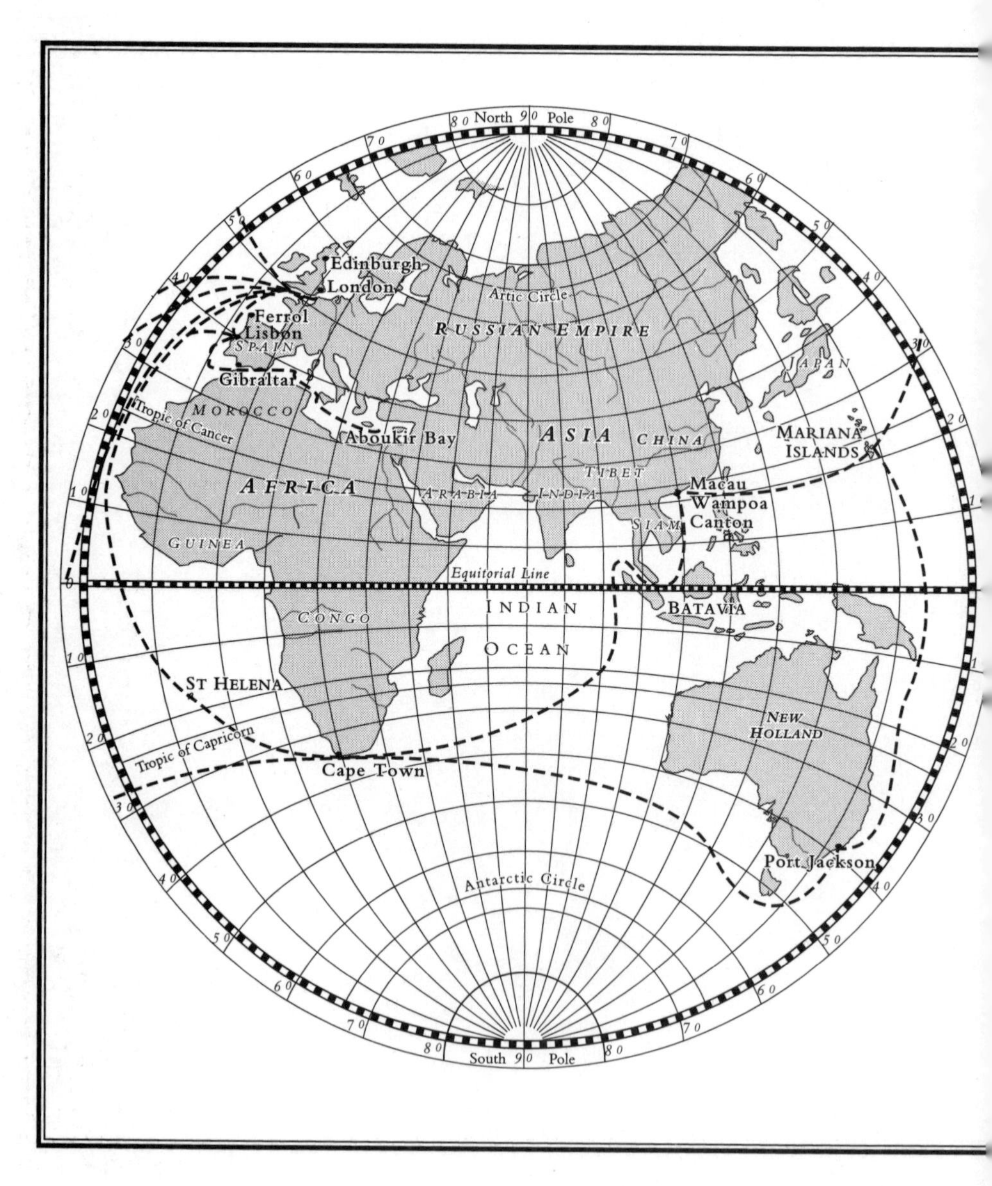

Map of the world as Nicol would ha

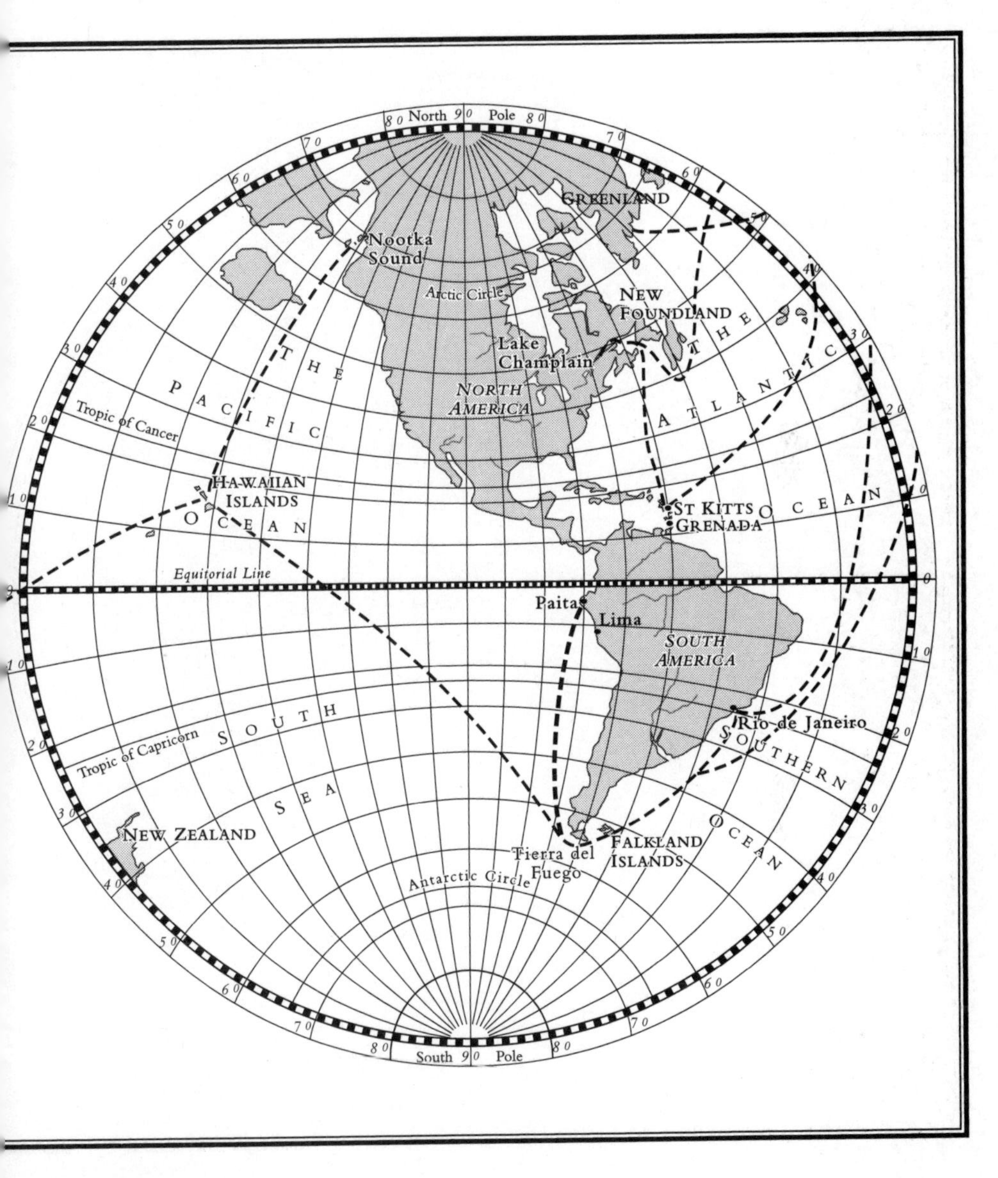

nown it, showing some of his journeys.

Introduction

by Tim Flannery

JOHN NICOL TWICE circled the globe, in the process visiting all six habitable continents. He fought American revolutionaries and Napoleon's navy, was in Hawaii when Cook's murderers were still young, in Port Jackson when Sydney consisted of about a thousand souls, and in the West Indies when African slaves were beginning to experiment with the music which would become blues and jazz. In short, as he roamed the world in the late eighteenth century, he saw the modern age in its infancy.

The world John Nicol records is not one of admirals, governors and high officials, for he was by his own admission a simple 'bungs'—an 'unlettered' cooper. He describes a world seen from below decks; a world peopled by slaves, convicts and Chinese barbers, many of whom Nicol counted among his friends. As such, his story is an extreme rarity. People like Nicol usually lacked the means to have their adventures recorded, and publishers were largely uninterested in such autobiographies. Indeed, a significant fraction of Nicol's compatriots would not even have lived to tell their stories. When he sailed, mortality rates of 15 per cent *per annum* were not looked upon as especially bad, yet Nicol survived twenty-five years at sea.[1]

The story of how this book came into existence is almost as remarkable as the one Nicol himself tells. Picture yourself in a street in Edinburgh with the freezing winter of 1822 just beginning to relax its grip. An old derelict totters feebly along, picking tiny fragments of coal from between the icy cobbles. These he places in the pocket of an old apron tied round his waist. They will be used to light a small fire, over which he will crouch, trying to fight off the chill. As he searches for his coals, the old man is approached by a 'very strange person' and so begins the encounter which, after a long and happenstance history, places this book in your hands today.[2]

The 'very strange person' was John Howell, who was to record and edit Nicol's work. Even in nineteenth-century Scotland Howell was an anomaly. He described himself as a 'polyartist'. Although a bookbinder by trade, he was an inveterate inventor and tinkerer by nature. The most enduring of his contrivances is the 'plough', a device used by bookbinders

1 Simmons, J. J. (III), 'Those Vulgar Tubes', *Studies in Nautical Archaeology* no. 1, Department of Archaeology, Texas University, 1991.

2 Nicol, John, *The Life and Adventures of John Nicol, Mariner, with a foreword and afterword by Alexander Laing*, Cassell & Company, London, 1937, 27.

well into the present century. Alexander Laing, who gave some biographical notes on Howell, remarked of this invention that 'many a careless binder has ruined good books by too exuberant cropping [with it].'[1]

Howell's other inventions included 'a reliable salve for the ringworm' and a method for the fabrication of false teeth. Transport also intrigued him. He invented a flying machine (the testing of which, from the roof of an old tannery, cost him a broken leg), and a sort of prototype submarine. This latter nearly led to fratricide, for John encouraged an unwilling brother to enter the 'large model of a fish' for its test run on the River Leith. The brother refused, however, and John took his place. A contemporary account reports that:

> Scarcely had the fish entered the water when it capsized: the keel turning upwards, and poor John was submerged. Sounds of an alarming kind were heard to issue from the belly of the fish, and no time was lost in dragging it to the bank, when the inventor was liberated from his perilous position; but it took nearly half an hour before 'suspended animation' was fully restored.[2]

Howell's other great interest lay in the exploits of military men and adventurers. He published five books, three of which concerned such people. The first, *Journal of a Soldier of the 71st, or Glasgow Regiment* was followed by *The Life and Adventures of John Nicol, Mariner* and,

1 *Life and Adventures*, 1937, 26.
2 ibid., 28.

finally, *The Life of Alexander Alexander Written by Himself*. Howell's method seems to have consisted of befriending old soldiers and sailors, then spending months writing down or editing their life stories. One wonders whether they moved into his house for the duration. Whatever the case, Howell's motives were noble ones, for he signed over royalties to his adoptees, and endeavoured to use their stories to obtain for them their well deserved pensions.

Howell's 1822 edition of *The Life and Adventures of John Nicol, Mariner* is a modest little book, measuring just sixteen centimetres by ten. Its only illustration is a simple drawing of Nicol himself—in all probability placed there to evoke the reader's pity. It shows the weatherbeaten and wistful countenance of one who has seen much of life. The book's rarity now suggests that the print run was small. Its only republication occurred in 1937 when Cassell issued an edition 'embellished with numerous original designs' by Gordon Grant, and with a foreword and afterword by Laing, who claims that *Life and Adventures* is the earliest reminiscence by an ordinary sailor that 'has any claim to permanence as literature'. The book, he says, 'acquainted me . . . with a distinct personality I should have felt far the poorer for not having known, and from time to time I have sought him out again, in his book, with the same pleasure I should take in looking up an old friend.'

John Nicol had 'seen more of the world than most persons in Edinburgh, perhaps in Britain' according to Howell, yet throughout his life he seems to have remained almost unworldly. This may stem from the fact that, like many seamen, he led a largely sheltered life. While at sea, his domestic and financial arrangements were made for him. Decisions were made by others, and there was little time for romance with all its complications. In these ways, going to sea was akin to joining a religious order.

Nicol was not a sailor of the rum, sodomy and the lash school. When he first went to sea he read his Bible daily and it troubled his conscience that he lost the habit. He was shy, did not drink heavily and was appalled by foul language. At times one wonders how this good and simple man mixed it with the recurrent brutality of life at sea.

Nicol's naivety shows through nowhere more clearly than in his first romance. After meeting a young woman on a coach journey he feels 'something uncommon arise in [his] breast'. After a number of efforts, he 'summonsed the resolution to take her hand in mine; I pressed it gently, she drew faintly back'. With little more encouragement than that, Nicol decides upon marriage and, were it not for a recalcitrant prospective father-in-law, may have succeeded in his designs. He was equally 'at sea' with the most important female in his life, a convict girl named Sarah Whitlam who became his great love. Yet time has shown that his assessment of Sarah Whitlam was hardly an accurate one.

Given the editorial role Howell played, one

wonders how much of *The Life and Adventures of John Nicol, Mariner* represents his input, for the beauty of the language sometimes makes the reader doubt whether it could be the work of an unlettered cooper. Laing speculates that Howell's influence on the book's style and content was minor. He notes that the two works published by Howell alone (*An Essay upon the War Galleys of the Ancients* and *The Life and Adventures of Alexander Selkirk*) 'lack the passages of terse grandeur which lifts Nicol's story, from time to time, to the level of great English prose'.[1] Howell was also a great respecter of facts, and is unlikely to have tampered with the subjects of Nicol's work. Nicol himself says that he will make his story as interesting as is in his power, 'consistent with truth'; its detail is in itself a guide to its authenticity. He remembers, for instance, how Chinese washer women kept a pig in 'a cage-like box fixed to the stern of their sampan.' On the Falkland Islands the geese he saw were 'very pretty, spreckled like a partridge.'

There is something very special about Nicol's prose, with its attention to minute detail, recalled decades after the events occurred. Perhaps this derives from Nicol's style, which is clearly in the great oral storytelling tradition of the sea, owing more to the long tradition of the storytelling bards than to the written prose of his contemporaries. The natural

1 *Life and Adventures*, 1937, 23.

rhythm and pattern of such language is a powerful aid to memory. The stories, told over and over, become ever more refined and compelling. Nicol even draws a picture of himself as raconteur, late in his life, when he takes a boat to London to attempt to gain his pension: 'I was at sea again . . . I had always a crowd round me listening to my accounts of the former voyages that I had made . . . I was very happy.' From such stories has come this vivid and romantic tale of travel to the hidden corners of the world.

A large part of the fascination of Nicol's book lies in his service as steward aboard the *Lady Juliana* transport which, as part of the second fleet, brought over two hundred female convicts to Australia in 1790. The logbook of the *Lady Juliana* is long lost, so Nicol's account is the main source of information for the voyage.[1] His time aboard the *Lady Juliana* (which he recollects as the *Lady Julian*) was formative, for Nicol fell in love with a convict girl named Sarah Whitlam. She was his first real love, and Nicol 'courted her for a week and upwards, and would have married her on the spot had there been a clergyman on board'. She was, he said, 'as kind and true a creature as ever lived'. Before the voyage was out she bore him a son, John.

On the evening of 3 June 1790 the *Lady Juliana*

1 Flynn, Michael, *The Second Fleet: Britain's Grim Convict Armada of 1790*, Library of Australian History, Sydney, 1993, 1–8.

entered Port Jackson after almost a year at sea. Nicol records how the landing was 'almost to our sorrow'. He knew his time with Sarah was running out. But it was a special moment, for that evening John Nicol and Watkin Tench—the great chronicler of the birth of European Australia, who had rowed out to meet the ship amid squalls and cloudbursts—stood together under the one set of sails. For Tench the arrival of the *Lady Juliana* was a moment of exquisite joy. 'News burst upon us like meridian splendour on a blind man,' he records as he learned for the first time of the French Revolution, the madness of George III and the loss of the *Guardian* supply ship. Nicol, characteristically, gives us a glimpse of an intensely human story inside this great historic moment. He doesn't care about revolutions, kings or shipwrecks. His thoughts are all about his imminent separation from his new family.

Nicol spent six weeks in Port Jackson with his beloved Sarah and their infant son. They were, perhaps, the happiest days of his life. Although his recollections of Port Jackson were thirty years old by the time they were written down, they are remarkably accurate. He records, for instance that there were only two 'natives' in the town at that time. They were Abaroo and Nanbaree, survivors of the smallpox epidemic who were then living with Surgeon White (Nanbaree) and the Reverend and Mrs Johnson (Abaroo). He also records some curious attributes of the 'sweet tea' which was drunk with such avidity by the first fleeters. Nicol wrote that 'it is infused and drank like the China tea. I liked it much. It requires no sugar and is both a bitter and a sweet'. He also regarded its medicinal qualities highly:

> There was an old female convict, her hair quite grey with age, her face shrivelled, who was suckling a child she had borne in the colony. Everyone went to see her, and I among the rest. It was a strange sight. Her hair was quite white. Her fecundity was ascribed to the sweet tea.

Tench and others tell us of this woman, but none do so with the descriptive vividness of Nicol. And none ascribe her fecundity to the tea!

As the hour of his departure approached, Nicol became desperate to stay with his wife and child. He was, however, contracted to return to England and the ship was short of hands. He relates that:

> It was not without the aid of the military we were brought on board. I offered to lose my wages but we were short of hands . . . The captain could not spare a man and requested the aid of the governor. I thus was forced to leave Sarah, but we exchanged faith. She promised to remain true.

Nicol spent the next few years trying to return to Port Jackson, but without success. While thus engaged, he heard from a runaway convict that Sarah had left the colony for Bombay. Nicol did not know what to make of this information, and nor do I. Sarah did not sail for Bombay until 1796, yet Nicol claims to have heard of it in 1791-92.[1] Was Sarah sending out misinformation, or had Nicol misremembered? Given his subsequent sailing schedule, the latter seems unlikely, for after 1794 Nicol was fighting in the French Revolutionary wars. Nicol visited Sarah's parents in Lincoln, but they could tell him nothing. Hoping for the best yet fearing betrayal, he tried to get a passage to Bombay, but could not find a berth, even as a paying passenger. In all his subsequent journeying, the possibility of being reunited with Sarah is continually on his mind. 'She was,' he says, 'still the idol of all my affections.'

In 1801 Nicol returned to his native Edinburgh, being 'too old to undertake any more love pilgrimages after an individual, as I knew not in what quarter of the globe she was, or whether she were dead or alive'. But what of Sarah and her son? The children of convicts were often removed from their parents, and little John's fate is not recorded. Sarah, in contrast, first appears in the records of the colony the day after Nicol's tearful departure, but the telling of that story must await its proper place.

Nicol's Australian interlude occupied a fraction of his twenty-five years at sea. Much of what he records elsewhere is of great interest to the contemporary reader, for he recalls events and cultures which were glossed over by his better educated and better

1 *The Second Fleet*, 461.

connected contemporaries. The importance of Nicol's work is magnified by the fact that he was far above the ordinary in his humanity, memory and wit. He also loved a song, and nowhere does this shine through more clearly than during his visit to Jamaica, where he lived for some time among slaves. He says of these poor people, 'I esteemed them in my heart' and they clearly reciprocated.

Nicol records that during his stay, he and the other crew were fed on a 'cut and come again' basis, and he always ensured that he took a little something extra to give to the plantation slaves. They in return invited him to a dance. Nicol was touched to find that these poorest of the poor had purchased some 'three bit maubi' as they called rum. They did not drink this luxury themselves, but bought it on his account, having heard that sailors prefer it. The vibrancy of the songs he heard that night shone on undimmed in Nicol's memory for over three decades:

I lost my shoe in an old canoe
Johnio, come Winum so;
I lost my boot in a pilot boat,
Johnio, come Winum so

and

My Massa a bad man,
My Missis cry honey,
Is this the damn nigger
You buy wi my money?
Ting a ring ting, ting a ring ting, tarro

The cruel treatment of the slaves clearly appalled Nicol. He records the beating of a pregnant woman and the part he and a colleague played in terminating it. He talks of a one-legged runaway blacksmith chained to his bench, and a slave forced to wear a barbarous collar of spikes. His anger at these outrages remained, like the songs, unblunted by the years.

Nicol's next voyage was more carefree. His journey in search of discovery and trade aboard the *King George* was to take him to Hawaii just after the murder of James Cook. Indeed, the *King George* was the first ship to arrive in the islands after Cook's discovery of them. Nicol records that:

> Almost every man on board took a native woman for a wife while the vessel remained ... The fattest woman I ever saw in my life our gunner chose for a wife. We were forced to hoist her on board. Her thighs were as thick as my waist. No hammock in the ship would hold her. Many jokes were cracked upon the pair.

He also records the wonderful facility of the Hawaiians to parody the Europeans:

> We had a merry facetious fellow on board called Dickson. He sung pretty well. He squinted and the natives mimicked him. Abenoue, King of Atooi, could cock his eye like Dickson better than any of his subjects. Abenoue called him Billicany, from his often singing 'Rule Britannia' . . . Abenoue loved him better than any man in the ship, and always

> embraced him every time they met on shore or in the ship, and began to sing, 'Tule Billicany, Billicany tule,' etc.

Then comes Nootka Sound, the Marianas, and finally back to Nicol's beloved Wampoa in China, which he visited three times. How can we believe that Nicol was befriended there by a Chinaman named Tommy Linn, a barber-surgeon who contracted to shave the entire crew of Nicol's ship during the duration of their stay? Nicol was really at home among the Chinese, and he was accepted into their bosom when he saved a child from drowning.

> The current was strong and the boy was carried down with rapidity. I leapt into the river and saved him with great difficulty . . . and soon had the pleasure of delivering him to his father who stood on the beach wringing his hands.
>
> I wished to go on board, but the Chinese would have me to his house where I was most kindly received and got my dinner in great style. I like their manner of setting out the table at dinner. All that is to be eaten is placed upon the table at once, and all the liquors at the same time. You have all before you and you may make your choice.

He also records, in a delightful manner, some examples of the lingua franca used between Chinese and European traders. Here were the antecedents of the diverse modern pidgins of Oceania, some of which are now the national languages of Pacific nations:

> Tommy Linn the barber . . . was a walking newspaper. His first word every morning was, 'Hey, yaw, what fashion?' and we used the same phrase to him. One morning he came, and the first thing he said was, 'Hey, yaw, what fashion? Soldier man's ship come to Lingcome bar.' We, after a few hours, heard that a man-of-war frigate had arrived . . .
>
> They are much alarmed at the appearance of a man-of-war ship, and they often say, 'Englishman too much cruel, too much fight.' There were some English seamen flogged for mutiny while we lay in the river. The Chinese wept like children for the men, saying, 'Hey, yaw, Englishman too much cruel, too much flog, too much flog.'

Nicol's final service was aboard a series of ships fighting in the French Revolutionary Wars. Nicol's ship the *Goliah* participated in the Battle of the Nile, one of Nelson's three great victories, and one of the most celebrated naval victories of all time. What is surprising is the presence of women and the role they played in the battle. Nicol writes:

> The women behaved as well as the men, and got a present for their bravery from the grand signior . . . I was much indebted to the gunner's wife who gave her husband and me a drink of wine every now and then which lessened our fatigue much. There were some of the women wounded, and one woman belonging to Leith died of her wounds and was buried on a small island in the

> bay. One woman bore a son in the heat of the action.

What a birth that must have been! After the guns ceased their booming, Nicol records what 'an awful sight it was. The whole bay was covered with dead bodies, mangled, wounded and scorched'. This carnage had been caused when the French war ship *L'Orient* blew up close to Nicol's *Goliath*. Such an event was rare in the naval warfare of the day.

At the termination of his service Nicol returned to Edinburgh, where he married his cousin Margaret. It was probably a match based more on affection and convenience than love. He had saved a relatively large sum (which was apparently kept sewn in his clothes) from his decades at sea, and this enabled him to set up a prosperous cooperage business. He also purchased a small cottage and for a time enjoyed married life. But then war (the Napoleonic Wars) broke out again, and the press gangs began their ghastly rounds. These gangs were sanctioned to kidnap and sell into forced labour any sailor they could find.

It is hard for us, in our egalitarian age, to understand just what a threat the press gangs represented to someone such as Nicol. The most vivid description of their rapacity comes from Admiral Anson's *Voyage Around the World*.[1] Although it was written sixty years

1 Walter, R., *A Voyage Round the World in the Years 1740, 1, 2, 3, 4 by George Anson, Esq.*, Alex Lawrie & Co., Edinburgh, 1741, 1804, 20.

earlier, little had changed by Nicol's time. The various efforts made to obtain marines for Anson all failed until:

> five hundred invalids [were] to be collected from the out pensioners of Chelsea college ... who, from their age, wounds, or other infirmities, are incapable of service in marching regiments ... But instead of five hundred, there came on board no more than two hundred and fifty nine; for all those who had limbs and strength to walk out of Portsmouth, deserted, leaving behind them only such as were literally invalids, most of them being sixty years of age, and some of them upwards of seventy.

This 'aged and diseased detachment' was destined to undertake a five-year-long voyage around the world, which was almost unequalled in its arduousness. They dropped like flies. The wounds some had received over fifty years before broke open afresh due to the scurvy. Few survived to see action, much less their homeland.

And so we find John Nicol, newly married at the age of forty-six, unable to sleep in his own bed for fear of being pressed. For eleven years he was forced to live the life of a fugitive in rural Scotland. Yet he remained loyal to king and country, and upon hearing the news of the victory at Trafalgar recalled:

> None but an old tar can feel the joy I felt. I wrought none the next day but walked about enjoying the feeling of triumph. Every now and then I felt the greatest desire to hurra aloud, and many an hurra my heart gave that my mouth uttered not.

To 'hurra' of course, would have alerted the press gangs to his being 'an old tar'.

Finally, at the age of fifty-eight, Nicol felt that it was safe to return home. His homecoming was a joyous one. Perhaps the excitement was too much for Margaret, his wife, for she did not long outlive it. Her death brought on another trial, for Nicol discovered that for years there had been 'more money going out than I by my industry could bring in . . . and a number of debits . . . had been contracted unknown to me'.

Nicol travelled to London in search of the pension he desperately needed and richly deserved. His fate in this endeavour would be familiar to anyone who has been shunted from one part of the bureaucracy to another. First he learned that his old friend Captain Portlock, who could have provided a testimonial of his service, had died six weeks earlier. He then went to Somerset House to gain a certificate of service. A clerk there sent him to Admiralty House where another clerk told him he had waited too long before applying. As a last ditch effort to gain the all-important certificate he went to see the governor of Greenwich Hospital, but he was on holiday in Scotland. Broke, Nicol returned to Edinburgh.

And so, in the early spring of 1822, at the age of sixty-seven, this fine old sailor was forced to walk the streets of his city, seeking fragments of coal to prevent himself from dying of cold. Had he not met John Howell he would have died in anonymity.

It is heartwarming to know that Howell's charity

really did make a difference to Nicol, for unlike so many of his fellows, he 'died like an admiral, in bed, having evenly rounded out his threescore years and ten'.[1] His funds were not exhausted even then, for a sum of 30 pounds was left to his relatives.

As great as Howell's gift was to Nicol, he left the world a far greater one, for Nicol's recollections offer a unique glimpse of an extraordinary world as it was seen through the eyes of a simple yet most acute watcher upon life. Nicol's tale still has the power to inspire us to adventure, and surely his prayers still go with those who love travel:

> Old as I am, my heart is still unchanged; and were I young and stout as I have been, again would I sail upon discovery—but, weak and stiff, I can only send my prayers with the tight ship and her merry hearts.

*

I have used the text of the original edition of *The Life and Adventures of John Nicol, Mariner*, published by William Blackwood in Edinburgh in 1822. I have modernised Nicol's spelling and punctuation, corrected the occasional error and added some footnotes, marked by an asterisk (*). Nicol's own notes are marked by a dagger (†).

1 *Life and Adventures*, 1937, 25.

A Most Interesting Character

by John Howell

EARLY IN THE spring of the year 1822 John Nicol, the narrator of these adventures, was pointed out to me as a most interesting character, and one who had seen more of the world than most persons in Edinburgh, perhaps in Britain.

He was walking feebly along with an old apron tied round his waist, in which he carried a few very small pieces of coal he had picked up in his wanderings through the streets. From the history I had got of his adventures, I felt grieved to see the poor old man. I requested him to call at my shop. He came in the evening. After a little conversation with him I was astonished at the information he possessed, and the spirit that awoke in the old tar.

I had no interest by which to serve myself. Money I had not to give. As the only means of being of permanent use to him, and perhaps of obtaining the pension he is by service entitled to, I thought of taking down a narrative of his life, from his own mouth. This

I have done, as nearly as I could, in his own words.

Even in the midst of all his present wants, he is a contented cheerful old man of sober habits, and bears an excellent character from those people who have employed him in his trade as a cooper. I have conversed with one of his shipmates who was with him in the *Edgar*, *Goliah* and *Ramilies*, who informs me he was as sober and steady a man as ever sailed.

I have never met with one possessed of a more tenacious memory or who gave a more distinct account of any occurrence he had witnessed, of which any gentleman may satisfy himself, as John will wait upon him with pleasure, upon application to the Publisher.

Edinburgh
12th November 1822

1

Author's Birth—Early Propensities—He Goes to London—Is Apprenticed to a Cooper—Enters the Navy—Smugglers—Arrives at Quebec.

Preface

TO THE PUBLIC it must appear strange that an unlettered individual, at the advanced age of sixty-seven years, should sit down to give them a narrative of his life. Imperious circumstances must plead my excuse. Necessity, even more than the importunity of well-wishers, at length compels me. I shall use my humble endeavour to make it as interesting as is in my power, consistent with truth.

My life, for a period of twenty-five years, was a continued succession of change. Twice I circumnavigated the globe; three times I was in China, twice in Egypt, and more than once sailed along the whole landboard of America from Nootka Sound to Cape Horn. Twice I doubled it—but I will not anticipate the events I am about to narrate.

Old as I am, my heart is still unchanged; and were I young and stout as I have been, again would I sail upon discovery—but, weak and stiff, I can only send my prayers with the tight ship and her merry hearts.

John Nicol

I WAS BORN in the small village of Currie, about six miles from Edinburgh, in the year 1755. The first wish I ever formed was to wander, and many a search I gave my parents in gratifying my youthful passion.

My mother died in child-bed when I was very young, leaving my father in charge of five children. Two died young and three came to man's estate. My oldest brother died of his wounds in the West Indies, a lieutenant in the navy. My younger brother went to America and I have never heard from him. Those trifling circumstances I would not mention, were I not conscious that the history of the dispersion of my father's family is the parallel of thousands of the families of my father's rank in Scotland.

My father, a cooper to trade, was a man of talent and information, and made it his study to give his children an education suited to their rank in life; but my unsteady propensities did not allow me to make the most of the schooling I got. I had read *Robinson Crusoe* many times over and longed to be at sea. We had been living for some time in Borrowstownness. Every moment I could spare was spent in the boats or about the shore.

When I was about fourteen years of age my father was engaged to go to London to take a small charge in a chemical work. Even now I recollect the transports my young mind felt when my father informed me I was to go to London. I counted the hours and minutes to the moment we sailed on board the

Glasgow and Paisley Packet, Captain Thompson master. There were a sergeant and a number of recruits, a female passenger, my father, brother and self, besides the crew. It was in the month of December we sailed, and the weather was very bad. All the passengers were seasick; I never was.

This was in the year 1769, when the dreadful loss was sustained on the coast of Yorkshire—above thirty sail of merchantmen were wrecked. We were taken in the same gale but rode it out. Next morning we could hardly proceed for wreck, and the whole beach was covered. The country people were collecting and driving away the dead bodies in wagons.

My father embraced this opportunity to prejudice me against being a sailor. He was a kind but strict parent and we dared not disobey him. The storm had made no impression upon my mind sufficient to alter my determination. My youthful mind could not separate the life of a sailor from dangers and storms, and I looked upon them as an interesting part of the adventures I panted after. I had been on deck all the time and was fully occupied in planning the means of escape. I enjoyed the voyage much, was anxious to learn everything, and was a great favourite with the captain and crew.

One of my father's masters was translating a French work on chemistry. I went to the printing office with the proofs almost every day. Once, in passing near the Tower, I saw a dead monkey floating in the river. I had not seen above two or three in my life. I thought it of great value.

I stripped at once and swam in for it. An English boy, who wished it likewise but who either would or could not swim, seized it when I landed, saying 'he would fight me for it'. We were much of a size. Had there been a greater difference, I was not of a temper to be easily wronged—so I gave him battle. A crowd gathered and formed a ring. Stranger as I was, I got fair play. After a severe contest, I came off victor. The English boy shook hands, and said, 'Scotchman, you have won it.'

I had fought naked as I came out of the water, so I put on my clothes and carried off the prize in triumph—came home and got a beating from my father for fighting and staying my message; but the monkey's skin repaid me for all my vexations.

I remained in London scarcely twelve months when my father sent me to Scotland to learn my trade. I chose the profession of a cooper to please my father. I was for some time with a friend at the Queensferry but, not agreeing with him, I served out my tedious term of apprenticeship at Borrowstownness. My heart was never with the business. While my hands were hooping barrels my mind was at sea and my imagination in foreign climes.

Soon as my period of bondage expired I bade my friends farewell and set out to Leith with a merry heart; and, after working journeyman a few months, to enable me to be a proficient in my trade, I entered on board the *Kent's Regard*, commanded by Lieutenant Ralph Dundas. She was the tender at this time (1776) stationed in Leith Roads.

Now I was happy, for I was at sea. To me the order to weigh anchor and sail for the Nore was the sound of joy.* My spirits were up at the near prospect of obtaining the pleasures I had sighed for since the first dawn of reason. To others it was the sound of woe, the order that cut off the last faint hope of escape from a fate they had been impressed into much against their inclination and interest. I was surprised to see so few who, like myself, had chosen it for the love of that line of life. Some had been forced into it by their own irregular conduct but the greater number were impressed men.**

Ogilvie's revenue cutter and the *Hazard* sloop of war had a short time before surprised a smuggling cutter delivering her cargo in St Andrew's Bay. The smuggler fought them both until all her ammunition was spent, and resisted their boarding her until the very last by every means in their power. A good many of the king's men were wounded, and not a few of the smugglers. When taken possession of they declared the captain had been killed in the action and thrown overboard. The remainder were marched to Edinburgh Castle and kept there until the evening before

* The Nore: a lighthouse near Hastings on the south-east coast of England.

** These were men who had been kidnapped by press gangs and forced into naval service.

we sailed. When they came on board we were all struck with their stout appearance and desperate looks; a set of more resolute fellows I have never in my life met with. They were all sent down to the press-room. The volunteers were allowed to walk the decks and had the freedom of the ship.

One night, on our voyage to the Nore, the whole ship was alarmed by loud cries of murder from the press-room. An armed force was sent down to know the cause and quell the riot. They arrived just in time to rescue, with barely the life, from the hands of these desperadoes, a luckless wretch who had been an informer for a long time in Leith. A good many in the press-room were indebted to him for their present situation.

The smugglers had learned from them what he was and with one accord had fallen upon him and beat him in a dreadful manner. When he was brought to the surgeon's berth there were a number of severe cuts upon his person. From his disgraceful occupation of informer, few on board pitied him. After a few days he got better and was able to walk, but was no more sent down to the press-room.

Upon our arrival at the Nore, a writ of *habeas corpus* was sent on board for one of the smugglers for a debt. We all suspected him to have been the captain, and this a scheme to get him off from being kept on board of a man of war.

I was sent on board the *Proteus*, twenty-gun ship, commanded by Captain Robinson, bound for New

York.* The greater number of the smugglers were put on board the same vessel. They were so stout, active, and experienced seamen that Captain Robinson manned his barge with them.

We sailed from Portsmouth with ordnance stores and 100 men to man the floating batteries upon Lake Champlain.**

I was appointed cooper, which was a great relief to my mind, as I messed with the steward in his room. I was thus away from the crew. I had been much annoyed and rendered very uncomfortable, until now, from the swearing and loose talking of the men in the tender. I had all my life been used to the strictest conversation, prayers night and morning. Now I was in a situation where family worship was unknown and, to add to the disagreeable situation I was in, the troops were unhealthy. We threw overboard every morning a soldier or a sheep.

At first I said my prayers and read my Bible in private, but truth makes me confess I gradually became more and more remiss, and before long I was a sailor like the rest; but my mind felt very uneasy and I made many weak attempts to amend.

We sailed with our convoy direct for Quebec. Upon our arrival the men, having been so long on salt provisions, made too free with the river water and

* The American War of Independence had begun.

** Lake Champlain: American Lake bordering New York and Vermont.

were almost all seized with the flux.* The *Proteus* was upon this account laid up for six weeks, during which time the men were in the hospital. After having done the ship's work, Captain Robinson was so kind as allow me to work on shore, where I found employment from a Frenchman who gave me excellent encouragement. I worked on shore all day and slept on board at night.

* The flux: dysentry.

2

Canada—Mode of Fishing—Serpents—Floats of Wood—Author Sails to the West Indies—Slavery—Arrives at Newfoundland.

CANADA IS A fine country. Provisions abound in it and the inhabitants are kind and humane. Salmon abound in the St Lawrence. The Indians come alongside every day with them, either smoked or fresh, which they exchange for biscuit or pork. They take them in wicker baskets wrought upon stakes stuck into the sand within the tide mark. The baskets have two entrances, one pointing up the river, the other pointing down. The entrances have no doors, but sharp-pointed wands prevent the exit of the fish or their returning: if once the head is entered the whole body must follow. They resemble in this the wire mouse trap used in Britain. Some have shutting doors, as in Scotland, that swing with the tide. When it is back, the Indians examine their baskets, and seldom find them without more or less fish.

The French eat many kinds of the serpents that abound in the country. Whether they are good eating I do not know, as I never could bring myself to taste them. They must be good, as it is not for want of other varieties they are made choice of. I often went of an evening with my master to catch them. We caught them with forked sticks; the Frenchman was very dexterous and I soon learned. We often caught two dozen in an evening. When we perceived one we ran the forks of the stick upon its neck, behind the head, and, holding it up from the ground, beat it upon the head with the other until we dispatched it. When we came home the heads were cut off and the snakes skinned. Their skins were very beautiful and many of the officers got scabbards made of them for their swords.

I was much surprised at the immense floats of wood that came gliding majestically down the river like floating islands. They were covered with turf, and wood huts upon them, smoke curling from the roofs, and children playing before the doors and the stately matron on her seat, sewing or following her domestic occupations, while the husband sat upon the front with his long pole, guiding it along the banks or from any danger in the river, and their batteau astern to carry them home with the necessaries they procured by the sale of their wood, the produce of their severe winter's labour.*

They had floated thus down the majestic St Lawrence hundreds of miles. It looked like magic and reminded me of the fairies I had often heard of, to see the children sporting and singing in chorus upon these floating masses, the distance diminishing the size of their figures and softening the melody of their voices, while their hardy enterprise astonished the mind upon reflection, and the idea of their enjoyment was dashed at the recollection of their hardships. They really are a cheerful race.

I can think of no pleasure more touching to the feelings and soothing to the mind than to lie upon the green banks and listen to the melodious voices of the

* Batteau: a light, flat-bottomed river boat used widely in Canada.

women of a summer evening as they row along in their batteaux, keeping time to the stroke of the oar. For hours I have lain over the breast-netting, looking and listening to them, unconscious of the lapse of time.

The time I had passed since my entrance into the St Lawrence was very pleasant. In our passage up we had run at an amazing rate—the trees and every object seemed to glide from us with the rapidity of lightning, the wind being fresh and direct. We passed the island of Antecost at a short distance and anchored at the island of Beak where the pilots live. It had an old sergeant, at the time, for governor, Ross his name, who had been with Wolfe at the taking of Quebec.

We then stood up the river, wind and tide serving, and passed next the island of Conder. It appeared a perfect garden. Then the Falls of Morant, the mist rising to the clouds. They appeared to fall from a greater height than the vane of our topmast, and made a dreadful roaring. We last of all made the island of Orleans, a most beautiful place. It is quite near the town and is, like the island of Conder, a perfect garden from end to end.

At length our men were all recovered and the stores landed. I bade farewell to my French master and friends on shore, and sailed for Gaspé Bay. We were joined here by the *Assistance*, fifty-gun ship, commanded by Captain Worth.

All the crew got a handsome treat from Governor O'Hara at the baptism of his family. They were beautiful children, five in number, the oldest a stately girl. None of them had yet been baptised, and the governor embraced the opportunity of the chaplain of the *Assistance* to have this necessary Christian rite performed, as there was not a clergyman at the station and the children had all been born in the Bay. The contrast between the situation of these children and their parents, and the people in Scotland, at the time, made a deep impression upon my mind; and I can say, at no period of my life had the privileges I had left behind appeared so valuable.

From Gaspe Bay we sailed with convoy for the West Indies. The convoy was loaded with salt fish. The American privateers swarmed around like sharks, watching an opportunity to seize any slow-sailing vessel. We took a few of them and brought the convoy safe to its destination.

While watering at St Kitt's we got free of the smugglers. The manner of their escape is the best comment upon their character. Captain Robinson went ashore in his barge. The crew, as I said before, was composed of them, coxswain and all. Soon after the captain left the water's edge they took to their heels. One of them became faint-hearted after he was away and returned. The others, that very night, while search was making for them, seized a boat belonging to the island and rowed over to St Eustatia, a Dutch neutral island, boarded, overpowered and carried off an American brig, and sold her at one of the French islands. None of them were ever taken that I heard of. The one that returned never again held up his head, as he was looked down upon by the crew.

While we lay at any of the West Indian islands our decks used to be crowded by the female slaves, who brought us fruit and remained on board all Sunday until Monday morning—poor things! And all to obtain a bellyful of victuals. On Monday morning the Jolly Jumper, as we called him, was on board with his whip; and, if all were not gone, did not spare it upon their backs.

One cruel rascal was flogging one on our deck, who was not very well in her health. He had struck her once as if she had been a post. The poor creature gave a shriek. Some of our men, I knew not which—there were a good many near him—knocked him overboard. He sunk like a stone. The men gave a hurra! One of the female slaves leaped from the boat alongside into the water and saved the tyrant, who, I have no doubt, often enough beat her cruelly.

I was one of the boarders. We were all armed, when required, with a pike to defend our own vessel should the enemy attempt to board; a tomahawk, cutlass and brace of pistols to use in boarding them. I never had occasion to try their use on board the *Proteus*, as the privateers used to strike after a broadside or two.

While we lay at St Kitt's I took the country fever and was carried to the hospital, where I lay for some days; but my youth, and the kindness of my black nurse, triumphed over the terrible malady. When able to crawl about the hospital, where many came in sick the one day and were carried out the next to be buried, the thoughts of the neglect of my Maker, and the difference in the life I had for some time led from the manner in which I had been trained up in my youth, made me shudder. With tears I promised myself to reform.

I could now see the land-crabs running through the graves of two or three whom I had left stout and full of health. In the West Indies the grave is dug no deeper than just to hold the body, the earth covering it only a few inches, and all is soon consumed by the land-crabs. The black fellows eat them. When I asked them why they eat these loathsome creatures their answer was, 'Why, they eat me.'

I returned on board free from the fever, but very weak. Soon after we took convoy for England, then sailed into Portsmouth harbour and were docked and repaired. While my weakness lasted, my serious impressions remained, but I must again confess: as I became strong in my body, the impressions upon my mind became weak.

As soon as the *Proteus* was repaired we took convoy for St John's, Newfoundland. On this voyage we had very severe weather. Our foremast was carried away and we arrived off St John's in a shattered state, weary and spent with fatigue. To add to our misfortunes we were three weeks lying before the harbour, and could not make it, on account of an island of ice that blocked up its mouth. During these three tedious weeks we never saw the sun or sky, the fogs were so dense. Had it not been for the incessant blowing of the fishermen's horns to warn each other, and prevent their being run down, we might as well have been in the middle of the ocean in a winter night. The bows of the *Proteus* could not be seen from her quarter-deck. We received supplies and intelligence from the harbour by the fishermen. At length this tedious fog cleared up, and we entered the harbour. The *Proteus*, having been an old East Indiaman, was now quite unfit for service; and the admiral caused her be made a prison-ship.

After this I was wholly employed on shore, brewing spruce for the fleet.* I had two and often three men under me to cut the spruce and firewood for my use. I was a man of some consequence even with the inhabitants, as I could make a present of a bottle of essence to them. They made presents of rum to me. I thus lived very happy, and on good terms with them.

Nothing surprised me more than the early marriage of the Newfoundland females. They have children at twelve years of age. I had some dealings with a merchant, and dined two or three times at his house. I inquired at him for his daughter, a pretty young woman whom I saw at table the first time. To my astonishment he told me she was his wife and the mother of three fine children.

* Spruce: a kind of beer made from spruce (*Picea*) and sugar, and slightly fermented.

In the winter, the cold on the Barrens, as the inhabitants call them, is dreadful. The Barrens are the spaces where there is no wood. Over these we must use our utmost speed to reach the woods. When once there, we are in comparative comfort; it is even warm among the trees. The thoughts of the Barrens again to be crossed is the only damp to our present enjoyment, as we are soon in a sweat from the exercise in cutting the wood.

When the snow first sets in it is necessary to remain at home until the weather clears up. Then the men put on their snow shoes, and three or four abreast thus make a path to the woods. In the middle of the day the sun hardens the path, and along these the wood is dragged upon sledges to the town by dogs. A person, not knowing the cause, would smile to see us urging on our dogs, ourselves pulling with one hand and rubbing our ears with the other. I am certain it would be a cure for tardiness of any kind to be forced to cross the Barrens in winter.

Numbers of the fishermen, who have gambled away their hard-won summer's wages, are forced thus to earn their winter's maintenance. At this time the greater part of the fishers were Irishmen, the wildest characters man can conceive. Gambling and every vice was familiar to them. Their quarrelling and fighting never ceased, and even murders were sometimes perpetrated upon each other. St Patrick's day is a scene of riot and debauchery unequalled in any town in Ireland.

I saw them myself march in line past an unfortunate man who had been killed in one of their feuds, and each man that passed him gave the inanimate body a blow, at the same time calling him by a term of abuse, significant of the party he had belonged to. It was unsafe to carry anything after nightfall. I have been attacked and forced to fight my way more than once. The respectable inhabitants are thus kept under a sort of bondage to this riotous race.

In the summer I was much annoyed by the mosquitos and yellow nippers, a worse fly; for they bite cruelly. They make such a buzzing and noise at night I could not close an eye without my mosquito dose, that is, rum and spruce.

3

Action between the Surprise *and* Jason*—Anecdotes—Miscellaneous Occurrences—Punishment for Neglect of Orders—Author Paid Off.*

I HAD NOW been eighteen months on shore when I was ordered by Admiral Montague on board the *Surprise*, twenty-eight-gun frigate, commanded by Captain Reeves. Her cooper had been killed a few days before in a severe action with an American vessel.

On board the *Surprise* we had a rougher crew than in the *Proteus*; ninety of them were Irishmen, the rest from Scotland and England. We kept cruising about, taking numbers of the America privateers. After a short but severe action we took the *Jason* of Boston, commanded by the famous Captain Manly, who had been commodore in the American service, had been taken prisoner and broke his parole. When Captain Reeves hailed and ordered him to strike, he returned for answer, 'Fire away! I have as many guns as you.' He had heavier metal but fewer men than the *Surprise*. He fought us for a long time.

I was serving powder as busy as I could, the shot and splinters flying in all directions, when I heard the Irishmen call from one of the guns (they fought like devils, and the captain was fond of them on that account), 'Halloo, Bungs, where are you?'*

I looked to their gun and saw the two horns of my study† across its mouth. The next moment it was through the *Jason's* side. The rogues thus disposed of my study, which I had been using just before the

* Bungs: slang name for a cooper.
† anvil.

action commenced and had placed in a secure place, as I thought, out of their reach. 'Bungs for ever!' they shouted when they saw the dreadful hole it made in the *Jason's* side. Bungs was the name they always gave the cooper.

When Captain Manly came on board the *Surprise* to deliver his sword to Captain Reeves, the half of the rim of his hat was shot off. Our captain returned his sword to him again, saying, 'You have had a narrow escape, Manly.'

'I wish to God it had been my head,' he replied.

When we boarded the *Jason*, we found thirty-one cavalry, who had served under General Burgoyne, acting now as marines on board the *Jason*.

A marine of the name of Kennedy, belonging to the *Surprise*, an intelligent lad and well-behaved, was a great favourite with the surgeon. They used to be constantly together reading and acquiring information. They came from the same place, had been at school together and were dear friends. Kennedy's relations were in a respectable line of life. I never learned the cause of his filling his present lowly situation. As it fell out, poor Kennedy was placed sentinel over the spirit-room of the *Jason*. He was, as I have said, an easy kind of lad and had not been long from home.

He allowed the men to carry away the spirits and they were getting fast drunk when the prize-master perceived it. Kennedy was relieved and sent on board the *Surprise*, and next morning put in irons on board the *Europa*, the admiral's ship, where he was tried by a court-martial and sentenced to be hanged on the fore-yardarm.

His offence, no doubt, was great, for the men would all have been so much the worse of liquor in a short time that the Americans could have recovered the *Jason* with ease. Yet we were all sorry for him, and would have done anything in our power to redeem him from his present melancholy situation. His friend the surgeon was inconsolable and did everything in his power. He drew up a petition to the admiral for pardon, stating his former good behaviour, his youth and good connections, and everything he could think of in his favour—but all would not do.

He was taken to the place of execution, the rope round his neck. The match was lit, the clergyman at his post. We were all aloft and upon deck to see him run up to the yardarm amidst the smoke of the gun, the signal of death.

When everyone looked for the command to fire, the admiral was pleased to pardon him. He was sent on board the *Surprise* more like a corpse than a living man. He could scarce walk and seemed indifferent to everything on board, as if he knew not whether he was dead or alive. He continued thus for a long time, scarce speaking to anyone. He was free and did no duty, and was the same on board as a passenger.

When the *Surprise* was in port Captain Reeves allowed a degree of licence to his men, but was a strict disciplinarian at sea, punishing the smallest fault. As we lay in the harbour after the capture of Captain Manly we got some prize money, and the crew were very merry. I, as cooper, was down in the steward's berth. (It was my duty as cooper to serve out the water and provisions at the regular times.) All my duty at the time was over and I was in my berth along with the steward, enjoying ourselves, when a noise and tumult on board roused us.

We were not touched with liquor; drunkenness was a vice I never was addicted to. We came upon deck. The crew were all fighting through amongst each other in their drink, English against Irish, the officers mostly on shore, and those on board looking on. I meant to take no share in the quarrel, when an Irishman came staggering up, crying, 'Erin go bragh!' and made a blow at me.

My Scottish blood rose in a moment at this provocation and I was as throng as the rest. How it ended I hardly recollect. I got a blow that stupefied me, and all was quiet when I came to myself, the liquor having evaporated from the others, and the passion from me.

Soon after this we hailed an American privateer commanded by a Captain Revel, and she struck. He was a different character from the gallant Manly. The weather was so foul and the sea ran so high, we could not send our boat on board, neither could theirs come on board of us. Captain Reeves ordered her under our quarter. As he sailed alongside, the weather still very stormy and night coming on, we were hailed by voices calling to us, scarcely to be distinguished in the rattling of our rigging and the howling of the blast. At length we made out with difficulty, that the American captain was going to make some prisoners he had walk overboard.

Captain Reeves, in great anger, ordered the privateer to place a light on her maintop—instead of which he placed one on a float and cast it adrift. The voices again hailed and let us know what had been done. Captain Reeves called to the American that he would sink her in a moment if he did not do as desired and come close under our lee. Towards morning the weather moderated, and we brought Revel and his prisoners on board the *Surprise*. He was a coarse, ill-looking fellow. His treatment of the prisoners made his own treatment the worse: while Manly dined every day at the captain's table, Revel messed by himself or where he chose with the prisoners.

We took convoy for Lisbon, thence to England where we brought Manly and Revel to be detained during the war in Mill Prison. Revel made his escape from the sergeant of marines on his way to the prison, for which the sergeant was tried by a court-martial and sentenced to be hanged, but was afterwards pardoned. It was nothing uncommon for us to take the same men prisoners once or twice in the same season.

We again took convoy for St John's. In the fleet was a vessel called the *Ark* commanded by Captain Noah. She was an armed transport. This we called *Noah's Ark*. In our voyage out an American privateer, equal in weight of metal but having forty-five men (the *Ark* only sixteen), bore down upon her. The gallant Noah, in his *Ark*, gave battle, we looking on, and after a sharp contest took the American and brought her alongside, her captain lying dead upon her deck. Captain Reeves, with consent of the crew, gave the prize to Noah, who carried her in triumph to Halifax and sold her.

One of our men was whipped through the fleet for stealing some dollars from a merchant ship he was assisting to bring into port. It was a dreadful sight: the unfortunate sufferer tied down on the boat and rowed from ship to ship, getting an equal number of lashes at the side of each vessel from a fresh man. The poor wretch, to deaden his sufferings, had drunk a whole bottle of rum a little before the time of punishment. When he had only two portions to get of his punishment, the captain of the ship perceived he was tipsy and immediately ordered the rest of the punishment to be delayed until he was sober. He was rowed back to the *Surprise*, his back swelled like a pillow, black and blue. Some sheets of thick blue paper were steeped in vinegar and laid to his back. Before he seemed insensible. Now his shrieks rent the air. When better he was sent to the ship, where his tortures were stopped and again renewed.

During the remainder of the war, our duty was the same, taking convoy and capturing American privateers. We came to England with convoy and were docked, then had a cruise in the Channel where we took the *Duke de Chartres*, eighteen-gun ship, and were ourselves chased into Monts Bay on the coast of Cornwall by a French sixty-four. We ran close inshore and were covered by the old fort which, I believe, had not fired a ball since before the time of Oliver Cromwell—but it did its duty nobly, all night the Frenchman keeping up his fire, the fort and *Surprise* returning it. When day dawned he sheered off, and we only suffered a little in our rigging. The only blood that was shed on our side was an old fogie of the fort who was shot by his own gun.

Quite weary of the monotonous convoy duty and having seen all I could see, I often sighed for the verdant banks of the Forth. At length my wishes were gratified by the return of peace. The *Surprise* was paid off in the month of March 1783. When Captain Reeves came ashore, he completely loaded the long-boat with flags he had taken from the enemy. When one of the officers inquired what he would do with them, he said, laughing, 'I will hang one upon every tree in my father's garden.'

4

Author Arrives in Scotland—Singular Adventure—He Returns to London—Enters a Greenland Ship—Whale Fishery.

I NO SOONER had the money that was due me in my hat than I set off for London direct and, after a few days of enjoyment, put my bedding and chest on board a vessel bound for Leith. Every halfpenny I had saved was in it but nine guineas, which I kept upon my person to provide for squalls. The trader fell down the river but, there being no wind and the tide failing, the captain told us we might sleep in London, only to be sure to be on board before eight o'clock in the morning. I embraced the opportunity and lost my passage.

As all my savings were in my chest, and a number of passengers on board whom I did not like, I immediately took the diligence to Newcastle.* There were no mails running direct for Edinburgh every day, as now. It was the month of March, yet there was a great deal of snow on the ground; the weather was severe, but not so cold as at St John's.

When the diligence set off there were four passengers: two ladies, another sailor and myself. Our lady companions, for the first few stages, were proud and distant, scarcely taking any notice of us. I was restrained by their manner. My companion was quite at home chatting to them, unmindful of their monosyllabic answers. He had a good voice and sung snatches of sea songs, and was unceasing in his endeavours to please. By degrees their reserve wore off and the conversation became general. I now

* Diligence: public stage coach.

learned they were sisters who had been on a visit to a relation in London and were now returning to their father, who was a wealthy farmer.

Before it grew dark we were all as intimate as if we had sailed for years in the same ship. The oldest, who appeared to be about twenty, attached herself to me and listened to my accounts of the different places I had been in with great interest. The youngest was as much interested by my volatile companion.

I felt a something uncommon arise in my breast as we sat side by side. I could think of nothing but my pretty companion. My attentions were not disagreeable to her and I began to think of settling, and how happy I might be with such a wife.

After a number of efforts I summoned resolution to take her hand in mine. I pressed it gently. She drew it faintly back. I sighed. She laid her hand upon my arm, and in a whisper inquired if I was unwell. I was upon the point of telling her what I felt, and my wishes, when the diligence stopped at the inn.

I wished we had been sailing in the middle of the Atlantic, for a covered cart drove up and a stout hearty old man welcomed them by their names, bestowing a hearty kiss upon each. I felt quite disappointed. He was their father. My pretty Mary did not seem to be so rejoiced at her father's kind salutation as might have been expected.

My companion, who was an Englishman, told me he would proceed no farther, but endeavour to win the hand of his pretty partner. I told him my present situation, that my chest and all I had was on board the Leith trader, and no direction upon it. On this account I was forced to proceed as fast as possible or I would have remained and shared his fortunes with all my heart. I took leave of them with a heavy heart, resolving to return. I could perceive Mary turn pale as I bade her farewell, while her sister looked joy itself when Williams told them he was to proceed no farther. Before the coach set off, I made him promise to write me an account of his success, and that I would return as soon as I had secured my chest and seen my father. He promised to do this faithfully.

I whispered Mary a promise to see her soon, and pressed her hand as we parted. She returned the pressure. I did not feel without hope. When the farmer drove off, Williams accompanying them, I only wished myself in his place.

When the coach reached Newcastle, I soon procured another conveyance to Edinburgh and was at Leith before the vessel. When she arrived I went on board and found all safe. I then went to Borrowstownness, but found my father had been dead for some time.

This was a great disappointment and grief to me. I wished I had been at home to have received his last blessing and advice, but there was no help. He died full of years; and that I may be as well prepared when I shall be called hence is my earnest wish. After visiting his grave and spending a few days with my friends, I became uneasy at not hearing from

Williams. I waited for three weeks; then, losing all patience, I set off myself to see how the land lay. I took leave of home once more, with a good deal of money in my pocket, as I had been almost a miser at home, keeping all for the marriage, should I succeed.

The spring was now advancing apace, when I took my passage in a Newcastle trader and arrived safe at the inn where I had last parted from Mary. It was night when I arrived and, being weary, soon went to bed. I was up betimes in the morning. When I met Williams, he was looking very dull. I shook hands, and asked, 'What cheer?'

He shook his head, and said, 'Why, Jack, we are on the wrong tack, and I fear will never make port. I had no good news to send, so it was of no use to write. I was at the farmer's last night. He swears, if ever I come near his house again, he will have me before the justice as an idle vagrant. My fair jilt is not much concerned, and I can scarce get a sight of her. She seems to shun me.'

I felt a chillness come over me at this information, and asked him what he meant to do.

'Why, set sail this day. Go to my mother, give her what I can spare, and then to sea again. My store is getting low here. But what do you intend to do, Jack?'

'Truth, Williams, I scarce know. I will make one trip to the farm, and if Mary is not as kind as I hope to find her I will be off too.'

Soon after breakfast I set off for the farmer's with an anxious heart. On my arrival I met Mary in the yard. She seemed fluttered at sight of me but, summoning up courage as I approached, she made a distant bow and coldly asked me how I did. I now saw there was no hope and had not recovered myself when her father came out, and in a rough manner demanded what I wanted and who I was. This in a moment brought me to myself and, raising my head, which had been bent towards the ground, I looked at him.

Mary shrunk from my gaze but the old man came close up to me, and again demanded what I wanted.

'It is of no consequence,' I answered. Then, looking at Mary, 'I believe I am an unwelcome visitor—it is what I did not expect—so I will not obtrude myself upon you any longer.' I then walked off as indifferent to appearance as I could make myself, but was tempted to look over my shoulder more than once. I saw Mary in tears and her father in earnest conversation with her.

I made up my mind to remain at the inn the rest of that day and all night, in hopes of receiving an appointment to meet Mary. I was loath to think I was indifferent to her—and the feeling of being slighted is so bitter I could have quarrelled with myself and all the world. I sat with Williams at the window all day. No message came. In the morning we bade adieu to the fair jilts with heavy hearts—Williams for his mother's and I for London.

After working a few weeks in London at my own business, my wandering propensities came as strong upon me as ever, and I resolved to embrace the first opportunity to gratify it, no matter whither, only let me wander. I had been many times on the different wharfs looking for a vessel, but the seamen were so plenty there was great difficulty in getting a berth.

I met by accident Captain Bond, who hailed me and inquired if I wished a berth. He had been captain of a transport in the American war. I had favoured him at St John's. I answered him, 'It was what I was looking after.'

'Then, if you will, come and be cooper of the *Leviathan* Greenland ship. I am captain. You may go to Squire Mellish and say I recommend you for cooper.'

I thanked him for his goodwill, went, and was engaged and on board at work next day.

We sailed in a short time for the coast of Greenland, and touched at Lerwick, where we took on board what men we wanted. In the first of the season we were very unsuccessful, having very stormy weather. I at one time thought our doom was fixed. It blew a dreadful gale and we were for ten days completely fast in the ice. As far as we could see all was ice, and the ship was so pressed by it everyone thought we must either be crushed to pieces or forced out upon the top of the ice, there ever to remain.

At length the wind changed and the weather moderated, and where nothing could be seen but ice, in a short time after, all as far as the eye could reach was open sea. What were our feelings at this change it were vain to attempt a description of—it was a reprieve from death.

The horrors of our situation were far worse than any storm I ever was in. In a storm upon a lea-shore, there, even in all its horrors, there is exertion to keep the mind up, and a hope to weather it. Locked up in ice, all exertion is useless. The power you have to contend with is far too tremendous and unyielding. It, like a powerful magician, binds you in its icy circle, and there you must behold, in all its horrors, your approaching fate, without the power of exertion, while the crashing of the ice and the less loud but more alarming cracking of the vessel serve all to increase the horrors of this dreadful sea-mare.

When the weather moderated we were very successful and filled our ship with four fish.* I did not like the whale-fishing. There is no sight for the eye of the inquisitive after the first glance and no variety to charm the mind. Desolation reigns around: nothing but snow, or bare rocks and ice. The cold is so intense and the weather often so thick. I felt so cheerless that I resolved to bid adieu to the coast of Greenland for ever, and seek to gratify my curiosity in more genial climes.

We arrived safe in the river and proceeded up to our situation. But how strange are the freaks of fate! In the very port of London, as we were hurrying to our station, the tide was ebbing fast when the ship missed stays and yawed round, came right upon the Isle of Dogs, broke her back and filled with water.

* These were bowhead whales.

There was none of us hurt and we lost nothing as she was insured. I was one of those placed upon her to estimate the loss sustained amongst the casks, and was kept constantly on board for a long time.

5

Voyage to Grenada—Treatment of the Negroes—Dancing and Songs—Long-Shorers Chiefly Scots and Irishmen—Anecdote of a Welshman.

MY NEXT VOYAGE was on board the *Cotton Planter* commanded by Captain Young, bound for the island of Grenada. I was very happy under Captain Young. He had been long in the Mediterranean trade where he had lost his health, and every year made a voyage to the West Indies to avoid the English winters. We sailed in the month of October, and arrived safe at St George's, Grenada.

I wrought a great deal on shore and had a number of blacks under me. They are a thoughtless, merry race; in vain their cruel situation and sufferings act upon their buoyant minds. They have snatches of joy that their pale and sickly oppressors never know. It may appear strange, yet it is only in the West Indian islands that the pictures of Arcadia are in a faint manner realised once in the week.

When their cruel situation allows their natural propensities to unfold themselves on the evenings of Saturday and Sabbath, no sound of woe is to be heard in this land of oppression—the sound of the Benji† and rattle, intermixed with song, alone is heard. I have seen them dancing and singing of an evening, and their backs sore from the lash of their cruel task-masters. I have lain upon deck of an evening, faint and exhausted from the heat of the day, to enjoy the

† The Benji is made of an old firkin [a small cask] with one end out, covered with shark skin, and beat upon with two pieces of wood. The rattles are made of a calabash shell, and a few small pebbles in it, fixed on a wooden handle; these they shake to the time of the Benji.

cool breeze of evening, and their wild music and song, the shout of mirth and dancing, resounded along the beach and from the valleys. There the negroes bounded in all the spirit of health and happiness while their oppressors could hardly drag their effeminate bodies along, from dissipation or the enervating effects of the climate.

These meetings are made up and agreed upon often long before they arrive. The poor and despised slaves will club their scanty earning for the refreshments and to pay Benji men. Many of them will come miles to be present. The females dress in all their finery for the occasion, and the males are decked with any fragments of dress they can obtain. Many of them are powdered. They all ape the manners of their masters as much as is in their power.

It is amusing to see them meet each other; they have so many congées, set phrases and kind inquiries in which Mama is the person most kindly inquired after.* They are as formal as dancing-masters, and make up to each other in civilities for the contempt heaped upon them by the whites.

The food allowed them by their masters is very poor. Half a salt herring, split down the middle, to each (they call it the one-eyed fish upon this account), horse beans and Indian corn constitute their fare. The Indian corn they must grind for themselves on Saturday after their day's task is done, which in general

* Congées: ways of saying hello and goodbye.

is to bring one burden of wood to the estate.

From Saturday until Monday morning they have to rest themselves and cultivate their patch of garden ground. Those who live near seaports prefer going to the mountains and gathering coconuts, plantains and other fruit which they sell. The slaves all bring any little fruit or vegetables they have to spare to market.

The sales by the whites, as well as blacks, are all made on the Sabbath day. The jailor of St George's is vendue-master by right of office, and none dare lift a hammer to sell without his permission.*

Captain Young did not keep his crew upon allowance. We had 'cut and come again' always. I often took a piece of lean beef and a few biscuits with me when I went to the plantation, as a present to the blacks. This the poor creatures would divide among themselves to a single fibre. As I had always been kind to them, they invited me and a few other seamen to one of their entertainments. I went with pleasure, to observe their ways more minutely. Upon my arrival I could hardly keep my gravity at their appearance, yet I esteemed them in my heart.

There was one black who acted as master of the ceremonies, but the Benji man appeared greater than any other individual. They all, before they commenced to dance, made their obeisance to him; the same at the conclusion. The master of ceremonies had an old cocked hat, and no courtier could have

* Vendue-master: auctioneer.

used it with more zeal. Many of the females had cast silk gowns which had belonged to their mistresses, and their heads powdered—but they were tawdry figures, though no lady or gentleman could have been more vain of their appearance or put on more airs.

The kind creatures had, upon our account, subscribed for three-bit maubi.† When they dance they accompany the Benji with the voice. Their songs were many of them *extempore*, and made on our ship or ourselves. My small gifts were not forgot. Their choruses are common. Their songs are of the simplest kind, as:

I lost my shoe in an old canoe,
  Johnio! come Winum so.
I lost my boot in a pilot boat,
  Johnio! come Winum so.

Others are satirical, as:

My Massa a bad man,
  My Missis cry honey,
Is this the damn nigger,
  You buy wi my money.
  Ting a ring ting, ting a ring ting, tarro.

† Maubi is a drink like ginger-beer they drink among themselves, but as they knew sailors liked stouter drink, they bought rum. The price was one shilling and sixpence the gallon. A bit is equal to sixpence. Rum they call three-bit maubi.

Missis cry nigger man
  Do no work, but eattee;
She boil three eggs in pan,
  And gi the broth to me.
  Ting a ring ting, ting a ring ting, tarro.

With such songs as these they accompany the Benji. I do not recollect to have ever heard them sing a plaintive song, bewailing their cruel fate. This made me wonder much, as I expected they would have had many bewailing their destiny. But joy seems on these occasions their only aim.

The dance went on with spirit. I would have joined with pleasure, but it was beyond my strength after my day's work and the heat of the climate. We parted in good time without the least appearance of intoxication. I never in my life was happier, had more attention paid to me, or was more satisfied with an entertainment.

They have one rhyme they use at work, and adjust their motions to it. They never vary it that I heard.

Work away, body, bo
Work aa, jollaa.

In this manner they beguile the irksomeness of labour, but the capricious driver often interrupts their innocent harmony with the crack of his cart whip. No stranger can witness the cruelty unmoved.

George Innes and I were proceeding through the plantation to inform the master the double moses was on the beach for sugar.† A black driver was flogging a woman big with child. Her cries rent the air, the other slaves declaring by their looks that sympathy they dared not utter. George ran to him and gave him a good beating, and swore he would double the gift if he laid another lash upon her. He had not dared when we returned.

There were two or three slaves upon the estate who, having once run away, had iron collars round their necks with long hooks that projected from them to catch the bushes should they run away again. These they wore night and day. There was a black slave, a cooper with a wooden leg, who had run away more than once. He was now chained to the block at which he wrought.

They are much given to talking and story-telling; the Scripture characters of the Old Testament are quite familiar to them. They talk with astonishment of Samson, Goliath, David, etc. I have seen them hold up their hands in astonishment at the strength of the white Buccaras. I have laughed at their personifications. Hurricane, they cannot conceive what it is. There are planters of the name of Kane on the island. Hurricane, they will say, 'He a strong white Buccara, he come from London.'

There was a black upon the estate who had been on the island of St Kitt's when Rodney defeated the

† The double moses is a large boat for taking on board the sugar casks. There are two, the single and double moses. The single holds only one hogshead, the double more.

French fleet. He had seen the action and was never tired speaking of it, nor his auditors of listening. He always concluded with this remark: 'The French 'tand 'tiff, but the English 'tand far 'tiffer. De all de same as game cock, de die on de 'pot.'

They are apt to steal, but are so very credulous they are easily detected. Captain Young gave a black butcher of the name of Coffee a hog to kill. When the captain went to see it, Coffee said, 'This very fine hog, Massa, but I never see a hog like him in all my life, he have no liver, no light.'*

Captain Young: 'That is strange, Coffee. Let me see in the book.' He took a memorandum book out of his pocket, turned over a few leaves, and looked very earnest. 'I see Coffee go to hell bottom—hog have liver and lights.'

Coffee shook like an aspen leaf, and said, 'O Massa, Coffee no go to hell bottom—hog have liver and lights.'

He restored them and, trembling, awaited his punishment. Captain Young only laughed, and made him a present of them.

I one time went with Captain Young to a planter's, where he was to dine, that I might accompany him back to the ship in the evening, as he was weakly. Upon our arrival I was handed over to a black who was butler and house steward. He had been in England and, as he said, seen London and King

* Light: lung.

George. He was by this become a greater man than by his situation among the other slaves, and was as vain in showing the little he knew as if he had been bred at college, and was perpetually astonishing the other slaves, whom he looked down upon, with the depth of his knowledge and his accounts of London and King George.

No professor could have delivered his opinions and observations with more pomp and dogmatism. One of the blacks inquired at me what kind of people the Welsh were. To enjoy the sport, as one of the crew, William Jones, a Welshman, was in company with me at the time, I referred him to the black oracle who, after considering a moment or two, replied with a smile of satisfaction upon his sooty features, 'The English have ships, the Irish have ships and the Scotch have ships, but Welshmen have no ships—they are like the negro man, they live in the bush.'

The Welshman started to his feet and would have knocked him down had I not prevented. He poured out a volley of oaths upon him.

He heard him with indifference, and his assertion was not the least shaken in the opinion of his hearers by the Welshman's violence—it, like many others of equal truth, was quoted and received as gospel. It was long a byword in the ship: 'Welshman live in the bush like negro man.'

Our cook having left the vessel, we were forced to take a long-shorer in his place. They are a set of idle dissipated seamen who will not work or take a berth.

They loiter along the harbours and get drunk by any means, no matter however base. Home they have none. The weather is so warm, they lie out all night and are content with little victuals. They are in general covered with rags and filth, the victims of idleness and disease. It is nothing uncommon to see their feet and ankles a mass of sores, their feet eaten by the jiggers until they resemble fowls' feet, having no flesh on them. Their minds chilled and totally sunk, death soon closes their career.

The next morning after the new cook came on board, he lay so long the captain's kettle was not boiled, nor the fire kindled. Paddy was quite indifferent when the cabin boy told him Captain Young must have the kettle immediately. He replied, 'Let him send his blasters and blowers here then.' Blasters and blowers was sent about his business immediately, and he cared not a fig.

I must confess the long-shorers are mostly composed of Irish and Scots. The very blacks despise them. They could make a good living by carrying water, as they could get a bit a burden. Many blacks get leave from the overseers to do this, giving them a bit a day, and earn as much as buy their freedom. An overseer may often have a dozen blacks thus employed, and his master not a bit the wiser, and the money his own gain.

We brought to England, as passenger from the island, a planter who was very rich and had a number of slaves. He had been a common seaman on board of a man-of-war, had deserted and lived on shore concealed until his ship sailed. He afterwards married a free black woman who kept a punch-house, who died and left him above three thousand pounds. With this he had bought a plantation and slaves, and was making money fast. He brought as much fresh provisions and preserves on board as would have served ten men out and out, and was very kind to the men in giving them liquor and fresh provisions.

6

Voyage of Discovery—Anecdote—Falkland Islands—Cape Horn—Owhyee—Atooi—Onehow—Manners of the Natives.

UPON OUR ARRIVAL in London I learned that my old officer, Lieutenant Portlock, now captain, was going out in the *King George*, as commander, in company with the *Queen Charlotte*, Captain Dixon, upon a voyage of discovery and trade round the world.

This was the very cruise I had long wished for. At once I made myself clean and waited upon Captain Portlock. He was happy to see me, as I was an excellent brewer of spruce-beer, and the very man he wished, but knew not where to have sent for me. I was at once engaged on the most liberal terms as cooper, and went away rejoicing in my good fortune. We had a charter from the South Sea Company and one from the India House, as it was to be a trading voyage for furs as well as discovery. This was in the year 1785.

With a joyful heart I entered on this voyage but, through an unforeseen accident, I had more to do than I engaged for. Our steward went on shore for a few necessary articles just before we sailed. He was a foolish lad, got tipsy, and the money sold him. Having spent it, he was ashamed to come on board again. The wind was fair, and I engaged to fill his place rather than delay the voyage one day, so eager was I upon it.

The first land we made was Santa Cruz in the island of Tenerife, where we stayed ten days getting fruit and provisions; then made the island of Sao Tiago (it belongs to the Portuguese) where we watered and took in fresh provisions. While here we caught a number of fish called bass, very like salmon, which we eat fresh. The island is badly cultivated but abounds in cattle. We exchanged old clothes for sheep, or anything the men wanted.

The Portuguese here are great rogues. I bought two fat sheep from one of them. The bargain was made and I was going to lead away my purchase when he gave a whistle and my sheep scampered off to the fields. The fellow laughed at my surprise. I had a great mind to give him a beating for his trick, and take my clothes from him, but we had strict orders not to quarrel with the people upon any account. At length he made a sign that I might have them again by giving a few more articles. I had no alternative but lose what I had given or submit to his roguery. I gave a sign I would. He gave another whistle and the sheep returned to his side. I secured them before I gave the second price.

With all their roguery they are very careless of their money, more so than any people I ever saw. In walking through the town I have seen kegs full of dollars, without heads, standing in the houses, and the door open without a person in the house to look after them.

Having watered, we run for the Falkland Islands. When we arrived we found two American vessels busy whaling. We hoisted our colours, the Anchor and Hope. The Americans took us for Spaniards and set off in all haste. When we landed we found a great number of geese ready plucked and a large fire burning, so we set to work and roasted as many as served us all, and enjoyed them much.

Next morning the Americans came near in their boats, and found out their mistake. Captain Portlock thanked them for their treat. We then had a busy time killing geese. There are two kinds, the water and upland. The water ones are very pretty, spreckled like a partridge. The penguins were so plenty we were forced to knock them out of our way as we walked along the beach.

The pelicans are plenty and build their nests of clay. They are near each other, like a honey-comb. I was astonished how each bird knew its own nest. They appear to hatch in the same nest until they are forced to change by the accumulation of dung. They are so tame I have stood close by when they arrived with their pouch distended with fish, and fed their young without being in the least disturbed.

We killed a number of hogs. Our doctor broke his double-barrelled gun in dispatching one, and sold it afterwards in China for £42. What was of more value to us was a great many iron hoops and beeswax, the remains of some wreck. We picked up some of the wax but took every inch of the hoops. They were more valuable than gold to us for trading with the natives.

When off Cape Horn we perceived an object floating at a small distance from the ship. Not one of us could make out what it was. All our boats being fast, two men went down into the water and swam to it, and made it fast in the slings. When it came on board it was a cask, but so overgrown with weeds and barnacles the bung-hole could not be discovered. I was set to work to cut into it. To our agreeable surprise it was full of excellent port wine. All the crew got a little of it and Captain Portlock gave us brandy in place of the rest.

We next made Staten Island; the weather was fine, but very cold.* We stood away for latitude 23° where we cruised about for some time in quest of islands laid down in our charts. We could find none, but turtle in great abundance. They were a welcome supply, but we soon tired of them, cook them as we could in every variety.

Not finding the islands, we bore away for the Sandwich Islands.** The first land we made was Owhyee, the island where Captain Cook was killed. The *King George* and *Queen Charlotte* were the first ships which had touched there since that melancholy event. The natives came on board in crowds and were happy to see us. They recognised Portlock and others who had been on the island before, along with Cook. Our decks were soon crowded with hogs, breadfruit, yams and potatoes. Our deck soon resembled shambles—our butcher had fourteen assistants.

I was as busy and fatigued as I could be cutting iron hoops into lengths of eight and nine inches which the

* Staten Island lies south of Tierra del Fuego.
** The Hawaiian Islands.

carpenter ground sharp. These were our most valuable commodity in the eyes of the natives. I was stationed down in the hold of the vessel, and the ladders were removed to prevent the natives from coming down to the treasury. The King of Owhyee looked to my occupation with a wistful eye; he thought me the happiest man on board to be among such vast heaps of treasure.

Captain Portlock called to me to place the ladder and allow the king to come down, and give him a good long piece. When the king descended he held up his hands and looked astonishment personified. When I gave him the piece of hoop of twenty inches long he retired a little from below the hatch into the shade, undid his girdle, bent the iron to his body and, adjusting his belt in the greatest haste, concealed it. I suppose he thought I had stole it. I could not but laugh to see the king concealing what he took to be stolen goods.*

We were much in want of oil for our lamps. The sharks abounding, we baited a hook with a piece of salt pork and caught the largest I ever saw in any sea. It was a female, nineteen feet long. It took all hands to hoist her on board; her weight made the vessel heel. When she was cut up we took forty-eight young ones out of her belly, eighteen inches long. We saw them go into her mouth after she was hooked.** The hook

* The king was more likely hiding it from his fellow Hawaiians.

** The fish seen apparently entering the mouth were probably not young sharks but remora (suckerfish) which habitually accompany larger marine organisms.

was fixed to a chain attached to our mainbrace, or we never would have kept her. It was evening when she snapped the bait; we hauled the head just above the surface, the swell washing over it. We let her remain thus all night and she was quite dead in the morning. There were in her stomach four hogs, four full-grown turtle, beside the young ones. Her liver, the only part we wanted, filled a tierce.*

Almost every man on board took a native woman for a wife while the vessel remained, the men thinking it an honour, or for their gain, as they got many presents of iron, beads or buttons. The women came on board at night and went on shore in the morning. In the evening they would call for their husbands by name. They often brought their friends to see their husbands, who were well pleased, as they were never allowed to go away empty.

The fattest woman I ever saw in my life our gunner chose for a wife. We were forced to hoist her on board. Her thighs were as thick as my waist. No hammock in the ship would hold her. Many jokes were cracked upon the pair.

They are the worst people to pronounce the English of any I ever was among. Captain Portlock they called *Potipoti*. The nearest approach they could make to my name was *Nittie*, yet they would make the greatest efforts, and look so angry at themselves and vexed at their vain efforts.

* A large cask of varying size.

We had a merry facetious fellow on board called Dickson. He sung pretty well. He squinted and the natives mimicked him. Abenoue, King of Atooi, could cock his eye like Dickson better than any of his subjects.* Abenoue called him Billicany, from his often singing 'Rule Britannia'. Abenoue learned the air and the words as near as he could pronounce them. It was an amusing thing to hear the king and Dickson sing. Abenoue loved him better than any man in the ship, and always embraced him every time they met on shore or in the ship, and began to sing, 'Tule Billicany, Billicany tule,' etc.

We had the chief on board who killed Captain Cook for more than three weeks. He was in bad health, and had a smelling-bottle with a few drops in it which he used to smell at. We filled it for him. There were a good many bayonets in possession of the natives, which they had obtained at the murder of Cook.

We left Owhyee and stood down to Atooi, where we watered and had a feast from Abenoue the King. We took our allowance of brandy on shore and spent a most delightful afternoon, the natives doing all in their power to amuse us. The girls danced, the men made a sham fight, throwing their spears. The women, standing behind, handed the spears to the men the same as in battle, thus keeping up a continued shower of spears. No words can convey an adequate

* Atooi: Kauai.

idea of their dexterity and agility. They thought we were bad with the rheumatism, our movements were so slow compared with their own. The women would sometimes lay us down and chafe and rub us, making moan and saying, 'O Rume! O Rume!' They wrestled, but the stoutest man in our ship could not stand a single throw with the least chance of success.

We next stood for Onehow, of which Abenoue was king as well as Atooi, to get yams.* This island grows them in abundance, and scarce any thing else. They have no wood upon the island but exchange their yams for it to build their canoes. While lying here it came to blow a dreadful gale. We were forced to cut our cables and stand out to sea, and leave sixteen men and boys. It was three weeks before we could return. When we arrived we found them well and hearty. These kind people had lodged them two and two in their houses, gave them plenty of victuals and liberty to ramble over the whole island.

The only man who was in the least alarmed for his safety was an old boatswain. He was in continual fear. The innocent natives could not meet to divert themselves, or even a few talk together, but the old sinner would shake with horror and called to his shipmates, 'Now, they are going to murder us—this is our last night.' He was a perfect annoyance to the others. He scarce ever left the beach but to go to some height to look out for the ships, and after looking till he was

* Onehow: Niihau.

almost blind he would seek out the other men to make his lamentations and annoy them with his fears of the loss of the ships or their being deserted by them.

At length we returned and took them on board, making presents to the king and his kind people for their unlimited hospitality. We now took an affectionate leave of these kind islanders.

As the summer now advanced apace we stood over to Cook's River, where we arrived in 1786, eleven months after we left England.* Upon our arrival a number of Russians came on board of us and made the captain a present of salmon, who in return gave them salt, an article they stood much in need of. One of our men, who spoke the Russian tongue, told them we were upon a voyage of discovery. We did not wish them to know we were trading in furs. We parted from them with mutual civilities.

At the entrance of Cook's River is an immense volcanic mountain which was in action at the time, and continued burning all the time we lay there, pouring down its side a torrent of lava as broad as the Thames. At night the sight was grand but fearful. The natives here had their spears headed with copper but, having no one on board who could speak their language, we had no means of learning where they obtained the copper.

While we lay here it was the heat of summer, yet the ice never melted and the snow was lying very deep

* Cook's River: Cook Inlet, Alaska.

on the heights. What a contrast from the delightful islands we had so lately left.

Our longboat, decked and schooner-rigged, proceeded up the river in hopes of finding an outlet, or inland sea. After proceeding with great difficulty and perseverance, until all hopes of success vanished, they returned. We then bore to the southward to Prince William's Sound to pursue our trade with the Indians. They are quite different from the Sandwich Islanders in appearance and habits. They are not cruel but great thieves.

I was employed on shore brewing spruce all day and slept on board at night. One night the Indians, after starting the beer, carried off all the casks: they were iron-hooped.* All our search was vain; no traces of them were to be discovered. To quarrel with the Indians would have defeated the object of our voyage. At length they were discovered by accident in the most unlikely place, in the following manner.

One of our boats had been on a trading excursion detained so long, we became alarmed for its safety. Captain Portlock sent some of our men armed to the top of a high hill to look out for the boat. To the surprise of the men, they found the staves and ends of the barrels, and some large stones they had used in breaking them to pieces. How great must their labour have been in rolling up the barrels and then in dashing them to pieces. Yet I have no doubt

* Starting: spilling.

they thought themselves richly rewarded in obtaining the iron hoops. The men brought back a stave or two with the ship's name branded on them to evidence the truth of their discovery. We then moved the brewing place to the other side of the island, within sight of the ship.

I was much annoyed by the natives for some time while working. They would handle the hoops, and every now and then a piece would vanish. There was only a quarter-master and boy with me. While the natives swarmed around I felt rather uncomfortable. They became more and more bold. The captain, seeing from the deck my disagreeable situation, hailed me to set Neptune, our great Newfoundland dog, upon them, saying he would fear them more than fifty men.

I obeyed with alacrity and hounded Neptune, who enjoyed the sport as much as I, to see the great fellows run, screaming like girls, in all directions. I was soon left to pursue my labour unmolested and whenever they grew troublesome Neptune, without orders, put them to the running and screaming. When one approached, if Neptune was near, he would stretch out his arms, and cry, '*Lally, Neptune*'—that is 'friend' in their language. The Indians here could pronounce every word we spoke almost as well as ourselves. This appeared the more strange after hearing the vain efforts of our friends the Sandwich Islanders.

One Sabbath day all the ship's company, except the captain, two boys and the cook, were on shore amusing themselves. During our absence an immense number of the natives came alongside and took complete possession of the vessel and helped themselves to whatever took their fancy. The captain, boys, and cook barricadoed themselves in the cabin and loaded all the muskets and pistols within their reach. Their situation was one of great danger.

The surgeon and myself were the first that arrived on the beach. The captain hailed us from the cabin window and let us know his disagreeable situation, telling us to force the Indians to put us on board. We having our muskets, they complied at once. Thus, by adding strength to the captain, we gained new assurance and, the others doing as we did, were put all on board as they came to the beach. The Indians offered no violence to the ship and when the crew were nearly all on board they began to leave the vessel, shipping off their booty.

Captain Portlock ordered us to take no notice of the transaction in way of hurting the Indians but to purchase back the articles they had taken away that were of use to us—but they had only taken what pieces of iron they found loose about the ship. After having hid the things they had stolen they began to trade as if nothing had happened, and we bought back what few bolts they had taken.

They had plundered the smith's tent in the same manner, although they looked upon him as a greater man than the captain. He was a smart young fellow and kept the Indians in great awe and wonder. They thought the coals were made into powder.* I have seen them steal small pieces and bruise them, then come back. When he saw this, he would spit upon the anvil while working the hot iron and give a blow upon it. They would run away in fear and astonishment when they heard the crack.

* Powder: gun powder.

7

Trading Voyages—Conduct of the Natives—Sandwich Islands—Language—Nootka Sound—Ships Sail for China.

ONE OR OTHER of our boats, often both, were absent for some time upon trading voyages. In one of these trips our boat was nearly cut off, and would in all probability, had it not been for the presence of mind of an American, one of the crew, Joseph Laurence. I never was more alarmed for my safety in the whole voyage.

We were rowing through a lagoon to get a near cut to the ship. The tide was ebbing fast, the boat took the ground, and before we could do anything to get her off the whole bay was dry. The natives surrounded the boat in great numbers and looked very mischievous. We knew not what to do.

In this dilemma, Laurence, who knew their ways, took a small keg of molasses and went to the beach. At the same time he sat down by it and began to sing and lick, inviting them to follow his example. They licked and listened to him for a good while, and even joined him in singing—but the molasses wore done and they were weary of his songs.

We looked about in great anxiety and discovered a small height that commanded the boat. To this we ran but dared not to fire, even while they were plundering the boat. They could have killed us all with spears and stones, had we even shot one hundred of them and wasted all our ammunition.

We stood like bears at the stake, expecting them every moment to commence the attack, resolved to sell our lives as dear we could. At length the wished return of tide came and we got to the boat, and she floated soon after. Then we cared not one penny for them. We began to trade and bought back the articles they had stolen. Even our compass we were forced to buy back. We set sail for the *King George*, resolved to be more circumspect in future and happy we had escaped so well.

The party who had taken possession of the vessel on the Sabbath day, the next time they came back had their faces blacked and their heads powdered with the down of birds. They had done this as a disguise, which showed they had a consciousness of right and wrong. Thinking we knew them not, as we took no notice of them, they were as merry and funny as any of the rest.

While the boats were absent on a trading voyage the canoe was sent to haul the seine for salmon. There were fourteen men and boys in it. About half way between the vessel and the shore she filled with water. Those who could swim made for the beach. The boys, and those who could not, clung to the canoe. Captain Portlock saw from the deck the danger they were in and requested the boatswain, who was an excellent swimmer, to go to their assistance. He refused.

The sailmaker and myself leapt into the water. I had a line fixed round my waist, as I swam first, which he supported at a short distance behind, to ease its weight. When I came up to the canoe they were nearly spent. I fixed the line to the canoe and we made a signal to the ship when those on board drew her to the vessel, John Butler and I attending to assist and encourage them. There was a son of Sir John Dick's and a son of Captain Gore's among the boys. Captain Portlock never could bear the boatswain afterwards. Before this he was a great favourite.

While in Prince William's Sound the boat went on an excursion to Snug Corner Cove at the top of the Sound. She discovered the *Nootka*, Captain Mairs, in a most distressing situation from the scurvy. There were only the captain and two men free from disease. Two and twenty Lascars had died through the course of the winter. They had caused their own distress by their inordinate use of spirits on Christmas eve. They could not bury their own dead. They were only dragged a short distance from the ship and left upon the ice. They had muskets fixed upon the capstan and man-ropes that went down to the cabin, that when any of the natives attempted to come on board they might fire them off to scare them.

They had a large Newfoundland dog whose name was Towser, who alone kept the ship clear of the Indians. He lay day and night upon the ice before the cabin window, and would not allow the Indians to go into the ship. When the natives came to barter they would cry, '*Lally Towser*,' and make him a present of a skin before they began to trade with Captain Mairs, who lowered from the window his barter, and in the same way received their furs.

The *Beaver*, the *Nootka's* consort, had been cut off in the beginning of the winter and none of her people were ever heard of. We gave him every assistance in our power in spruce and molasses, and two of our crew to assist in working the vessel, Dickson and George Willis, who stopped at Canton until we arrived—then, wishing him well, took our leave of him. Captain Portlock could have made a fair prize of him, as he had no charter and was trading in our limits, but he was satisfied with his bond not to trade on our coast; but the bond was forfeit as soon as we sailed, and he was in China before us.

We now stood for Nootka Sound, but encountered a dreadful gale and were blown off the coast and suffered much in our sails and rigging which caused us to stand for the Sandwich Islands to refit—which gave us great joy.

The American coast is a hostile region compared with the Sandwich Islands. The American Indians are very jealous, and if any of our men were found with their women, using the least freedom, they would take his life if it was in their power; but their women are far from being objects of desire, they are so much disfigured by slitting their lips and placing large pieces of wood in them shaped like a saucer. I have seen them place berries upon it, and shake them into their mouth as a horse would corn out of a mouth-bag, or lick them in with their tongue. The men have a bone eight inches long, polished and stuck through the gristle of their nose. We called it their sprit-sailyard. We had suffered a good deal of hardship on this coast, and bade it adieu with joy.

Soon as we arrived at Owhyee our old acquaintance flocked on board to welcome us, each with a present. Then such a touching of noses and shaking of hands took place. '*Honi, honi*'—that is, touch nose, and 'How are you?'—were the only words to be heard. Our deck was one continued scene of joy. I was now picking up the language pretty fast and could buy and sell in it, and knew a great number of words that were very useful to me. There is a great likeness in many of their words to the Latin:

Sandwich Islands	*English*
terra	earth
nuna	moon
sola	sun
oma	man
leo	dog

Noue is their word for large, *maccou* for a fish-hook. When they saw our anchors they held up their hands and said, '*Noue maccou.*' During our wintering this second time, almost the same scenes were re-acted.

Having refitted and taken in provisions, we again set sail for Cook's River, Prince William's and Nootka Sound to obtain more fur skins. We were pretty successful. While on shore in Prince William's Sound, brewing spruce beer, I and the quartermaster made an excursion up the river and discovered a large space covered with snake-root, which is of great value in China.* My comrade, who had been in China,

* This was probably ginseng (*Panax spp.*) which has a forked root.

informed me of its value. It is the sweetest smelling plant I ever was near when it is growing. We set to work and dug up as much as we chose and dried it, letting no one know, for lessening the value of what we got. It was got safe on board the day before we sailed and we sold it well at Wampoa.*

We parted company from the *Queen Charlotte*. She had been absent for a long time. When a party of Indians came to the *King George*, having in their possession a pair of buckles that belonged to one of the people on board our consort, we became alarmed for her, thinking she had been cut off. We immediately set sail for Nootka Sound, leaving a large quantity of salmon half dried. After waiting in Nootka Sound, our place of rendezvous, for some time, and she not appearing, we immediately set sail for Owhyee, but got no word of our consort until we came to Atooi, when we perceived Abenoue in his single canoe, making her scud through the water, crying, '*Tattoo for Potipoti*,' as he jumped upon deck with a letter from Captain Dixon, which removed our fears and informed us he had discovered an island and got a very great number of skins and had sailed for China. We watered and laid in our provisions as quick as we could to follow her.

Abenoue, soon after he came on board, told the captain he had seen Billicany, and squinted so like Dickson we knew at once Mairs had been there in the

* Wampoa: a port town just outside Canton.

Nootka. Dickson afterwards told us Mairs would not have got anything from Abenoue had he and Willis not been with him.

Abenoue had a son called Poinoue—in English 'Large Pudding'. I thought him well named. He had the largest head of any boy I ever saw. His father wished Captain Portlock to take him to England but Poinoue did not wish to go. He leapt overboard just as we sailed and swam back to his father.

It was with a sensation of regret I bade a final adieu to the Sandwich Islands. Even now I would prefer them to any country I ever was in. The people so kind and obliging, the climate so fine and provisions so abundant—all render it a most endearing place.

Owhyee is the only place I was not ashore in. Captain Portlock never went himself and would not allow his crew to go. The murder of Cook made him timorous of trusting too much to the islanders. At Atooi and Onehow we went on shore, one watch one day, the other the next.

After taking on board as much provisions as we could stow we sailed for China. At the Ladrones, or Mariana Islands, a number of pilots came on board. The captain agreed with one. The bargain was made in the following manner. He showed the captain the number of dollars he wished by the number of cass, a small brass coin, the captain taking from the number what he thought too much, the pilot adding when he thought it too little. He was to pilot the *King George* to the island of Macau. From thence we sailed up the

Bocca Tigris to Wampoa, where we sold our cargo of skins.* We were engaged to take home a cargo of tea for the East India Company.

* Bocca Tigris: the estuary at the head of which Canton is situated.

8

China—Manners of the Chinese—Food—Religion—Punishments—Evasion of Duty—St Helena—Author Arrives in England.

I WAS AS happy as any person ever was to see anything. I scarcely believed I was so fortunate as really to be in China. As we sailed up the river, I would cast my eyes from side to side. The thoughts and ideas I had pictured in my mind of it were not lessened in brilliancy, rather increased. The immense number of buildings that extended as far as the eye could reach, their fantastic shapes and gaudy colours, their trees and flowers so like their paintings, and the myriads of floating vessels, and above all the fanciful dresses and gaudy colours of their clothes—all serve to fix the mind of a stranger upon his first arrival. But upon a nearer acquaintance he is shocked at the quantity of individual misery that forces itself upon his notice, and gradually undoes the grand ideas he had formed of this strange people.

Soon as we cast anchor the vessel was surrounded with sampans. Every one had some request to make. Tartar girls requested our clothes to wash, barbers to shave the crews, others with fowls to sell; indeed, every necessary we could want. The first we made bargain with was a barber, Tommy Linn. He agreed to shave the crew for the six months we were to be there for half a dollar from each man, and he would shave every morning, if we chose, on board the ship, coming off in his sampan.

The Tartar girls washed our clothes for the broken meat or what rice we left at mess. They came every day in their sampans and took away the men's shirts, bringing them back the next, and never mixed the clothes. They all spoke less or more English and would jaw with the crew as fast as any women of their rank in England. They had a cage-like box fixed to the stern of their sampan in which was a pig who fed and fattened there at his ease.

Our ears were dinned with the cry of the beggars in their sampans, '*Kamscha me lillo rice*'. I have seen the mandarins plunder these objects of compassion when they had been successful in their appeals to the feelings of the seamen. I was surprised at the minute subdivision of their money. Their cass is a small piece of base coin with a square hole in it, three of which are a kandarin; sixty cass one mace; one mace equal to sevenpence English money. The cass is of no use out of the country, and when a seaman changes a dollar he receives no other coin from the wily Chinese.

I was on shore for a good while at Wampoa, making candle for our voyage home. I had a number of Chinese under me. My greatest difficulty was to prevent them from stealing the wax. They are greater and more dexterous thieves than the Indians. A bambooing for theft, I really believe, confers no disgrace upon them.

They will allow no stranger to enter the city of Canton. I was different times at the gate, but all my ingenuity could not enable me to cross the bar, although I was eight days in the suburbs. The Tartars are not even allowed to sleep on shore. They live in junks and other craft upon the river. If employed on shore they must be away by sunset, but may land again at sunrise in the morning.

The Chinese, I really believe, eat anything there is life in. Neptune was constantly on shore with me at the tent. Every night he caught less or more rats. He never eat them, but laid them down when dead at the tent door. In the morning the Chinese gave vegetables for them and were as well pleased as I was at the exchange.

After the candles were made I removed to Banks Hall to repair the cooper work, and screen sand and dry it, to pack the tea boxes for our voyage home. One day a boy was meddling rather freely with the articles belonging to me. Neptune bit him. I was extremely sorry for it, and after beating him dressed the boy's hurt which was not severe. I gave the boy a few cass, who went away quite pleased. In a short time after I saw him coming back, and his father leading him. I looked for squalls, but the father only asked a few hairs out from under Neptune's foreleg, close to the body. He would take them from no other part, and stuck them all over the wound.* He went away content. I had often heard, when a person had been tipsy the evening before, people tell him to take a hair of the dog that bit him, but never saw it in the literal sense before.

A short time before we sailed all the crew got two months' pay advance for private trade, and purchased

* Perhaps this was a folk preventative against rabies.

what articles they chose. The dollars are all stamped by the captain, as the Chinese are such cheats they will dexterously return you a bad dollar and assert, if not marked, it was the one you gave.

With all their roguery they are not ungrateful. One day two Chinese boys were playing in our boat. One of them fell overboard. The current was strong and the boy was carried down with rapidity. I leapt into the river and saved him with great difficulty, as the current bore us both along until my strength was almost spent. By an effort I got into the smooth water, and soon had the pleasure of delivering him to his father, who stood on the beach wringing his hands.

I wished to go on board, but the Chinese would have me to his house where I was most kindly received and got my dinner in great style. I like their manner of setting out the table at dinner. All that is to be eaten is placed upon the table at once, and all the liquors at the same time. You have all before you and you may make your choice. I dined in different houses and the same fashion was used in them all. The Chinese never thought he could show me kindness enough.

We buried our chief-mate, Mr Macleod, whose funeral I attended, upon French Island.

Almost every junk has a mandarin on board who keeps order and collects the revenue and tyrannises over the poor Chinese. They pay money for the liberty of doing anything to obtain a living. Tommy Linn paid seventy dollars for leave to practise as barber and surgeon upon the river.

They cure every disease by herbs. When any sailor or officer was so imprudent as visit Loblob Creek and received the reward of their folly, our surgeons could not cure them, yet the Chinese barber did so with ease.*

Every new moon all the men in China must have their heads shaved. If they do not the mandarin makes them suffer for it.

They have the longest nails to their fingers I ever saw. Many of their nails are half as long as the rest of the finger, they take so much care of them and keep them so white and clean. They, I really believe, would almost as soon have their throats cut as their nails. A Chinese will hold, by their means, more dollars in one hand than an Englishman will hold in both of his. Shaking hands will never be the fashion in China.

When the day is wet or thick, which rarely happens, the Chinese will say, 'Joss too much angry.' Then the paper sacrifices begin. The whole river is in a smoke. Every junk, down to the small sampan, must burn, under the direction of the mandarin, a certain quantity of paper to please 'Joss' their god. The rich must burn fine gilt paper, the poor coarser paper. The mandarin is the sole judge of the quantity and quality—from him there is no appeal. He himself burns no paper; a small piece of touchwood serves his turn. There he will stand in a conspicuous place, and look as steadfast upon it as a statue, until it is all burnt out.

* Loblob Creek: the local red-light district.

They are the most oppressed people I ever was amongst. They must want even a wife if they are not rich enough to pay the tax imposed by the mandarin. They are summary in their justice. Wherever the theft is committed, there the mandarin causes the culprit to be laid upon his back and beat upon the belly with a bamboo the number of times he thinks adequate to the offence. If the offence is great, they are sent to the Ladrone Islands, their place of banishment for thieves. There they live by piloting vessels and fishing but are not allowed to come up farther than Macau. They are cowardly and cruel. Six half-drunk sailors would clear a whole village; but when they catch one of them drunk and by himself, then they bamboo him in the cruellest manner.

Tommy Linn the barber was the agent we employed. He brought us any article we wanted from the city and, like his brethren in Europe, was a walking newspaper. His first word every morning was, 'Hey, yaw, what fashion?' and we used the same phrase to him. One morning he came, and the first thing he said was, 'Hey, yaw, what fashion? Soldier man's ship come to Lingcome bar.' We, after a few hours, heard that a man-of-war frigate had arrived at the mouth of the river. They are allowed to come no higher up. Tommy had seen the red coats of the marines.

They are much alarmed at the appearance of a man-of-war ship, and they often say, 'Englishman too much cruel, too much fight.' There were some

English seamen flogged for mutiny while we lay in the river. The Chinese wept like children for the men, saying, 'Hey, yaw, Englishman too much cruel, too much flog, too much flog.'

Having completed our cargo, we fell down the river. As we came near to the chop-house where the chop-marks are examined (the men having many articles on board in their private trade that had not paid duty, which the Chinese would have seized), we fell upon the old stratagem. When their boat put off two of us fell a fighting and we made the whole deck a scene of riot. These timorous Chinese custom-house-officers did not offer to come on board, but called out, 'Hey, yaw, what fashion? Too much baubry, too much baubry,' and put back to the chop-house.

By this manoeuvre we paid not one farthing of duty for our skins which we sold in China—the officers dared not come on board. We landed them as soon as possible and, when once in the factory, all was safe.

We set sail for St Helena where we made a present to the governor of a number of empty bottles. He in return gave us a present of potatoes, a valuable gift to us. While here, I and a number of the crew were nearly poisoned by eating albicores and bonettos.* We split and hung them in the rigging to dry. The moon's rays have the effect of making them

* Albicores and bonettos: fish similar to tuna and mackerel.

poisonous. My face turned red and swelled, but the others were far worse. Their heads were swelled twice their ordinary size—but we all recovered.

In a few days we set sail for England where I arrived without any remarkable occurrence after an absence of three years, having in that time circumnavigated the globe. We came into the river in the month of September 1788.

9

Author Engaged as Steward of a Convict Ship—Anecdotes of Female Convicts—Sails for New South Wales—Attaches Himself to Sarah Whitlam—Singular Punishment—Crossing the Line—Miscellaneous Occurrences—Port Jackson—St Helena.

I NOW RETURNED to Scotland with a sensation of joy only to be felt by those who have been absent for some time. Every remembrance was rendered more dear, every scene was increased in beauty. A piece of oaten cake tasted far sweeter in my mouth than the luxuries of eastern climes.

I was for a time reconciled to remain. The love of country overcame my wandering habits. I had some thought of settling for life, as I had saved a good deal of my pay. In the middle of these musings, and before I had made up my mind, a letter I received from Captain Portlock upset all my future plans and rekindled my wandering propensities with as great vigour as ever.

The letter requested me to come to London without delay, as there were two ships lying in the river bound for New South Wales: the *Guardian* and *Lady Julian*, in either of which I might have a berth.* The *Guardian* was loaded with stores and necessaries for the settlement. There was a vine-dresser and a person to superintend the cultivation of hemp on board. She sailed long before us. The *Lady Julian* was to take out female convicts.

I would have chosen the *Guardian*, only she was a man-of-war, and as I meant to settle in Scotland upon our return I could not have left her when I chose. My only object was to see the country, not to remain at sea. I therefore chose the *Lady Julian*, as she was a

* This was the *Lady Juliana* which sailed with the second fleet.

transport, although I did not by any means like her cargo—yet to see the country I was resolved to submit to a great deal.

I was appointed steward of the *Lady Julian*, commanded by Captain Aitkin, who was an excellent humane man and did all in his power to make the convicts as comfortable as their circumstances would allow. The government agent, an old lieutenant, had been discharged a little before I arrived for cruelty to the convicts. He had even begun to flog them in the river. Government, the moment they learned the fact, appointed another in his place.

We lay six months in the river before we sailed, during which time all the jails in England were emptied to complete the cargo of the *Lady Julian*. When we sailed there were on board 245 female convicts.* There were not a great many very bad characters. The greater number were for petty crimes, and a great proportion for only being disorderly, that is, street-walkers, the colony at the time being in great want of women.

One, a Scottish girl, broke her heart and died in the river. She was buried at Dartford. Four were pardoned on account of his Majesty's recovery. The poor young Scottish girl I have never yet got out of my mind. She was young and beautiful, even in the convict dress, but pale as death, and her eyes red with weeping.

* The *Lady Juliana* actually carried 226 convicts.

She never spoke to any of the other women or came on deck. She was constantly seen sitting in the same corner from morning to night. Even the time of meals roused her not. My heart bled for her—she was a countrywoman in misfortune. I offered her consolation but her hopes and heart had sunk. When I spoke she heeded me not, or only answered with sighs and tears. If I spoke of Scotland she would wring her hands and sob until I thought her heart would burst. I endeavoured to get her sad story from her lips but she was silent as the grave to which she hastened. I lent her my Bible to comfort her but she read it not. She laid it on her lap after kissing it, and only bedewed it with her tears. At length she sunk into the grave of no disease but a broken heart. After her death we had only two Scottish women on board, one of them a Shetlander.

I went every day to the town to buy fresh provisions and other necessaries for them. As their friends were allowed to come on board to see them, they brought money; and numbers had it of their own, particularly a Mrs Barnsley, a noted sharper and shoplifter.* She herself told me her family for one

* Elizabeth Barnsley was fashionably dressed and 'had every appearance of gentility' when she visited an expensive draper's shop in Bond Street in February 1788, in the company of Ann Wheeler. They bought some muslin and Irish cloth, but a shop assistant noticed that Wheeler had slipped a whole bolt of muslin under her cloak and muff. Both women were convicted of theft, and Elizabeth spent over a year in

hundred years back had been swindlers and highwaymen. She had a brother, a highwayman, who often came to see her as well dressed and genteel in his appearance as any gentleman. She petitioned the government agent and captain to be allowed to wear her own clothes in the river, and not the convict dress. This could on no account be allowed, but they told her she might wear what she chose when once they were at sea.

The agent, Lieutenant Edgar, had been with Captain Cook, was a kind humane man and very good to them. He had it in his power to throw all their clothes overboard when he gave them the convict dress, but he gave them to me to stow in the after hold, saying, 'They would be of use to the poor creatures when they arrived at Port Jackson.'

Those from the country came all on board in irons, and I was paid half a crown a head by the country jailors, in many cases, for striking them off upon my anvil, as they were not locked but riveted. There was a Mrs Davis, a noted swindler, who had obtained great quantities of goods under false names and other equally base means.*

* Two women with the surname of Davis were on board the *Lady Juliana*. The younger, Ann, was sentenced to seven

---

Newgate prison where she paid half a crown a week to stay in a relatively comfortable part of the prison. She joined her husband in Sydney where she bore him two sons. The family presumably returned to England after 1795. (See Michael Flynn, *The Second Fleet: Britain's Grim Convict Armada of 1790*, Library of Australian History, Sydney, 1993, 150.)

We had one Mary Williams, transported for receiving stolen goods.* She and other eight had been a long time in Newgate where Lord George Gordon had supported them. I went once a week to him and got their allowance from his own hand all the time we lay in the river.

One day I had the painful task to inform the father and mother of one of the convicts that their daughter, Sarah Dorset, was on board. They were decent-looking people, and had come to London to inquire after her. When I met them they were at Newgate. The jailor referred them to me. With tears in her eyes the mother implored me to tell her if such a one was on board. I told them there was one of that name. The father's heart seemed too full to allow him to speak but the mother with streaming eyes blessed God that they had found their poor lost child, undone as she was.

* Two convicts named Mary Williams sailed with Nicol. The one apparently referred to by Nicol had a tragic story to tell. Desperate to pay the rent of half a crown per week due on her room, she pawned a pair of sheets, two blankets and a pillow belonging to the room. She was sentenced to seven years' transportation but spent eighteen months in Newgate prison waiting for the sentence to be carried out. She was twenty-four when she embarked on the *Lady Juliana*. (See *The Second Fleet*, 613.)

---

years' transportation for trying to sell stolen clothing. The older, Deborah, had been sentenced to death (later commuted to transportation) for stealing jewellery from Mr Timothy Topping of Chislehurst. It is probably Deborah that Nicol is talking of here. (See *The Second Fleet*, 235-36.)

I called a coach, drove to the river and had them put on board. The father, with a trembling step, mounted the ship's side, but we were forced to lift the mother on board. I took them down to my berth and went for Sarah Dorset. When I brought her the father said in a choking voice, 'My lost child!' and turned his back, covering his face with his hands. The mother, sobbing, threw her hands around her. Poor Sarah fainted and fell at their feet. I knew not what to do. At length she recovered and in the most heart-rending accents implored their pardon.

She was young and pretty and had not been two years from her father's house at this present time, so short had been her course of folly and sin. She had not been protected by the villain that ruined her above six weeks, then she was forced by want upon the streets and taken up as a disorderly girl, then sent on board to be transported. This was her short but eventful history. One of our men, William Power, went out to the colony when her time was expired, brought her home and married her.*

I witnessed many moving scenes, and many of the most hardened indifference. Numbers of them would

* Sarah Dorset was convicted of stealing a greatcoat from a London pub. She was sentenced to seven years' transportation. Sarah in fact bore a son to Edward Powell, a seaman on the *Lady Juliana*. Powell did return to Sydney in 1793 but he then married Elizabeth Fish, a free woman, who returned with him to England. Sarah became housekeeper to John Woodward, butcher. The couple had three children. Sarah died in New South Wales in 1838. (See *The Second Fleet*, 248.)

not take their liberty as a boon. They were thankful for their present situation, so low had vice reduced them. Many of these from the country jails had been allowed to leave it to assist in getting in the harvest, and voluntarily returned.

When I inquired their reason, they answered, 'How much more preferable is our present situation to what it has been since we commenced our vicious habits? We have good victuals and a warm bed. We are not ill treated or at the mercy of every drunken ruffian as we were before. When we rose in the morning we knew not where we would lay our heads in the evening, or if we would break our fast in the course of the day. Banishment is a blessing for us. Have we not been banished for a long time, and yet in our native land, the most dreadful of all situations? We dared not go to our relations whom we had disgraced. Other people would shut their doors in our faces. We were as if a plague were upon us, hated and shunned.'

Others did all in their power to make their escape. These were such as had left their associates in rapine on shore and were hardened to every feeling but the abandoned enjoyments of their companions. Four of these made their escape on the evening before we left England through the assistance of their confederates on shore. They gave the man on watch gin to drink as he sat on the quarterdeck, the others singing and making fun. These four slipped over her bows into a boat provided for their escape. I never heard if they were retaken. We sailed without them.

Mrs Nelly Kerwin, a female of daring habits, banished for life for forging seamen's powers of attorney and personating their relations, when on our passage down the river, wrote to London for cash to some of her friends.* She got a letter informing her it was waiting for her at Dartmouth. We were in Colson Bay when she got this letter. With great address she persuaded the agent that there was an express for him and money belonging to her lying at Dartmouth. A man was sent who brought on board Nell's money, but no express for the agent. When she got it she laughed in his face and told him he was in her debt for a lesson. He was very angry, as the captain often told him Kerwin was too many for him.

We had on board a girl pretty well behaved, who was called by her acquaintance a daughter of Pitt's.**

* Eleanor Kirvein kept a 'house of entertainment for sailors' at Gosport. An important part of her business was 'bomb-boating'—providing credit and accommodation for sailors and finding them berths on outward-bound ships. She was convicted of forging the will of a seaman and was sentenced to death. After a 'panel of matrons' found her to be pregnant her sentence was commuted to transportation for seven years. She married Henry Palmer, a convict, in July 1790. A few months later he was killed by a falling tree. She sailed for India, a free woman, in 1793. Michael Flynn notes that she was probably one of the few convict mothers who lived to see the children they left behind. (See *The Second Fleet*, 386.)

** William Pitt (1759-1806) was the current prime minister of Great Britain.

She herself never contradicted it. She bore a most striking likeness to him in every feature and could scarce be known from him as to looks. We left her at Port Jackson.

Some of our convicts I have heard even to boast of the crimes and murders committed by them and their accomplices, but the far greater number were harmless unfortunate creatures, the victims of the basest seduction. With their histories, as told by themselves, I shall not trouble the reader.

When we were fairly out to sea, every man on board took a wife from among the convicts, they nothing loath. The girl with whom I lived, for I was as bad in this point as the others, was named Sarah Whitlam. She was a native of Lincoln, a girl of a modest reserved turn, as kind and true a creature as ever lived. I courted her for a week and upwards, and would have married her on the spot had there been a clergyman on board.

She had been banished for a mantle she had borrowed from an acquaintance. Her friend prosecuted her for stealing it, and she was transported for seven years.*

* Sarah Whitlam, who was born in 1767, was in fact convicted of the theft of a large amount of cloth and clothing, including six yards of black chintz cotton, a raven grey Coventry tammy gown, a pink quilted petticoat, a pair of stays, a fine white lawn apron, a chocolate ground silk handkerchief, a woman's black silk hat and a pair of leather shoes. Flynn speculates that her loot would have filled a cart and may have been stolen from a shop. (See *The Second Fleet*, 610.)

I had fixed my fancy upon her from the moment I knocked the rivet out of her irons upon my anvil, and as firmly resolved to bring her back to England when her time was out, my lawful wife, as ever I did intend anything in my life. She bore me a son in our voyage out.

What is become of her, whether she is dead or alive, I know not. That I do not is no fault of mine, as my narrative will show.

But to proceed. We soon found that we had a troublesome cargo, yet not dangerous or very mischievous—as I may say, more noise than danger. When any of them, such as Nance Ferrel who was ever making disturbance, became very troublesome we confined them down in the hold and put on the hatch.* This, we were soon convinced, had no effect as they became in turns outrageous, on purpose to be confined. Our agent and the captain wondered at the change in their behaviour.

I, as steward, found it out by accident. As I was overhauling the stores in the hold I came upon a hogshead of bottled porter with a hole in the side of it and, in place of full, there were nothing but empty bottles in it. Another was begun and more than a box of candles had been carried off. I immediately told the captain, who now found out the

* Elizabeth Farrell was convicted of stealing clothing and linen from a house in East Smithfield. She eventually went to Van Diemen's Land where she lived comfortably with her husband John Hall, a first-fleet convict. She died in Hobart in 1827. (See *The Second Fleet*, 268.)

cause of the late insubordination and desire of confinement.

We were forced to change the manner of punishing them. I was desired by the agent Lieutenant Edgar, who was an old lieutenant of Cook's, to take a flour barrel and cut a hole in the top for their head and one on each side for their arms. This we called a wooden jacket. Next morning, Nance Ferrel, as usual, came to the door of the cabin and began to abuse the agent and captain. They desired her to go away between decks and be quiet. She became worse in her abuse, wishing to be confined and sent to the hold, but to her mortification the jacket was produced, and two men brought her upon deck and put it on.

She laughed and capered about for a while, and made light of it. One of her comrades lighted a pipe and gave it her. She walked about strutting and smoking the tobacco, and making the others laugh at the droll figure she made. She walked a minuet, her head moving from side to side like a turtle.

The agent was resolved she should be heartily tired, and feel in all its force the disagreeableness of her present situation. She could only walk or stand—to sit or lie down was out of her power. She began to get weary and begged to be released. The agent would not until she asked his pardon, and promised amendment in future. This she did in humble terms before evening, but in a few days was as bad as ever. There was no taming her by gentle means. We were forced to tie her up like a man, and give her one dozen with the cat-o'-nine-tails, and assure her of a clawing every offence. This alone reduced her to any kind of order.

How great was the contrast between her and Mary Rose. Mary was a timid modest girl who never joined in the ribaldry of the rest, neither did she take up with any man upon the voyage. She was a wealthy farmer's daughter who had been seduced under promise of marriage by an officer, and had eloped with him from her father's house. They were living together in Lincoln when the officer was forced to go abroad and leave her. He, before he went, boarded her with their landlady, an infamous character, who, to obtain the board she had received in advance without maintaining the unfortunate girl, swore she had robbed her of several articles.

Poor Mary was condemned by her perjury and sentenced to be transported. She had disgraced her friends and dared not apply to them in her distress. She had set the opinions of the world at defiance by her elopement, and there was no one in it who appeared to befriend her, while in all its bitterness she drank the cup of her own mixing. After the departure of the *Lady Julian* her relations had discovered the fate of their lost and ruined Mary. By their exertions the whole scene of the landlady's villainy was exposed, and she stood in the pillory at Lincoln for her perjury.

Upon our arrival we found a pardon lying at Port Jackson, and a chest of excellent clothes sent by the magistrates for her use in the voyage home. She lodged all the time I was there in the governor's house and every day I took her allowance to her. She was to sail in the first ship for London direct, the *Lady Julian* being bound for China. During the tedious voyage out I took her under my protection. Sarah and she were acquaint before they saw each other in misfortune. Mary washed the clothes and did any little thing for Sarah when she was confined, which she was long before we reached Port Jackson.*

The first place we stopped at was Santa Cruz in the island of Tenerife for water. As we used a great

* Mary Rose had the most extraordinary career of any of the convict women mentioned by Nicol. At sixteen she was sentenced to seven years' transportation for stealing clothes. Fortune had smiled upon her, however, in giving her such a romantic and patriotic name. It seems that it never failed to elicit sympathy in her hour of need. Michael Flynn observes that Nicol's view of her 'mixes fact with romantic fiction' but that 'he was not the only one to fall under her spell'.

Following her imprisonment in Lincoln an anonymous poet penned a romantic ballad to publicise her plight. This it seems was associated with a plea for clemency from no less a person than Sir Joseph Banks! Nicol's assertion that a pardon and clothing were waiting for her in Port Jackson is clearly impossible, as no vessel arrived in the settlement from England between the first and second fleets.

Nicol may have been misled by the fact that Governor Phillip was aware of Banks' plea, and arranged for Rose to marry 'one of the best men in this place'. Less than a year later Phillip lamented to Banks that 'my desire of making her better has only been the means of ruining the poor devil who married her'. Rose lived on in Sydney until at least 1825. (See *The Second Fleet*, 508.)

quantity the agent, at the captain's request, had laid in tea and sugar in place of beef or pork allowed by government. We boiled a large kettle of water that served the whole convicts and crew every night and morning. We allowed them water for washing their clothes, any quantity they chose, while in port. Many times they would use four and five boatloads in one day.

We did not restrain the people on shore from coming on board through the day. The captains and seamen who were in port at the time paid us many visits. Mrs Barnsley bought a cask of wine and got it on board with the agent's leave. She was very kind to her fellow convicts who were poor. They were all anxious to serve her. She was as a queen among them.

We had a number of Jewesses on board. One, Sarah Sabolah, had a crucifix, and the others soon got them and passed themselves for Roman Catholics, by which means they got many presents from the people on shore and laid up a large stock for sea.*

We next stood for Sao Tiago, accompanied by two slave ships from Santa Cruz to Sao Tiago, who sailed thus far out of their course for the sake of the ladies. They came on board every day when the weather would permit. At length they stood for the coast to pick up their cargo of human misery. We watered

* Sarah Sabolah cannot be traced. The name may have been an assumed one.

again and made all clear for a new start. Our Jewesses played off the same farce with their crucifixes, and with equal success.

We then stood for Rio de Janeiro where we lay eight weeks taking in coffee and sugar, our old stock being now reduced very low. I was employed on shore repairing flour casks to receive it. The Jewesses made here a good harvest, and the ladies had a constant run of visitors. I had received fifty suits of child-bed linen for their use—they were a present from the ladies of England. I here served out twenty suits. Mrs Barnsley acted as midwife and was to practise at Port Jackson, but there was no clergyman on board. When in port the ladies fitted up a kind of tent for themselves.

In crossing the line we had the best sport I ever witnessed upon the same occasion. We had caught a porpoise the day before the ceremony which we skinned to make a dress for Neptune with the tail stuffed. When he came on deck he looked the best representation of a merman I ever saw, painted, with a large swab upon his head for a wig. Not a man in the ship could have known him. One of the convicts fainted, she was so much alarmed at his appearance, and had a miscarriage after. Neptune made the boys confess their amours to him, and I was really astonished at the number. I will not describe the ceremony to fatigue the reader, as it has been often described by others.*

* The ceremony of crossing the Equator was an occasion of much merriment. Often the oldest and ugliest sailor was

From Rio de Janeiro we sailed for the Cape of Good Hope, where we took on board seventy-three ewes and a ram for the settlement. We were detained a long time here as we found that the *Guardian* had struck upon an island of ice, and was so severely injured that she was deserted by most of her crew, who were never heard of afterwards. The captain and those who remained with him in the ship were only saved by being towed into the Cape by an American vessel. What detained us was the packing of flour and other necessaries for the colony, as we knew it must be in great want, the *Guardian* being loaded with supplies for it.

At length we sailed for Port Jackson. We made one of the convicts shepherdess, who was so fortunate in her charge of the flock as not to lose one. While we lay at the Cape we had a narrow escape from destruction by fire. The carpenter allowed the pitch-pot to boil over upon the deck, and the flames rose in an alarming manner. The shrieks of the women were dreadful, and the confusion they made running about drove everyone stupid. I ran to my berth, seized a pair of blankets to keep it down until the others drowned it with water. Captain Aitkin made me a handsome present for my exertions.

The captain had a quantity of linen on board, and during the voyage had kept above twenty of the

---

dressed up as King Neptune's wife, and another as Neptune himself. Many liberties were taken with the crew and the officers.

convicts making shirts to sell at Port Jackson. He got them made cheap and sold them to great advantage upon our arrival as the people of the colony were in want of every necessity.

At length, almost to our sorrow, we made the land upon the 3rd of June 1790, just one year all but one day from our leaving the river. We landed all our convicts safe. My charge as steward did not expire for six weeks after our arrival, as the captain, by agreement, was bound to victual them during that time.

It is a fine country and everything thrives well in it. A sergeant of marines supplied the *Lady Julian* with potatoes and garden stuffs for half a crown a day. There were thirty-six people on board and we had as much as we could use. There were only two natives in the town at the time, a boy and a girl.* These had been brought in by a party of the settlers, having been left by their parents. I saw but little of the colony, as my time was fully occupied in my duties as steward, and any moments I could spare I gave them to Sarah.

The days flew on eagles' wings, for we dreaded the hour of separation which at length arrived. It was not without the aid of the military we were brought on board. I offered to lose my wages but we were short of hands, one man having been left sick at Rio de Janeiro, and we had lost our carpenter

* They were Abaroo and Nanbaree, survivors of the smallpox epidemic, who were then living with Surgeon White (Nanbaree) and the Reverend and Mrs Johnson (Abaroo).

who fell overboard. The captain could not spare a man and requested the aid of the governor. I thus was forced to leave Sarah, but we exchanged faith. She promised to remain true, and I promised to return when her time expired and bring her back to England.*

I wished to have stolen her away, but this was impossible, the convicts were so strictly guarded by the marines. There were no soldiers in the colony at this time. With a heavy heart I bade adieu to Port Jackson, resolved to return as soon as I reached England. We would have remained some time longer, but Captain Aitkin was very unwell and the mate was anxious to complete the voyage.

They have an herb in the colony they call sweet tea.** It is infused and drank like the China tea. I liked it much. It requires no sugar and is both a bitter and a sweet. There was an old female convict, her hair quite grey with age, her face shrivelled, who was suckling a child she had borne in the colony. Everyone went to see her, and I among the rest. It was a strange sight. Her hair was quite white. Her fecundity was ascribed to the sweet tea.

* John Nicol and Sarah Whitlam parted for the last time on 25 July 1790. On 26 July Sarah married John Coen Walsh, a first-fleet convict. She signed the marriage register with a cross. In June 1796 the couple sailed for England via India with their two sons. Walsh was back in Australia by 1801 but there are no further records of Sarah Whitlam.

** *Smilax glyciphylla.*

I brought away with me two bags of it as presents to my friends, but two of our men became very ill of the scurvy and I allowed them the use of it, which soon cured them but reduced my store. When we came to China I showed it to my Chinese friends, and they bought it with avidity and importuned me for it and a quantity of the seed I had likewise preserved. I let them have the seed, and only brought a small quantity of the herb to England.

Upon our arrival at Wampoa I renewed my acquaintance with my Chinese friends, and was as happy as I could be with the thoughts of Sarah's situation upon my mind—but this was the dullest voyage I ever made. I changed my berth in the ship, but all would not do. Everything brought her endearing manners to my recollection. To leave her a convict was a great aggravation to my grief. Had I left her by choice for a voyage I could have thought of her with pleasing regret and anxious hope of seeing her soon. But to leave her exposed to temptation in the very worst company the world could produce was too much to think of with composure. I left with her my Bible, the companion of all my voyages, with our names written in it. She used to read it often, when I never thought of it.

So much did these thoughts prey upon my mind I almost resolved to lose my wages by leaving the *Lady Julian* at Rio or the Cape. But to be so far from home, without one penny in my pocket to pay her passage to England, would have been madness, as I could not bear the idea of bidding for ever farewell to Scotland, the place where my wanderings were always intended to cease.

I made up my mind to come to England in the *Lady Julian*, and get a berth out the first opportunity, and by that time her term of transportation would be expired. We touched at St Helena on our way to England. When we arrived I was paid off and immediately made every inquiry for a ship for New Holland, but there was none, nor any likely to be soon.

10

Author Engaged on Board a South Sea Whaler—Miscellaneous Occurrences—Grief at the Conduct of Sarah—Seal-Fishing—Sea Lions—Unexpectedly Meets a Countryman at Paita—Transactions There.

THERE WAS A vessel called the *Amelia*, Captain Shiels, fitting out as a south-sea whaler. She belonged to Squire Enderborough, Paul's Wharf, London. I got myself engaged as cooper of her. The whole crew were on shares. I, as cooper, had a larger share than a seaman, but this was not my present aim, neither did I think of gain.

I had all my money secured about my person, sewed into my clothes, ready for a start, and with it to pay the passage of Sarah and my son to England. My intention was, when we arrived at Rio de Janeiro on our return home, to fall sick and endeavour to obtain my share from the captain and allow the vessel to sail without me, or to claim it when I reached England. From Rio I could easily get a ship to the Cape. From the Cape to New South Wales I had the only chance of a vessel. I would have remained until the *Amelia* reached the Cape, but she might not even anchor there. These were my views in entering on board the *Amelia*.

In two months after my leaving the *Lady Julian* I was again at sea in hopes of reaching Port Jackson by some means or other. In our first offset we were stranded upon the Red Sand near the Nore. While we lay in distress, the Deal men came out and wished to make a wreck of us by cutting away our masts.* I, with

* Deal was one of the 'cinque ports' near Dover. The men of Deal were pilots, lifeboat men and smugglers known for 'hovelling', or taking disabled ships.

alacrity, aided the captain and stood guard with a brace of pistols, and threatened to blow out the brains of the first man of them that offered to set his foot upon our deck.

The weather fortunately was moderate. We, having no longboat, carried out our anchor between two boats into deep water, and as the tide flowed we got her off. To my great disappointment we were forced to put back into dock to have her examined by removing the copper sheathing. All the crew left her except myself, as the engagement was broken by our return to dock, and the men would not continue in her as they thought no good would come of the voyage. Her stranding was an omen of her bad luck.

There was no ship in the river for New South Wales, and the Indiamen would not sail until about the month of March. The *Amelia* would still be the first vessel. I had no inducement, therefore, to leave her.

We were soon again ready for sea, and set sail with an entire new crew. The first land we made was the island of Buena Vista which belongs to the Portuguese, where we took in livestock, and salt to salt down our seal skins, then stood for Sao Tiago and took in more livestock; from thence to the Falkland Islands for geese and swine. We next made Staten Island, and passed the Straits of Magellan and Straits le Mair, but did not go through either of them. We doubled the Cape then stood down to our fishing ground which was between latitude 18° and the Line.

We had nothing to do but commence, as we had been busy all the voyage preparing and fitting our tackle. Our boilers were fitted up before we left England as in the south seas the spermaceti is all boiled upon the deck. The boiler is built up with fire brick, and a space left between the lower tier and the deck about nine inches high, quite watertight. When once the fire is kindled, which is never after allowed to go out until the ship is fully fished, the space between the bricks and the deck is kept full of water. There are two plug-holes (one on each side) so that when the water heats and would melt the pitch, upon whatever tack the ship may be, the plug is drawn from the under side and the space immediately filled with cold water from the higher side. Great attention is required to watch the boilers. We do not require to carry out fuel to boil our oil, as the refuse of the oil is used ever after the first fire is kindled.

The ashes of the fire is better than any soap. Let our clothes be ever so black and greasy, as they must be from our employment, one shovel full of ashes in a tub of water will make them as clean as when we bought them.

During the fishing we lived wholly upon turtle and were heartily tired of them. We were very fortunate in our fishing. We caught one whale from which we obtained 125 pounds weight of ambergrease, the largest quantity ever brought to England by one ship.

Upon the fishing ground we found the *Venus*, Captain Coffin. She had taken out convicts to Port

Jackson and there was a convict on board at the time. He had concealed himself in her until she was at sea, and by this means made his escape from the colony. He used to hide himself from me but, the other men assuring him I would not inform, he had the courage to speak to me at length, and inquired if ever I had been at Port Jackson.

I told him I had in the *Lady Julian*. He answered he had seen me there. My heart beat high with anxiety. I feared, yet wished, to hear of Sarah Whitlam.

At length I inquired. How shall I express my grief when informed she had left the colony for Bombay. Thus were my worst fears realised. Unconstant woman! Why doubt my faith? Yet dear, and never to be forgotten, I resolved to follow her to India. I could not speak to him so broke off the conversation for the present and left him in greater despondency than I left Port Jackson. My grief was not then mixed with doubts of her constancy. She had only three years to serve when I left her, and these were not yet expired. How she got away he could not inform me.

Every time we met I renewed my inquiries. He was so uniform in his replies, and assured me of its truth so solemnly, I was forced to believe the unpleasant truth. I inquired for my son John, but he could give me no information to be relied on. He believed she had taken him with her but, as the children are taken from the convicts and maintained at school by the government, he knew not her son from the others, and did not see her go away.

I now had no inducement to go to Port Jackson and for a few days scarce cared what became of me. My love for her revived stronger at this time than any other since I left her. I even gave her praise for leaving it. She did so to be out of bad company, my mind would whisper, and I resolved to get to Bombay as soon as possible, and endeavour to find her out.

As my usual buoyancy of spirits returned, I pursued my labours with all the ardour of a seaman. After taking a sufficient quantity of spermaceti we stood as far down as latitude 3° to the Island of Lopes where we killed thirty thousand seals.* We had a busy time chasing and killing them. When we had a sufficient number we began to kill sea-lions to get their skins for the ship's use. One of their skins was a sufficient load for two men. We used to stand in a gap of the rocks in the morning and knock them down with our clubs as they approached the sea, then stab them with our long knives.

George Parker our mate made a blow at one and missed him. He made a snap at George and sent his tusk right through his arm, a little above the wrist, and walked away at his leisure with him into the sea, Parker roaring like a bull from the pain and terror. Robert Wyld, perceiving his danger, rushed into the water to rescue him, and was up to the armpits before

* Island of Lopes: Lobos Island in northern Peru.

he succeeded in dispatching the unwieldy monster. He then dragged them both on shore where, with difficulty, the tusk was drawn from between the bones, it was so firmly jammed.

We soon after sailed three degrees to the north of the Line to the River Tambo where we anchored, and the captain ascended the river nine miles in his boat, to which I belonged, to the town of Tambo. We had an American Indian for a pilot. He appeared to worship the alligators as he kept constantly bowing and muttering to them, and a busy time he had of it as they were very numerous.

The governor of the town and people were very kind and civil to us. We remained all night at the governor's house, feasting like kings. Captain Shiels made him a present of some porter and a cheese and a few other things, for which he would have given us as many bullocks as we chose. We only took one which was as much as we could use fresh, there being only sixteen hands in the ship. We watered in the river then crossed the Line to the city of Paita, where we anchored in a beautiful bay, quite land-locked and as smooth as a mill-pond.

We scarcely had made all tight when a boat came alongside, and inquired if there was a Scotchman on board. The captain allowed me to go as I was the only one in the ship. I was conducted to a baker's shop in the town and into an elegant room, where a sickly-looking person, but elegantly dressed, rose and met me, shaked hands, and said, 'How's a' wi' you?'

My ears tingled and my heart leapt for joy to hear the accents of my native tongue so unexpectedly. I looked hard at him but had never seen him before. I thanked him and we sat down together and began a long conversation. We talked of Old Scotland and the talk was all on my side for a long while, he had so many questions to put, and he seemed to devour every word I spoke while joy beamed in his sickly features.

At length I got his own history. He was a native of Inverness and had been bred to the sea and, coming to the West Indies, had engaged in the contraband trade carried on along the Spanish main; had been taken prisoner and carried to Montevideo; from thence to Lima where he had been long in prison and suffered many hardships but, being a Roman Catholic, he was not sent to the mines. He had found means to obtain his liberty and afterwards win the love of a rich Spanish lady who procured him his pardon and afterwards married him. He was now very rich and had a ship of his own, besides immense property, but having fallen sick at Paita he had ordered his vessel to proceed on her voyage and send his servants to carry him overland to Lima. He was expecting them every day.

He treated me nobly and made me a handsome present when he went away, which he did while we lay at Paita. I was astonished at the number of servants and horses that came for him. His saddle would have bought fifty horses. The stirrups were solid gold, and every part was loaded with it. The maker seemed to have studied more to lay on gold than taste in the ornaments. He made the most enticing offers to induce me to go with him, but Sarah was dearer to me than all the riches in the world.

The governor and people of Paita were so kind to us we passed our time very agreeably. All their houses were open to us. They forced presents of fruit upon us, and gave us as much accadent as we chose to drink.*

The governor treated us with a Spanish play. These entertainments are through the day. During the performance we were served with wine, sweet-meats and fruits, but not understanding the language we paid more attention to the refreshments than the play. The governor was one of the kindest gentlemen I ever saw. He told us he loved the English for their humanity; he had been in the town when Lord Anson plundered it.** Ever since they do not keep their saints and plate in the church, but in the town-house which is no stronger than the church. You may see them carrying it back and forward every day.

The governor was very anxious to learn English. I could buy and sell in Spanish. Upon this account he took great notice of me. I had a Spanish and English dictionary on board. I gave it him, and he made me a

* Accadent: spiritous liquor.

** Admiral Anson sailed upon a voyage around the world in the years 1740–44, during which he plundered Paita but showed the inhabitants great mercy.

handsome present he was so much pleased with it—and he made rapid progress in his study.

He was the first that told me of the King of France's death. He said, drawing his hand across his neck, 'The people have cut the neck of de Roi de Française.' I understood what he meant, but did not believe the information.

I wore in general, when ashore, a black jacket with black horn buttons. A priest I used often to meet at the governor's took a fancy to the buttons and offered me any price for them. I soon cut off my buttons, and gave them to him. I had breeches and vest with the same buttons; off went they, every one. A Jew would have counted it a good bargain.

Amidst all their kindness they are very superstitious. I must have lain in the streets all night one evening I missed the boat, had not a Portuguese who was with me told them I was an Irishman. 'O bon Irelandois! O bon Christian!' they cried and made me welcome, gave me the best in the house, happy to entertain so good a Christian as an Irishman.

While everything was going on to our wish, and our ambergrease selling well, we were forced to leave Paita in great haste. One of our men, getting himself tipsy, told the people openly we were selling ambergrease and had still a great quantity to sell. The governor immediately sent for the captain and informed him of his danger. He himself was not against the sale but should word reach Lima they would order a frigate to Paita and make a prize of us. We were too much afraid of this to tarry longer than get in what supplies we stood in need of, for which the governor would accept no payment.

I went with other two to take leave of the governor. As we proceeded along we saw two ladies swinging in a net, and a female servant keeping it in motion. We stood looking at them a few minutes before they perceived us. As soon as they did they desired the servant to cease, came down and bade us come into the house where they treated us with fruit and wine, and would scarce allow us to go away so soon as we wanted. The ladies here have a pale and sickly look. All their movements are languid. Even the men are far from being active. Everyone moves as if he wished someone to carry him.

11

Rio de Janeiro—Portuguese Seamen—Lisbon—Author Arrives in London—Visits Sarah's Parents—Enters a Vessel Bound for China—Anecdote.

WHEN WE SAILED we had two booms over our stern, and a net made fast to them filled with pumpkins, melons and other vegetables, the gift of these kind Spaniards. We stood direct for Rio de Janeiro, where Captain Shiels intended to remain for some time as he had completed his cargo so soon. He would have lost the bounty had he arrived before the time specified in the act of parliament.

There were a great number of Portuguese vessels lying at Rio de Janeiro at this time. No accounts had been received from Lisbon for six months, and it was believed the French had taken Portugal. I counted every day we remained as so much of my time lost, and wearied very much. At length a ship arrived from Lisbon and all the Portuguese prepared to sail. The governor's linguist came on board the *Amelia* and requested, as a personal favour, that Captain Shiels would allow four of his men to go on board the Commodore to assist in the voyage home, as it would be a winter's passage.

I immediately volunteered. I hoped by this means to reach England sooner and obtain more money for Sarah, as I would receive a full share of the *Amelia* in England the same as if I had continued in her. Had I know the delays, the fatigue and vexations I was to endure from these execrable superstitious Portuguese sailors, I never would have left the *Amelia* for any reward the Commodore could have given me—and he was very kind to us. He knew our value, and his whole reliance was upon us. We were to work the ship, and fight the ship should an enemy lay us alongside. He had been forty years trading between Lisbon and Rio de Janeiro, and in all that time never had made a winter's voyage.

The Portuguese are the worst sailors in the world in rough or cold weather, and we had plenty of both, but worse than all we had a black fellow of a priest on board to whom the crew paid more attention than the captain. He was for ever ringing his bell for mass and sprinkling holy water upon the men. Whenever it blew harder than ordinary they were sure to run to the quarterdeck to the black priest. We were almost foundered at one time by this unseamanlike conduct. The whole crew ran to the quarterdeck, kneeling down, resigned to their fate, the priest sprinkling holy water most profusely upon them, while we four Englishmen were left to steer the vessel and hand the sails. It required two of the four to steer, so that there were only two to hand the sails. The consequence was she broached to. William Mercer and I ran and cut the foregeers, and allowed the yard to swing. At the same time, the captain, mate and boatswain hauled in the forebrace and she righted in a moment. Had her commons not been very high, she must have filled while she lay upon her beam ends. The sea was all over her deck round the hatch, but so soon as she righted and we were going to make sail the Portuguese left their priest and lent us a hand.

We were wrought almost to death and never could have made out the voyage had we not been well fed and the captain given us plenty of liquor. The black priest rung his bell at his stated time whatever we were doing, and the Portuguese would run to their berths for their crosses. Often the main tack was left half hauled aboard at the sound of his bell, and the vessel left to drift leeward until prayers were over. As two men could do nothing to the sail when the wind was fresh, after prayers they would return and begin bawling and hauling, calling upon their saints as if they would come to assist.

We were thus almost driven to distraction by them and could scarce keep off our hands from boxing their ears. Many a hearty curse they and their saints got. Then they would run to the captain or priest and make complaint that the Englishmen had cursed Saint Antonio or some other of the saints. I often wondered the captain did not confine the priest to his cabin in foul weather, as he was sure to be busiest then. When they complained, the captain took our part and overawed the Portuguese, or I really believe they would have thrown us overboard. They often looked at us as if they could have eat us without salt, and told us to our face we were 'star pork', that is, all the same as swine—that we knew nothing of God or the saints.

I showed them my Bible and the names of the saints. They were quite surprised. Had I made another voyage I would have made converts of many of them. I was bald headed and they called me an English padre. Often the bell rang while we were at dinner. They inquired why I would not go to mass. 'I mess with the Coussinero,' I replied.* They began to think I had the best religion. They seemed to think the foul weather was all upon our account, and the virgin and saints sent it because they employed heretics on board.

We had a supercargo on board as passenger, who had made his fortune in the slave trade and was returning home to Portugal. He took unwell and died. At his funeral there were the following manoeuvres gone through. Everyone had a candle in his hand, and all stood in a double line upon the deck. There were even lanthorns hung over the ship's side to light him to the bottom. The body was carried along the double line, the priest chanting, and every one touched him before he was thrown overboard. The captain requested us to do as the others did. Says Will Mercer, 'Captain, I will throw him overboard for you, if you please.'

At length, after a tedious voyage of three months, I got out of this vile crew. When we reached the Tagus the Portuguese began to quarrel and knock us about.** We stood our ground the best way we could until the captain got five of them sent on shore under a guard of soldiers. We remained at the captain's house until we got our wages. The owners gave us a doubloon a piece over and above our agreement for saving the ship, as the captain did us every justice to the owners at the time, saying, 'If the English were as

* Coussinero: cook.

** The Tagus is the estuary Lisbon is situated on.

careful of their souls as they are of their bodies, they would be the best people in the world.'

I had many conversations with the captain concerning the ignorance of the Portuguese people in general, and asked why the priest did not inform them better. He said, 'Were we to inform them they would soon turn the priest about his business and rise against the government. They must only get knowledge little by little.'

We assisted at a religious ceremony before we came away, at the special request of our kind friend the captain. The foresail that was set when she broached to was given as an offering to the church, as the black priest told them it was through it they were saved. Although the worst sailor in the world knew it was the sail that would have sunk us, they dared not contradict the priest. The whole ship's crew carried it through the streets of Lisbon upon handkerchiefs to the church where it was placed upon the altar with much mummery. We came away and left them but the owners of the vessel bought back the sail again, after the priests had blessed it to their minds, as the church had more use for money than foresails.

William Mercer and I entered on board a brig bound for London, which was to sail in a few days, during which time we rambled about through the filthy streets of Lisbon. The higher orders of the Portuguese are very kind and civil. I was too late one evening to get on board the brig. A Portuguese merchant noticed my perplexity, for it is no pleasing thing to have a lodging to seek in Lisbon at a latish hour. Without my requesting him, he took me to his own house, gave me an excellent supper and bed. Had I been a gentleman of his acquaintance he could not have been kinder or paid me more attention. He ordered his servant to call me at any hour in the morning I chose.

As war was now looked for we were afraid for the press.* The Portuguese captain, at our request, got each of us a protection from the British consul at Lisbon. With a joyful heart I set sail for London to look out for an Indiaman that I might get to Bombay and inquire for Sarah, for she was still the idol of all my affections. At this time I was all anxiety to reach England. I often hoped she had reached her father's house and there was pining at my absence. I used for days to flatter myself with these dreams.

When we arrived at Gravesend a man-of-war's boat came on board to press any Englishmen there might be on board. William and I did not choose to trust to our protections now that we were in the river. So we stowed ourselves away among some bags of cotton where we were almost smothered but could hear every word that was said. The captain told the lieutenant he had no more hands than he saw, and they were all Portuguese. The lieutenant was not very particular, and left the brig without making much search.

* Britain had by now entered the French Revolutionary Wars.

When the boat left the vessel we crept from our hiding hole, and not long after a custom-house officer came on board. When we cast anchor, as I had a suit of long clothes in my chest that I had provided, should I have been so fortunate as have found Sarah at Port Jackson, to dash away with her a bit on shore, I put them on immediately and gave the custom-house officer half a guinea for the loan of his cocked hat and powdered wig. The long gilt-headed cane was included in the bargain.

I got a waterman to put me on shore. I am confident my own father, had he been alive, could not have known me with my cane in my hand, cocked hat and bushy wig. I inquired at the waterman the way to the inn where the coach set out from for London; I at the same time knew as well as him. I passed for a passenger. At the inn I called for a pint of wine, pens and ink, and was busy writing any nonsense that came in my head until the coach set off. All these precautions were necessary. Had the waterman suspected me to be a sailor he would have informed the press-gang in one minute. The waiters at the inn would have done the same.

By these precautions I arrived safe in London but did not go down to Wapping until next day, where I took up my old lodgings, still in my disguise. My landlord went on board and brought on shore my bedding and chest. I left them under his charge while I went to Lincoln to Sarah's parents where I made every inquiry—but they knew not so much of her as I did myself. The last information they had obtained was from the letter I had put in the post office for them before I sailed in the *Amelia*.

I immediately returned to London where, to my disappointment, I found there was not a berth to be got in any of the Indiamen who were for Bombay direct. They were all full. I then, as my next best, went to be engaged as cooper on board the *Nottingham* for China direct, depending on providence if we were ever to meet again. To find some way to effect my purpose, my landlord took me to be impressed. He got the six guineas allowed the bringer, which he returned to me. He was from Inverness, as honest a man as ever lived. I had always boarded in his house when in London.

A curious scene happened at my entry. There were a few more impressed on the same day, one an old tar. When asked by Captain Rogers, in his examination, how they hauled the main tack aboard, he replied, 'I can't tell, your honour, but I can show.' He clapped his foot into Captain Rogers' pocket, at the same instant leaped on his shoulders, tore his coat to the skirts, saying, 'Thus we haul it aboard.'

Captain Barefoot of the *Nottingham* and the other captains laughed heartily, as well as Rogers, who said rather peevishly, 'You might have shown, without tearing my coat.'

'How could I, your honour?' was the reply.*

* Perhaps this was the only means the old tar had of showing his displeasure at being pressed.

12

Arrival at the Cape of Good Hope—Singular Incident—Java—Wampoa—Chinese Artificers—Music—Returns to England, and is Impressed—Leith Roads—Mutiny—Storm at Sea.

I THUS AGAIN set off as cooper of the *Nottingham* in 1793. Nothing worthy of notice happened. As I have gone over the same voyage before I will not detain the reader, but one circumstance that I witnessed off the Cape of Good Hope I cannot avoid mentioning as a dreadful example of what man will dare, and the perils he will encounter, to free himself from a situation he dislikes.

A man-of-war had been washing her gratings when the India fleet hove in sight. (They are washed by being lowered overboard and allowed to float astern.) Four or five men had slipped down upon them, cut them adrift and were thus voluntarily committed to the vast Atlantic without a bit of biscuit or a drop of water or any means of guiding the gratings they were floating upon in the hope of being picked up by some vessel. They held out their arms to us and supplicated in the wildest manner to be taken on board.

The captain would not. The *Nottingham* was a fast sailing ship and the first in the fleet. He said, 'I will not. Some of the stern ships will pick them up.' While he spoke these unfortunate and desponding fellow creatures lessened to our view, while their cries rung in our ears. I hope some of the stern ships picked them up. Few things I have seen are more strongly impressed upon my memory than the despairing looks and frantic gestures of these victims in quest of liberty. Next morning the frigate they had left came alongside of us and inquired if we had seen them. The captain gave an indirect answer to their inquiries, as well he might.

When we arrived at Java and anchored at Batavia I made every inquiry for a country ship, and would have left the *Nottingham* in a moment had there been one.* All my money was concealed upon my person for a start. I thought of falling sick and remaining until a country ship came, but I might really have become what I feigned in this European's grave, as I must have remained in the hospital. Had I walked about the city in health, the Dutch would soon have kidnapped me. I was thus once more baffled.

Indeed, I must confess, I did not feel the same anguish now I had endured before. It was now four years since I had left her in the colony, and her leaving it so soon, without waiting for me, showed she cared less about me than I cared for her. Not to write to her parents I had often thought very neglectful of her. I made up my mind not to leave the *Nottingham* at such risks, but to return in her to England and settle, as I had now some cash and had seen all I could see, and just make one more call at her friends in Lincoln, in my way to Scotland, and be ruled by the information I there obtained.

We sailed for Wampoa, where I was kindly received by my Chinese friends. I now paid more attention and saw things without the glare of novelty and have no cause to alter anything I said before. I had always, while at home, thought them the best tradesmen and most ingenious of people. I am

* Batavia: Jakarta.

inclined to think they have been overrated in regard to their abilities. Some things they do very neat, but considering the things they have to do them with it is no wonder. I mean their varnishes and colours, native productions.

Let the following facts that I can vouch for speak for themselves. In my own line they are unable to make any article with two ends, such as barrels. They have only reached the length of a tub. These they dool, that is pin with bamboos, the joints of the staves as well as the bottom. When a cask that comes from Europe is to be broached they cannot even bore and place the crane on it. A foreign cooper must go on shore and do it. Many a half dollar I have got for this service myself from the Chinese merchants.

I do not believe they can make a nail with a head. Many thousand of their nails I have had through my hands, and never saw one with a head upon it such as we have in England. Their nails are either sprigs or simply bent like a crow's toe. They are the worst smiths of any people, and can do nothing with a bar of iron if thick. I and the other coopers always kept the cuttings of our hoops which they bought with avidity—but larger pieces they would scarce take from us.

A vessel, the *Argyll*, while we were there in the *King George*, had lost her rudder in the voyage out and could not sail without a new one. There was not a smith in Canton who could forge the ironwork. The captain of the ship applied to the armourer of the *King*

George who took it in hand and in three weeks gained one hundred dollars by the job.

They appear to me to be excellent copiers, but not inventors. One of our officers sat for a painter to draw his picture and told the Chinese not to make him ugly. 'How can make other than is?' was the reply. He had no idea of altering a single feature to add to the looks of the object he was painting. All was a slavish copy of what was before his eyes. If you want anything made out of the common they must have one of the same as a pattern or they will not take it in hand. And what is further proof of their want of invention is, when you see one house you have seen every house of the same rank, or any other articles of their manufacture you have seen all. There is scarcely any variety and you need give yourself no trouble looking for others if the price pleases.

There is no change of fashion: the oldest articles you can fall in with are the same make and fashion as the newest, and a traveller who visited the country two hundred years ago could know no difference but in the men. They would be new, the old having died; the present race, I may say, wearing their dress and inhabiting their houses without the least change in the general appearance.

The only instrument of music I saw was a bagpipe, like the small Lowland pipe, on which they play well. Their gongs cannot be called a musical instrument. When John Tuck, the deputy emperor, appears (he is called so by the seamen on account of his having a gallows on board the grand boat which is as large as a seventy-four-gun ship and crowded with attendants), his band consists only of bagpipes. Their gongs are only used that I heard to make *tchin, tchin* to Joss in bad weather and at their paper sacrifices; and every vessel, down to the smallest sampan, has a Joss on board.

The deputy emperor comes once every year to view the fleet and pay his respects to the commodore. It is the grandest sight upon the river. Not so much as a sampan is allowed to move. He makes a present to every ship in the fleet of bullocks, wine, schamsee and flour. The officers start the schamsee overboard—it is a pernicious liquor distilled from rice. The flour is so coarse it is given to the hogs.

They measure every ship and can tell to a quarter chest how much she will hold. The first American sloop that came, she having only one mast, the Chinamen said, 'Hey, yaw, what fashion? How can measure ship with one mast?'—they having been accustomed to measure ships with more masts than one. They measure between the masts the breadth and depth of the ship.

I went up the river to the Dutch Folly, a fort lying waste opposite Canton in the middle of the river. The Dutch pretended they wished to build an hospital for their sick and got leave to do so, but their design was discovered by the bursting of a large barrel full of shot, and the Chinese put a stop to their undertaking, which now lies waste.

The Chinese sell all their fish, frogs, rats and hogs alive, and all by weight. Their frogs are bred and fed by them and are the largest I ever saw. When we bought our sea stock the hogs came on board in the baskets in which they were weighed.

The Chinese women are seldom seen in the streets. They walk very ill, and their gowns sweep the ground. Their hair is very prettily done up in the form of a crown on the top of their heads and fastened with a large gold or silver pin. The Tartar women are to be met at every step.

The cargo being complete, we fell down the river using our old precaution to keep off the Chinese chop-officers, and they retired with the same exclamation, 'Hey, yaw, what fashion? Too much baubry. Too much baubry.'

Nothing uncommon happened until we reached the Downs. I had allowed my beard to grow long and myself to be very dirty to be as unlikely as possible when the man-of-war boats came on board to press the crew. As we expected, they came. I was in the hold, sorting among the water casks, and escaped. They took every hand that would answer. I rejoiced in my escape but my joy was of short duration. One of the men they had taken had a sore leg. The boat brought him back—and I had the bad luck to be taken and he was left. Thus were all my schemes blown into the air.

I found myself in a situation I could not leave, a bondage that had been imposed upon me against my will, and no hopes of relief until the end of the war—not that I disliked it, but I had now become weary of wandering for a time and longed to see Scotland again. My heart always pointed to my native land. Remonstrance and complaint were equally vain.

I therefore made up my mind to it, and was as happy as a man in blasted prospects can be. I was taken on board the *Venerable*, Admiral Duncan. She was the flagship and commanded by Captain Hope, now Admiral Hope. The *Venerable's* boats had made a clean ship of the *Nottingham*. She was forced to be brought up the river by ticket-porters and old Greenwich men. Next morning sixty of us who had belonged to the *Nottingham* were turned over to the *Edgar*, seventy-four, Captain Sir Charles Henry Knowles. This was on the 11th June 1794. I was stationed in the gunner's crew.

We went upon a cruise to the coast of Norway, then touched at Shetland for fresh provisions. Afterwards we sailed for Leith Roads. I now felt all the inconveniencies of my confinement. I was at home in sight of the place where I wished all my wanderings to cease. Captain Barefoot of the *Nottingham* had wrote to Sir C. H. Knowles in my behalf, and he was very kind to me. I asked leave to go on shore to see my friends which he consented to, but Lieutenant Collis would not allow me, saying 'it was not safe to allow a pressed man to go on shore at his native place'.

Had I been allowed, I did not intend to leave the *Edgar*. I would not have run away for any money, upon my kind captain's account. My uncle came on board and saw me before we sailed, and I was visited by my other friends, which made me quite happy.

While we lay in Leith Roads, a mutiny broke out in the *Defiance*, seventy-four. The cause was, their captain gave them five-water grog; now the common thing is three-waters. The weather was cold. The spirit thus reduced was, as the mutineers called it, as thin as muslin and quite unfit to keep out the cold. No seaman could endure this in cold climates. Had they been in hot latitudes they would have been happy to get it thus for the sake of the water, but then they would not have got it.

The *Edgar* was ordered alongside the *Defiance* to engage her, if necessary, to bring her to order. We were saved this dreadful alternative by their returning to duty. She was manned principally by fishermen, stout resolute dogs. When bearing down upon her my heart felt so sad and heavy, not that I feared death or wounds, but to fight my brother, as it were. I do not believe the *Edgar's* crew would have manned the guns. They thought the *Defiance* men were in the right, and had they engaged us heartily as we would have done a French seventy-four, we could have done no good, only blown each other out of the water, for the ships were of equal force; and if there were any odds the *Defiance* had it in point of crew. Had I received my discharge and one hundred guineas I could not have felt my heart lighter than I did when we returned to our anchorage. And the gloom immediately vanished from every face in the ship.

We shortly after sailed on a cruise in the north seas and encountered a dreadful gale on the 17th October. I never was in such danger in all my life. The *Edgar* was only newly put in commission, and her rigging was new and not properly seasoned. We in a few hours carried away our bowsprit and foremast in this dreadful night, then our mizen and main topmast. With great difficulty we cut them clear. Soon after our mainmast loosened in the step, and we every moment expected it to go through her bottom. Then no exertion could have saved us from destruction. The carpenter, by good fortune, got it secured.

We lost all our anchors and cables in our attempts to bring her to, save one. At length it moderated a little, when we rigged jury masts and made for the Humber where we brought to with our only remaining anchor—when the *Inflexible*, Captain Savage, hove in sight and took us in tow. When in this situation the coasters, as they passed, called to the *Inflexible*, 'What prize have you got in tow?' A fresh gale sprung up and the *Inflexible* was forced to cast us off.

The weather moderated again and we proceeded up the Swain the best way we could into Blackstakes, Chatham. My berth during the storm, as one of the gunner's crew, was in charge of the powder on deck we used in firing our guns of distress. The ship rolled so much we were often upon our beam ends, and rolled a number of our guns overboard. We were forced to start all our beer and water to lighten the ship, but we rode it out, contrary to our expectation, and were shortly after turned over, captain and all, to the *Goliah*, seventy-four guns, and sailed to join Sir John Jervis in the blockade of Toulon. We boarded a Spanish ship and found on board thirty Austrian prisoners. They every man entered with us as marines.

13

Action off Cape St Vincent—Blockade of Cadiz—Action at Aboukir Bay—Anecdotes of the Battle—Subsequent Occurrences—Landing of the British Army in Egypt—Ophthalmia—Return to England.

WE NEXT SAILED for St Forensa Bay in the island of Corsica to water, but found the French in possession of the watering-place, and could get none. I belonged to the launch and had charge of the powder and match. I was constantly on shore when any service was to be done in destroying stores, spiking guns, blowing up batteries, and enjoyed it much. We carried off all the brass guns, and those metal ones that were near the edge of the rocks we threw into the sea. This was excellent sport to us but we were forced to leave it and sail to Gibraltar for water and provisions; but could obtain no supplies and sailed for Lisbon where we got plenty, having been on short allowance for some time before.

While we lay at Lisbon we got private intelligence overland that the Spanish fleet was at sea. We with all dispatch set sail in pursuit of them. We were so fortunate as come in sight of them by break of day, on the 14th of February, off Cape St Vincent. They consisted of twenty-five sail, mostly three-deckers. We were only eighteen but we were English, and we gave them their valentines in style.

Soon as we came in sight, a bustle commenced not to be conceived or described. To do it justice, while every man was as busy as he could be the greater order prevailed. A serious cast was to be perceived on every face but not a shade of doubt or fear. We rejoiced in a general action; not that we loved fighting, but we all wished to be free to return to our homes and follow our own pursuits. We knew there was no other way of obtaining this than by defeating the enemy. 'The hotter war the sooner peace,' was a saying with us. When everything was cleared, the ports open, the matches lighted and guns run out, then we gave them three such cheers as are only to be heard in a British man-of-war. This intimidates the enemy more than a broadside, as they have often declared to me. It shows them all is right, and the men in the true spirit baying to be at them.

During the action, my situation was not one of danger but most wounding to my feelings and trying to my patience. I was stationed in the after-magazine, serving powder from the screen, and could see nothing—but I could feel every shot that struck the *Goliah*, and the cries and groans of the wounded were most distressing as there was only the thickness of the blankets of the screen between me and them. Busy as I was, the time hung upon me with a dreary weight. Not a soul spoke to me but the master-at-arms as he went his rounds to inquire if all was safe. No sick person ever longed more for his physician than I for the voice of the master-at-arms. The surgeon's-mate at the commencement of the action spoke a little, but his hands were soon too full of his own affairs.

Those who were carrying run like wild creatures and scarce opened their lips. I would far rather have been on the decks amid the bustle, for there the time flew on eagle's wings. The *Goliah* was sore beset; for some time she had two three-deckers upon her. The men stood to their guns as cool as if they had been exercising. The admiral ordered the *Britannia* to our assistance. Iron-sides, with her forty-twos, soon made them sheer off.† Towards the close of the action the men were very weary. One lad put his head out of the porthole, saying, 'Damn them, are they not going to strike yet?' For us to strike was out of the question.

At length the roar of the guns ceased and I came on deck to see the effects of a great sea engagement—but such a scene of blood and desolation I want words to express. I had been in a great number of actions with single ships in the *Proteus* and *Surprise* during the seven years I was in them. This was my first action in a fleet and I had only a small share in it. We had destroyed a great number and secured four three-deckers. One they had the impiety to call the *Holy Ghost* we wished much to get, but they towed her off. The fleet was in such a shattered situation we lay twenty-four hours in sight of them, repairing our rigging.

It is after the action the disagreeable part commences. The crews are wrought to the utmost of their strength. For days they have no remission of their toil, repairing the rigging and other parts injured in the action. Their spirits are broke by fatigue. They have no leisure to talk of the battle and, when the usual

† The *Britannia* is a first-rate, carrying 110 guns. She was the only ship that carried forty-two-pounders on her lower deck, and thirty-two on her middle deck. She was the strongest built ship in the navy. The sailors upon this account called her 'Iron-Sides'.

round of duty returns, we do not choose to revert to a disagreeable subject. Who can speak of what he did where all did their utmost? One of my mess-mates had the heel of his shoe shot off. The skin was not broke yet his leg swelled and became black. He was lame for a long time.

On our return to Lisbon we lost one of the fleet, the *Bombay Castle*. She was stranded and completely lost. All her crew were saved. We were in great danger in the *Goliah*. Captain Sir C. H. Knowles was tried for not lending assistance, when he needed it himself. The court-martial honourably acquitted him. Collis, our first lieutenant, told us not to cheer when he came on board, but we loved our captain too well to be restrained. We had agreed upon a signal with the cox-swain, if he was, as he ought to be, honourably acquitted. The signal was given and in vain Collis forbade. We manned the yards and gave three hearty cheers. Not a man on board but would have bled for Sir C. H. Knowles. To our regret we lost him to our ship at this very time. He was as good a captain as I ever sailed with. He was made admiral, and went home in the *Britannia*.

Captain Foley took command of the *Goliah* and we joined the blockade of Cadiz where we remained, sending our boat to assist at the bombardments and covering them, until Admiral Nelson came out again and picked out thirteen seventy-fours from the fleet. The *Goliah* was one. She was the fastest sailing ship in the fleet. We did not stay to water but got a supply from the ships that were to remain, and away we set under a press of sail, not knowing where.

We came to an anchor in the Straits of Messina. There was an American man-of-war at anchor. Captain Foley ordered him to unmoor that the *Goliah* might get her station, as it was a good one near the shore, but Jonathan would not budge, but made answer, 'I will let you know I belong to the United States of America and I will not give way to any nation under the sun but in a good cause.'*

So we came to an anchor where we could. We remained here but a short time when we got intelligence that the French fleet were up the Straits. We then made sail for Egypt but missed them, and came back to Syracuse and watered in twenty-four hours. I was up all night filling water. The day after we left Syracuse we fell in with a French brig who had just left the fleet. Admiral Nelson took her in tow and she conducted us to where they lay at anchor in Aboukir Bay.**

We had our anchors out at our stern port with a spring upon them, and the cable carried along the ship's side, so that the anchors were at our bows, as if there was no change in the arrangement. This was to prevent the ships from swinging round, as every ship was to be brought to by her stern. We ran in between the French fleet and the shore to prevent any

* Jonathan: A generic name for an American.
** Aboukir Bay: near Alexandria in Egypt.

communication between the enemy and the shore. Soon as they were in sight a signal was made from the admiral's ship for every vessel as she came up to make the best of her way, firing upon the French ships as she passed, and 'every man to take his bird' as we joking called it.

The *Goliah* led the van. There was a French frigate right in our way. Captain Foley cried, 'Sink that brute, what does he there?' In a moment she went to the bottom and her crew were seen running into her rigging. The sun was just setting as we went into the bay, and a red and fiery sun it was. I would, if had I had my choice, been on the deck. There I would have seen what was passing and the time would not have hung so heavy, but every man does his duty with spirit, whether his station be in the slaughterhouse or the magazine.†

I saw as little of this action as I did of the one on the 14th February off Cape St Vincent. My station was in the powder magazine with the gunner. As we entered the bay we stripped to our trousers, opened our ports, cleared, and every ship we passed gave them a broadside and three cheers. Any information we got was from the boys and women who carried the powder. The women behaved as well as the men, and got a present for their bravery from the grand signior.

† The seamen call the lower deck near the mainmast the slaughterhouse, as it is amidships and the enemy aim their fire principally at the body of the ship.

When the French admiral's ship blew up, the *Goliah* got such a shake we thought the after-part of her had blown up until the boys told us what it was. They brought us every now and then the cheering news of another French ship having struck, and we answered the cheers on deck with heartfelt joy. In the heat of the action a shot came right into the magazine but did no harm as the carpenters plugged it up and stopped the water that was rushing in.

I was much indebted to the gunner's wife who gave her husband and me a drink of wine every now and then, which lessened our fatigue much. There were some of the women wounded, and one woman belonging to Leith died of her wounds and was buried on a small island in the bay. One woman bore a son in the heat of the action. She belonged to Edinburgh.

When we ceased firing I went on deck to view the state of the fleets, and an awful sight it was. The whole bay was covered with dead bodies, mangled, wounded and scorched, not a bit of clothes on them except their trousers. There were a number of French, belonging to the French admiral's ship the *L'Orient*, who had swam to the *Goliah* and were cowering under her forecastle. Poor fellows, they were brought on board and Captain Foley ordered them down to the steward's room to get provisions and clothing.

One thing I observed in these Frenchmen quite different from anything I had ever before observed. In the American war, when we took a French ship, the *Duke de Chartres*, the prisoners were as merry as if they had taken us, only saying, '*Fortune de guerre*'—you take me today, I take you tomorrow. Those we now had on board were thankful for our kindness but were sullen and as downcast as if each had lost a ship of his own.

The only incidents I heard of are two. One lad who was stationed by a salt box on which he sat to give out cartridges and keep the lid close—it is a trying berth—when asked for a cartridge, he gave none, yet he sat upright. His eyes were open. One of the men gave him a push. He fell all his length on the deck. There was not a blemish on his body yet he was quite dead, and was thrown overboard. The other, a lad who had the match in his hand to fire his gun. In the act of applying it a shot took off his arm. It hung by a small piece of skin. The match fell to the deck. He looked to his arm and, seeing what had happened, seized the match in his left hand and fired off the gun before he went to the cockpit to have it dressed. They were in our mess or I might never have heard of it. Two of the mess were killed and I knew not of it until the day after. Thus terminated the glorious first of August, the busiest night in my life.

Soon after the action the whole fleet set sail with the prizes, and left the *Goliah* as guard ship. We remained here until we were relieved by the *Tigre*, seventy-four, when we sailed for Naples to refit. After refitting we sailed for Malta to join in the blockade, where we remained eight months without any occurrence worthy of notice. At length the *Goliah* became so leaky we were forced to leave our station and sail for Gibraltar where, after watering, we sailed for England.

We got some marines from the Rock to reinforce the *Goliah's* complement—one of them a tall stout Englishman who had been cock of the Rock.* He was very overbearing. There are often quarrels at the ship's fires when the men are boiling their kettles. We had a stout little fellow of an Irishman, who had been long in the *Goliah*. The marine pushed his kettle aside. Paddy demanded why he did so.

'Because I choose to do it.'

'I won't allow you while the life is in me,' was the reply.

'Do you wish to fight?' said the Englishman.

'Yes, and I do,' said Paddy. 'I will take the Gibraltar rust out of you or you shall beat the life out of my body before we are done.'

A fight was made up in a minute, and they went well forward on the deck to be out of sight of the officers. To it they went and fought it out, we forming a ring and screening them from observation. Paddy was as good as his word, for he took the rust off the marine so well he was forced to give in, and we were all happy to see the lobster-back's pride taken out of him.

On our arrival she was put out of commission, and the crew turned over to the *Royal William*, the guard

* The Rock: Gibraltar.

ship, and had two or three days' liberty on shore by the admiral's order.

I was next drafted on board the *Ramilies* and sailed for Belleisle, but remained only a short time in her when I was turned over to the *Ajax*, Captain Alexander F. Cochrane, upon preferment.* We sailed for Ferrol and attempted to cut out some vessels but did not succeed, then stood for Algiers to water, having a fleet of transports with troops on board under convoy. The troops were commanded by Sir Ralph Abercromby. Having watered, we sailed with the army to Mamarice Bay, and the troops were encamped upon a fine piece of ground, with a rivulet running through the centre. The French had just left the place, having first done all the mischief in their power.

While we lay here an engineer named William Balcarras went in a frigate to reconnoitre the French works. He landed and, having attained his object, was coming off in his boat when he was followed by another from the shore and shot dead before he reached the frigate.

We left Mamarice Bay and sailed to Rhodes, where we took in forage for the cavalry. We then sailed for Alexandria and landed the troops.

I belonged to one of the boats. Captain A. F. Cochrane was beach-master, and had the ordering of the troops in the landing. We began to leave the ships about twelve o'clock and reached the shore about

* Belleisle is in the Bay of Biscay.

sunrise in the morning. We rowed very slow with our oars muffled. It was a pleasant night. The water was very still and all was as silent as death. No one spoke but each cast an anxious look to the shore, then at each other, impatient to land. Each boat carried about one hundred men and did not draw nine inches of water.

The French cavalry were ready to receive us, but we soon forced them back and landed eight thousand men the first morning. We had good sport at landing the troops as the Frenchmen made a stout resistance. We brought back the wounded men to the ships.

For some time we supplied the troops on shore with provisions and water. After the advance of the troops into the country I was with the seamen on shore, assisting at the siege of Alexandria and working like a labourer in cutting off the branch of the Nile that supplied the city with water. One of the *Ajax's* boats, at Sir Ralph Abercromby's request, carried him after receiving his wound, on board the hospital ship.

Of all the countries I was ever in, in all my wanderings, I could not remain in Egypt. The air is so dry and I felt so disagreeable. It is, on the whole, sandy and barren, yet what I saw of it that was cultivated is very agreeable. For some days before the town surrendered I had been so bad with the flux I was forced to go on board. After the town surrendered and the operations of the army ceased we sailed for Malta. At this time I was blind with the ophthalmia and continued thus for six weeks.

My sufferings were most acute. I could not lie down for a moment, for the scalding water that continually flowed from my eyes filled them and put me to exquisite torture. I sat constantly on my chest with a vessel of cold water bathing them. If I slept I awoke in an agony of pain. All the time the flux was most severe upon me and the surgeon would not dry it up, as it, he said, relieved my eyes. When we came to Malta a French surgeon cured me by touching the balls of my eyes with tincture of opium, but the pain of the application was very severe. Thank God, however, I soon after recovered my health and spirits.

From Malta we sailed to Gibraltar where we watered, then sailed for England where, to my joy, I found that peace was concluded. We were all paid off shortly after our arrival. I was ship's corporal when I was discharged.

14

Author Arrives in Edinburgh—Marries and Settles as a Cooper—Forced to Leave his Business from Danger of Impressment—Retires to Cousland—Subsequent Occurrences—Returns to Edinburgh from Inability to Work at Cousland—Failure of Prospects—Present Situation.

I WAS ONCE more my own master, and felt so happy I was like one bewildered. Did those on shore only experience half the sensations of a sailor at perfect liberty after being seven years on board ship without a will of his own, they would not blame his eccentricities but wonder he was not more foolish.

After a few days my cooler reason began to resume its power and I began to think what should be my after pursuits. It was now seven years since I had been pressed from the *Nottingham.* In that time the thoughts of Sarah had faded into a distant pleasing dream. The violent desire I at one time felt to repossess her was now softened into a curiosity to know what had become of her.

As I was now possessed of a good deal of pay and prize-money due, when I received it I went down by Lincoln to make inquiry, but no one had heard of her since I was there myself, nine years before. So all my inquiries after her terminated and I proceeded to Scotland, determined to settle, as I was now too old to undertake any more love pilgrimages after an individual, as I knew not in what quarter of the globe she was or whether she was dead or alive.

I arrived in Edinburgh just twenty-five years after I had left it to wander over the globe. I had been only twice there, once at the end of the American war when I found my father dead and my brothers wanderers. After my return from the voyage with Captain Portlock I remained only a few days and just passed through the city. When in the *Edgar*, I never had been on shore.

I scarce knew a face in Edinburgh. It had doubled itself in my absence. I now wandered in elegant streets where I had left corn growing. Everything was new to me. I confess I felt more sincere pleasure and enjoyment in beholding the beauties of Edinburgh than ever I felt in any foreign clime, for I now could identify myself with them. I was a Scotchman and I felt as if they were my own property. In China, in Naples, in Rio de Janeiro or even in London I felt as a stranger, and I beheld with only the eye of curiosity.

Here I now looked on with the eye of a son who is witnessing the improvements of his father's house. Little did I at this time think I should wander in these very streets to pick up a few coals to warm my aged limbs! But everything is wisely ordered by that Power who has protected me in dangers when I thought not of Him.

I felt myself, for a few weeks after my arrival, not so very happy. As I had anticipated, there was scarcely a friend I had left that I knew again. The old were dead, the young had grown up to manhood and many were in foreign climes. The Firth of Forth which in my youth appeared a sea to my inexperienced mind, Arthur Seat and the neighbouring hills, now seemed dwindled to insignificance in comparison to what I had witnessed in foreign parts. Because they were my native scenery I felt hurt that any other country should possess more imposing objects of their kind. But they were Scotch and I loved them still.

I could not settle to work but wandered up and

down. At length I fell in with a cousin of my own. We had been playfellows and a friendly intimacy had continued until I went to sea. I fixed my affections on her and we were married. I gave her my solemn promise never again to go to sea during her life. I then thought sincerely of settling and following my trade. I bought a house in the Castle Hill and furnished it well, then laid in a stock of wood and tools. I had as much work as I could do for a soap work at the Queensferry. For one year my prospects were as good as I could have wished, and I was as happy as ever I had been in my life.

But in a few months after the war broke out again and the press-gang came in quest of me.* I could no longer remain in Edinburgh and avoid them. My wife was like a distracted woman and gave me no rest until I sold off my stock in trade and the greater part of my furniture and retired to the country. Even until I got this accomplished I dared not to sleep in my own house, as I had more than one call from the gang.

I went to Cousland, nine miles from Edinburgh in the parish of Cranstoun, and put up at one Robert Moodie's, a small public house, not knowing what was to be my next pursuit. I could obtain no employment as a cooper unless I lived in a large or seaport town, and there I could not remain. I at length applied to Mr Dickson and got work from him at the lime quarries. My berth was to bore and charge the stones with

* Britain had entered the Napoleonic Wars.

gunpowder to facilitate the work. I continued to live at Robert Moodie's, my wife Margaret paying me an occasional visit, until I got a house of my own from Mr Dickson, when she came out to reside constantly with me.

I hoped that every month would put a period to the war and I would be allowed to return to Edinburgh. But peace still seemed to recede from Britain. Year after year I looked for it in vain. When the weather was good, night after night have I sat after my day's labour by the old windmill in Bartholomew's field, first gazing upon Edinburgh that I dared not reside in, then upon the vessels that glided along the Forth. A sigh would escape me at my present lot. My promise to Margaret kept me from them (my word has ever been my bond) or I should assuredly have gone to sea again. I was like a bird in a cage, with objects that I desired on every side but could not obtain.

The cultivation of the small garden attached to my cottage occupied my mind for some time. I was becoming a little more reconciled to my lot when the press-gang came out even to Cousland and took away a neighbour of the name of Murray. He had a large family and, through the interest of the minister and neighbouring gentlemen, he got off. His impressment was a great blow to my tranquillity for many months. For a long time I slept every night either in Dalkeith or Musselburgh, and during the day a stranger could not appear near the quarry without causing the most disagreeable sensations to me. At length this cause of uneasiness wore off likewise, and I settled down to my usual calm expectations of peace—but year followed year and my prospects were unaltered.

I now began to see the great alterations that had taken place in the country from the time I had been in it, when a boy, about the year 1766. At that time I had resided for some time with my uncle at Edmonstone. The country was very little inclosed. The farmers lived with their servants. Now the country was inclosed and the farmers were gentlemen.*

At Dalkeith fair, when the crops were off the ground, it was called 'long halter time'. The cattle during the fair got leave to stray at large while the farmers, their wives, daughters and servants were all at the fair, only one woman being left at home. Now the farmers, if they went to the fair, it was to sell or buy, not to make merry. Their wives and daughters would have thought themselves disgraced if they were seen at the fair. They no longer messed with their servants but lived like noblemen by themselves. If a servant had occasion to speak to his master, he must address him as if he had been an admiral—this to me appeared strange at first.

As Mr Dickson knew I was anxious for the news, he was so kind as give me a reading of the newspapers when he was done. The other workmen assembled in

* Inclosing was the annexing of common fields, meadows and pastures into consolidated farms.

my cottage on the evenings I got them and I read aloud. Then we would discuss the important parts together. The others were not friendly to the government, save one, an old soldier who had been in the East Indies. He and I always sided together. I had broke His Majesty's bread for fourteen years and would not, upon that account, hear his government spoken against.

I had but poor help from the old soldier and I had them all to contend with, but when I was like to be run down I bothered them with latitudes and longitudes and the old soldier swore to all I said and we contrived to keep our ground, for we had both been great travellers. When they spoke of heavy taxes I talked of China. When they complained of hard times I told them of West Indian slaves—but neither could make any impression on the other.

When Murray was pressed and I was forced to skulk like a thief, they thought they had a great triumph over me and did not spare their taunts. One would ask what I thought of British freedom; another if I could defend a government which did such things?

I was at no loss for my answer. I told them, 'Necessity had no law.' Could the government make perfect seamen as easily as they could soldiers there would be no such thing as pressing of seamen, and that I was happy to be of more value than them all put together, for they would not impress any of them, they were of so little value compared with me.

When the news of the victory of Trafalgar arrived

I had my triumph over them in return. None but an old tar can feel the joy I felt. I wrought none the next day but walked about enjoying the feeling of triumph. Every now and then I felt the greatest desire to hurra aloud, and many an hurra my heart gave that my mouth uttered not.

For eleven years I lived at Cousland. Year followed year, but still no views of peace. I grew old apace and the work became too heavy for me. I was now fifty-eight years of age, and they would not have taken me had I wished to enter the service. I therefore removed to Edinburgh, and again began to work for myself. My first employers had failed in business long before. The times were completely changed. I could not get constant employment for myself. I therefore wrought for any of the other masters who were throng, but the cooper business is so very poor I have been oftener out of employment than at work. Few of them keep journeymen. They, like myself, do all their work with their own hands.

I never had any children by my cousin during the seventeen years we lived together. Margaret during all that time never gave me a bad word or made any strife by her temper—but all have their faults. I will not complain, but more money going out than I by my industry could bring in has now reduced me to want in my old age.

At her death, which happened four years ago, I was forced to sell all my property except a small room in which I live, and a cellar where I do any little work I am so fortunate as obtain. This I did to pay the expenses of her funeral and a number of debts that had been contracted unknown to me. As my poverty will not allow me to pay for a seat in a church, I go in the evenings to the Little Church, but my house is in the Tolbooth parish.

Doctor Davidson visits me in his ministerial capacity. These, I may say, are the only glimpses of sunshine that ever visit my humble dwelling. Mr Mackenzie, my elder, is very attentive in giving me tickets of admission to the sermons that are preached in the school house in the Castle Hill. In one of Doctor Davidson's visits, he made me a present of a few shillings. It was a great gift from God. I had not one penny at the time in the house.

In the month of August, last year, a cousin of my own made me a present of as much money as carried me to London. I sailed in the *Hawk*, London smack. I was only a steerage passenger but fared as well as the cabin passengers. I was held constantly in tow by the passengers. My spirits were up. I was at sea again. I had not trode a deck for twenty years before. I had always a crowd round me listening to my accounts of the former voyages that I had made. Everyone was more kind to me than another. I was very happy.

Upon my arrival in London I waited upon my old captain, Portlock, but fortune was now completely against me. He had been dead six weeks before my arrival. I left the house, my spirits sunk with grief for his death and my own disappointment, as my chief dependence was upon his aid. I then went to Somerset House for the certificate of my service: seven years in the *Proteus* and *Surprise* in the American War, and seven in the *Edgar*, *Goliah*, *Ramilies* and *Ajax* in the French War.

I was ordered to go to the Admiralty Office first and then come back to Somerset House. When I applied at the Admiralty Office a clerk told me I had been too long of applying. I then went down to the Governor of Greenwich Hospital. I was not acquainted with him, but I knew the Governor of Greenwich would be a distressed seaman's friend. His servant told me he was in Scotland. I then waited upon Captain Gore whose son's life I had saved, but he was not at home. It was of no use to remain in London as my money wore down apace. I took my passage back to Edinburgh in the *Favourite*, London smack, and arrived just four weeks from my first setting out on this voyage of disappointment. What can I do? I must just take what fortune has still in store for me.

At one time, after I came home, I little thought I should ever require to apply for a pension, and therefore made no application until I really stood in need of it.

I eke out my subsistence in the best manner I can. Coffee made from the raspings of bread (which I obtain from the bakers) twice a day is my chief diet. A few potatoes or anything I can obtain with a few pence constitute my dinner. My only luxury is tobacco which I have used these forty-five years. To beg I never will submit. Could I have obtained a small pension for my past services, I should then have reached my utmost earthly wish and the approach of utter helplessness would not haunt me as it at present does in my solitary home. Should I be forced to sell it, all I would obtain could not keep me and pay for lodgings for one year. Then I must go to the poor's house, which God in his mercy forbid. I can look to my death bed with resignation but to the poor's house I cannot look with composure.

I have been a wanderer and the child of chance all my days, and now only look for the time when I shall enter my last ship, and be anchored with a green turf upon my breast, and I care not how soon the command is given.

SERVICE OF JOHN NICOL

SHIPS' NAMES.	WHERE.	PERIOD.
Proteus and *Surprise*	American War, West Indies	1776–83
Leviathan	Greenland	1784
Cotton Planter	West Indies	1784–85
King George	South Seas and China	1785–88
Lady Juliana	New South Wales and China	1789–91
Amelia	South Sea	1791–92
Nottingham	China	1793–94
Edgar, *Goliah*, *Ramilies* and *Ajax*	French War, Egypt, Mediterranean	1794–1801

Index